PSYCHOLOGY OF EMOTIONS, MOTIVATIONS AND ACTIONS

THE PSYCHOLOGY OF HUMAN BEHAVIOR

PSYCHOLOGY OF EMOTIONS, MOTIVATIONS AND ACTIONS

Additional books in this series can be found on Nova's website
under the Series tab.

Additional E-books in this series can be found on Nova's website
under the E-book tab.

HEALTH PSYCHOLOGY RESEARCH FOCUS

Additional books in this series can be found on Nova's website
under the Series tab.

Additional E-books in this series can be found on Nova's website
under the E-book tab.

PSYCHOLOGY OF EMOTIONS, MOTIVATIONS AND ACTIONS

THE PSYCHOLOGY OF HUMAN BEHAVIOR

ROBERT G. BEDNARIK
EDITOR

nova publishers
New York

For permission to use material from this book please contact us:
Telephone 631-231-7269; Fax 631-231-8175
Web Site: http://www.novapublishers.com

Library of Congress Cataloging-in-Publication Data

The psychology of human behavior / editor, Robert G. Bednarik (Convener, President and Editor, International Federation of Rock Art Organisations (IFRAO) Australia).
pages cm
Includes index.
ISBN: 978-1-62257-901-3 (hbk.)
1. Psychology. 2. Behaviorism (Psychology) I. Bednarik, Robert G.
BF121.P8273 2013
150--dc23

2012034755

Published by Nova Science Publishers, Inc. † New York

CONTENTS

PREFACE

Robert G. Bednarik

This collection of articles about the psychology of human behavior is dominated by the topic of how the extant behavior of modern humans may have developed, thus establishing an empirical framework for comprehending human ethology. An etiology of human behavior clearly has to be grounded in an understanding of its historical development through time, which is an aspect that has so far not received adequate consideration in the scientific literature, be it that of psychology, psychiatry, human evolution, neuroscience, cognitive science, or paleoanthropology. In this volume that issue is decisively and comprehensively addressed. It presents the latest thoughts by leading researchers working in this general field, who provide distinctively interdisciplinary approaches informed by the most recent research in such disciplines as the neurosciences, evolutionary psychology, Pleistocene archaeology, paleoart studies and primatology. Such a comprehensive and up-to-date overview of how the behavior of the human genus may have developed has not been attempted before, and it has long been overdue.

The principal tenor of the book is established in the first chapter, by Robert G. Bednarik, titled "The origins of modern human behavior". He first explains why the favored models of the human past provided by Pleistocene archaeology are unreliable, when interpretation of behavior is extracted from unrepresentative archaeological samples and untestable propositions about the meaning of the empirical evidence. He points out the inconsistencies between dominant archaeological interpretational models of the distant human past and the findings of a number of sciences, especially concerning the supposedly very late appearance of cognitive modernity. He then examines several specific recent archaeological interpretations of human behavior in the Pleistocene, illustrating their limited credibility by presenting scientific refutations. This brings into play the relatively recent rise of countless neuropathologies and unfavorable genetic as well as somatic conditions that collectively define modern humans as a species subjected to rapid deterioration in various ways, but most specifically through intensive neotenization. Bednarik attributes these developments, which defy all rules of natural selection, to the rising influence of cultural choices and subtle selective breeding, i.e., to unintentional self-domestication. It is against this revolutionary revision to received beliefs about recent human evolution that he then proceeds to examine the roles of theory of mind, self-awareness, and consciousness. Using evidence from clinical psychiatry, he analyzes how humans construct their "self", and how human behavior derives from their constructs of reality. He examines the potential of homology in exploring the limits of hominin cognition, in lieu of deductions made from perceived technology alone. The provisional etiology of modern human behavior he offers shows that, in the sense that the neural structures involved in moderating behavioral patterns were substantially in place, modern behavior began in the order of a million years ago. However, fully modern human behavior did not appear until recent centuries, because the ontogenic development of human brains has changed significantly over the course of recent history.

This finding derives strong support from Patricia A. Helvenston's second chapter, "Differences between oral and literate cultures: What we can know about Upper Paleolithic minds". Helvenston presents a detailed and magisterial treatise based on the differences between the minds generated by oral and literate cultures. She demonstrates with numerous examples from traditional societies around the world that their members experience a reality quite different from that of a modern Westerner. Since Paleolithic cultures were non-literate, she contends that the implicit assumptions of most archaeologists, that the mind of Upper Paleolithic hominins was similar to the modern mind, must be false. She thus confirms the validity of the similar proposal in the previous chapter, and enriches it with an overwhelming wealth of ethnographic data. This includes not only observations among recent indigenous cultures, but also historically accessible societies, such as those of the Middle Ages or ancient Greece. Most pre-modern peoples' thought processes were dominated by what neuroscientists term "magical thinking", which lacks the sustained application of cause and effect reasoning. Helvenston also demonstrates that the use of literacy changes the workings of the human brain ontogenically. The language of oral societies, for instance, differs from that of literate communities, in the former's common use of mnemonic devices such as metaphor, proverb, and ritual, just as their beliefs and lives tend to be dominated by animism and omens. These beliefs often include quite peculiar convictions, such as the denial of natural death: all deaths are thought to be caused by malevolent agents. Lack of literacy also involves different ways of categorizing and organizing than those promoted by literacy, and the absence of advanced algorithms or computation. In view of the neuroscientifically demonstrated ontogenic plasticity of the brain, Helvenston's central hypothesis is a persuasive, and is a valuable correction of archaeologists' misconceptions in conflating their own minds with those of the people they seek to study.

The third chapter, "The comparative psychology of human uniqueness: A cognitive behavioral review" by Robert A. Dielenberg, continues this exploration of hominin behavior but focuses on a much earlier timeframe. It takes the investigation right to the nonhuman primates, in an authoritative, comprehensive, and state-of-the-art synopsis of the relevant information primatology can bring to bear on this volume's themes. As a neuroscientist, Dielenberg presents a mass of evidence illustrating the psychology of apes and monkeys in numerous areas. He compares what is known about the tool use, mirror self-recognition, theory of mind, causal reasoning, imitation, teaching, and cooperative behavior of extant nonhuman primates, and then scrutinizes their language and symboling abilities. He adds mental time travel and metacognition to explore the limits of ape and monkey cognition, assessing each of these variables judiciously and comparing them with those documented in present humans. Although he notes a number of areas requiring more research, Dielenberg particularly singles out two research topics as remaining well under-represented in the work to date: volitional control and innovation. His far-reaching survey shows that the cognitive abilities of primates generally differ only in degree, not in kind. Although apes can infer some physical unseen causation, they lack the ability to infer properties of things based on observations of the material world. This prevents their access to a realm of imagination and ideas, which is the basis of the cumulative nature of human culture. This difference, perhaps more than any other, explains why ape culture remains largely static, whereas the snowballing effect of human culture becomes increasingly influential as hominins progress though time. Thus Dielenberg coins the axiomatic proposition that the proclivity to attribute causation to unseen agents is the hallmark of the human species.

Derek Hodgson's chapter four, "Grappling with an enigma: The complexity of human behavior as a multidimensional phenomenon", also emphasizes the significance of the neurosciences and of a multidisciplinary approach to the topic of this volume. The primary objective of his chapter is to remind the reader of the often self-inflicted limitations imposed by scholars interested in understanding the human past, especially those from archaeology. He contends that such limitations have not only led to distorted appraisals of human cognitive evolution, but have also hampered a more exploratory and open assessment of the evidence. His commendably balanced approach takes account of concepts such as disembodied cognition, which he deems important to understanding human behavior. He concurs with authors of previous chapters that the notion of "modern human behavior", so crucial to the dominant paradigms in Pleistocene archaeology, should not be regarded as fixed or restricted to a particular set of traits gleaned from the archaeological record. Hodgson emphasizes the importance of elevated population levels during phases of the Pleistocene, and the benefits from greater social interaction these are likely to have entailed. In this respect he negates the replacement scenario, which perceives a distinctive population bottleneck explaining the supposed appearance of a new species. The influence of population levels and densities on human behavior, he argues, provides a more parsimonious way of disambiguating the archaeological record than traditional approaches. Indeed, human behavior is a flexible commodity that responds to environmental effects and socio-cultural factors in comparatively complex ways. Thus Hodgson regards what is defined as "modern human behavior" as being determined by the fluctuating and complex nature of social relationships, which may not always be either materially visible or embodied. One of his key findings is that, although the *content* of imagination may be determined more by culture than biology, the *capacity* to imagine owes more to biology than culture.

The next chapter is by Ben Watson, titled "Rock art and human behavior". In it he demonstrates how rock art around the world can reveal fundamental psychological and behavioral characteristics of humans separated by vast temporal and spatial spans. Similarly, the study of human ethology can show how the nature of hunter-gatherer rock art may be influenced by perceptual sensitivities to specific visual forms and patterns. For instance, a preference for abstract-geometric graphics may reflect significant aspects of the natural world, including forms of biological importance or sign stimuli eliciting innate neurophysiological responses. Hunter-gatherers require only minimal visual cues for the identification of animal species, and categorization of fauna may be neurologically differentiated at a relatively early stage of visual processing. Experience of fauna in everyday life and the pre-existence of innate neural structures concerned with animals help to explain their prevalence in rock art as determining factors in their perception, recognition, identification, and recall, as well as the greater likelihood of meaningful associations and concepts being attributed to them. Watson considers that the choice of particular animals for symbolic roles may be understood as influenced by their visual salience, mediated by shared human perceptual-neurophysiological structuring and associated behavioral responses. Neural structures may respond to certain types of animals, explaining a bias toward their choice for depiction, and suggest innate reasons for their appearance in rock art. Inherent perceptual sensitivity to animal forms could also explain the exaggeration and emphasis of particular features of animals, Watson observes. Thus neural substrates underlying typical human behavioral responses to animals and their parts may provide a particularly important basis for their representation in paleoart. Importantly, in addition to genetic predispositions and susceptibilities, this imprinting appears to be largely stable in humans, resulting in cross-cultural constants.

Finally, Ashley Craig, Elaine Blumgart, and Yvonne Tran, in their chapter "Coping with the adversity of chronic disorder: The development of resilience", consider how individuals affected by permanent deleterious conditions manage the ensuing behavioral effects. They list a number of such impairments and the circumstances facilitating resilience in the face of the adversities they engender. Craig et al. then focus on one of them, a person's involuntary disruptions to the fluency of their speech (chronic stuttering), and present a detailed analysis of the condition. They report that stuttering is believed to be related to a genetic-based speech processing capacity deficit, usually beginning in infancy. It can lead to adverse conditions, such as avoidant behavior and social disengagement. The study by Craig and his colleagues compares 200 adult sufferers with an equal number of unaffected individuals, carefully selecting their samples to match the relevant demography. The stuttering sample was found to present significantly elevated levels of distress behavior across a broad range of psychopathology, including interpersonal sensitivity, anxieties, somatization, obsessive compulsiveness tendencies, depressive mood, hostility, psychoticism tendencies and paranoid ideation. These variables were statistically analyzed, taking into account age, demography, stuttering severity, health risks, self-efficacy, physical role domain, vitality, social support, and income group, and comparing the resilient with the non-resilient sub-groups on the basis of these variables. The study found that the main factors preventing psychopathology in sufferers are greater sense of perceived self-mastery over stress, greater access to helpful social support, and superior social functioning.

The distinctly interdisciplinary format of this volume thus succeeds in providing an inkling of the complexity of dealing with human behavior, and the reasons for its complexity relative to the behavior of other animal species. While it provides a first credible insight into the etiology of human behavior, it also demonstrates unambiguously the paucity of reliable knowledge about what drives it. As this book shows, any explanation of the psychology of human behavior that omits to explain its derivation is akin to trying to understand an illness from its symptoms alone. Medicine has long understood that symptoms are useful in diagnosis, even though they are not necessary unfailing in that role; but to deal effectively with illness, its etiology should be understood. This is the very essence of modern medical science. In psychology, that understanding remains profoundly lacking, because until now psychology and psychiatry have largely focused on categorizing symptoms and trying to understand neuropathologies by intuition-like assertion. The etiologies of such conditions have only recently begun to be subjected to sustained attention, and understanding of their ancestries and derivational histories had until now not even been attempted in any consequential form. In this sense, the present book is a pioneering effort, but it also succeeds in exposing the massive lacunae in the relevant scientific knowledge. These significant gaps are to some extent attributable to the shortcomings of Pleistocene archaeology and palaeoanthropology; tellingly, prominent neuroscientist Todd M. Preuss has referred to *Homo sapiens* as 'the undiscovered primate' in 2000. This volume endorses his view, but presents a small increment in remedying the condition he succinctly diagnosed. The etiology of that condition is much easier to establish than that of human behavior: it is attributable to over-specialization, *déformation professionnelle*, and the rising quarantining of disciplines isolating them from others. This book makes an effort to remedy this state.

In: The Psychology of Human Behavior
Editor: Robert G. Bednarik

ISBN: 978-1-62257-901-3

Chapter 1

The Origins of Modern Human Behavior

Robert G. Bednarik*
International Federation of Rock Art Organizations (IFRAO),
Caulfield South, Australia

Abstract

To explain human behavior through its present-day manifestations is like considering illness through its symptoms instead of its causes. A psychology that explores human behavior purely by analyzing its observed extant expressions, without recourse to how or why these may have developed, lacks a scientific context, which demands causal explanations. In this chapter, it is attempted to show that an etiology of human behavior would be achievable if a better-targeted database could be extracted from Pleistocene archaeology and paleoanthropology. Nevertheless, a rudimentary model of how and why hominin behavior patterns developed in the Pleistocene is presented here. In particular, "behavioral normality" is explored through the available empirical information and the rise of brain illnesses during the most recent history of our species. The establishment of self-awareness and consciousness is considered, as well as the role of "theory of mind" in the development of behavioral patterns. The advent of extra-cranial storage of symbolic and cultural meanings is also of relevance, as well as the development of constructs of reality in the cognitive evolution of hominins. In considering this etiological context of modern human behavior it is demonstrated that a judicious utilization of relevant data obtainable from the archaeological record can yield a realistic paradigm.

Introduction

In essence, psychology is the study of the human "mind" and behavior, generally through experiments, observations and questionnaires, but can also include animal studies,

* Convener and Editor, International Federation of Rock Art Organizations (IFRAO), P.O. Box 216, Caulfield South, VIC 3162, Australia, robertbednarik@hotmail.com

particularly ethology. The humanist concept of "mind" is broadly intended to refer to conscious experience and intelligent thought but lacks a clear-cut definition as a specific entity. Instead of assuming that mind exists, it may be more productive to ask, what are the neural and endocrine processes that make up the system that has traditionally been called the human mind, how do they work, and how can their interplay be described. Not surprisingly, psychology is widely seen as a "soft science," or as lacking the overarching or universal theory required of a proper science (Kuhn 1962). Its principal shortcoming, however, is perhaps that it is essentially observing and recording "symptoms," and from them creating taxonomies and remedies. But this does not constitute a valid etiology of conditions, even though they are expressed by "normal" or "aberrant" behavior. In considering the psychology of human behavior, as this volume professes to attempt, it is not adequate to describe such behavior in normative terms that are, for all practical purposes, its own results. In the first instance it is necessary to inquire into the primary causal explanations: what are the features in the human neural system that elicit observable effects?

This task, of course, falls to the neurosciences and endocrinology rather than traditional and essentially humanist psychology. However, there is a more important dimension to these issues: just as disease can only be understood from the perspective of its etiology rather than through its symptoms, any effective comprehension of human behavior involves the investigation of its origins. As Marks and Nesse (1994: 259) observed, "even if we knew every connection of every neuron, every action of every transmitter, our understanding would remain inadequate until we also knew the function for which those mechanisms were shaped." Inevitably, no such comprehension is possible without involving evolutionary psychology and indeed the field of hominin ethology—the study of the behavior of the human ancestors. This chapter will attempt to address that issue on the basis of the current, albeit quite limited and in certain ways flawed, knowledge.

The replacement of humanist psychology with scientific modes of investigation is a symptom of the inevitable general process of supplanting the "soft sciences" with the "hard" (Becher 2001; Bednarik 2011a), a slow but inevitable course. Just as astrology was replaced with astronomy, or phrenology with neuroscience, in many of its practices traditional psychology lacks the rigor of a scientific discipline. Phenomena that are of interest to it, such as emotion, thinking, or personality, cannot be quantified effectively and with a semblance of objectivity (Panksepp 1998: 9). The improbably high support research has reported for initial hypotheses in psychology and psychiatry (Sterling 1959; Klamer et al. 1989; Fanelli 2010) is several times that yielded in the hard sciences, indicating systematic bias. The logical and methodological rigor employed to test hypotheses varies systematically across disciplines and fields. Papers in psychology, psychiatry, and business studies report positive testing of hypotheses five times as often as space science, while the biological disciplines rank intermediate. Studies applying behavioral and social methodologies on people rank 3.4 times higher than physical and chemical studies on non-biological material, using the same index of confirmation bias (Press and Tanur 2001). The social sciences are thus qualitatively different from the hard sciences (Shipman 1988; Latour 2000; Simonton 2004; Bishop 2007; Bednarik 2011a), and psychology and psychiatry, in particular, "pretend to be sciences, offering allegedly empirical observations about the functions and malfunctions of the human mind" (Szasz 2006).

Another "social science" of importance in the context of considering the origins of human behavior is Pleistocene archaeology, the field professing to study traces of early human behavior. The available information of archaeology is much more circumscribed than the limitations of available data would demand, for reasons that will shortly be considered. In addition to the dearth of knowledge itself, systematic misapplication of it to conform to preconceived notions of what the data should show is widespread (Bednarik 2012). Of all the "soft sciences," archaeology is arguably the softest. In contrast to the other humanities, archaeology, especially Pleistocene archaeology, offers no falsifiability. By its very nature, it cannot generate propositions that are testable—at least not without the help of hard sciences, usually physics or the earth sciences. It is then not a matter of a low rate of refutations, as in psychology or psychiatry, but hypotheses are not even presented as internally falsifiable propositions. Instead they are rated on the basis of "authority" (Lewis-Williams 1993). Some archaeologists themselves have defined the discipline as a political pursuit (Trigger 1984, 1989; Kohl and Fawcett 2000; Silberman 2000); it creates narratives about past cultures and societies for the presently dominant powers, the states. In this it is guided by Darwinist rationale: the apparent overall technological and somatic improvements foster the concept of inevitable "progress," be it cultural or somatic. This is a flawed notion even before it is examined closely. Both cultures and societies clearly evolve *and devolve* (Henrich 2004), and corresponding but also different effects can be observed in the human species as such (Bednarik 2011b), if degeneration were seen as devolution. The idea that evolution yields some "ideal" ultimate state permeates all of archaeology and colors all of its models, with the glorious descendents of the "African Eve" representing the final purpose of the evolutionary ascent: a creature in the image of a deity. In this nauseating self-glorification our species ignores that it is rapidly "devolving," as will be shown below.

The concept of a relentless progress derives from this self-delusion, guiding Pleistocene archaeologists in their expectations and thereby contaminating all hypothesis-building the field is capable of generating. In reality, cultural development is not a continuous upward process; there is no ultimate goal, and there are examples of cultural and technological "devolution." For instance after the Tasmanian Aborigines were separated from the Australian mainland tribes by the island's sundering toward the end of the Pleistocene, their cultural and technological abilities declined gradually (Jones 1977, 1978). Complex systems science predicts that the volume of information that can be stably maintained over time is limited by the propensity for introducing error in generational information transmission (Andersson 2011). This effect was first noted in the relationship between the length of genetic sequences and the rate of error in RNA replication (Eigen and Schuster 1977). As the mutation rate increases beyond a crucial point, the system of short-term memory carriers can no longer maintain a long-term memory. If cognition were the main constraint on technology—the mantra Pleistocene archaeologists are committed to—any early appearance of sophistication would be impossible, except by a "running ahead of time." But locally narrow specializations, such as in maritime technology, or technological forays during a small number of generations that failed to persist in the long run, may have had limited prospects of being retained over time. Technological conservatism was adaptive for hominins, complex systems science predicts. Most importantly, intelligence was driven by social factors, not by technology, which was not limited by some cognitive potential maximum sophistication. After all, cognitive evolution cannot be driven by selection for its technological effects, because cognitive capabilities simply must precede any technological expressions they might reasonably lead to (Alvard 2003). Andersson (2011) predicts that hominins must generally have been smarter than their technological traces—which are in any case significantly misinterpreted—might lead us to believe. As he points out, this is the case today with modern humans, and it applies equally to other extant primates. In short, lowest common denominator technology, the kind archaeology might be able to recover, is no measure of cognitive potential, or of potential technological sophistication. The problem, according to complex systems theory, is in long-term transmission and maintenance of innovations and innovative practices. Neither Pleistocene archaeology nor paleoanthropology has applied any of these crucial points, and so they continue to deliver tainted explanations for their data.

The problem with these under-developed disciplines is identified by Kuhn (1962) who has shown that, in its earliest stages of development, a discipline can be completely fragmented theoretically and methodologically. Its course can be determined by different schools of thought that interpret the same phenomena in radically different ways. This is a condition that seems to characterize many fields in the social sciences and possibly some of the biological sciences as well (see also Cole 2001; Bednarik 2011a), but is particularly prominent in Pleistocene archaeology (Bednarik 2011b, 2011c, 2012). Data describing human or non-human behavior are inherently noisy in any discipline, and are open to alternative interpretations. Among the unconscious biases involved is that the human subjects of behavioral study can be subconsciously aware of researchers' expectations, and behave accordingly (Barber 1976; Shipman 1988; Latour 2000), and the tendency to hypothesize after the results is known (Kerr 1998).

The State of Pleistocene Archaeology and Paleoanthropology

There are a number of profound problems in science that, if solved, are guaranteed to revolutionize human comprehension of the world. Are non-carbon-based life forms possible? How does the brain create linguistic representations, or how does recursive language work? Is a unified theory of physics possible? What about string theory? How does self-awareness work, what is the self? Many of these most fundamental issues are connected with humans themselves, simply because these ultimately affect all other dimensions of human understanding. Some of them appear to have been solved, such as the question how human nature came about (Bednarik 2011b). Here it will be attempted to respond to the question, how did "modern human behavior" as we know it originate.

Since the origins of human behavior cannot possibly be considered without the relevant historical context, which is inevitably created by archaeology and paleoanthropology, it is requisite that this chapter begins by examining the quality of the information these disciplines are capable of providing. The inadequacies of mainstream Pleistocene archaeology (Bednarik 2012) range from the inability to create emic knowledge or testable propositions to a litany of epistemic, taxonomic, and ethical problems that have led to an historical trajectory of the discipline marked by an endless list of mistakes and blunders. One of the earliest was the categorical rejection, by all archaeologists, of customs official Jacques Boucher de Crèvecœur de Perthes' (1846) proposition that humans coexisted with Pleistocene fauna, thus delaying the acceptance of the Paleolithic for several decades. In fact the matter had to be resolved by two geologists, Prestwich (1859) and Falconer. Next, all archaeologists rejected the proposition of fossil humans, when teacher Johann Carl Fuhlrott (1859) presented the remains from the Neanderthal. Again it took several decades to decide in favor of the non-archaeologist. Then Marcelino Santiago Tomás Sanz de Sautuola's (1880) proposal of Pleistocene cave art was so brusquely rejected by all archaeologists that it drove this amateur into a premature death. It took decades before the notion of Paleolithic art was grudgingly accepted by archaeology, after several other non-archaeologists had presented indisputable evidence (Cartailhac 1902). In the meantime, physician Eugene Dubois proposed that he had found the remains of a species intermediate between apes and humans in Java, only to be greeted by a chorus of derision and rejection from physical anthropologists and archaeologists. It took again several decades before his *Homo erectus* found acceptance. By then the titled and publicly funded academics had already embraced the finds from Piltdown as the "missing link," and it took them almost four decades to realize that they had been duped by a simple hoax. And it took again a non-archaeologist, Kenneth Oakley (Weiner et al. 1953) to reveal this. When anatomist Raymond Dart presented the first australopithecine remains in 1925, they were not rejected; they were simply ignored, in the safe knowledge that humans had evolved, very fittingly, in God's own country, England. The full viciousness of the discipline of archaeology is well illustrated by the Glozel affair, which began in 1924 with the discovery of the extensive site complex by teenager Émile Fradin. It led to the attempted salting of the site by celebrated archaeologist Dorothy Garrod in November 1927, and to Fradin being beaten by police and indicted for fraud in 1928, action prompted by the president of the French Prehistoric Society, Felix Regnault. Fradin was only exonerated in March 1932, and since then the authenticity of the Glozel finds has been proven by avocational archaeologists.

These are only some of the more prominent examples, but they show the general pattern: all important ideas in archaeology, especially Pleistocene archaeology, have been presented by people other than professional archaeologists, and they were typically rejected by the entire academic discipline. In most cases these serious errors of judgment were eventually corrected through the work of non-archaeologists. Anyone suggesting that archaeology might have learnt from this historical trajectory is mistaken. On the contrary, the frequency of erroneous announcements by professional archaeologists and paleoanthropologists has increased in recent decades, as has their viciousness whenever they found themselves contradicted by scientists. When in 1995 all commenting archaeologists claimed that a series of petroglyph sites in the lower Côa valley of northern Portugal and at nearby Siega Verde in Spain are of the Upper Paleolithic (Zilhão 1995), several scientists subjected themselves to a fully blind test and found that the Côa rock art is relatively recent, most being only a few centuries old (Watchman 1995, 1996; Bednarik 1995a). For this they were severely attacked, threatened, abused, and defamed, and their science was declared fraudulent by the archaeologists. While the evidence in favor of the scientists has since increased, no credible evidence for the archaeologically claimed age has come forth. A recent quantification of the fluvial erosion of dated inscriptions and petroglyphs at nearby Siega Verde has shown conclusively that both are generally less than 200 years old (Bednarik 2009). Another recent example (there are many others) of an archaeological and paleoanthropological blunder concerns the attribution of some primate bones found in the cave Liang Bua in Flores, Indonesia (Morwood et al. 2004). Since they have been reported, the bones have been attributed to a gibbon-like creature, an australopithecine, a relative of *Homo georgicus* or *Homo habilis*, a dwarf *Homo erectus*, or a modern microcephalic human. In other words, the collective opinion is that these primate remains are of a creature somewhere between an ape and a modern human. To know that, one does not need paleoanthropologists, it is obvious to anyone; and this shows the significant problems with their guesswork discipline. The unseemly spectacle of unscholarly behavior accompanying these debates does little to inspire confidence in them. But the perhaps greatest example of a recent blunder by Pleistocene archaeologists refers to the most debated archaeological issue of recent decades, and one that is of central importance in the present chapter: the origins of "modern" humans (bearing in mind that "we have never been modern"; Latour 1993).

The notion that the "Upper Paleolithic" was introduced into Europe from Africa has been around for a long time, for instance Dorothy Garrod of Glozel fame had believed in this invasion. In 1973 Professor Reiner Protsch "von Zieten" proposed that modern humans arose in sub-Saharan Africa, presenting a series of false datings (Terberger and Street 2003; Schulz 2004) of presumed "modern" fossil specimens over the following years (Protsch 1973, 1975; Protsch and Glowatzki 1974; Protsch and Semmel 1978; Henke and Protsch 1978). This was developed into the "Afro-European *sapiens*" model (Bräuer 1984), and a few years later the "African Eve" complete replacement scenario appeared (Cann et al. 1987; Stringer and Andrews 1988); followed by the Pennisi (1999) model, the "wave theory" (Eswaran 2002), the Templeton (2002) model, and the "assimilation theory" (Smith et al. 2005), among others. Of these, the mitochondrial Eve model is the most extreme, contending that the purported African invaders were a new species, unable to interbreed with the rest of humanity. They are said to have replaced all other humans, be it by exterminating or out-competing them. However, there were significant problems with the African Eve theory right from the start. The computer modeling of Cann et al. (1987) was botched and its haplotype trees were fantasies that could not be provided with time depth even if they were real. Based on 136 extant mitochondrial DNA samples, it arbitrarily selected one of 10^{267} alternative and equally credible haplotype trees (which are very much more than the number of elementary particles of the entire universe, about 10^{70}!). Maddison (1991) then demonstrated that a re-analysis of the Cann et al. model could produce 10,000 haplotype trees that were actually more parsimonious than the single one chosen by these authors. Yet no method could even guarantee that the most parsimonious tree result should even be expected to be the correct tree (Hartl and Clark 1997: 372). Cann et al. had also mis-estimated the diversity per nucleotide (single locus on a string of DNA), incorrectly using the method developed by Ewens (1983) and thereby falsely claiming greater genetic diversity of Africans, compared to Asians and Europeans (they are in fact very similar: 0.0046 for both Africans and Asians, and 0.0044 for Europeans). Even the premise of genetic diversity is false, for instance it is greater in African farming people than in African hunters-foragers (Watson et al. 1996), yet the latter are not assumed to be ancestral to the former (see e.g. Ward et al. 1991). Cann et al.'s assumption of exclusive maternal transference of mitochondria was also false, and the constancy of mutation rates of mtDNA was similarly a myth (Rodriguez-Trelles et al. 2001, 2002). As Gibbons (1998) noted, by using the modified putative genetic clock, Eve would not have lived 200,000 years ago, as Cann et al. had claimed, but only 6000 years ago. The various genetic hypotheses about the origins of "Moderns" that have appeared over the past few decades placed the hypothetical split between these and other humans at times ranging from 17,000 to 889,000 years BP. They are all contingent upon purported models of human demography, but these and the timing or number of colonization events are practically fictional: there are no sound data available for most of these variables. This applies to the contentions concerning mitochondrial DNA ("African Eve") as much as to those citing Y-chromosomes ("African

Adam"; Hammer 1995). The divergence times projected from the diversity found in nuclear DNA, mtDNA, and DNA on the non-recombining part of the Y-chromosome differ so much that a time regression of any type is extremely problematic. Contamination of mtDNA with paternal DNA has been demonstrated in extant species (Gyllensten et al. 1991; Awadalla et al. 1999; Morris and Lightowlers 2000; Williams 2002), in one recorded case amounting to 90% (Schwartz and Vissing 2002). Interestingly, when this same "genetic clock" is applied to the dog and implies its split from the wolf occurred 135,000 years ago, archaeologists reject it because there is no paleontological evidence for dogs prior to about 15,000 years ago (Napierala and Uerpmann 2010; but see Germonpré et al. 2009). The issues of base substitution (Lindhal and Nyberg 1972) and fragmentation of DNA (Golenberg et al. 1996) have long been known, and the point is demonstrated, for instance, by the erroneous results obtained from the DNA of insects embedded in amber (Gutierrez and Marin 1998). Other problems with interpreting or conducting analyses of paleogenetic materials are alterations or distortions through the adsorption of DNA by a mineral matrix, its chemical rearrangement, microbial or lysosomal enzymes degradation, and lesions by free radicals and oxidation (Geigl 2002; Carlier et al. 2007).

Since 1987 the genetic distances in nuclear DNA (the distances created by allele frequencies) proposed by different researchers or research teams have produced conflicting results (e.g. Vigilant et al. 1991; Barinaga 1992; Ayala 1996; Brookfield 1997), and some geneticists concede that the models rest on untested assumptions; others even oppose them (e.g. Barinaga 1992; Hedges et al. 1992; Maddison et al. 1992; Templeton 1992, 1993, 1996, 2002, 2005; Brookfield 1997). The key claim of the replacement theory (the "Eve" model), that the "Neanderthals" were genetically so different from the "Moderns" that the two were separate species, has been under severe strain since Gutierrez et al. (2002) demonstrated that the pair-wise genetic distance distributions of the two human groups overlap more than claimed, if the high substitution rate variation observed in the mitochondrial D-loop region (see Walberg and Clayton 1981; Torrini et al. 1994; Zischler et al. 1995) and lack of an estimation of the parameters of the nucleotide substitution model are taken into account. The more reliable genetic studies of living humans have shown that both Europeans and Africans have retained significant alleles from multiple populations of Robusts (Hardy et al. 2005; Garrigan et al. 2005; cf. Templeton 2005). After the Neanderthal genome yielded results that seemed to include an excess of Gracile single nucleotide polymorphisms (Green et al. 2006), more recent analyses confirmed that "Neanderthal" genes persist in recent Europeans, Asians, and even Papuans (Green et al. 2010). "Neanderthals" (use of this term here is only to comply with established jargon and implies no approval; the term "Robusts" is preferable) are said to have interbred with the ancestors of Europeans and Asians, but not with those of Africans (Gibbons 2010; cf. Krings et al. 1997). The African alleles occur at a frequency averaging only 13% in non-Africans, whereas those of other regions match the Neanderthaloids in ten of twelve cases. "Neanderthal genetic difference to humans must therefore be interpreted within the context of human diversity" (Green et al. 2006: 334). This suggests that gracile Europeans and Asians evolved largely from local robust populations, and the replacement model has thus been decisively refuted. While this may surprise those who subscribed to Protsch's "African hoax," it had long been obvious from previously available evidence. For instance Alan Mann's finding that tooth enamel cellular traits showed a close link between Neanderthaloids and present Europeans, which both differ from those of Africans (Weiss and Mann 1978), had been ignored by the Eve protagonists, as has much other empirical evidence (e.g., Roginsky et al. 1954; Yakimov 1980). In response to the initial refutations of the Eve model, Cann (2002) made no attempt to argue against the alternative proposals of long-term, multiregional evolution.

But faulty genetics are only one aspect of the significant shortcomings of the replacement model; it also lacks any archaeological, paleoanthropological, technological, or cultural evidence (Bednarik 1991, 1992, 1995b, 1997a, 1997b, 2008a, 2011b, 2011c). Nothing suggests that Upper Paleolithic culture or technology originated in sub-Saharan Africa, or that such traditions moved north through Africa into Eurasia. The early traditions of Mode 4 ("Upper Paleolithic") technocomplexes evolved in all cases *in situ*, and the Graciles of Australia, Asia, and Europe emerged locally from Robusts, as they did in Africa. By the end of the Middle Pleistocene, 135,000 years ago, all habitable regions of the Old World continents can be safely assumed to have been occupied by hominins. At that time, even extremely inhospitable parts, such as the Arctic (Schulz 2002; Schulz et al. 2002; see also Pavlov et al. 2001), were inhabited by highly adapted Robusts. Therefore the notion that African immigrants from the tropics could have displaced these with their identical technologies is demographically absurd. Wherever robust and gracile populations coexisted, from the Iberian Peninsula to Australia, they shared technologies, cultures, even ornaments. Moreover, the established resident populations in many climatic regions would have genetically swamped any intrusive population bringing with it a much smaller number of adaptive alleles. Introgressive hybridization (Anderson 1949), allele drift based on generational mating site distance (Harpending et al. 1998), and genetic drift (Bednarik 2011d) through episodic genetic isolation during climatically unfavorable events (e.g. the Campagnian Ignimbrite event, or the Heinrich Event 4; Barberi et al. 1978; Fedele et al. 2002, 2003; Fedele and Giaccio 2007) account for the mosaic of hominin forms found.

Mode 4 technocomplexes (Foley and Lahr 1997) first appear across Eurasia between 45,000 and 40,000 years ago, perhaps even earlier (Felgenhauer et al. 1959), at which time they existed neither in Africa nor in Australia. In fact right across northern Africa, Mode 3 traditions continued for more than twenty millennia, which renders it rather difficult to explain how Eve's progeny managed to cross this zone without leaving a trace. None of the many tool traditions of the early Mode 4 which archaeologists have "identified" across Europe have any precursors to the south, including the Aurignacian, Châtelperronian, Uluzzian, Proto-Aurignacian, Olschewian, Bachokirian, Bohunician, Streletsian, Gorodtsovian, Brynzenian, Spitzinian, Telmanian, Szeletian, Eastern Szeletian, Kostenkian, Jankovichian, Altmühlian, Lincombian or Jerzmanovician (Bednarik 2011b). Some of these "cultures" have provided skeletal human remains of Robusts, including "Neanderthals" (Gábori-Csánk 1993; Bader 1978; Smith et al. 1999; Smith et al. 2005; Ahern et al. 2004), but there are no unambiguous associations between "anatomically modern human" remains (Graciles) and "early Upper Paleolithic" assemblages (Bednarik 2008b). This is another massive blow to the replacement proponents, who relied on the unassailability of their belief that some of these traditions, especially the Aurignacian, were by Graciles—having fallen victim to Protsch's hoax. Moreover, these "cultures," as they are called, are merely etic constructs, "observer-relative or institutional facts" (Searle 1995); as "archaeofacts" they have no real, emic existence. They are entirely made up of invented (etic) tool types and based on the fundamental misunderstanding of Pleistocene archaeology that tools are diagnostic for identifying cultures. Indeed, the *cultural* variables of Pleistocene archaeology have never received much attention, or been employed in creating a cultural nomenclature. At this point it becomes apparent that the received but probably false taxonomy of Pleistocene cultures has been matched with equally unrealistic ethnic entities, and the entire system begins to crumble. Cultures are undeniably defined by cultural variables, not by tools or technologies, and for that reason alone the cultures of the Pleistocene have clearly not been identified correctly. Archaeologists misuse the term "culture" in several senses, calling any sediment layer that contains charcoal a "cultural layer"; most charcoal in the ground was not even deposited by humans. Not only have archaeologists invented cultures on the basis of non-cultural diagnostics, even if that were not so, cultures would still not define peoples. The simplistic notion that one can trace ethnic differences through tool assemblages, a cornerstone of received Pleistocene archaeology, is therefore a major epistemic impediment in the discipline. Pleistocene archaeology as it is conducted is incapable of providing a cultural history, as it relegates the cultural information available (such as rock art) to marginal rather than central status, forcing it into the false technological framework it has created. Instead of beginning with a chronological skeleton of paleoart traditions and then placing tool assemblages into it, invented tool types forming invented cultures of invented ethnic and even genetic groups form the temporal backbone of the academic narrative. The result is a collection of origins myths for groups, nations, and for "modern humans" generally.

But there are several other impediments preventing the field from attaining scientific credibility. They are only mentioned in passing here (but see Bednarik 2012). Just as archaeology destroys the sediments it excavates, its deconstruction, objectification, and academic appropriation of the beliefs of other societies are injurious to them (Piotrowski and Ross 2011). Indigenous metaphysics cannot even be effectively translated into forms decipherable within a Western construct of reality (Berger and Luckmann 1966; Pinker 2002) without significant corruption. "Who has the right to frame and interpret the past of others?" (Lyons 2002: 127; cf. Barkan and Bush 2002: 2; Brown 2003: 184; McNiven and Russell 5005). Archaeological narratives are framed within the ever-changing kaleidoscope of Western society's prejudices and preconceptions, shaped by their social constructs rather than contributing to their shaping. Archaeologists, the "molesters of the past" (Campbell 2006), manage the remains and monuments of the defeated, marginalized, and superseded cultures for the victorious states whose servants they are, and who validate them. The political uses made of archaeology's "findings have facilitated ethnic clashes and cleansing, bigotry and nationalism far more often than they have promoted social justice" (Kohl and Fawcett 1995). Acquisition of knowledge about the ontologies of indigenous societies is integral to dispossession, to diminishment of indigenous values and sovereignty, and to gaining power through "interpretation."

Any recourse by referring to the ideal of academic freedom and the prerogatives of science is unjustified: the discipline refuses academic freedom to others by restricting access to its resources and opposing avocational researchers at every opportunity, and it maintains a non-scientific epistemology by eschewing principles of falsifiability. Its premises are rated by the perceived authority of the proposer, not according to testability, the most fundamental requirement in the sciences. Excavation inevitably results in the destruction of all spatial contexts and other relevant information, therefore the pronouncements of the excavator (e.g. the plan and section drawings) have to be accepted on authority; they are not testable data. Moreover, excavation can only yield non-random samples, another limitation in conflict with the requirements of scientific method. The remains secured from an excavation cannot be expected to be *representative* of anything other than themselves; their composition is merely accidental, besides having been significantly affected by taphonomy (Bednarik 1994). Similarly, most finds are made accidentally, and there is not much control over the historical sequence of key discoveries. Since the order in which they are made is largely random, the dogma is similarly haphazard at any point in history. Therefore endeavors to preserve this intrinsically false dogma, which characterize so much effort in archaeology, are fundamentally anti-scientific. In this way the practices of the discipline conspire to keep it from attaining credibility, rather as if it had been designed to yield mostly questionable narratives. It is also an academic pursuit that defines its sphere of interest not by some concrete terms of reference, but self-referentially: archaeological subjects are defined so by what senior archaeologists take an interest in (Lewis-Williams 1993).

The Available Database

All of this suggests that there are inherent problems with the way Pleistocene archaeology and paleoanthropology create their narratives of the human past. The gatekeepers of human evolution and paleo-ecology have not provided a consistent and comprehensive explanation of why humans are the way they are, or how they became what they are today. This leaves any endeavor to discuss the origins of human behavior with the choice of either abandoning that quest due to the incommensurability issues of the orthodox model, or approaching the data more circumspectly, excising from it what has been formulated in compliance with the orthodox dogma and reviewing critically the rest. Archaeology, of course, does not recover behavior. It may find traces caused by human behavior, it may employ uniformitarian analogy to explain such traces, but in the absence of refutability of any resulting hypotheses these are posited outside of science. One may cull from the wealth of available archaeological data that part that seems reliable, and attempt to generate better-supported hypotheses than those which traditional archaeology has offered. They are indeed likely to be more credible, but the fundamental problem of the lack of falsifiability remains.

There is, however, another way to pursue these issues, and it is the one adopted here. To circumvent the lack of archaeology's falsifiability one could recruit relevant hard sciences to provide testable propositions that could test otherwise untestable hypotheses. In certain areas this has long been done in archaeology, especially in the dating of occupation horizons and specific objects. The sciences recruited here were the earth sciences, palynology, nuclear physics and a few others. None of the hard sciences gradually taking over from the humanities (especially from psychology and psychiatry), which should be of particular relevance in considering behavior, have been sustainably brought into correlation with the question of early (Pliocene and Pleistocene) human behavior. In particular neuroscience and cognitive science need to be introduced to attempt a first etiology of hominin behavior. This should render possible the formulation of assertions that may be testable within the hard sciences, rather than by simple appeal to archaeological plausibility. The process would still be precarious, but should result in greatly improved resolution of the issues and possible solutions. It needs to start from the general rule of science that propositions must be presented in such a way that they can be disproved by some conceivable spatio-temporally located event exemplifying a possibility which the proposition would exclude. The credibility or veracity of any outcomes could be greatly enhanced if the experiment departed from a considerably improved reliability of the underlying empirical archaeological database. Therefore this is attempted here before delving into the subject of the origins of human behavior.

In revising the empirical database of Late Pleistocene (130,000 to 10,000 years ago) archaeology it is essential to excise any aspects (statistics, interpretations, "institutional facts," etc.) that derive from the now discredited replacement hypothesis. As Christopher Hitchens once stated, "that which can be asserted without evidence can be dismissed without evidence." Applying instead the scientific methods of taphonomic logic (Bednarik 1994) and complex systems theory (Andersson 2011) unambiguously demands some form of gradualism in determining the human ascent. This development would be expected to have been punctuated by phases of "evolution" and occasional "devolution," with the former obviously dominating. The notion of devolution shows that the term "cultural evolution" is a misnomer, because whereas biological evolution is not teleological, having no ultimate purpose (therefore all biological development is evolutionary), cultures obviously can develop backwards (to a more primitive state) when ideas drop out of the "meme pool."

A skeletal framework can be established by initially inferring some key developments in the broadest possible sense. For instance, language ability: the most dramatic somatic development in human evolution is encephalization, the phenomenal increase in cranial volume, which is unparalleled in biology. Its evolutionary cost is massive, for instance in its obstetric demands (O'Connell et al. 1999). Just as the required increase in the size of the birth canal competes with the physical fitness of females, the enforced premature birth competes with the mobility of the band. Human infants are born in fetal form, unable to cling to a mother, and the prolonged period of their dependence on the mother and the group severely limits breeding frequency, and therefore reduces a woman's potential number of viable births. To suggest that such a severe impediment to reproductive fitness (Joffe 1997) as this abnormally enlarged organ was tolerated by evolutionary selection without some very significant compensatory development is biologically naïve. That major benefit might have been the advanced communication required to underwrite societal complexity (Falk 2009; Bickerton 1990, 1996, 2010). Therefore the null hypothesis should be that language ability and the development of speech can be correlated with the rapid increase in brain size, which commenced over two million years ago. Relevant are several empirical factors: the hyoid bone of juvenile australopithecine remains from Dikika, Ethiopia (Alemseged et al. 2006), and from a putative *Homo erectus* from Castel di Guido, Italy (Capasso et al. 2008), although their mere presence does not prove speech. Laryngeal movement is more important, as is the presence of Broca's and Wernicke's areas, which have both been claimed to be detectable on cranial endocasts of *Homo habilis* (Falk 1983). Ultimately, however, the presence of speech in early hominins has not been demonstrated somatically at this stage.

This provides an initial appreciation of where the goalposts might need to be located in that respect. The timing of a few other key developments helps sketching out a realistic framework, including the advent of colonizing sea crossings, roughly a million years ago (Bednarik 1997a, 2003a); and most especially the gradual introduction of the extra-cranial storage of symbolic information, commencing perhaps around the same time (see below). Both these indicators have provided solid empirical information through specific phenomena on the archaeological record. The concept of storage of symbolism outside the brain, i.e., in a variety of objects and their properties, was first proposed by Gregory (1970: 148), who realized that this would be a relatively stable and permanent expression. This idea of an external, "surrogate cortex" was developed further by Goody (1977), Carruthers (1990, 1998), and eventually Donald (1991, 2001; Donald et al. 1993). It was Donald (1991: 308–333; 2001: 305–315) who coined the name "exogram," derived from the concept of the engram (Bednarik 1987), which is a hypothesized but not demonstrated persistent protoplasmic alteration of neural tissue thought to occur upon stimulation, and accounting for memory. This idea was mooted by Semon (1904, 1921: 24); used by authors such as Lashley (1950); and much later reinvented by Dawkins (1976) who called the memory trace a "meme." In fact Semon had already used the term "mnemic trace" in 1904, but it seems Dawkins was unaware of all of this. Similarly, Donald's three stages of cultural evolution were foreshadowed by Fairservice (1975). Donald, consequently, defines an "exogram" as an *external* memory record of an idea, a made, symbolic invention that may have undergone a process of repeated examination, testing, and improvement. However, this idea was also previously stated; Bednarik (1987) had related the notion of engrams to permanent externalizations of ideas (finger fluting patterns in caves), but without naming them. Donald (1991: Table 8.1) observes that engrams would be impermanent, of constrained format, fixed physical medium, limited capacity and size, and not easily refinable. In these and other characteristics they would differ fundamentally from exograms, which are often permanent, are unconstrained and reformatable, can be of any medium, have virtually unlimited capacity and size, and can be subjected to unlimited iterative refinement.

Donald's lack of familiarity with the empirical information on early symboling (Bednarik 1992, 2003; Hodgson 2003), combined with his inadequate understanding of anthropology (Brace 1993, 1996, 1999) and neglect of cognitive ethology (Cynx and Clark 1993) detract greatly from his work. For instance he accepts Lieberman's (Lieberman and Crelin 1971; Lieberman et al. 1972, 1992) notions of Neanderthal vocal capabilities, which were refuted (Falk 1975, 1987; Arensburg et al. 1989, 1990; cf. Laitman et al. 1992; Bickerton 1993, 1996, 2010; Dunbar 1996; Aitchison 1996; Falk 2009) and today are absurdities. Nevertheless, Donald's work has prompted the development of an academic cottage industry in the cognitive sciences, extended cognition studies (Clark and Chalmers 1998; Adams and Aizawa 2001, 2008; Malafouris 2004; Rupert 2004; Aizawa and Adams 2005; Block 2005; Prinz 2006). However, the formulation of Donald's concept of exograms provides a valuable benchmark for the determination of hominin capacities, because some forms of them attributable to specific times can survive for very long periods of time. These, collectively, represent one of the most instructive forms of empirical evidence for the cognitive evolution of humans, for the origins of human modernity (Bednarik 2011b, 2011c), and for the proliferation of symboling ability during the Middle Pleistocene (c. 780,000 to 130,000 years ago). Taphonomy (determining the selective survival of material evidence) sees to it that most exograms would never survive from the Pleistocene (Bednarik 1994), and most of those that could would not be recognizable as having functioned as exograms. However, there are several classes of such materials that can, under fortunate circumstances, remain not only recoverable, but are recognizable as exograms. Middle Pleistocene examples have been classified into beads, petroglyphs, portable engravings, proto-sculptures, pigments and manuports (Bednarik 1992, 2003a). Most of these classes of evidence offer no utilitarian explanations and they begin appearing with Mode 1 and Mode 2 technocomplexes (hand-axe-free and handaxe Lower Paleolithic tool traditions), i.e., about the same time in human evolution as the first evidence of pelagic crossings, up to one million years ago. There are even indications that some utilitarian artifacts began to be invested with non-utilitarian properties during the "Acheulian" traditions of that time. Notably the development of the hand-axes to excessive perfection and symmetry has been suggested to be well beyond the necessary (Gamble 1997; Wynn 2002), and implies the introduction of a sense of perfection (Bednarik 2011c). Similarly, in some cases it has been suggested that the presence of prominent fossil casts on a few such Acheulian hand-axes is intentional; i.e., that the tool was deliberately worked around this natural inclusion (Oakley 1981). Vast numbers of late Acheulian hand-axes imply such outstanding workmanship and knapping skill that they appear to have been status symbols rather than mere tools. This would suggest that their incredible perfection was an exogrammic message.

While these interpretations are plausible, they are not testable, which also applies to the proposition that pigment use is necessarily proof of exogram use. Ochre and hematite pigments were certainly used extensively by people of Acheulian technology (Bednarik 1992, 2003a), but such substances can also serve utilitarian purposes. Similarly, a variety of arguments can be invented to deny that manuports (unusual natural and unmodified objects that were transported by humans, such as crystals, fossils, and strikingly shaped stones), portable engravings, and proto-sculptures acted as exograms. However, this position cannot be sustained for some classes of evidence, notably beads and petroglyphs of the Lower Paleolithic. They are far too sophisticated to be dismissed as coincidences, flukes, or evidence of a "running ahead of time" (Vishnyatsky 1994) in human evolution. While it is possible to deny the intentionality of simple engravings on bone, ivory and stone to preserve the replacement model of recent human evolution, the secure identification of beads and pendants is largely uncontroversial. Small objects, drilled through with stone tools, could be either beads or pendants; or they could be small utilitarian objects such as buckles or quangings (pulling handles used in sealing) as the Inuit use (Boas 1888: Figs 15, 17, 121d; Nelson 1899: Pl. 17; Kroeber 1900: Fig. 8). Such utilitarian objects are generally of distinctive shape, use-wear, and material; they need to be very robust. Small objects that were drilled through either in the center or close to one end (e.g. teeth perforated near the root); that are too small or too fragile to be utilitarian objects; or that lack the typical wear patterns of such articles; can be safely assumed to be beads or pendants (Bednarik 1997c). An example of such complete lack of ambiguity are the disc beads made from ostrich eggshell. These are extremely common in the ethnography of southern African people (Woodhouse 1997), and in the archaeological record they are found from there to China and Siberia (Bednarik 1993a; Bednarik and You 1991; Grün and Beaumont 2001; Kumar et al. 1988; Mason 1988; Morris 2000; Wendt 1974; Woodhouse 1997). Of a significantly greater antiquity are the over forty similar ostrich eggshell beads from El Greifa site E, in Wadi el Adjal, Libya (Bednarik 1997c). They come from a substantial sequence of Acheulian occupation deposits representing many millennia of continuous occupation of a littoral site, on the shore of the huge Fezzan Lake of the Pleistocene (Ziegert 2007). However, the Libyan beads, about 200,000 years old, may well be exceeded in age by many other finds, such as the pendants from the Repolusthöhle, in the Austrian Alps (Mottl 1951), or the several hundred centrally perforated fossils from Acheulian deposits in France and England (Bednarik 2005). First reported by Boucher de Perthes (1846), Prestwich (1859: 52) and Smith (1894), they remained widely ignored for the entire 20th century and were correctly identified as *Porosphaera globularis* only in 2005, and their extensive modification and wear as beads were only then recognized. The crinoid fossils from a site in Israel are another example of Acheulian beads (Goren-Inbar et al. 1991).

Amazingly all these numerous beads managed to survive for hundreds of millennia, only to be ignored or rejected by archaeologists, according to whose beliefs such complex symbolic objects could not possibly have existed in those early times. Firstly, their use demonstrates self-consciousness with all its implications, itself an important factor in cognitive evolution. But they also demand the existence and communication of complex symbolic meanings, without which beads cannot possibly exist. Whatever their practical purpose may have been (decorative, communicative, emblemic, economic, protective, commemorative, ideological, etc.), their function was always symbolic: they demonstrate essentially modern cognition, irrespective of considerations of physical evolution or technology. Contrary to Malafouris (2008) who sees "the self as emerging through the ornament [bead]," self-awareness, including autonoetic awareness, must precede bead use, because without self-awareness (and several other precursory conditions) beads lack any justification for existence. Hominins did not first make beads and then find a way to make them relevant. The example Malafouris cites, the forty-one late Middle Stone Age shells from Blombos Cave in South Africa, are certainly not the "landmark" in cognitive evolution he sees in them. Not only are they preceded by earlier beads and pendants several times as old (Bednarik 1997b, 1997c, 2001, 2005, 2008c), self-awareness predates them in the primate ancestry by dozens of million of years. The view that the first appearance of "the human ability to be reflectively conscious of one's own perspective on the world" must be deducible from archaeological finds is itself archaeocentric. Beads are exograms conveying complex meanings, and they imply other faculties still. For instance beads and pendants involve the use of cordage, which in turn almost demands the facility of knotting—both of which also are practically required for the construction of seagoing rafts (Bednarik 1997a, 1999, 2003b). And as replicative archaeology would have shown archaeologists, the making of beads, especially from ostrich eggshell, involves some rather complex technological steps (Bednarik 1997c). But they were certainly not the first exograms used by hominins.

Another form of evidence illustrating the cognitive status of Lower Paleolithic humans that has been largely ignored by Pleistocene archaeology is the occurrence of petroglyphs safely dated to that period by excavation. So far limited to about 550 cupules (hemispherical cup-marks hammered into hard rock panels, also known from practically all subsequent periods up to the 20th century) and three linear petroglyphs at two sites in central India, these constitute the earliest known rock art in the world (Bednarik 2008d). They were found in two quartzite caves, Auditorium Cave at World-Heritage listed Bhimbetka (Bednarik 1993b), and Daraki-Chattan (Kumar 1996; Bednarik et al. 2005). There are, however, first indications that some of the earliest cupules in southern Africa could be of the Fauresmith tool tradition, which is also Lower Paleolithic (Beaumont and Bednarik 2010), but here better evidence of age is still required. Replicative archaeology has established that to produce one of these cupules on the rock in question requires in excess of 30,000 strokes with the types of hammer stones demonstrated to have been used (Kumar 2010). Moreover, cupules are generally limited to the smallest possible size, relative to their depth, which implies rather obsessive behavior in the service of a production that provided no tangible benefits for the maker, and no apparent selective advantages. Indeed, it is the features driven by obsessive behavior that are the very basis of human civilizations. The compulsion for perfection underlying such products as beads and cupules is the very same drive that underpins all of modern culture and all its institutions—not least of all academia and science. Without this obsessive behavior the human ascent would not have been possible. Apes, apparently, feel no impulse to improve their simple sleeping nests or implements, and there is no such obsession evident in the stone tools of the human ancestors from the australopithecines to *Homo erectus*, i.e., until the template of the hand-axe began to be developed beyond the purely functional. Since that time, and coinciding with the development toward robust *Homo sapiens*, the phenomenon of "progress"—reified by the search for improvement—has been the principal determinant of human cultural evolution (Bednarik 2011b, 2011c). It began perhaps at an imperceptibly slow pace, gradually acquiring momentum, until in recent millennia it became an overpowering force driving humanity's relentless technological ascent. Today's human society would be unthinkable without it. On the archaeological record this development can be first identified in time through such objects as beads and pendants, cupules, and the evolving ability to harness the forces of nature: e.g., wind, waves, currents, and buoyancy, as manifested in the earliest demonstrated maritime colonization events (Bednarik 1997a, in press); or the first evidence of the controlled use of fire (Beaumont 2011).

Archaeological Interpretations of Human Behavior

The hypothesis of the introduction and rise of exograms has attracted almost no interest from archaeologists, and the available empirical information relating to it has been either ignored or explained away. Exograms have generally been interpreted in terms that are comprehensible within the simplistic worldview of archaeology, usually as "primitive art." There is no scientific reason to refer to anything of the Pleistocene as "art," which is why the material in question is preferably called "paleoart": it is no more "art" than a peanut is either a pea or a nut. The word simply defines art-like manifestations of the deep past, without implying what they are or what their roles were.

Archaeologists have also espoused numerous premature and untestable hypotheses about paleoart, such as the notion that it was introduced by shamans. Despite isolated claims for Holocene evidence (e.g. Porr and Alt 2006), it remains profoundly unknown at what point in human history the practices defined as shamanism were introduced. But there are alternative, logical methods of investigating the role of shamanism in rock art. In the entire ethnographic world literature there is not a single report of a shaman having produced rock art. There are, however, numerous cases of rock art production having been observed and recorded, or where the authors of the "art" may be known to us (e.g. Haskovec and Sullivan 1986; Bednarik 1998: 26; Novellino 1999). In all such cases no shamans were involved, and the utilitarian or ceremonial purpose of the rock art, where it is known, lacks any connection with shamanism. Indeed, one of the most obvious prerequisites for considering what the characteristics of shamanic art might be is a definition of its ethnographically demonstrated idiosyncrasies. In the absence of such an explicit index any definitive way of identifying authentically shamanic art traditions is lacking. Moreover, most of the world's rock art occurs in regions from which no shamanic practices are known ethnographically. Although none of this demonstrates that no rock art was ever produced by shamans, the proposition that significant quantities of rock art are the work of shamans (Lewis Williams and Dowson 1988) is unwarranted by the empirical data, and it is of course untestable. Thus the scientific null hypothesis, that most rock art is not shamanic, has empirical support; the archaeologically favored shamanic hypothesis has none.

The altered states in (North American) shamanism were perhaps first recognized by Oesterreich (1935: 295). Peters and Price-Williams (1980: 397) examined them across 42 cultures. Loeb (1924), Radin (1937), and Devereux (1961) defined shamans variously as epileptic, hysteric or neurotic, whereas Silverman (1967) introduced the notion that shamanism is an acute form of schizophrenia. His hypothesis attracted immediate criticism (Handelman 1968; Weakland 1968; Boyer 1969) and was followed by later work rejecting it. Lex (1984) suggested that the popularity of the notion that schizophrenia provides an explanation for shamanic experiences and behavior appears to emanate from distorted and romantic interpretations of the significance of hallucinatory symptoms. Noll (1983), in examining altered states of consciousness, demonstrated that the anthropological "schizophrenia metaphor" of shamanism and its altered states is untenable. Significant phenomenological differences exist between the shamanic and schizophrenic states of consciousness. Despite these authoritative rebuttals the notion that there is a connection between shamanism and schizophrenia continued to be pursued in recent years (e.g. Polimeni and Reiss 2002; El-Mallakha 2006) and has given rise to various archaeological theses. For instance Whitley (2009) attributes both early rock art and shamanism to bipolar disorder.

Of particular concern are the endemic modes of polemic presented by the shamanists. Rather than citing ethnographic information they reinterpret the original texts "creatively" (Hromnik 1991; Solomon 1999, 2000; Le Quellec 2006; Helvenston 2012) and replace key terminology with their own preferred words. For instance, Lewis-Williams replaces the terms "sorcerer," "witchdoctor," "medicine man," or "healer" (and even "teacher") with his preferred word "shaman," even though there are very significant differences between these concepts. But he believes that is what the ethnographers (e.g., Bleek 1933, 1935, 1936; How 1962; Katz 1976, 1982; Katz and Biesele 1986; Lee 1967; Marshall 1969; Orpen 1874; Prins 1990) meant when they wrote of sorcerers and medicine men, and that they were too ignorant to understand metaphors. He also mistranslates the word "medicine man" used by an old Xhosa or Mpondomise woman in relation to the rock art painters (Lewis-Williams 1986; cf. Jolly 1986). He further conflates hallucinogen-induced trance with trance involving no drugs, confusing analogical effects with identical causes (Lewis-Williams 2002). Similarly, he continues to ignore the advice of those genuinely engaged in the study of authentic shamanism (Eliade 1964; De Heusch 1965; Rouget 1980; Hamayon 1982, 1990, 1995; Hultkrantz 1993; Francfort et al. 2001), although he lacks first-hand knowledge of shamanism.

However, shamanism is not the only frivolous explanation of rock art, the perhaps most numerous representative of exograms surviving from the Pleistocene. Other speculations concern proposals that rock art and other evidence of "modern behavior" were introduced through various brain illnesses. As noted, such hypotheses began appearing in the first half of the 20th century, explaining shamanism as the result of epilepsy, hysteria, neuroses, and schizophrenia (see e.g. Kroeber 1940; Demerath 1942; Devereux 1956; Silverman 1967; Scheff 1970; Le Barre 1970, 1972). This fashion of presenting essentially unsupported theories of this kind has continued to the present time, with the most recent proposals including the attribution of paleoart and all archaeological indicators of "modernity" to autism and Asperger's syndrome. Indeed, the human brain disease autism (Hermelin and O'Connor

1970; Frith 1989; Hughes et al. 1997; Baron-Cohen 2002, 2006; Allman et al. 2005; Grinker 2007; Brasic 2009a, 2009b, 2010; Balter 2007; Burack et al. 2009; Bednarik and Helvenston 2012; Helvenston and Bednarik 2011) has been proposed to have been instrumental in introducing Pleistocene paleoart so often that it is hardly an original idea (Kellman 1998, 1999; Humphrey 1998; Haworth 2006; Spikins 2009; Bogdashina 2003, 2010: 159–160; cf. Marr 1982; Treffert 2010), and yet some of its most ardent promoters seem to think they discovered it. This illustrates how inadequately these proposals were researched. There are, of course, many other explanations of hominin behavior in the archaeological literature, but before they are considered it needs to be appreciated that the discipline *is not capable of detecting behavior*. It merely records objects and their physical contexts; it can within limits also estimate the ages of remains; but its etic explanations and interpretations lack any emic credibility. Some of its inherent limitations could be overcome by introducing more rigorous practices, especially "taphonomic logic" (Bednarik 1994) and the "metamorphology" developed from it (Bednarik 1995c). However, these proposals have attracted virtually no enthusiasm in archaeology, which itself implies fundamental structural problems in the field. Preservation of the dogma has precedence, simply because a paradigmatic shift is thought to be too traumatic for the discipline. That may well be true but the question is: is it better to facilitate the promotion of precipitate models, such as those of a mythical African Eve or the involvement of brain diseases in the recent (Final Pleistocene) development of human cognition, enculturation and technology?

As the author has exhaustively investigated the African Eve hoax elsewhere (Bednarik 1991, 1992, 1997b, 2003a, 2008a, 2008b, 2011b, 2011c, 2001d) he focuses here on the second issue, that of the contribution of neuropathologies to the human ascent.

The Rise of Brain Illnesses

Although Humphrey's (1998) paper presents no convincing case for a nexus between Pleistocene cave art and *autism*, he does raise some very pertinent and interesting points. One concerns the deeply ingrained belief that the "Upper Paleolithic" artists shared our modern "mind." Pleistocene archaeologists often use such terms as "modern behavior" or "modern mind" but it is becoming increasingly apparent that there is no agreement as to what they mean. Some authors refer to human modernity as a set of abilities one can reasonably expect to find a million years ago, even earlier (Bednarik 2011b, 2011c). Others favor a much more narrow definition, attributing a "pre-modern mind" even to the cave artists of the early Upper Paleolithic (see Humphries 1998 and debate therein) and suggesting the "modern mind" to postdate 20,000 years BP. Bearing in "mind" that it is not clear what the mind is (what is its appearance, weight, or composition?) and that this is probably intended as a shorthand generic term for mental processes occurring in the human brain, the concept of "modernity of mind" is fraught with various difficulties. It is therefore doubtful that a scientific (testable) case can be made for a connection between the exceptional skills sometimes (but very rarely) found in autistics (Waterhouse 1988; Mottron and Belleville 1993, 1995; Mottron et al. 1999; Happé and Vital 2009) and the abilities of the graffitists of the Franco-Cantabrian caves.

Humphrey's challenge of archaeologists' "received view" (Dennett 1998)—to show why they assume that Upper Paleolithic paleoartists must have shared present-day perception and reality—is of particular interest. So is Dennett's observation that "It will be interesting to see if the defenders of the received view have such facts in reserve to salvage their case, or whether they will have to fall back on simply citing various eminent opinions in favor of the received view." Certainly the responses of archaeologists following the presentation of Humphrey's hypothesis have failed to offer such "facts." Another fascinating aspect of Humphrey's contentions arises when he quotes Mithen as stating "that modern humans … were capable of the type of symbolic thought and sophisticated visual representation that was beyond Neanderthals." Two issues arise from this statement. First, the art of the "Aurignacians" provides no proof whatsoever of symbolic thought, which seems to be believed by nearly all Pleistocene archaeologists. It only provides evidence of depiction, no more. That is not to say that the "Aurignacians" were not capable of symboling, but the proof for that is to be (and can be) found elsewhere. Second, we have no evidence of any kind that "Aurignacian" palaeoart was produced by "anatomically modern humans," because all Late Pleistocene human remains of Europe predating, say, 26,000 years are either of Robusts (usually called Neanderthals there) or of intermediate forms (Bednarik 1995b, 2007, 2008a, 2011b, 2011c). Therefore Mithen's claim is probably wrong on both counts and merely expresses the inherent defects of the replacement hypothesis.

Humphrey presents only a single example of an autistic child with advanced artistic abilities (Selfe 1977), although some others have long been known (e.g. Pring and Hermelin 1993; Kellman 1998, 1999; Happé and Frith 2010), and he seems unaware of other authors pursuing the same issue. Moreover, his hypothesis suffers from his lack of awareness that such abilities in children are certainly not limited to autistic savants, but are also well known as "precocious realism" in the art of non-autistic children (Selfe 1983; Drake and Winner 2009; O'Connor and Hermelin 1987, 1990; contra Snyder and Thomas 1997). Seen in that overall context, Humphrey's hypothesis loses its appeal. If his suggestion that the palaeoart of the early "Upper Paleolithic" implies an absence of language use, because of their naturalism, were applied to, say, the realistic rock art attributed to the San Bushmen, its absurdity becomes apparent. Similarly, he seems to be unaware that throughout the world, the images we tend to regard as naturalistic are preceded by traditions that lack iconographic elements. Finally, the extremely rare occurrence of autistics with exceptional depictive abilities does not explain why 99.99% of autistic spectrum disorder (ASD) patients lack them. After all, ASD has recently become a very common illness, affecting one in 110 children now (Weintraub 2011; locally even as high as one in 38). The epidemic increase in this diagnosis, from one in 5000 in 1975, cannot be entirely attributed to changing diagnostic criteria (cf. Buchen 2011). The explanation offered in Bednarik (2011b) is perhaps the most eligible.

Similarly, Spikins' (2009) "different minds theory" suffers from an inadequate consideration of the relevant empirical evidence a more careful review of paleoart would reveal. Spikins explains "modern behavior" as the rise in cognitive variation within populations through social mechanisms for integrating "different minds." She focuses particularly on one form of autism, *Asperger's syndrome*, because it does not inhibit the effective use of language or cognitive development, and the associated attention to detail enables patients to compensate for the deficit of empathy. Subjects with autistic conditions (as well as in schizophrenia; Brüne 2006) have cognitively based deficiencies in "theory of mind" (ToM, see below). Contradicting the scientific evidence, Spikins' hypothesis misuses the term "species" by maintaining that *Homo sapiens neanderthalensis* is a separate species, when in fact it is a subspecies (different species cannot produce fertile offspring with each other). She believes that the earliest evidence of symbolic communication appears in South

Africa 165,000 years ago. Leaving aside the issue that symbolic communication, like behavior or intention, cannot be demonstrated by archaeology, only conjectured, she ignores both the inferred use of symbolic communication by Lower Paleolithic hominins (suggested by language use, seafaring, use of beads, palaeoart of various types) and the experimentally demonstrated symbolic communication ability of extant animals other than humans.

This does not necessarily render Spikins' hypothesis false, because it could still be validly applied to a model of hominin evolution based on empirical data rather than archaeological myths (Bednarik 2008a, 2011b). Her main contention is that autism is a spectrum of differences displayed across the modern population, and that modern behavior arose when autistic modes of thinking were integrated into the practices of human societies. She emphasizes the analytical and mathematical thinking in Asperger's, a form of "mild autism" (Rodman 2003; Bednarik and Helvenston 2012), and attributes to it the changes she detects in technology: "Rigid analytical thinking (both by autistic individuals and through their influence) might improve technology and foraging efficiency." She cites projectile weapons, bladelets, bone artifacts, hafting, "elaborate fire use," exploitation of marine resources and large game, apparently unaware that all of these have been demonstrated from the Lower Paleolithic, together with palaeoart and "personal ornamentation." Nevertheless, she feels that these are all attributable to the "attention to detail, exceptional memory, a thirst for knowledge and narrow obsessive focus" of autistics, particularly when coupled with their desire for social isolation.

However, these proficiencies are obviously not limited to people with ASD, a condition that also happens to include diagnostic characteristics such as inflexibility in thinking, difficulty with planning and organization, and rigorous adherence to routine (Pickard et al. 2011), which impede originality and innovative thought. The creativity Spikins invokes is normally impoverished in ASD patients (Frith 1972; Craig and Baron-Cohen 1999; Turner 1999), unless fostered, and the savant skills ascribed to them need to be nurtured and are specific to the ordered cultural context of modern life (Baron-Cohen 2000; Folstein and Rosen-Sheidley 2001; Thioux et al. 2006). Moreover, the neuropsychiatric disorders of humans, absent in other extant primates (Rubinsztein et al. 1994; Walker and Cork 1999; Enard et al. 2002a; Olson and Varki 2003; Marvanová et al. 2003; Bednarik and Helvenston 2012; Sherwood et al. 2011), are a deleterious by-product of recent evolution (Bednarik 2011b, 2011c, 2011d, in press; Bednarik and Helvenston 2012; Helvenston and Bednarik 2011; Pickard et al. 2011). The phylogenetic timing of the introduction of ASD is the crucial issue here: *to influence society the illness had to exist, but to do so, society and selective processes had to first tolerate it*. The lack of social skills typical of ASD in societies heavily reliant upon social dynamics would tend to select against it, socially as well as genetically. Thus Spikins' hypothesis runs up against the classical Keller and Miller (2006) paradox, the resolution to which will be considered below because it applies to all neuropathologies. Spikins fails to take into consideration the complexities of their genetic bases and how or why they arose in the first place. Until now (Bednarik 2011b, 2011c), no solution had been provided for this, which renders her stab in the dark without reference frame and scientific justification.

Schizophrenia (Os and Kapur 2009) is a polygenetic disorder (Cardno and Gottesman 2000; Kennedy et al. 2003; Riley and Kendler 2006). However, because its underlying physiological abnormalities remain inadequately understood, a properly integrated etiologic and pathophysiologic model does not yet exist. Schizophrenia is a disease of decreased cellular connectivity in the brain, precipitated by environmental stress during brain development, among those with genetic vulnerability (Ayalew et al. 2012). Although numerous schizophrenia susceptibility genes have been identified (NRG1, NRG3, DTNBP1, COMT, CHRNA-7, SLC6A4, IMPA2, HOPA12bp, DISC1, TCF4, MBP, MOBP, NCAM1, NRCAM, NDUFV2, RAB18, ADCYAP1, BDNF, CNR1, DRD2, GAD1, GRIA1, GRIA4, GRIN2B, HTR2A, RELN, SNAP-25, TNIK, HSPA1B, ALDH1A1, ANK3, CD9, CPLX2, FABP7, GABRB3, GNB1L, GRMS, GSN, HINT1, KALRN, KIF2A, NR4A2, PDE4B, PRKCA, RGS4, SLC1A2, SYN2; Yoshikawa et al. 2001; Spinks et al. 2004; Cho et al. 2005; Li et al. 2006; Xu et al. 2006; Ayalew et al. 2012), they are of small or non-detrimental individual effects. Susceptibility alleles only constitute increasing risk for schizophrenia through aggregating, be it by chance, assortative mating, or by other mechanisms (Cannon 2005). Carriers of small numbers of schizophrenia susceptibility genes are far more numerous (about 15% of any population) than cases of the actual disorder (0.3–1%), and the advantages selected for in first-degree relatives of schizophrenia patients have been suggested to include creativity (Horrobin 2001). According to Crow (1997), schizophrenia and language are linked to cerebral asymmetry, and the hemispherical dominance for language led to the collateral hemispheric lateralization and psychosis (Crow 1995a 1995b). However, this notion is countered by several indices, not only the obvious error of linking language origins with the falsity of speciation of Graciles (see above, and Falk 2009; Bickerton 2010). For instance, the planum temporale, presenting a left-right asymmetry favoring the left (Geschwind and Levitsky 1968), which has been related to language reception, is also present in great apes (Gannon et al. 1998, 2001). Moreover, the detection of the FOXP2 gene on chromosome 7 of two Robusts from El Sidrón in Spain (Krause et al. 2007; cf. Enard et al. 2002b; Zhang et al. 2002; Sanjuan et al. 2006), but absence of such schizophrenia susceptibility alleles as NRG3 in Robusts refutes the idea (in fact schizophrenia may have appeared much later than Graciles; Bednarik and Helvenston 2012).

Children later diagnosed with schizophrenia had persistent reading impairment and low IQ scores (Karlsson 1984; Crow et al. 1995), and all cultures perceive the illness as a serious maladaptive dysfunction (Pearlson and Folley 2008). Introvertive anhedonia, a typical symptom of schizophrenia (Schuldberg 2000), decreases creative activity significantly, thus providing a clear separation between creative and clinical cohorts. However, as in autism, there is a spectrum within which schizophrenia is merely the extreme form. For instance, first-degree relatives of psychotic patients have been consistently shown to be notably creative (Heston 1966; Karlsson 1970). Elevated levels of some of the schizotypal traits are commonly observed in individuals that are active in the creative arts (Schuldberg 1988, 2000; Brod 1997; Nettle 2001). Schizotypal diathesis, which may lead to actual illness under specific environmental factors (Tsuang et al. 2001) but in most cases does not, is therefore more convincingly implicated in creativity, much in the same way as mild forms of autism can yield high-performing individuals. Schizophrenia is associated with drastically reduced probability of reproduction (Bassett et al. 1996; Avila et al. 2001), through significantly diminished fertility, mediated by reduced survival and social competence (Brüne 2006), reduced attractiveness for mating and lower marriage rates, as well as possibly via reduced fertility once married. The notion that artistic production has its origins in "costly displays" (Miller 2000, 2001; Varella et al. 2011) would therefore seem to exclude the involvement of schizophrenic artists. Of potential interest would be how schizotypy relates to mating behavior, e.g., through an increase in extra-pair copulations, a higher turnover of relationships, or less time between relationships.

However, the involvement of schizotypy in shamanism deserves further examination. The discovery of the rubber hand illusion (RHI) in schizophrenic patients (Peled et al. 2003) has considerable implications for the notion of out-of-body experiences (Thakkar et al. 2011). It has been suggested that a weakened sense of the self may contribute to psychotic experiences. The RHI illustrates proprioceptive drift, which is observed to be significantly greater in schizophrenia patients than in a control sample, and can even lead to an out-of-body experience, linking "body disownership" and psychotic experiences. In summary, there is no credible empirical evidence linking schizophrenia with palaeoart production, just as there is none linking shamanism with it or with schizophrenia. Nevertheless, susceptibility to proprioceptive drift can be shown to be linked to schizotypy, and may well account for certain experiences of shamans.

Finally, Whitley (2009) proposed that rock art arose from "mad geniuses" via shamanism, attributing it to *bipolar disorder*, but without any credible justification or empirical evidence. This disease differs from schizophrenia in some ways: it is not neurodegenerative with advanced age, and there is decreased neuronal and glial density in association with glial hypertrophy (Rajkowska 2009). Both illnesses are highly heritable (Edvardsen et al. 2008), as shown by monozygotic twin studies (Kieseppä et al. 2004), and they are clearly polygenic as indicated by the wide spectrum of their manifestations. The bipolar range stretches from bipolar I through bipolar II and to mild forms of cyclothymia. It is reflected in the lack of resolution in decisively determining the genetic basis, although regions of interest identified in linkage studies include chromosome 18, 4p16, 12q23-q24, 16p13, 21q22 and Xq24-q26 (Craddock and Jones 1999; Craddock et al. 2005; Saito et al. 2001), and genes DRD4, SYNJ1 and MAOA have been implicated (Muglia et al. 2002; Stopkova et al. 2004; Andres et al. 2004; Cho et al. 2005; Preisig et al. 2005; Jansson et al. 2005). Just as autism and schizophrenia comprise spectra rather than discrete illnesses, much the same applies to bipolar disorders, and probably for the same reasons: numerous genetic predispositions (Schulze 2010) and a range of environmental factors determine any patient's specific condition. However, bipolar illness is a very serious disorder and even today is not well controlled in many patients (Helvenston 2012). Like schizophrenia and other brain illnesses it would have severely affected the life prospects of sufferers in the Pleistocene, and the likeliness of passing on their genes, as they would have been completely disabled to even survive for periods of time.

Human "Devolution"

This raises the perhaps most fundamental problem with the shamanic, bipolar, schizophrenic, Asperger's, autistic and similar archaeological "explanations" of rock art and human modernity: their advocates make no attempt to determine whether these conditions actually existed in the Pleistocene. This is not just a question of clarifying when neuropathologies began to have a significant impact on the human genome, but more importantly, why they were not selected against. The mental and cognitive developments in the human brain rendered humans vulnerable to neurodegenerative diseases as well as frontal lobe connectivity problems, to demyelination or dysmyelination, Mendelian disorders—in fact to thousands of syndromes and disorders endemic to humans (Bednarik 2011b). Why their rise was not vigorously selected against by natural evolution is the classic *Keller and Miller* (2006) *paradox*, which was resolved only recently (Bednarik 2007, 2008a, 2008b). In a species fully subject to the canons of natural selection such numerous disadvantageous mutations would be suppressed vigorously. They include thousands of Mendelian (single gene) disorders, but also countless somatic changes, such as cleidocranial dysplasia or delayed closure of cranial sutures, malformed clavicles and dental abnormalities (genes RUNX2 and CBRA1 refer), type 2 diabetes (gene THADA), or the microcephalin D allele, introduced approximately 37,000 years ago through a single progenitor copy (but could be as recent as 14,000 years ago, at 95% confidence interval; Evans et al. 2005). Another contributor to microcephaly, the ASPM allele, appeared around 5800 years BP (Evans et al. 2005; Mekel-Bobrov et al. 2005).

It should be clarified that the contradictory nature of the notion of "devolution" indicates that the concept of "evolution" is misused in cultural studies. Devolution cannot occur in biology, because any change, any development is evolutionary, or attributable to genetic adaptation in populations. The confusion arises because archaeology uses the term analogically but in the sense of "development toward more complex forms," and perceives human history as a teleological process. This is just one example of the incommensurabilities between scientific and humanistic meanings of terminology, which shows that effective communication is almost impossible between the two (Bednarik 2011a). Here, the term "devolution" is placed in quotation marks and refers to both somatic and neural developments that are not the outcome of natural selection and lead to inferior characteristics, rather than adaptively better genetic or physiological fitness.

The suspension of human evolution determined by natural selection and genetic drift (Bednarik 2011d) has remained completely unrecognized until recently, in part because Pleistocene archaeology and paleoanthropology have pursued the replacement hypothesis with such fervor that they failed to notice that it was initially based on a hoax by a German archaeologist. However, it has no genetic, skeletal or cultural justification whatsoever (Bednarik 2008a). That hypothesis demands that natural selection and genetic drift governed recent evolution and speciation, when in fact the emergence of the Graciles involved no speciation; they and the Robusts are one species (Green et al. 2010). The distinctive changes during the final third of the Late Pleistocene are almost entirely the result of self-domestication caused by the determination of breeding patterns by rising cultural imperatives that have been identified (Bednarik 2008b). Domestication promotes unfavorable alleles (e.g. Horrobin 1998, 2001; Andolfatto 2001; Lu et al. 2006), and it can even account for otherwise unexplained features, such as the abolition of estrus in females. If it was under the auspices of this process that predispositions for brain illnesses were protected from natural selection, such pathologies must postdate these developments, and it would be expected that most appeared less than 40,000 years ago and are endemic to the subspecies *Homo sapiens sapiens* (Bednarik 2008a, 2011b; Helvenston and Bednarik 2011). Where relevant genetic indications are already available, they confirm this prediction. For instance the genes CADPS2 and AUTS2, involved in autism, appear with Graciles, and NRG3 (schizophrenia) is also absent in Robusts. Using the human haplotype map to test for selective sweeps in regions associated in genome scans with psychosis, such as 1q21, is promising (Voight et al. 2006). Such selective sweeps tend to yield relatively recent etiologies, of less than 20,000 years. Some conditions, such as schizophrenia, have been suggested to be much more recent (Bednarik and

Helvenston 2012), and so far no known relevant susceptibility alleles have been reported from Robust remains.

Therefore at this stage none of the more severe brain illnesses should be expected to be found in hominin populations prior to the partial suspension of natural selection, which on present indications may have begun, initially on a small scale, between 50,000 and 30,000 years ago. It is therefore unlikely that by the time the first known cave art was created (Bednarik 2007), any of the brain diseases to which it has been attributed could have even taken root. Moreover, the establishment in the human genome of thousands of deleterious alleles during the Final Pleistocene is certainly not the only detrimental change identifying the transition from robust to gracile human forms. Indeed, most of these changes have been maladaptive. They include significantly reduced brain volume (by ~13%) and cranial as well as other skeletal robusticity, and greatly reduced physical strength. Most importantly, hominin neotenization, which had already had a slight effect in previous physical evolution, accelerated rapidly between fifty and thirty millennia ago, to the point of prompting the notion of replacement, which nearly all archaeologists were duped by.

Neoteny, pedomorphism, fetalization, or juvenilization defines the retention into adulthood of juvenile or fetal physiology (Gould 1979; Ashley Montagu 1989; Thiessen 1997). Humans resemble chimpanzees anatomically most closely in the latter's fetal stage (Haldane 1932; De Beer 1940; Ashley Montagu 1960). The skull of an unborn ape is thin-walled, globular and lacks the prominent tori of the adult ape, thus resembling the cranium of a modern human. Upon birth its robust features develop rapidly. The slow closing of the cranial sutures in humans is another neotenous feature (genes RUNX2 and CBRA1 refer). The face of the ape embryo forms an almost vertical plane, as it does in the modern human all the way through adulthood, which is not the case in mature apes. Even the brains of fetal apes and adult humans are much more similar to each other, in terms of proportion and morphology, than they are to those of adult apes. Both the fetal chimpanzee and the adult human have hair on the top of the head and on the chin, but are otherwise largely naked. All male adult apes have a penis bone, but it is categorically absent in both fetal chimpanzees and all humans. The atrophy of the penis bone in humans appears to have been compensated for by the organ's significantly increased length and thickness, relative to apes (Badcock 1980: 47). Similarly, in female chimpanzees, the *labia majora* are an infantile feature; in humans they are retained for life. The hymen, too, is present only in the neonate ape, but in the absence of penetration is retained for life in human females. The organs of the lower abdomen, such as rectum, urethra, and vagina, are typically aligned with the spine in most adult mammals, including apes; only in fetal apes and humans do they point forward relative to the spine. The human ovary reaches full size at the age of five, which is the age of sexual maturity of the apes (De Beer 1940: 75). The legs of fetal apes are relatively short, while the arms are about as long in relation to the body as in humans. In the apes, the arms become much longer after birth. Human hands and feet resemble those of embryonic apes closely, but differ significantly from both hands and feet of mature apes. In fact the human foot, especially, retains the general structure found in unborn apes, which rather contradicts the hypothesis that it is an adaptation to upright walking. It could equally well be the case that upright walk is an adaptation to the neotenous foot of hominins, a possibility never considered by paleoanthropology. Even the shape of the cartilage of the ear in humans is a neotenous feature.

Neoteny is a phylogenic development in which fetal characteristics remain into adulthood, and specific processes of anatomical maturation are retarded (de Beer 1940). "But neoteny does not only contribute to the production of large structural change; it is also the cause of the retention of plasticity" or "morphological evolvability" (de Beer 1930: 93). Adaptively useful novelties supposedly become available as maturation genes are freed by pedomorphosis. In hominin evolution encephalization and neoteny are quite probably related, perhaps through supervenience (Bednarik 2011b). It is self-evident that, relative to the neonate ape, the newborn human is not remotely as far developed. In the first year after birth, the human brain more than doubles in both volume and weight. It continues to grow, approaching adult size by the age of three, but goes on expanding slightly more up to adolescence and even beyond. This extraordinary development, unheard of in the rest of the animal kingdom, compares with that of other primates, with rhesus monkey and gibbon achieving 70% of adult brain size at birth, the remaining 30% in the subsequent six months. In the larger apes, the size of the brain approaches adult size after the first year of life.

In the human genus neotenous traits include an exceedingly large brain, thinness of skull bones, flattened and broadened face, lack of tori, relatively large eyes, smallish nose, small teeth and jaws, and limbs that are proportionally short relative to the torso, especially the arms (Gould 1977; Ashley Montagu 1989; de Panafieu 2007). The acquisition of some of these characteristics involved enormous evolutionary costs, and most are decidedly detrimental to a primate. As in the case of adverse changes to the neural and endocrine systems, these deleterious developments need to be explained, because many of them completely contradict the principles of evolution. These have been suspended and replaced by the rules of domestication: systematic sexual selection in favor of specific characteristics, which were determined by cultural factors rather then those determining evolutionary fitness. In other words, in the most recent history of hominins, natural selection became increasingly moderated, and eventually almost replaced, by cultural selection (Bednarik 2008a, 2011c).

This process can be observed in the rapid gracilization among skeletal remains, especially in the females, beginning about 40,000 years ago (Bednarik 2008b, 2011b, 2011d). It was the females who led the neotenization in recent humans, and neoteny, although occurring in both genders, has remained more strongly expressed in women than in men. Its typical features are smaller body size, more delicate skin and skeleton, smaller mastoid features, significantly reduced or absent tori, less hair but retention of fetal hair, higher pitch of voice, more forward tilt of head but more backward tilt of pelvis, smoother ligament attachments and narrower joints, but they include also increased longevity, lower amount of energy expended at rest, faster heartbeat and prolonged development period (Ashley Montagu 1960). Few of these features present any appreciable evolutionary benefits.

One of the very few significant differences between humans and other animals is that no animal, including all other primates, has any preferences in mate selection of youth, specific body ratios (e.g. hips vs waist), facial features and symmetry, skin tone or hair color. In modern humans these culturally determined factors are undeniably crucial in the preference of mating partners, therefore they must have been introduced at some time in the past. Apart perhaps from facial symmetry, which may imply high immunocompetence (Grammer and Thornhill 1994; Shackelford and Larsen 1997), there are no biological advantages in these strongly developed *cultural* biases. Facial "attractiveness," for instance, is a cultural construct found in all extant societies (Cunningham et al. 1995), and in female humans, neotenous facial features are strongly preferred by males (Jones 1995, 1996). These include, irrespective of cultural context, neonate large eyes, shiny hair, small noses, reduced lower facial regions, thin jaws, and high foreheads (Perrett et al. 1994; Sforza et al. 2009), which are all distinctive neonate features. Obviously such pronounced preferences in female mate selection will inevitably effect significant somatic changes in populations that are totally unrelated to environmental variables. Such changes can be best observed in the hominins of central Europe, such as those from many Czech sites, of the period from about 35,000 to 25,000 years ago (Bednarik 2008b). Darwin's laws of evolutionary theory were supplanted by Mendelian laws of inheritance (Mendel 1866), and humans domesticated themselves, albeit unintentionally, through selective breeding favoring specific physical characteristics (Bednarik 2008a, 2008b, 2011b, 2011c, 2011d). However, this "devolution" in the most recent phylogenic history of humans is not limited to physiology; neoteny was also favored psychologically (Charlton 2006). The neotenous psychological traits of individuals of outstanding mental faculties derive precisely from the "retention of plasticity" or "morphological evolvability" de Beer (1930) had already referred to. The baby-faced students Zebrowitz et al. (1998) refer to tend to outperform their less-neotenized peers academically today.

Domestication is the collective genetic alteration of the physiology, behavior or life cycle of species through selective breeding. Humans are not the only initiators of domestication, many animal species, vertebrate and invertebrate, from mammals to ants, have domesticated others, for instance to modify foods undigestible by the domesticators, or for their labor, or simply to serve as staple food source (Bednarik 2011b). Selective breeding defies natural evolution in the sense that it can rapidly change the characteristics of a population without any natural selection in the Darwinian sense occurring. Selection for single traits inevitably results in changes in numerous others, and these changes tend to be deleterious. For instance domestication of animals typically results in decreased cranial volume relative to body size, a decrease that can be as much as 30–40 %. Neotenous physical traits arising from the domestication of animals include changes in reproductive cycles (estrus), fewer or shortened vertebra, curly tails (Trut 1999), loss of hair, larger eyes, rounded forehead, and shortened muzzle (Bertone 2006). Many of these (and others) reflect the gracilization noted in humans, and that also applies to the changes in behavior, toward playfulness, behavioral plasticity, exploratory pattern and pathology (note the juvenile behavior of a dog vs that of a wolf).

Therefore the first major factor in understanding early human behavior is that what are perceived as certain modern patterns very probably appeared together with the rapid somatic changes of the last part of the Late Pleistocene. They are then essentially attributable to human neotenization, which demonstrably accelerated markedly at that time. In many ways this process resembles devolution, and it occurred almost entirely outside the canons of Darwinian evolution. This does not, however, imply that modernity in human behavior should be expected to have appeared as one single package during that time, which archaeologists in Eurasia call the "early Upper Paleolithic," and which witnessed rapid gracilization of all human populations in four continents (Bednarik 2011c). To consider the origins of human behavior it does not suffice to focus on these last forty or so millennia. What transpires from the above is that *it was human behavior itself* that determined the most recent course in the development of the species, from robust *Homo sapiens* (such as *H. sapiens neanderthalensis*) to *H. sapiens sapiens*. This immediately raises the question: what were the preceding developments that set the stage for this final phase? If a viable and comprehensive etiological history of human behavior is to be formulated, it will be necessary to consider the possible antecedent developments that could have led to the final ascent of culturally induced neoteny.

THEORY OF MIND, SELF-AWARENESS, AND CONSCIOUSNESS

Three factors demanding attention in any speculation about early hominin behavior are theory of mind (ToM), the issue of self-awareness, and consciousness. ToM defines the ability of any animal to attribute mental states to oneself and others, and to understand that conspecifics have beliefs, desires, and intentions; and that these may be different from one's own (Premack and Woodruff 1978; Baron-Cohen 1991; Frith and Happé 1994; Ozonoff and Miller 1995; Happé et al. 1996; Happé 1997; Baron-Cohen et al. 1997; Jarrold et al. 2000; Jacques and Zelazo 2005; Bednarik 2011b). Each organism can only prove the existence of his or her own "mind" through introspection, and has no direct access to others' "minds." The presumption that other cognizing organisms have beliefs, intents, desires, pretending, knowledge, etc. is the basis of a ToM. Although present in numerous species, at greatly differing levels, it has perhaps attracted most attention in the study of two groups, children and great apes, and the level they conceive of mental activity in others, attribute intention to, and predict the behavior of others (Call and Tomasello 1998). It is thought to be largely the observation of behavior that can prompt a ToM.

The discovery of mirror neurons in macaques in the 1990s (Di Pellegrino et al. 1992; Rizzolatti et al. 1996) has provided much impetus in the exploration of how a ToM is formed (Gallese and Goldman 1998; Iacoboni et al. 2005). Mirror neurons are activated both when specific actions are executed and when identical actions are observed, providing a neural mechanism for the common coding between perception and action (but see Hickok 2009). One of the competing models to explain ToM, simulation theory (Gordon 1986, 1996; Preston and de Waal 2002), is said to derive much support from the mirror neurons, although it predates their discovery by a decade. These neurons are seen as the mechanism by which individuals simulate others in order to better understand them. However, mirror neurons have so far not been shown to produce actual behavior (Provine 2009). Motor command neurons in the prefrontal complex send out signals that orchestrate body movements, but some of them, the mirror neurons, also fire when merely watching another individual—not necessarily a conspecific—perform a similar act. It appears that the visual input prompts a "virtual reality" simulation of the other individual's actions. However, ToM and "simulation," though related, may have different phylogenic histories (Somerville and Decety 2006; Keysers and Gazzola 2007), and the roles of mirror neurons may be much more complex than anticipated; they may be involved in the formulation of constructs of reality (Bednarik 2011b). Ramachandran (2009a) has speculated about the roles of mirror neurons in cognitive evolution (Oberman and Ramachandran 2009), in empathy, imitation (cf. Ferrari et al. 2009), and language acquisition (cf. Rizzolatti and Arbib 1998). His examples of germane evidence include anosognosia in a small cohort of right hemisphere stroke patients, which prompts denial of paralysis in other patients; and the suppression of the MU brain wave in humans when their hand is moved.

Neurological conditions have shown that the self is not the monolithic entity it believes itself to be (see Dielenberg, this volume). These conditions include out-of-body-experiences, apotemnophilia (alienation of a body part, especially a limb, which derives from alienation due to a congenital defect in the right parietal), transsexuality, Cotard's syndrome (patient is convinced to be dead), the Capgras delusion (because visual and emotional brain areas are disconnected, patient experiences familiar entities as substitutes or imposters), or akinetic mutism (patient is completely unresponsive, unable to talk or walk, despite being fully awake; caused by damage to the anterior cingulate) (Ramachandran 2009b). It has been shown above that susceptibility to proprioceptive drift, demonstrated by the rubber hand illusion (Peled et al. 2003), probably accounts for out-of-body-experiences (Thakkar et al. 2011). This is one of the examples Ramachandran cites, and this susceptibility varies considerably among individuals. It is probably connected with low levels of "body ownership" and schizotypy, and such conditions can induce the belief that the patient is outside of his/her body, e.g., floating above it and actually seeing the body. Other conditions confirm that the brain's right parietal lobe contains in the superior parietal lobule an internal image of the body. Pathology affecting this body image has psychologically demonstrable, dramatic effects. For instance it is thought to be the underlying cause of anorexia nervosa and somatoparaphrenia (or apotemnophilia; cf. anosognosia). The latter syndrome, found in about 5% of right hemisphere stroke patients, leads these to deny their own paralysis. Some of these patients even deny the similar paralysis in fellow patients, which as noted is probably attributable to the function of the mirror neurons. Ramachandran (2009a) suggests that, to make a judgment about somebody else's movements, one has to run a virtual reality simulation of the corresponding movements in one's own brain. Other phenomena probably involving mirror neurons are contagious acts such as yawning and laughing, or the odd fact that one cannot tickle oneself (Provine 2009). There is, however, nothing trivial about the gravity of these various insights, an importance that cannot possibly be overstated. They seem to bring into focus the most profound question an intelligent organism appears to be able to contemplate: how does the brain form a construct of external reality? They raise the possibility that Plotkin's (2002) concept of an imagined world made real was closer to factuality than even he anticipated. Ultimately it must be recognized that, so far, there has not been a viable universal theory of how the neuronal mechanisms and systems of the brain create reality from the sensory input of the phenomenal world, which after all underlies all human comprehension of the world. These above considerations suggest that, put simply, the parietal lobe might be creating a virtual-reality-like model of the external world, much in the same way as it forms a mental image of the body.

But these considerations lead too far from the present concerns (and their adequate treatment would involve a separate book; cf. Bednarik in prep.), which are limited to the "more manageable" topics of ToM and self-awareness. It must also be mentioned that there is evidence against attributing ToM to mirror neurons. Brain regions implicated in it are the anterior paracingulate cortex, the superior temporal sulci and the temporal poles bilaterally (Gallagher and Frith 2003), among others. But the mirror neurons are located in the inferior frontal cortex and superior parietal lobe. Also, macaques lack a developed ToM despite having mirror neurons. Both ontogenically and phylogenically, a ToM is acquired gradually, and precursory behaviors to a ToM are recognized. Understanding attention (Baron-Cohen 1991), understanding of others' intentions (Dennett 1987), and imitative experience with conspecifics (Horowitz 2003) are hallmarks of a ToM. The "false-belief task" (Wimmer and Perner 1983), which establishes the ability of an individual to attribute false beliefs to a conspecific, is seen as a key indicator of the level of development of ToM. In humans it occurs normally around the age of four, but while it is found in children with Down syndrome, it is absent in most of those with autistic spectrum disorder (Baron-Cohen et al. 1985; Leslie 1991), and a link with mirror neurons is suggested (Williams et al. 2001; Oberman et al. 2005; Oberman and Ramachandran 2007). Another such test (Gopnik 1988; Gopnik and Astington 1988) can be passed by most 5-year-olds (see also Zaitchik 1990; Leslie and Thaiss 1992; Sabbagh and Moses 2006). These abilities would seem to mark the threshold of human ToM, but since precursory behaviors indicative of ToM are found widely among non-human species, such behavior would be expected in human phylogeny well before the australopithecines. Similarly, in a realistic model well-developed stages of ToM would need to be attributed to such species as *Homo habilis* or *Homo erectus*. The ontogenic parallels are relatively well understood. Intentional behavior can be detected by infants 5–9 months old (Woodward 1999), while at 15 months infants can classify actions according to their goals (Csibra et al. 2003). The same abilities are available to chimpanzees and orangutans (Call and Tomasello 1998), but apparently not to monkeys (Jellema et al. 2000). Between 18 and 24 months, the child establishes joint attention (Franco and Butterworth 1996), as well as engages in pretend-play, and it develops an ability to understand desires (Wellman and Wooley 1990; Rapacholi and Gopnik 1997; Wellman and Liu 2004). Again, apes use gaze monitoring to detect joint attention (Hare et al. 2000), but monkeys apparently do not. But it is with the appearance of "metarepresentation," the ability to explicitly represent representations as representations (Leslie 1994; Baron-Cohen 1995; Perner and Garnham 2001), and with recursion that human ToM emerges, as these are lacking in the great apes (Suddendorf 1999; Call and Tomasello 1999). Similarly, the apes have so far provided very tenuous indications of episodic memory or future planning (Suddendorf and Busby 2003). Episodic memory, which is identified with autonoetic consciousness, can be impaired in humans, e.g., in amnesia, Asperger's syndrome, or in older adults (Gardiner 2001). It can be attributed to differential activity in the medial prefrontal and medial parietal cortices, imaging studies of episodic retrieval have shown (Lou et al. 2004).

Homology would then suggest that precursory ToM behavior such as the detection of intention, goals, and joint attention would have appeared in human ancestors during the Miocene, while metarepresentation and recursion are likely to have emerged in the Pliocene. Planning of future action, self-representation, complex syntax and creative thought are rendered possible by these, as well as metamemory and counterfactual reasoning (Shimamura et al. 1990; Suddendorf 1999; De Villiers 2000; Shimamura 2000; Saxe and Kanwisher 2003; Samson et al. 2004). It is roughly at the age of 40 months that the child surpasses the ToM level of the other great apes. Thus the executive control over cognition unique to humans, together with metarepresentation and recursion, should have developed in the last 5 to 7 million years. Although the brain areas accounting for the latter two faculties remain unidentified, executive control resides in the frontal lobes. Since the frontal and temporal areas have experienced the greatest degree of enlargement in humans (Semendeferi et al. 2001; Bednarik and Helvenston 2012), uniquely human abilities would be expected to be most likely found there, although inter-connectivity rather than discrete loci may be the main driving force of cognitive evolution. But it is precisely the expansion of association cortices that has made the human brain disproportionately large (Preuss 2000).

Turning to self-awareness, the sentience of one's own knowledge, attitudes, opinions, and existence, it is again obvious that various levels apply to different species. Some of the great apes, the elephants, and bottlenose dolphins are among the species that have passed the mirror test (Gallup 1970; Mitchell 1993, 1997, 2002; Heyes 1998; Gallup et al. 2002; Keenan et al.

2003; but see Swartz 1997; De Veer and Van Den Bos 1999; Morin 2003 for critical reviews), and interestingly they are much the same species shown to possess von Economo neurons (Seeley et al. 2006; Butti et al. 2009; Hakeem et al. 2009). This is perhaps not so much a relationship of direct supervenience; the connection may be via social complexity. Von Economo neurons seem to occur in relatively large species with large brains and extensive social networks (Bednarik 2011b) and have recently been identified in macaques (Evrard et al. 2012), and it may be that constructs of individuality evolved in tandem with these networks. Indeed, it is difficult to see how social complexity could have evolved beyond that of ants, bees, or termites without some level of self-awareness, just as the advent of self-awareness is hard to account for. Self-awareness is seen as a superior, more developed form of consciousness. The hallmark of consciousness may be a transparent representation of the world from a privileged egocentric perspective (Trehub 2009) but this does not reveal how it could have come about. Consciousness focuses attention on the organism's environment, merely processing incoming external stimuli (Dennett 1991; Farthing 1992), whereas self-awareness focuses on the self, processing both private and "public" information about selfhood. The capacity of being the object of one's own attention defines self-awareness, in which the individual is a reflective observer of its internal milieu and experiences its own mental events (Gallup 1998; Gallup and Platek 2002; Carver 2002). What is regarded as the "self" is inherently a social construct (Seyfarth and Cheney 2000), shaped by the individual's culture and immediate conspecifics (Leary and Buttermore 2003). But the self is not the same as consciousness (Natsoulas 1998), as shown by the observation that many attributes seen as inherent in the self are not available to conscious scrutiny. People invent the neurological computation of the boundaries of personhood from their own behavior and from the narratives they form, which also determine their future behavior. Thus it needs to be established how the chain of events from sensory input is established and how behavior is initiated, controlled, and produced (Carruthers 2002; Koch 2004; Nelson 2005; Clowes 2007). It appears that subcortical white matter, brainstem, and thalamus are implicated in consciousness (Fernández-Espejo et al. 2011), although it is assumed that unconsciousness mainly involves the cortical brain (Velly et al. 2007) and the thalamus is not believed to drive consciousness. Ultimately consciousness is self-referential awareness, the self's sense of its own existence, which may explain why its etiology remains unsolved. Hofstadter (2007) likens this quest to finding a self-consistent set of axioms for deducing all of mathematics, which Kurt Gödel has shown to be impossible, due to the self-referential nature of mathematical statements.

Internally directed aspects of cognition, such as ToM, episodic memory, self-evaluation, and self-awareness derive from the default mode network (DMN), which is considered to be a functionally homogeneous system (Sestieri et al. 2011). Relative to ToM, conscious self-awareness is even less understood and accounted for ontologically. Neuroscience and neuropsychology favor the view that it is located primarily in a neural network of the prefrontal, posterior temporal, and inferior parietal of the right hemisphere (Stuss et al. 2001; Decety and Sommerville 2003; Gusnard 2005; but see critiques in Morin 2002, 2004; Morin and Michaud 2007). In humans, a diminished state of self-awareness occurs for instance in dementia, sleep, or when focusing upon strong stimuli (Cavanna and Trimble 2006). Ultimately self-awareness must be the result of interplay of many variables, starting from the input of the proprioceptors to the engagement of several brain regions. It includes the operation of distal type bimodal neurons (moderating anticipation and execution; Maravita et al. 2003). What can be said about it is that it can be safely attributed to all hominoids and hominins, and there is a reasonable expectation that it became progressively more established with time. In contrast to the dogmatic rejection of Lower Paleolithic beads by some archaeologists, from a biological perspective it is rather surprising that such artifacts, quintessential to defining self-awareness archaeologically, appear so late on the available record (during the Acheulian traditions). As in so many other issues, biological, empirical, and scientific perceptions clash irreconcilably with the fictitious narratives of Pleistocene archaeology (Bednarik 1992, et passim).

Thus the relevant scientific information would provide a rough framework for a first attempt to formulate a preliminary etiology of hominin behavior, in which archaeological dogma, however, has no place. Lower levels of ToM certainly have to be expected in the Miocene and Pliocene ancestors of humans (i.e., for much of the last 20 million years) and beyond, and could reasonably be presumed to have developed further during these periods (Foley 1997). The behavior of these primates must be assumed to have been attuned to the level of ToM and self-awareness that was available to them. In view of the dysteleological nature of evolution, the archaeological, teleologically guided assumption of a development of increased complexity cannot apply to a natural system. If it did, the system would cease to be natural (governed by Darwinian evolution alone). On the other hand, *culture can develop teleologically*, via incremental improvements involving a moderating intellect of gradually increasing autonomy. Therefore hominin intellect is neither archaeologically recoverable nor can it be inferred from stone tools, which is the underlying "lithocentric" mantra of most scholars in the field. The sciences, on the other hand, are perfectly capable of providing some of the crucial goalposts, and since these account perfectly for the most dramatic aspect of hominin evolution, encephalization, they need to gain priority in explaining the human ascent, including how modern behavior originated. Given that natural selection can only select expressed characteristics, not latent ones, the indices Pleistocene archaeology fields in its speculations about behavior, cognition, or even technology are inevitably flawed. The absurdity of archaeology's "explosion" or "great leap" around 40,000 years ago illustrates this, when it is contrasted with the empirical observation that the human brain approached its modern size many hundreds of millennia ago. Just as language can only be selected for after it has appeared, so can larger brain size, and to suggest, as archaeology implies, that for millions of years this brain increased relentlessly without being much used, is unacceptable to the biological sciences.

Conclusion

According to these deliberations, distinctive precursors of modernity in human behavior were present several million years ago, and since then have become gradually more established. At the upper end of the time scale, the rapid neotenization and incidental self-domestication of the human line over the last forty or so millennia (Bednarik 2008a, 2008b, 2011b) were such that they would have completed the journey to fully modern behavior. However, in the task of beginning to formulate a first outline of the etiology of human behavior these are merely preludial considerations. Much of modern behavior is driven by a set of powerful imperatives, especially the desires for security, peer approval, and "respect."

There are the desires to be taken seriously, the desire of belonging (to a place, group, or whatever), to believe in something (which is cognitively easier than not to do so). There are also desires to be useful, for control, for love, and for more of what is desired, which contrast with what is essential for survival. Defining these and other properties in neuroscientific terms is well beyond present means, and the biases likely to occur when a narrow-minded organism deigns to study itself must also be considered. Human priorities in studying the neotenous ape define the shortcomings of such an approach, particularly when they are dominated by a Western righteousness that has yet to learn that all human groups exist, and have existed, in different constructs of reality. As Helvenston argues cogently in this volume, conflating literate minds with the oral minds that inhabited the human past, which "cognitive archaeology" does without realizing, is the result of one such epistemological impairment.

"Modern behavior," therefore, does not refer to the behavior of modern Westerners, or to that of any other extant human group. Instead it is defined by the state of the neural structures that are involved in moderating behavioral patterns, which ultimately are determined by inhibitory and excitatory stimuli in the brain. The many behaviors mapped onto these structures are more different than the countless languages that have been mapped onto similarly inherent systems of language centers. After all, human behavior is not only determined by the intrinsic structures giving rise to it; these are demonstrably influenced by ontogenic experiences of the individual and their effects on these neural configurations. Just as there can be no doubt about the ontogenic plasticity of behavior, it follows that the behavior of all individuals must be different, each reflecting individual experience—just as the precise realities in which human individuals exist must all differ from one another. As Malafouris (2008) states, "the functional structure and anatomy of the human brain is a dynamic construct remodeled in detail by behaviourally important experiences." Cultural activity modifies the chemistry and structure of the brain through affecting the flow of neurotransmitters and hormones (Smail 2007) and the quantity of gray matter (Maguire et al. 2000; Draganski et al. 2004). For instance the general introduction of writing in recent centuries has dramatically changed the brain of adult humans. Although they start out as infants with brains similar to non-literate peoples, these brains are gradually reorganized as demanded by the thinking implicit in literacy, which is totally different from the thought patterns found in oral societies (Helvenston, this volume). The use of all symbol systems (be they computer languages, conventions for diagrams, styles of painting) influence perception and thought (Goodman 1978). Therefore the complexity of the issue cannot be overestimated, but this does not change the underlying proposition that there must have been dominant patterns of hominin behavior at any point in history. These would have been determined by the interplay of specific behavioral imperatives: social norms and pressures, the range of behavioral options perceived to be available to the individual, given a specific set of beliefs. These beliefs would have been formed by many influences, such as society's framework and individual life experience, i.e., ontogenic factors specific to the individual.

In a scientific sense, behavior is the outcome not only of neuronal activity; other factors are also involved, especially the endocrine system. The hypothalamus alone controls the neurotransmitter dopamine and the hormones somatostatin, oxytocin, vasopressin; and the growth hormone-releasing, thyrotropine-releasing, gonadotropin-releasing, and corticotropin-releasing hormones. Then there is the pituitary gland just below it (Figure 1), whose anterior section controls the hormones for growth, thyroid-stimulation, and adrenocorticotropic,

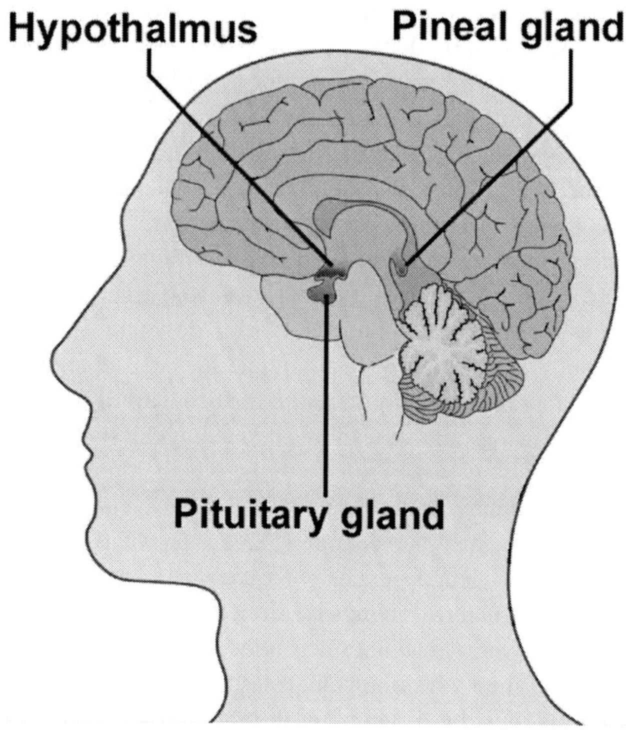

Figure 1. The locations of human brain glands.

follicle-stimulating, luteinizing, and luteotropic hormones; its intermediate section maintains melanocyte-stimulating hormone; and the posterior section provides oxytocin, vasopressin and anti-diuretic hormones. The pineal gland controls melatonin. Specific neurons can have considerable influence on behavior, for instance the von Economo neurons have already been mentioned. The tonically active neurons, functioning as a gating mechanism between the matrisome and the striosome regions, modulate the orbital frontal cortex and anterior cingulate by adjusting the degree to which the thalamus drives both areas (Bednarik 2011b: 177). But still other substances of the brain can influence behavior. For example the protein tau, a component of intracellular neurofibrillary tangles, has profound effects as neurons and synapses die and axons degenerate in Parkinson's disease. The current Human Microbiome Jumpstart Reference Strains Consortium (2010) has even offered the suggestion that gut microbiota may be involved in neural development and function, e.g., in mood disorders (Forsythe et al. 2010). Similarly, *Helicobacter pylori*, a bacterium implicated in ulcers and stomach cancer, may help trigger Parkinson's disease. In short, human behavior is the result of an exceedingly complex etiology that currently defies comprehensive explanation.

Nevertheless, this paper has attempted a scientific definition of the broad parameters of the likely behavior of hominins to probe the origins of modern behavior. It has done this not by offering speculative musings about specific behavior patterns, but by introducing relevant issues from the biosciences, thus facilitating the formulation of propositions that are testable within these. Archaeological appeal to plausibility has been explicitly excluded as being merely a stratagem to preserve a false dogma. That dogma demands that modern behavior appeared with the purported speciation to recent Graciles and is expressed in the Final

Pleistocene cave art of southwestern Europe (from 32,000 years BP onwards); therefore any preceding evidence of human modernity must be either false, incorrectly dated, or its presenters must be mistaken. All of the assumptions underpinning this notion are false: the first Upper Paleolithic cave art is not the work of Graciles (Bednarik 2007); the amount of Middle Paleolithic rock art surviving today is probably much greater than that of Upper Paleolithic rock art (Bednarik 2010); and empirical evidence of "behavioral modernity" precedes the Graciles by hundreds of millennia (Bednarik 2011c). Attempts to sustainably bring the neurosciences and cognitive sciences into correlation with archaeological narratives of Pleistocene human behavior have been made, but have been severely hampered by false archaeological models, especially the replacement hypothesis. Human modernity, be it somatically, culturally, or behaviorally, did not appear as a single package at a particular time, but emerged as a series of progressive developments culminating in the recent neotenization episode in the last part of the Late Pleistocene. Human behavior 30,000 years ago would have certainly differed dramatically from today's patterns, and yet it was fully modern in the sense that the biological structures producing patterns of behavior were largely similar to todays. However, these similarities had been developing for eons prior to the emergence of that glorious crown of evolution, *Homo sapiens sapiens* (Bednarik 2011b).

The core trait under selection in the evolution of cognition is not tool use, or even ToM; it is high order control capacity (Christensen in prep.). ToM, self-awareness, consciousness, technology, and culture were all available to non-human species, but were not developed to an integrated system of a self-reflective brain that observes itself and then makes conscious decisions based on excitatory/inhibitory neural functions. For instance, the sleeping nests or tools of the great apes were not improved upon; there was no volition to do so. Therefore volition becomes the prompter, and it needs to be explained how its ability to derive abstract goals from the prefrontal cortex arose (R. Dielenberg, pers. comm.). The answer, it is proposed here, lies in the rise of cultural behavior and its growing conscious comprehension of cause and effect (Bednarik 2011b). This development apparently took place in the Early Pleistocene. By the beginning of the Middle Pleistocene, 780,000 years ago, human behavior as a neurological process was well established, in the sense that the neural structures involved in moderating behavioral patterns were substantially in place. Fully modern human behavior, however, did not appear until recent centuries, because the ontogenic development of human brains has changed significantly over the course of recent centuries (for instance through the widespread introduction of literacy). Therefore the archaeological claims placing the advent of modern behavior 30 or 40 millennia ago are false, however such behavior is defined. It can be safely assumed, as a null hypothesis, that for much of the Pleistocene and for most of the Holocene, human behavior was modern in the sense that it used much the same structures as today, but it was certainly not modern in its expressions. Indeed, even among contemporary conspecifics, behavior can differ widely, for instance according to the conventions of symbol use (see Helvenston, this volume) and sophistication of cause and effect reasoning. The use of symbols or exograms changes with time, while fully coherent cause and effect reasoning is a recent introduction and not yet accessible to most of humanity, whose cognition remains widely dominated by what neuroscience terms "magical thinking."

REFERENCES

Adams, F., and Aizawa, K. (2001). The bounds of cognition. *Philosophical Psychology* 14, 43–64.

Adams, F., and Aizawa, K. (2008). *The bounds of cognition*. Malden: Blackwell Publishing.

Ahern, J. C. M., Karavanic, I., Paunović, M., Janković, I., and Smith, F. H. (2004). New discoveries and interpretations of fossil hominids and artifacts from Vindija Cave, Croatia. *Journal of Human Evolution* 46, 25–65.

Aitchison, J. (1996). *The seeds of speech: Language origin and evolution*. Cambridge, UK: Cambridge University Press.

Aizawa, K., and Adams, F. (2005). Defending non-derived content. *Philosophical Psychology* 18, 661–669.

Alemseged, Z., Spoor, F., Kimbel, W. H., Bobe, R., Geraads, D., Reed, D., and Wynn, J. G. (2006). A juvenile early hominin skeleton from Dikika, Ethiopia. *Nature* 443(7109), 296–301.

Allman, J. M., Watson, K. K., Tetreault, N. A., and Hakeem, A. Y. (2005). Intuition and autism: A possible role for von Economo neurons. *Trends in Cognitive Science* 9(8), 367–373.

Alvard, M. S. (2003). The adaptive nature of culture. *Evolutionary Anthropology* 12, 136–149.

Anderson, E. (1949). *Introgressive hybridization*. New York: John Wiley and Sons.

Andersson, C. (2011). Paleolithic punctuations and equilibria: Did retention rather than invention limit technological evolution? *PaleoAnthropology 2011*, 243–259; doi:10.4207/PA.2011.ART55.

Andolfatto, P. (2001). Adaptive hitchhiking effects on genome variability. *Current Opinion in Genetics and Development* 11, 635–641.

Andres, A. M., Soldevila, M., Navarro, A., Kidd, K. K., Oliva, B., and Bertranpetit, J. (2004). Positive selection in MAOA gene is human exclusive: Determination of the putative amino acid change selected in the human lineage. *Human Genetics* 115, 377–386.

Arensburg, B., Schepartz, L. A., Tillier, A.-M., Vandermeersch, B., and Rak, Y. (1990). A reappraisal of the anatomical basis for speech in the Middle Pleistocene hominids. *American Journal of Physical Anthropology* 83, 137–146.

Arensburg, B., Tillier, A.-M., Vandermeersch, B., Duday, H., Schepartz, L. A., and Rak Y. (1989). A Middle Palaeolithic human hyoid bone. *Nature* 338, 758–760.

Ashley Montagu, M. F. (1960). *An introduction to physical anthropology*. Springfield, IL: Thomas.

Ashley Montagu, M. F. (1989). *Growing young*. Westport, CT: Bergin and Garvey.

Avila, M., Thaker, G., and Adami, H. (2001). Genetic epidemiology and schizophrenia: A study of reproductive fitness. *Schizophrenia Research* 47, 233–241.

Awadalla, P., Eyre-Walker, A., and Maynard Smith, J. (1999). Linkage disequilibrium and recombination in hominid mitochondrial DNA. *Science* 286, 2524–2525.

Ayala, F. J. (1996). Response to Templeton. *Science* 272, 1363–1364.

Ayalew, M., Le-Niculescu, H., Levey, D. F. , Jain, N. , Changala, B. , Patel, S. D. , Winiger, E. , Breier, A. , Shekhar, A. , Amdur, R. , Koller, D. , Nurnberger, J. I. , Corvin, A. , Geyer, M. , Tsuang, M. T. , Salomon, D. , Schork, N. J. , Fanous, A. H. , O'Donovan, M.

C. , and Niculescuet, A. B. (2012) Convergent functional genomics of schizophrenia: from comprehensive understanding to genetic risk prediction, *Molecular Psychiatry*, DOI: 10.1038/mp.2012.37.

Badcock, C. R. (1980). *The psychoanalysis of culture*. Oxford: Basil Blackwell.

Bader, O. N. (1978). *Sungir: Verkhnepaleoliticheskaya stoyanka*. Moscow: Izdatel'stvo "Nauka."

Balter, M. (2007). A mind for sociability. *ScienceNow Daily News* July 27, p. 1.

Barber, T. X. (1976). *Pitfalls in human research*. New York: Pergamon Press.

Barberi, F., Innocenti, F., Lirer, L., Munno, R., Pescatore, T. S., and Santacroce, R. (1978). The Campanian Ignimbrite: A major prehistoric eruption in the Neapolitan area (Italy). *Bulletin of Volcanology* 41, 10–22.

Barinaga, M. (1992). "African Eve" backers beat a retreat. *Science 255*, 686–687.

Barkan, E., and R. Bush (2002). Introduction. In E. Barkan and R. Bush (Eds.), *Claiming the stones, naming the bones: Cultural property and the negotiation of national and ethnic identity* (pp. 1–13). Los Angeles: Getty Research Institute.

Baron-Cohen, S. (1991). Precursors to a theory of mind: Understanding attention in others. In A. Whiten (Ed.), *Natural theories of mind: Evolution, development and simulation of everyday mindreading* (pp. 233–251). Oxford: Basil Blackwell.

Baron-Cohen, S. (1995). *Mindblindness: An essay of autism and theory of mind*. Cambridge, MA: MIT Press.

Baron-Cohen, S. (2000). Is Asperger syndrome /high-functioning autism necessarily a disability? *Development and Psychopathology* 12, 489–500.

Baron-Cohen, S. (2002). The extreme male brain theory of autism. *Trends in Cognitive Sciences* 6(6), 248–254.

Baron-Cohen, S. (2006). Two new theories of autism: Hyper-systemizing and assortative mating. *Archives of Disease in Childhood* 91, 2–5.

Baron-Cohen, S., Jolliffe, T., Mortimore, C., and Robertson, M. (1997). Another advanced test of theory of mind: Evidence from very high functioning adults with autism or Asperger syndrome. *Journal of Child Psychology and Psychiatry* 38, 813–822.

Baron-Cohen, S., Leslie, A. M., and Frith, U. (1985). Does the autistic child have a "theory of mind"? *Cognition* 21(1), 37–46.

Bassett, A. S., Bury, A., Hogkinson, K. A., and Honer, W. G. (1996). Reproductive fitness in familial schizophrenia. *Schizophrenia Research 21*, 151–160.

Beaumont, P. B. (2011). The edge: More on fire-making by about 1.7 million years ago at Wonderwerk Cave in South Africa. *Current Anthropology* 52(4), 585–595.

Beaumont, P. B., and Bednarik, R. G. (2010). On a search for ancestral rock art in the south-eastern Kalahari, South Africa. *Pré actes du congrès, IFRAO Ariège 2010*, Pleistocene art of Africa, DVD, Lacombe, Tarascon-sur-Arège.

Becher, T. (2001). *Academic tribes and territories: Intellectual enquiry and the culture of disciplines*. Buckingham: Open University Press.

Bednarik, R. G. (1987). Engramme und Phosphene. *Zeitschrift für Ethnologie* 112(2), 223–235.

Bednarik, R. G. (1991). "African Eve" a computer bungle. *The Artefact 14*, 34–35.

Bednarik, R. G. (1992). Palaeoart and archaeological myths. *Cambridge Archaeological Journal* 2(1), 27–43.

Bednarik, R. G. (1993a). About Palaeolithic ostrich eggshell in India. *Indo-Pacific Prehistory Association Bulletin* 13, 34–43.
Bednarik, R. G. (1993b). Palaeolithic art in India. *Man and Environment* 18(2), 33–40.
Bednarik, R. G. (1994). A taphonomy of palaeoart. *Antiquity* 68, 68–74.
Bednarik, R. G. (1995a). The age of the Côa valley petroglyphs in Portugal. *Rock Art Research* 12(2), 86–103
Bednarik, R. G. (1995b). Concept-mediated marking in the Lower Palaeolithic. *Current Anthropology* 36(4), 605–634.
Bednarik, R. G. (1995c). Metamorphology: In lieu of uniformitarianism. *Oxford Journal of Archaeology* 14(2), 117–122.
Bednarik, R. G. (1997a). The origins of navigation and language. *The Artefact* 20, 16–56.
Bednarik, R. G. (1997b). The global evidence of early human symboling behaviour. *Human Evolution* 12(3), 147–168.
Bednarik, R. G. (1997c). The role of Pleistocene beads in documenting hominid cognition. *Rock Art Research* 14(1), 27–41.
Bednarik, R. G. (1998). The technology of petroglyphs. *Rock Art Research* 15(1), 23–35.
Bednarik, R. G. (1999). Maritime navigation in the Lower and Middle Palaeolithic. *Comptes Rendus de l'Académie des Sciences Paris, Earth and Planetary Sciences* 328, 559–563.
Bednarik, R. G. (2001). Beads and pendants of the Pleistocene. *Anthropos* 96, 545–555.
Bednarik, R. G. (2003a). The earliest evidence of palaeoart. *Rock Art Research* 20(1), 89–135.
Bednarik, R. G. (2003b). Seafaring in the Pleistocene. *Cambridge Archaeological Journal* 13(1), 41–66.
Bednarik, R. G. (2005). Middle Pleistocene beads and symbolism. *Anthropos* 100(2), 537–552.
Bednarik, R. G. (2007). Antiquity and authorship of the Chauvet rock art. *Rock Art Research* 24(1), 21–34.
Bednarik, R. G. (2008a). The mythical Moderns. *Journal of World Prehistory* 21(2), 85–102.
Bednarik, R. G. (2008b). The domestication of humans. *Anthropologie* 46(1), 1–17.
Bednarik, R. G. (2008c). Beads and the origins of symbolism. *Time and Mind: The Journal of Archaeology, Consciousness and Culture* 1(3): 285–318.
Bednarik, R. G. (2008d). Cupules. *Rock Art Research* 25(1), 61–100.
Bednarik, R. G. (2010). Australian rock art of the Pleistocene. *Rock Art Research* 27(1), 95–120.
Bednarik, R. G. (2011a). Rendering humanities sustainable. *Humanities 1*(1), 64–71; doi:10.3390/h1010064; *http://www.mdpi.com/2076-0787/1/1/64/*
Bednarik, R. G. (2011b). *The human condition*. New York: Springer.
Bednarik, R. G. (2011c). The origins of human modernity. *Humanities* 1(1), 1–53; doi:10.3390/h1010001; http://www.mdpi.com/2076-0787/1/1/1/.
Bednarik, R. G. (2011d). Genetic drift in recent human evolution? In K. V. Urbano (Ed.), *Advances in genetics research, Volume 6* (pp. 109–160). New York: Nova Science Publishers.
Bednarik, R. G. (2012). *Creating the human past*.
Bednarik, R. G. (In press). *The first mariners*.
Bednarik, R. G. (In prep.). *Human constructs of reality*.

Bednarik, R. G., and Helvenston, P. A. (2012). The nexus between neurodegeneration and advanced cognitive abilities. *Anthropos* 107(2).

Bednarik, R. G., Kumar, G., Watchman, A., and Roberts, R. G. (2005). Preliminary results of the EIP Project. *Rock Art Research* 22, 147–197.

Bednarik, R. G., and You Yuzhu (1991). Palaeolithic art from China. *Rock Art Research* 8(2), 119–123.

Berger, P. L., and Luckmann, T. (1966). *The social construction of reality: A treatise in the sociology of knowledge*. Garden City, NY: Anchor Books.

Bertone, J. (2006). *Equine geriatric medicine and surgery*. St Louis, MI: W. B. Saunders.

Bickerton, D. (1990). *Language and species*. Chicago: University of Chicago Press.

Bickerton, D. (1993). Putting cognitive carts before linguistic horses. Behavioural and Brain Sciences 16*, 749–750.*

Bickerton, D. (1996). *Language and human behaviour*. London: UCL Press.

Bickerton, D. (2010). *Adam's tongue: How humans made language, how language made humans*. New York: Hill and Wang.

Bishop, R. C. (2007). *The philosophy of the social sciences: An introduction*. London: Continuum International Publishing Group.

Bleek, D. F. (1933). Beliefs and customs of the /Xam Bushmen. Part VI: Rain-making. *Bantu Studies* 7, 375–392.

Bleek, D. F. (1935). Beliefs and customs of the /Xam Bushmen. Part VII: Sorcerers. *Bantu Studies* 9, 1–47.

Bleek, D. F. (1936). Beliefs and customs of the /Xam Bushmen. Part VIII: More about sorcerers and charms. *Bantu Studies* 10, 131–162.

Block, N. (2005). Review of Alva Noë. *Journal of Philosophy* 102, 259–272.

Boas, F. (1888). *The Central Eskimo*, reprinted 1964. Lincoln: University of Nebraska Press.

Bogdashina, O. (2003). *Sensory perceptual issues in autism and Asperger's syndrome*. London: Jessica Kingsley Publishers.

Bogdashina, O. (2010). *Autism and the edges of the known world: Sensitivities, language and constructed reality*. London and Philadelphia: Jessica Kingsley Publishers.

Boucher de Perthes, J. (1846). *Antiquités celtiques et antédiluviennes*. Paris.

Boyer, L. B. (1969). Shamans: To set the record straight. *American Anthropologist* 71, 307–309.

Brace, C. L. (1993). "Popscience" versus understanding the emergence of the modern mind. Review of *Origins of the modern mind: Three stages in the evolution of culture and cognition*, by Merlin Donald. *Behavioral and Brain Sciences* 16(4), 750–751.

Brace, C. L. (1996). Racialism and racist agendas: Review of *Race, evolution and behavior: A life history perspective*, by J. Philippe Rushton. *American Anthropologist* 98(1), 176–177.

Brace, C. L. (1999). An anthropological perspective on "race" and intelligence: The non-clinal nature of human cognitive capabilities. *Journal of Anthropological Research* 55(2), 245–264.

Brasic, J. R. (2009a). Autism. *E Medicine Medscape*. Internet address: *http://emedicine.medscape.com/article/912781-print.*

Brasic, J. R. (2009b). Asperger's syndrome. *E Medicine Medscape*. Internet address: *http://emedicine.medscape.com/article/912296-print.*

Brasic, J. R. (2010). PET Scanning in autism spectrum disorders. *E Medicine Medscape, Neurology*. Internet address: *http://emedicine.medscape.com/article/1155568-print.*

Bräuer, G. (1984). Präsapiens-Hypothese oder Afro-europäische Sapiens-Hypothese? *Zeitschrift für Morphologie und Anthropologie* 75, 1–25.

Brod, J. H. (1997). Creativity and schizotypy. In G. Claridge (Ed.), *Schizotypy: Implications for illness and health* (pp. 274–299). Oxford: Oxford University Press.

Brookfield, J. F. Y. (1997). Importance of ancestral DNA ages. *Nature* 388, 134.

Brown, M. F. (2003). *Who owns native culture?* Cambridge, MA: Harvard University Press.

Brüne, M. (2006). Theory of mind and social competence in schizophrenia. *Clinical Neuropsychiatry* 3, 32–38.

Buchen, L. (2011). When geeks meet. *Nature* 479(7371), 25–27.

Burack, J. A., Charman, T., Yurmiya, N., and Zelazo, P. R. (Eds.) (2009). *The development of autism: Perspectives from theory and research*. London: Taylor and Francis/Routledge.

Butti, C., Sherwood, C. C., Hakeem, A. Y., and Allman, J. M. (2009). Total number and volume of von Economo neurons in the cerebral cortex of cetaceans. *Journal of Comparative Neurology* 515(2), 243–259.

Call, J., and Tomasello, M. (1998). Distinguishing intentional from accidental actions in orangutans (*Pongo pygmaeus*), chimpanzees (*Pan troglodytes*), and human children (*Homo sapiens*). *Journal of Comparative Psychology* 112(2), 192–206.

Call, J., and Tomasello, M. (1999). A nonverbal false belief task: The performance of children and great apes. *Child Development* 70(2), 381–395.

Campbell, F. (2006). Molesting the past. *The Weekend Australian*, 25 February, R15.

Cann, R. L. (2002). Tangled genetic routes. *Nature* 416, 32–33.

Cann, R. L., Stoneking, M., and Wilson, A. C. (1987). Mitochondrial DNA and human evolution. *Nature* 325, 31–36.

Cannon, T. D. *(2005).* The inheritance of intermediate phenotypes for schizophrenia. Current Opinion in Psychiatry 18, 135–140.

Capasso, L., Michetti, E., and d'Anastasio, R. (2008). A *Homo erectus* hyoid bone: Possible implications for the origin of the human capability for speech. *Collegium Antropologicum* 32(4), 1007–1011.

Cardno, A. G., and Gottesman, I. I. (2000). Twin studies of schizophrenia: From bow-and-arrow concordances to star wars Mx and functional genomics. *American Journal of Medical Genetics* 97, 12–17.

Carlier, L., Couprie, J., Maire, A. le, Guilhaudis, L., Milazzo, I., Gondry, M., Davoust, D., Gilquin, B., and Zinn-Justin, S. (2007). Solution structure of the region 51-160 of human KIN17 reveals an atypical winged helix domain. *Protein Science* 16, 2750–2755.

Carruthers, M. (1990). *The book of memory*. Cambridge, UK: Cambridge University Press.

Carruthers, M. (1998). *The craft of thought*. Cambridge, UK: Cambridge University Press.

Carruthers, P. (2002). The cognitive functions of language. *Behavioral and Brain Sciences* 25, 657–674.

Cartailhac, E. (1902). Les cavernes ornées de dessins. La grotte d'Altamira, Espagne. "Mea culpa d'un sceptique." *L'Anthropologie* 13, 348–354.

Carver, C. S. (2002). Self-awareness. In M. R. Leary and J. P. Tangney (Eds.), *Handbook of self and identity* (pp. 179–196). New York: Guilford Press.

Cavanna, A. E., and Trimble, M. R. (2006). The precuneus: A review of its functional anatomy and behavioral correlates. *Brain* 129, 564–583.

Charlton, B. G. (2006). The rise of the boy-genius: Psychological neoteny, science and modern life. *Medical Hypotheses* 67, 679–681

Cho, H. J., Meira-Lima, I., Cordeiro, Q., Michelon, L., Sham, P. C., Vallada, H., and Collier, D. A. (2005). Population-based and family-based studies on the serotonin transporter gene polymorphisms and bipolar disorder: A systematic review and meta-analysis. *Molecular Psychiatry* 10, 771–781.

Christensen, W. (in prep.). The evolutionary origins of volition. In D. Spurrett, H. Kincaid, D. Ross, and L. Stephens (Eds.), *Distributed cognition and the will: Individual volition and social context*. Cambridge, MA: MIT Press.

Clark, A., and Chalmers, D. (1998). The extended mind. *Analysis* 58(1), 10–23.

Clowes, R. A. (2007). Self-regulation model of inner speech and its role in the organisation of human conscious experience. *Journal of Consciousness Studies* 14, 59–71.

Cole, S. (2001). *What's wrong with sociology?* New Brunswick, NJ: Transaction Publishers.

Craddock, N., and Jones, I. (1999). Genetics of bipolar disorder: Review article. *Journal of Medical Genetics* 26, 585–594.

Craddock, N., O'Donovan, M. C., and Owen, M. J. (2005). The genetics of schizophrenia and bipolar disorder: Dissecting psychosis. *Journal of Medical Genetics* 42, 193–204.

Craig, J., and Baron-Cohen, S. (1999). Creativity and imagination in autism and Asperger Syndrome. *Journal of Autism and Developmental Disorders* 29, 319–326.

Crow, T. J. (1995a). A Darwinian approach to the origins of psychosis. The British Journal of Psychiatry 167, 12–25.

Crow, T. J. *(1995b).* A theory of the evolutionary origins of psychosis. European Neuropsychopharmacology *5(suppl.),* 59–63.

Crow, T. J. *(1997).* Schizophrenia as failure of hemispheric dominance for language. Trends in Neurosciences 20, 339–343.

Crow, T. J., Done, D. J., and Sacker, A. *(*1995). Childhood precursors of psychosis as clues to its evolutionary origins. European Archives of Psychiatry and Clinical Neuroscience 245, 61–69.

Csibra, G., Biro, S., Koos, O., and Gergely, G. (2003). One-year-old infants use teleological representations of actions productively. Cognitive Science 27(1), 111–133.

Cunningham, M., Roberts, A., and Vu, C. (1995). "Their ideas of beauty are, on the whole, the same as ours": Consistency and variability in the cross-cultural perception of female physical attractiveness. *Journal of Personality and Social Psychology* 68, 261–279.

Cynx, J., and Clark, S. J. (1993). Ethological foxes and cognitive hedgehogs. Behavioural and Brain Sciences 16, 756–757.

Dart, R. A. (1925). *Australopithecus africanus*: The man-ape of South Africa. *Nature* 115, 195–199.

Dawkins, R. (1976). The selfish gene. *Oxford: Oxford University Press.*

De Beer, G. R. (1930). *Embryology and evolution*. Oxford: Oxford University Press.

De Beer, G. R. (1940). *Embryos and ancestors*. Oxford: Oxford University Press.

Decety, J., and Somerville, J. A. (2003). Shared representations between self and others: a social cognitive neuroscience view. *Trends in Cognitive Science* 7, 527–533.

De Heusch, L. (1965). Possession et chamanisme. Essai d'analyse structurale. In *Les religions africaines traditionnelles (Rencontres internationales de Bouaké)* (pp. 139–170). Paris: Seuil.

Demerath, N. J. (1942). Schizophrenia among primitives. *American Journal of Psychiatry* 98, 703–707.

Dennett, D. C. (1987). Reprint of intentional systems in cognitive ethology: The Panglossian paradigm defended. *The Brain and Behavioral Sciences* 6, 343–390.

Dennett, D. C. (1991). *Consciousness explained.* Boston, MA: Little, Brown.

Dennett, D. C. (1998). Comment on N. Humphrey, "Cave art, autism, and the evolution of the human mind." *Cambridge Archaeological Journal* 8(2), 184–185.

de Panafieu, J.-B. with P. Gries (2007). *Evolution.* New York: Seven Stories Press.

De Veer, M. W., and Van Den Bos, R. (1999). A critical review of methodology and interpretation of mirror self-recognition research in nonhuman primates. *Animal Behavior* 58, 459–468.

Devereux, G. (1956). Normal and abnormal: The key problem of psychiatric anthropology. In J. B. Casagrande and Y. Gladwin (Eds.), *Some uses of anthropology: Theoretical and applied* (pp. 23–48). Washington, DC: Anthropological Society of Washington.

Devereux, G. (1961). Shamans as neurotics. *American Anthropologist* 63, 1088–1090.

De Villiers, J. (2000). Language and theory of mind: What are the developmental relationships? In S. Baron-Cohen, H. Tager-Flusberg and D. Cohen (Eds.), *Understanding other minds: Perspectives from developmental cognitive neuroscience* (2nd edn, pp. 83–123). Oxford: Oxford University Press.

Di Pellegrino, G., Fadiga, L., Fogassi, L., Gallese, V., and Rizzolatti, G. (1992). Understanding motor events: A neurophysiological study. *Experimental Brain Research* 91, 176–180.

Donald, M. (1991). *Origins of the modern mind: Three stages in the evolution of culture and cognition.* Cambridge, MA: Harvard University Press.

Donald, M. (2001). *A mind so rare: The evolution of human consciousness.* New York: W.W. Norton.

Donald, M. et al. (1993). Précis of "Origins of the modern mind: Three stages in the evolution of culture and cognition." *Behavioral and Brain Sciences* 16, 737–791.

Draganski, B., Gaser, C., Bush, V., Schuierer, G., Bogdahn, U., and May, A. (2004). Changes in grey matter induced by training. *Nature* 427(6972), 311–312.

Drake, J., and Winner, E. (2009). Precocious realists: Perceptual and cognitive characteristics associated with drawing talent in non-autistic children. *Philosophical Transactions of the Royal Society of London, B Biological Science* 364(1522), 1449–1458.

Dunbar, R. (1996). *Grooming, gossip and the evolution of language.* London: Faber and Faber.

Edvardsen, J., Torgersen, S., Røysamb E., et al. (2008). Heritability of bipolar spectrum disorders. Unity or heterogeneity. *Journal of Affective Disorders* 106(3), 229–240.

Eigen, M., and Schuster, P. (1977). The hypercycle. A principle of natural self-organization. *Naturwissenschaften* 64, 541–565.

Eliade, M. (1964). *Shamanism: Archaic techniques of ecstasy.* Princeton, NJ: Princeton University Press.

El-Mallakha, R. S. (2006). Schizophrenia and the origins of shamanism among the Kwakiutl maritime cultures of northwest North America: A hypothesis. *Schizophrenia Research* 86, 329–330.

Enard, W., Khaitovich, P., Klose, J., Heissig, F., Zöllner, S., Giavalisco, P., Nieselt-Struwe, K., Muchmore, E., Varki, A., Ravid, R., Doxiadis, G. M., Bontrop, R. E., and Pääbo, S. (2002a). Intra- and interspecific variation in primate gene expression patterns. *Science* 296(5566), 340–343.

Enard, W., Przeworski, M., Fisher, S. E., Lai, C. S., Wiebe, V., Kitano, T., Monaco, A. P., and Pääbo, S. (2002b). Molecular evolution of FOXP2, a gene involved in speech and language. *Nature* 418, 869–872.

Eswaran, V. (2002). A diffusion wave out of Africa. *Current Anthropology* 43(5), 749–774.

Evans, P. D., Gilbert, S. L., Mekel-Bobrov, N., Vallender, E. J., Anderson, J. R., Vaez-Azizi, L. M., Tishkoff, S. A., Hudson, R. R., and Lahn, B. T. *(2005).* Microcephalin, a gene regulating brain size, continues to evolve adaptively in humans. Science 309(5741), 1717–1720.

Evrard, H. C., Forro, T., and Logothetis, N. K. (2012). Von Economo neurons in the anterior insula of the macaque monkey. *Neuron* 74(3), 482–489.

Ewans, W. J. (1983). The role of models in the analysis of molecular genetic data, with particular reference to restriction fragment data. In B. S. Weir (Ed.), *Statistical analysis of DNA sequence data* (pp. 45–73). New York: Marcel Dekker.

Fairservice, W. A., Jr (1975). *The threshold of civilization.* New York: Scribner.

Falk, D. (1975). Comparative anatomy of the larynx in man and chimpanzee: Implications for language in Neanderthal. *American Journal of Physical Anthropology* 43, 123–132.

Falk, D. (1983). Cerebral cortices of east African early hominids. *Science* 221, 1072–1074.

Falk, D. (1987). Hominid paleoneurology. *Annual Review of Anthropology* 16, 13–30.

Falk, D. (2009). *Finding our tongues: Mothers, infants and the origins of language.* New York: Basic Books.

Fanelli, D. (2010). "Positive" results increase down the hierarchy of the sciences. *PloS ONE* 5(4), e10068; doi:10.1371/journal.pone.0010068.

Farthing, G. W. (1992). *The psychology of consciousness.* New Jersey: Prentice Hall.

Fedele, F. G., and Giaccio, B. (2007). Paleolithic cultural change in western Eurasia across the 40,000 BP timeline: Continuities and environmental forcing. In P. Chenna Reddy (ed.), *Exploring the mind of ancient man. Festschrift to Robert G. Bednarik* (pp. 292–316). New Delhi: Research India Press.

Fedele, F. G., Giaccio, B., Isaia, R., and Orsi, G. (2002). Ecosystem impact of the Campanian Ignimbrite eruption in Late Pleistocene Europe. *Quaternary Research* 57, 420–424.

Fedele, F. G., Giaccio, B., Isaia, R., and Orsi, G. (2003). The Campanian Ignimbrite Eruption, Heinrich Event 4, and Palaeolithic change in Europe: A high-resolution investigation. In *Volcanism and the earth's atmosphere* (pp. 301–325). Washington, DC: Geophysical Monograph 139, American Geophysical Union.

Felgenhauer, F. (1959). Das Paläolithikum von Willendorf in der Wachau, Niederösterreich. Vorbericht über die monographische Bearbeitung. *Forschungen und Fortschritte* 33(3), 152–155.

Fernández-Espejo, D., Bekinschtein, T., Monti, M. M., Pickard, J. D., Junque, C., Coleman, M. R., and Owen, A. M. (2011). Diffusion weighted imaging distinguishes the vegetative state from the minimally conscious state. *NeuroImage* 54(1), 103–112.

Ferrari, P. F., Bonini, L., and Fogassi, L. (2009). From monkey mirror neurons to mirror-related behaviours: Possible direct and indirect pathways. *Philosophical Transactions of the Royal Society*, *B* 364, 2311–2323.

Foley, R. (1997). *Humans before humanity*. London: Blackwell.

Foley, R., and Lahr, M. M. (1997). Mode 3 technologies and the evolution of modern humans. *Cambridge Archaeological Journal* 7, 3–36.

Folstein, S. E., and Rosen-Sheidley, B. (2001). Genetics of autism: Complex aetiology for a heterogeneous disorder. *Nature Reviews Genetics 2*, 943–955.

Forsythe, P., Sudo, N., Dinan, T., Taylor, V. H., and Bienenstock, J. (2010). Mood and gut feelings. *Brain, Behavior, and Immunity* 24(1), 9–16.

Francfort, H. P., and Hamayon, R. N., with Bahn, P. (Eds) (2001). *The concept of shamanism, uses and abuses*. Bibliotheca Shamanistica, Vol. 10, Budapest: Akadémiai Kiadó.

Franco, F., and Butterworth, G. (1996). Pointing and social awareness: Declaring and requesting in the second year. *Journal of Child Language* 23(2), 307–336.

Frith, U. (1972). Cognitive mechanisms in autism: Experiments with color and tone sequence production. *Journal of Autism and Childhood Schizophrenia 2*, 160–173.

Frith, U. (1989). *Autism: Explaining the enigma*. Oxford: Blackwell.

Frith, U., and Happé, F. G. E. (1994). Autism: Beyond "theory of mind." *Cognition* 50, 115–132.

Fuhlrott, C. J. (1859). Menschliche Überreste aus einer Felsengrotte des Düsselthals. Ein Beitrag zur Frage über die Existenz fossiler Menschen *Verhandlungen des Naturhistorischen Vereins Preussen und Rheinland Westphalen* 16, 131–153.

Gábori-Csánk, V. (1993). *Le Jankovichien: Une civilisation paléolithiques en Hongrie*. Liège: ERAUL 53.

Gallagher, H. L., and Frith, C. D. (2003). Functional imaging of "theory of mind." *Trends in Cognitive Sciences* 7(2), 77–83.

Gallese, V., and Goldman, A. (1998). Mirror neurons and the simulation theory of mind-reading. *Trends in Cognitive Science* 2(12), 493–501.

Gallup, G. G., Jr. (1970). Chimpanzees: Self recognition. *Science* 167(3914), 86–87.

Gallup, G. G., Jr. (1998). Self-awareness and the evolution of social intelligence. *Behavioural Processes 42*, 239–247.

Gallup, G. G., Jr., Anderson, J. L., and Shillito, D. P. (2002). The mirror test. In M. Bekoff, C. Allen, and G. M. Burghardt (Eds.), *The cognitive animal: Empirical and theoretical perspectives on animal cognition* (pp. 325–333). Chicago: University of Chicago Press.

Gallup, G. G., Jr., and Platek, S. M. (2002). Cognitive empathy presupposes self-awareness: Evidence from phylogeny, ontogeny, neuropsychology, and mental illness. *Behavioral and Brain Sciences* 25(1), 36–37.

Gamble, C. (1997). Handaxes and Palaeolithic individuals. In N. Ashton, F. Healey and P. Pettitt (Eds.), *Stone Age archaeology* (pp. 105–109). Monograph 102, Oxford: Oxbow Books.

Gannon, P. J., Holloway, R. L., Broadfield, D. C., and Braun, A. R. (1998). Asymmetry of chimpanzee planum temporale: Humanlike pattern of Wernicke's brain language area homolog. *Science* 279, 220–222.

Gannon, P. J., Kheck, N. M., and Hof, P. R. (2001). Language areas of the hominoid brain: A dynamic communicative shift on the upper east side planum. In D. Falk and K. R. Gibson

(Eds.), *Evolutionary anatomy of the primate cerebral cortex* (pp. 216–240). New York: Cambridge University Press.

Gardiner, J. M. (2001). Episodic memory and autonoetic consciousness: a first-person approach. *Philosophical Transactions: Biological Sciences* 356 (1413), 1351–1361.

Garrigan, D., Mobasher, Z., Severson, T., Wilder, J. A., and Hammer, M. F. (2005). Evidence for archaic Asian ancestry on the human X chromosome. *Molecular Biological Evolution* 22, 189–192.

Geigl, E.-M. (2002). Why ancient DNA research needs taphonomy. Paper presented to Conférence ICAZ, *"Bioshere to Lithosphere."*

Germonpré, M., Sablin, M. V., Stevens, R. E., Hedges, R. E. M., Hofreiter, M., Stiller, M., and Després, V. R. (2009). Fossil dogs and wolves from Palaeolithic sites in Belgium, the Ukraine and Russia: Osteometry, ancient DNA and stable isotopes. *Journal of Archaeological Science* 36(2), 473–490.

Geschwind, N., and Levitsky, W. (1968). Human brain: Left-right asymmetries in temporal speech region. *Science* 161, 186–187.

Gibbons, A. (1998). Calibrating the mitochondrial clock. *Science* 279, 28–29.

Gibbons, A. (2010). Close encounters of the prehistoric kind. *Science* 328, 680–684.

Golenberg, E. M., Bickel, A., and Weihs, P. (1996). Effect of highly fragmented DNA on PCR. *Nucleic Acids Research* 24, 5026–5033.

Goodman, N. (1978). *Ways of worldmaking*. Indianapolis, IN: Hackett Publishing Company.

Goody, J. (1977). *The domestication of the savage mind*. Cambridge, UK: Cambridge University Press.

Gopnik, A. (1988). Conceptual and semantic development as theory change. *Mind and Language* 3(3), 197–217.

Gopnik, A., and Astington, J. W. (1988). Children's understanding of representational change and its relation to the understanding of false belief and the appearance-reality distinction. *Child Development* 59, 26–37.

Gordon, R. (1986). Folk psychology as simulation. *Mind and Language* 1, 158–171.

Gordon, R. (1996). "Radical" simulationism. In P. Carruthers and P. K. Smith (Eds.), *Theories of theories of mind* (pp. 11–21). Cambridge, UK: Cambridge University Press.

Goren-Inbar, N., Lewy, Z., and Kislev, M. E. (1991). The taphonomy of a bead-like fossil from the Acheulian of Gesher Benot Ya'aqov, Israel. *Rock Art Research* 8(1), 83–87.

Gould, S. J. (1977). *Ontogeny and phylogeny*. Cambridge: Belknap Press.

Gould, S. J. (1979). A biological homage to Mickey Mouse. *Natural History* 88(5), 30–36.

Grammer, K., and Thornhill, R. (1994). Human facial attractiveness and sexual selection: The role of symmetry and averageness. *Journal of Comparative Psychology* 108, 233–242.

Green, R. E., Krause, J., Ptak, S. E., Briggs, A. W., Ronan, M. T., Simons, J. F., Du, L., Egholm, M., Rothberg, J. M., Paunovic, M., and Pääbo, S. (2006). Analysis of one million base pairs of Neanderthal DNA. *Nature* 444, 330–336.

Green, R. E., Krause, J., Briggs, A. W., Maricic, T., et al. (2010). A draft sequence of the Neandertal genome. *Science* 328, 710–722.

Gregory, R. L. (1970). *The intelligent eye*. London: Weidenfeld and Nicolson.

Grinker, R. R. (2007). *Unstrange minds: Remapping the world of autism*. New York: Basic Books.

Grün, R., and Beaumont, P. (2001). Border Cave revisited: A revised ESR chronology. *Journal of Human Evolution* 40, 467–482.

Gusnard, D. A. (2005). Being a self: considerations from functional imaging. *Consciousness and Cognition* 14, 679–697.

Gutierrez, G., and Marin, A. (1998). The most ancient DNA recovered from amber-preserved specimen may not be as ancient as it seems. *Molecular Biological Evolution* 15, 926–929.

Gutierrez, G., Sanchez, D., and Marin, A. (2002). A reanalysis of the ancient mitochondrial DNA sequences recovered from Neandertal bones. *Molecular Biological Evolution* 19, 1359–1366.

Gyllensten, U., Wharton, D., Josefsson, A., and Wilson, A. C. (1991). Paternal inheritance of mitochondrial DNA in mice. *Nature* 352, 255–257.

Hakeem, A. Y., Sherwood, C. C., Bonar, C. J., Butti, C., Hof, P. R., and Allman, J. M. (2009). Von Economo neurons in the elephant brain. *Anatomical Record* 292(2), 242–248.

Haldane, J. B. S. (1932). *The causes of evolution*. London: Longmans, Green and Co.; and New York: Harper Brothers.

Hamayon, R. (1982). Des chamanes au chamanisme. *L'Ethnographie* 78(2–3), 13–48.

Hamayon, R. (1990). *La chasse à l'âme. Esquisse d'une théorie du chamanisme sibérien.* Paris: Société d'Ethnologie, Mémoire 1.

Hamayon, R. (1995). Le chamanisme sibérien: Réflexions sur un médium. *La Recherche* 275, 416–422.

Hammer, M. F. (1995). A recent common ancestry for human Y chromosomes. *Nature* 378, 376–378.

Handelman, D. (1968). Shamanizing on an empty stomach. *American Anthropologist* 70, 353–356.

Happé, F. G. E. (1997). Central coherence and theory of mind in autism: Reading homographs in context. *British Journal of Developmental Psychology* 15, 1–12.

Happé, F., Ehlers, S., Fletcher, P., Frith, U., Johansson, M., Gillberg, C., Dolan, R., Frackowiak, R., and Frith, C. (1996). Theory of mind in the brain: Evidence from a PET scan study of Asperger syndrome. *Neuroreport 8*, 197–201.

Happé, F., and Frith, U. (eds) (2010). *Autism and talent.* Oxford: Oxford University Press.

Happé, F., and Vital, P. (2009). What aspects of autism predispose to talent? *Philosophical Transactions of the Royal Society of London, B Biological* Science 364(1522), 1369–1375.

Hardy, J., Pittman, A., Myers, A., Gwinn-Hardy, K., Fung, H. C., Silva, R. de, Hutton, M., and Duckworth, J. (2005). Evidence suggesting that *Homo neanderthalensis* contributed the H2 *MAPT* haplotype to *Homo sapiens*. *Biochemical Society Transactions* 33, 582–585.

Hare, B., Call, J., Agnetta, B., and Tomaselli, M. (2000). Chimpanzees know what conspecifics do and do not see. *Animal Behaviour* 59, 771–785.

Harpending, H. C., Batzer, M. A., Gurven, M., Jorde, L. B., Rogers, A. R., and Sherry, S. T. (1998). Genetic traces of ancient demography. *Proceedings of the National Academy of Sciences, USA* 95, 1961–1967.

Hartl, D., and Clark, A. (1997). *Principles of population genetics*. Sunderland, MA: Sinauer.

Haskovec, I.P., and Sullivan, H. (1986). Najambolmi: The life and work of and Aboriginal artist. *Unpubl. report to Australian National Parks and Wildlife Service, Canberra.*

Haworth, K. (2006). Upper Paleolithic art, autism, and cognitive style: Implications for the evolution of language. *Semiotica* 162, 127–174.

Hedges, S. B., Kumar, S., Tamura, K., and Stoneking, M. (1992). Human origins and analysis of mitochondrial DNA sequences. *Science* 255, 737–739.

Helvenston, P. A. (2012). Deciphering ancient minds: The mystery of San Bushman rock art. A critical book review. *Rock Art Research* 29(2).

Helvenston, P. A., and Bednarik, R. G. (2011). Evolutionary origins of brain disorders in *Homo sapiens sapiens*. *Brain Research Journal* 3(2), 113–139.

Henke, W., and Protsch, R. (1978). Die Paderborner Calvaria—ein diluvialer *Homo sapiens*. *Anthropologischer Anzeiger* 36, 85–108.

Henrich, J. (2004). Demography and cultural evolution: How adaptive cultural processes can produce maladaptive losses—the Tasmanian case. *American Antiquity* 69(2), 197–214.

Hermelin, B., and O'Connor, N. (1970). *Psychological experiments with autistic children*. Oxford and New York: Pergamon Press.

Heston, J. J. (1966). Psychiatric disorders in foster home reared children of schizophrenic mothers. *The British Journal of Psychiatry* 112, 819–825.

Heyes, C. M. (1998). Theory of mind in nonhuman primates. *Behavioral and Brain Sciences* 21(1), 101–134.

Hickok, G. (2009). Eight problems for the mirror neuron theory of action understanding in monkeys and humans. *Journal of Cognitive* Neuroscience *21*(7), 1229–1243.

Hofstadter, D. (2007). *I am a strange loop*. New York: Basic Books.

Hodgson, D. (2003). The biological foundations of Upper Palaeolithic art: stimulus, percept and representational imperatives. *Rock Art Research* 20(1), 3–22.

Horowitz, A. (2003). Do humans ape? Or do apes human? Imitation and intention in humans and other animals. *Journal of Comparative Psychology* 17, 325–336.

Horrobin, D. F. (1998). Schizophrenia: The illness that made us human. *Medical Hypotheses* 50, 269–288.

Horrobin, D. F. (2001). *The madness of Adam and Eve: How schizophrenia shaped humanity*. London: Bantam.

How, M. W. (1962). *The mountain Bushmen of Basutoland*. Pretoria: Van Schaik.

Hromnik, C. A. (1991). A testament to the shamanistic hallucinatory trance theory of the southern African rock art. *Rock Art Research* 8(2), 99–108.

Hughes, C., Soares-Boucaud, I., Hochmann, J., and Frith, U. (1997). Social behaviour in pervasive developmental disorders: Effects of informant, group and "theory-of-mind." *European Child and Adolescent Psychiatry* 6(4), 191–198.

Hultkrantz, Å. (1993). Introductory remarks on the study of shamanism. *Shaman* 1(1), 3–14.

Humphrey, N. (1998). Cave art, autism, and the evolution of the human mind. *Cambridge Archaeological Journal* 8(2), 165–191.

Iacoboni, M., Molnar-Szakacs, I., Gallese, V., Buccino, G., and Mazziotta, J. C. (2005). Grasping the intentions of others with one's own mirror neuron system. *PLoS Biology* 3(3), 529–535.

Jacques, S., and Zelazo, P. D. (2005). Language and the development of cognitive flexibility: Implications for theory of mind. In J. W. Astington and J. A. Baird (Eds.), *Why language matters for theory of mind* (pp. 144–162). Toronto: Oxford University Press.

Jansson, M., McCarthy, S., Sullivan, P. F., Dickman, P., Andersson, B., Oreland, L., Schalling, M., and Pedersen, N. L. (2005). MAOA haplotypes associated with thrombocyte-MAO activity. *BMC Genetics* 6, 46.

Jarrold, C., Butler, D. W., Coltington, E. M., and Jimenez, F. (2000). Linking theory of mind and central coherence bias in autism and the general population. *Developmental Psychology* 36, 126–138.

Jellema, T., Baker, C. I., Wicker, B., and Perrett, D. I. (2000). Neural representation for the perception of the intentionality of actions. *Brain and Cognition (Special Issue: Cognitive Neuroscience of Actions)* 44(2), 280–302.

Joffe, T. H. (1997). Social pressures have selected for an extended juvenile period in primates. *Journal of Human Evolution* 32, 593–605.

Jolly, P. (1986). A first generation descendant of the Transkei San. *South African Archaeological Bulletin* 41, 6–9.

Jones, D. M. (1995). Sexual selection, physical attractiveness and facial neoteny: Cross-cultural evidence and implications. *Current Anthropology* 36(5), 723–748.

Jones, D. M. (1996). An evolutionary perspective on physical attractiveness. *Evolutionary Anthropology* 5(3), 97–109.

Jones, R. (1977). The Tasmanian paradox. In R. V. S. Wright (Ed.), *Stone tools as cultural markers* (pp. 189–204). Canberra: Australian Institute for Aboriginal Studies.

Jones, R. (1978). Why did the Tasmanians stop eating fish? In R. A. Gould (Ed.), *Explorations in ethnoarchaeology* (pp. 11–47). Albuquerque: University of New Mexico Press.

Karlsson, J. L. (1970). Genetic association of giftedness and creativity with schizophrenia. *Hereditas* 66, 177–181.

Karlsson, J. L. *(1984).* Creative intelligence in relatives of mental patients. Hereditas 100*,* 83–86.

Katz, R. (1976). Educating for transcendence. !Kia-healing with the Kalahari !Kung. In R. B. Lee and I. DeVore (Eds.), *Kalahari hunter-gatherers. Studies of the !Kung San and their neighbors* (pp. 281–301). Boston: Harvard University Press.

Katz, R. (1982). *Boiling energy: Community healing among the Kalahari !Kung*. Cambridge, MA: Harvard University Press.

Katz, R., and M. Biesele (1986). !Kung healing: The symbolism of sex roles and culture change. In M. Biesele, R. Gordon and R. Lee (Eds.), *The past and present of !Kung ethnography: Critical reflections and symbolic perspectives. Essays in honour of Lorna Marshall* (pp. 195–230). Hamburg: Helmut Buske Verlag.

Keenan, J. P., Falk, D., and Gallup, G. C., Jr. (2003). *The face in the mirror: The search for the origins of consciousness*. New York: Harper Collins Publishers.

Keller, M. C., and Miller, G. (2006). Resolving the paradox of common, harmful, heritable mental disorders: Which evolutionary genetic models work best? *Behavioral and Brain Sciences* 29, 385–452.

Kellman, J. (1998). Ice Age art, autism and vision: How we see/how we draw. *Studies in Art Education* 39(2), 117–131.

Kellman, J. (1999). Drawing with Peter: Autobiography, narrative, and the art of a child with autism. *Studies in Art Education* 40(3), 258–274.

Kennedy, J. L., Farrer, L. A., Andreasen, N. C., Mayeux, R., and St George-Hyslop, P. (2003). The genetics of adult-onset neuropsychiatric disease: Complexities and conundra? Science 302, 822–826.

Kerr, N. L. (1998). HARKing: Hypothesizing after the results are known. *Personality and Social Psychology Review* 2, 196–217.

Keysers, C., and Gazzola, V. (2007). Integrating simulation and theory of mind: From self to social cognition. *Trends in Cognitive Sciences* 11(5), 194–196.

Kieseppä, T., Partonen, T., Haukka, J., Kaprio, J., and Lönnqvist, J. (2004). High concordance of bipolar I disorder in a nationwide sample of twins. *American Journal of Psychiatry* 161(10), 1814–1821.

Klamer, A., Solow, R. M., and McCloskey, D. N. (1989). *The consequences of economic rhetoric*. New York: Cambridge University Press.

Koch, C. (2004). *The quest for consciousness*. Greenwood Village, CO: Roberts and Company Publishers.

Kohl, P. L., and Fawcett, C. (2000). Archaeology in the service of the state: Theoretical considerations. In P. L. Kohl and C. Fawcett (eds), *Nationalism, politics, and the practice of archaeology* (pp. 3–18). Cambridge, UK: Cambridge University Press.

Krause, J., Lalueza-Fox, C., Orlando, L., Enard, W., Green, R. E., Burbano, H. A., Hublin, J.-J., Hänni, C., Fortea, J., Rasilla, M. de la, Bertranpetit, J., Rosas, A., and Pääbo, S. (2007). The derived FOXP2 variant of modern humans was shared with Neandertals. *Current Biology* 17(21), 1908–1912.

Krings, M., Stone, A., Schmitz, R. W., Krainitzki, H., Stoneking, M., and Pääbo, S. (1997). Neandertal DNA sequences and the origin of modern humans. *Cell* 90, 19–30.

Kroeber, A. L. (1900). The Eskimo of Smith Sound. *Bulletin of the American Museum of Natural History* 12, 265–327.

Kroeber, A. L. (1940). Psychotic factors in shamanism. *Character and Personality* 8, 204–215.

Kuhn, T. S. (1962). *The structure of scientific revolutions* (1st edn, 2nd edn 1970). Chicago: University of Chicago Press.

Kumar, G. (1996). Daraki-Chattan: A Palaeolithic cupule site in India. *Rock Art Research* 13(1), 38–46.

Kumar, G. (2010). Understanding the creation of early cupules by replication, with special reference to Daraki-Chattan in India. In R. Querejazu Lewis and R. G. Bednarik (Eds.), *Mysterious cup marks: Proceedings of the First International Cupule Conference* (pp. 59–66). BAR International Series 2073, Oxford: Archaeopress.

Kumar, G., Narvare, G., and Pancholi, R. K. (1988). Engraved ostrich eggshell objects: New evidence of Upper Palaeolithic art in India. *Rock Art Research* 5(1), 43–53.

Laitman, J., Reidenberg, J. S., and Gannon, P. J. (1992). Fossil skulls and hominid vocal tracts: New approaches to charting the evolution of human speech. In J. Wind, B. Chiarelli, B. Bichakjian and A. Nocentini (Eds.), *Language origin: A multidisciplinary approach* (pp. 395–407). Dordrecht: Kluwer.

Lashley, K. (1950). In search of the engram. *Society of Experimental Biology Symposium* 4, 454–482.

Latour, B. (1993). *We have never been modern*. Cambridge, MA: Harvard University Press.

Latour, B. (2000). When things strike back: A possible contribution of "science studies" to the social sciences. *British Journal of Sociology* 51, 107–123.

Leary, M. R., and Buttermore, N. R. (2003). The evolution of the human self: Tracing the natural history of self-awareness. *Journal of the Theory of Social Behaviour* 33(4), 365–404.

Le Barre, W. (1970). *The ghost dance: Origins of religion*. New York: Delta.

Le Barre, W. (1972). Hallucinogens and the shamanic origins of religion. In P. T. Furst (Ed.), *The flesh of the gods* (pp. 261–278). New York: Praeger.

Lee, R. B. (1967). Trance cure of the !Kung Bushmen. *Natural History* 76(9), 31–37.

Le Quellec, J.-L. (2006). The sense in question: Some Saharan examples. *Rock Art Research* 23(2), 165–170.

Leslie, A. M. (1991). Theory of mind impairment in autism. In A. Whiten (Ed.), *Natural theories of mind: Evolution, development and simulation of everyday mindreading* (pp. 63–77). Oxford: Basil Blackwell.

Leslie, A. M. (1994). Pretending and believing: Issues in the theory of ToMM. *Cognition* 50, 211–238.

Leslie, A., and Thaiss, L. (1992). Domain specificity in conceptual development. *Cognition* 43, 225–251.

Lewis-Williams, J. D. (1986). The last testament of the Southern San. *South African Archaeological Bulletin* 41, 10–11.

Lewis-Williams, J. D. (1993). Southern African archaeology in the 1990s. *South African Archaeological Bulletin* 48, 45–50.

Lewis-Williams, J. D. (2002). *The mind in the cave: Consciousness and the origins of art.* London and New York: Thames and Hudson.

Lewis-Williams, J. D., and Dowson, T. A. (1988). The signs of all times: Entoptic phenomena in Upper Palaeolithic art. *Current Anthropology* 29, 201–245.

Lex, B. W. (1984). The context of schizophrenia and shamanism. *American Ethnologist* 11(1), 191–192.

Li, D., Collier, D. A., and He, L. (2006). Meta-analysis shows strong positive association of the neuregulin 1 (NRG1) gene with schizophrenia. *Human Molecular Genetics* 15, 1995–2002.

Lieberman, P., and Crelin, E. S. (1971). On the speech of Neanderthal man. *Linguistic Inquiry* 2, 203–222.

Lieberman, P., Crelin, E. S., and Klatt, D. H. (1972). Phonetic ability and related anatomy of the newborn, adult human, Neanderthal man, and the chimpanzee. *American Anthropologist* 74, 287–307.

Lieberman, P., Laitman, J. R., Reidenburg, L. S., and Gannon, P. J. (1992). The anatomy, physiology, acoustics and perception of speech: Essential elements in analysis of the evolution of human speech. *Journal of Human Evolution* 23, 447–467.

Lindhal, T., and Nyberg, B. (1972). Rate depurination of native deoxyribonucleic acid. Biochemistry 11(19), 3610–3618.

Loeb, E. M. (1968). The shaman of Niue. *American Anthropologist* 26, 393–402.

Lou, H. C., Luber, B., Crupain, M., Keenan, J. P., Nowak, M., Kjaer, T. W., Sackeim, H. A., and Lisanby, S. H. (2004). Parietal cortex and representation of the mental self. *Proceedings of the National Academy of Sciences, USA* 101(17), 6827–6832.

Lu, J., Tang, T., Tang, H., Huang, J., Shi, S., and Wu, C.-I. (2006). The accumulation of deleterious mutations in rice genomes: A hypothesis on the cost of domestication. *Trends in Genetics* 22, 126–131.

Lyons, C. L. (2002). Objects and identities: Claiming and reclaiming the past. In E. Barkan and R. Bush (Eds.), *Claiming the stones, naming the bones: Cultural property and the negotiation of national and ethnic identity* (pp. 116–137). Los Angeles: Getty Research Institute.

Maddison, D. R. (1991). African origin of human MtDNA re-examined. *Systematic Zoology* 40, 355.

Maddison, D. R., Ruvolo, M., and Swofford, D. L. (1992). Geographic origins of human mitochondrial DNA: Phylogenetic evidence from control region sequences. *Systematic Biology* 41, 111–124.

Maguire, E. A., Gadian, D. G., Johnsrude, I. S., Good, C. D., Ashburner, J., Frackowiak, R. S. J., and Frith, C. D. (2000). Navigation-related structural change in the hippocampi of taxi drivers. *Proceedings of the National Academy of Sciences, USA* 97(8), 4398–4403.

Malafouris, L. (2004). The cognitive basis of material engagement: Where brain, body and culture conflate. In E. DeMarrais, C. Gosden and C. Renfrew (Eds.), *Rethinking materiality: The engagement of mind with the material world* (pp. 53–62). Cambridge, UK: McDonald Institute for Archaeological Research.

Malafouris, L. (2008). Beads for a plastic mind: the "blind man stick" (BMS) hypothesis and the active nature of material culture. *Cambridge Archaeological Journal* 18(3), 401–414.

Maravita, A., Spence, C., and Driver, J. (2003). Multisensory integration and the body schema: close to hand and within reach. *Current Biology 13*, R531–539.

Marks, I. M., and Nesse, R. M. (1994). Fear and fitness: An evolutionary analysis of anxiety disorders. *Ethology and Sociobiology* 15, 247–261.

Marr, D. (1982). *Vision.* San Francisco: W. H. Freeman.

Marshall, L. (1969). The medicine dance of the !Kung Bushmen. *Africa* 39, 347–381.

Marvanová, M., Ménager, J., Bezard, E., Bontrop, R. E., Pradier, L., and Wong, G. (2003). Microarray analysis of nonhuman primates: Validation of experimental models in neurological disorders. *The FASEB Journal* 17, 929–931.

Mason, R. (1988). Cave of Hearths, Makapansgat, Transvaal. *University of the Witwatersrand, Archaeological Research Unit, Occasional Papers* 21, 1–713.

McNiven, I. J., and Russell, L. (2005). *Appropriated pasts: Indigenous peoples and the colonial culture of archaeology*. Walnut Creek, CA: AltaMira Press.

Mekel-Bobrov, N., Gilbert, S. L., Evans, P. D., Vallender, E. J., Anderson, J. R., Tishkoff, S. A., and Lahn, B. T. (2005). Ongoing adaptive evolution of ASPM, a brain size determinant in *Homo sapiens*. *Science* 309(5741), 1720–1722.

Mendel, J. G. (1866). Versuche über Pflanzen-Hybriden. *Verhandlungen des naturforschenden Vereines in Brünn* 4, 3–47.

Miller, G. F. (2000). *The mating mind: How mate choice shaped the evolution of human nature*. New York: Doubleday.

Miller, G. F. (2001). Aesthetic fitness: How sexual selection shaped artistic virtuosity as a fitness indicator and aesthetic preference as mate choice criteria. *Bulletin of Psychology and the Arts* 2(1), 20–25.

Mitchell, R. W. (1993). Mental models of mirror-self-recognition: Two theories. *New Ideas in Psychology* 11, 295–325.

Mitchell, R. W. (1997). Kinesthetic-visual matching and the self-concept as explanations of mirror-self-recognition. *Journal for the Theory of Social Behaviour* 27, 18–39.

Mitchell, R. W. (2002). Subjectivity and self-recognition in animals. In M. R. Leary and J. P. Tangney (Eds.), *Handbook of self and identity* (pp. 567–595). New York: Guilford Press.

Morin, A. (2002). Right hemispheric self-awareness: A critical assessment. *Consciousness and Cognition* 11, 396–401.

Morin, A. (2003). Let's face it. *Evolutionary Psychology* 1, 177–187.

Morin, A. (2004). A neurocognitive and socioecological model of self-awareness. *Genetic, Social, and General Psychology Monographs* 130, 197–222.

Morin, A., and Michaud, J. (2007). Self-awareness and the left inferior frontal gyrus: Inner speech use during in self-related processing. *Brain Research Bulletin* 74(6), 387–396.

Morris, A. A. M., and Lightowlers, R. N. (2000). Can paternal mtDNA be inherited? *The Lancet* 355, 1290–1291.

Morris, D. (2000). Tsodilo — worked ostrich eggshell dated. *The Digging Stick* 17(2), 10.

Morwood, M. J., Soejono, R. P., Roberts, R. G., Sutikna, T., Turney, C. S. M., Westaway, K. E., Rink, W. J., Zhao, J.-X., Bergh, G. D. van den, Due, R. A., Hobbs, D. R., Moore, M. W., Bird, M. I., and Fifield, L. K. (2004). Archaeology and age of a new hominin from Flores in eastern Indonesia. *Nature* 431, 1087–1091

Mottl, M. (1951). Die Repolust-Höhle bei Peggau (Steiermark) und ihre eiszeitlichen Bewohner. *Archaeologica Austriaca* 8, 1–78.

Mottron, L., and Belleville, S. (1993). A study of perceptual analysis in a high-level autistic subject with exceptional graphic abilities. *Brain and Cognition* 23, 279–309.

Mottron, L., and Belleville, S. (1995). Perspective production in a savant autistic draughtsman. *Psychological Medicine* 25, 639–648.

Mottron, L., Belleville, S., and Ménard, E. (1999). Local bias in autistic subjects as evidenced by graphic tasks: Perceptual hierarchization or working memory deficit. *Journal of Child Psychology and Psychiatry* 40, 743–756.

Muglia, P., Petronis, A., Mundo, E., Lander, S., Cate, T., and Kennedy, J. L. (2002). Dopamine D4 receptor and tyrosine hydroxylase genes in bipolar disorder: Evidence for a role of DRD4. *Molecular Psychiatry* 7, 860–866.

Napierala, H., and Uerpmann, H.-P. (2010). A "new" Palaeolithic dog from central Europe. *International Journal of Osteoarchaeology*, DOI: 10.1002/oa.1182.

Natsoulas, T. (1998). Consciousness and self-awareness. In M. D. Ferrari and R. J. Sternberg (Eds.), *Self-awareness: Its nature and development* (pp. 12–33). The Guilford Press: New York.

Nelson, E. W. (1899). The Eskimo about Bering Strait. In *Eighteenth Annual Report of the Bureau of American Ethnology to the Secretary of the Smithsonian Institution, 1896–97*, Part I, 19–526.

Nelson, K. (2005). Emerging levels of consciousness in early human development. In H. S. Terrace and J. Metcalfe (Eds.), *The missing link in cognition: Origins of self-reflective consciousness* (pp. 116–141). Oxford: Oxford University Press.

Nettle, D. (2001). *Strong imagination: Madness, creativity and human nature*. Oxford: Oxford University Press.

Noll, R. (1983). Shamanism and schizophrenia: A state-specific approach to the "schizophrenia metaphor" of shamanic states. *American Ethnologist* 10(3), 443–459.

Novellino, D. (1999). Towards an understanding of Pälaqwan rock drawings: Between visual and verbal expression. *Rock Art Research* 16(1), 3–24.

Oakley, K. P. (1981). Emergence of higher thought, 3.0–0.2 ma B.P. *Philosophical Transactions of the Royal Society of London B* 292, 205–211.

Oberman, L. M., Hubbard, E. M., McCleery, J. P., Altschuler, E. L., Ramachandran, V. S., and Pineda, J. A. (2005). EEG evidence for mirror neuron dysfunction in autism spectrum disorders. *Cognitive Brain Research* 24, 190–198.

Oberman, L. M., and Ramachandran, V. S. (2007). The simulating social mind: the role of the mirror neuron system and simulation in the social and communicative deficits of autism spectrum disorders. *Psychological Bulletin* 133, 310–327.

Oberman, L., and Ramachandran, V. S. (2009). Reflections on the mirror neuron system: Their evolutionary functions beyond motor representation. In J. A. Pineda (Ed.), *Mirror neuron systems: The role of mirroring processes in social cognition* (pp. 39–62). New York: Humana Press.

O'Connell, J. F., Hawkes, K., and Jones, N. G. B. (1999). Grandmothering and the evolution of Homo erectus. *Journal of Human Evolution 36*, 461–485.

O'Connor, N., and Hermelin, B. (1987). Visual and graphic abilities of the idiot savant artist. *Psychological Medicine* 17, 79–90.

O'Connor, N., and Hermelin, B. (1990). The recognition failure and graphic success of idiot savant artists. *Journal of Child Psychology and Psychiatry* 31, 203–215.

Oesterreich, T. K. (1935). *Obsession and possession by spirits both good and evil* (transl. D. Ibberson). Chicago: De Laurence.

Olson, M. V., and Varki, A. (2003). Sequencing the chimpanzee genome: Insights into human evolution and disease. *Nature Reviews Genetics* 4, 20–28.

Orpen, J. M. (1874). A glimpse into the mythology of the Maluti Bushmen. *Cape Monthly Magazine (n.s.)* 9, 1–13.

Os, J. van, and Kapur, S. (2009). Schizophrenia. *The Lancet* 374(9690), 635–645.

Ozonoff, S., and Miller, J. N. (1995). Teaching theory of mind—a new approach in social skills training for individuals with autism. *Journal of Autism and Developmental Disorders* 25, 415–433.

Panksepp, J. (1998). *Affective neuroscience: The foundation of human and animal emotions.* New York: Oxford University Press.

Pavlov, P., Svendsen, J. I., and Indrelid, S. (2001). Human presence in the European Arctic nearly 40,000 years ago. *Nature* 413, 64–67.

Pearlson, G. D., and Folley, B. S. (2008). Schizophrenia, psychiatric genetics, and Darwinian psychiatry: An evolutionary framework. Schizophrenia Bulletin 34(4), 722–733.

Peled, A., Pressman, A., Geva, A. B., and Modai, I. (2003). Somatosensory evoked potentials during a rubber-hand illusion in schizophrenia. *Schizophrenia Research* 64(2–3), 157–163.

Pennisi, E. (1999). Genetic study shakes up Out of Africa Theory. *Science* 283, 1828.

Perner, J., and Garnham, W. A. (2001). Actions really do speak louder than words—but only implicitly. Young children's understanding of false belief in action. *British Journal of Developmental Psychology* 19(3), 413–432.

Perrett, D. I., May, K. A., and Yoshikawa, S. (1994). Facial shape and judgements of female attractiveness. *Nature* 368, 239–242.

Peters, L. G., and Price-Williams, D. (1980). Towards an experiental analysis of shamanism. *American Ethnologist* 7, 398–418.

Pickard, C., Pickard, B., and Bonsall, C. (2011). Autistic spectrum disorder in prehistory. *Cambridge Archaeological Journal* 21(3), 357–364.

Pinker, S. (2002). *The blank slate. The modern denial of human nature*. Putnam: Penguin.

Piotrowski, S., and Ross, A. (2011). Aboriginal epistemologies and interpretations of art and place. *Australian Archaeology* 73, 33–40.

Plotkin, H. (2002). *The imagined world made real: Towards a natural science of culture.* London: Penguin Books.
Polimeni, J., and Reiss, J. P. (2002). How shamanism and group selection may reveal the origins of schizophrenia. *Medical Hypotheses* 58(3), 244–248.
Porr, M., and Alt, K.W. (2006). The burial of Bad Dürrenberg, central Germany: Osteopathology and osteoarchaeologyof a late Mesolithic shaman's grave. *International Journal of Osteoarchaeology* 16, 395–406.
Preisig, M., Ferrero, F., and Malafosse, A. (2005). Monoamine oxidase a and tryptophan hydroxylase gene polymorphisms: Are they associated in bipolar disorder? *American Journal of Pharmacogenetics* 5, 45–52.
Premack, D. G., and Woodruff, G. (1978). Does the chimpanzee have a theory of mind? *Behavioral and Brain Sciences* 1, 515–526.
Press, J. S., and Tanur, J. M. (2001). *The subjectivity of scientists and the Bayesian approach.* New York: John Wiley and Sons.
Preston, S. D., and de Waal, F. B. M. (2002). Empathy: Its ultimate and proximate bases. *Behavioral and Brain Sciences* 25, 1–72.
Prestwich, J. (1859). On the occurrence of flint-implements, associated with the remains of extinct mammalia, on undisturbed beds of a late geological period. *Proceedings of the Royal Society of London* 10, 50–59.
Preuss, T. M. (2000). What's human about the human brain. In M. S. Gazzaniga (Ed.), *The new cognitive neurosciences* (pp. 1219–1234). Cambridge, MA: MIT Press.
Pring, L., and Hermelin, B. (1993). Bottle, tulip and wineglass: Semantic and structural picture processing by savant artists. *Journal of Child Psychology and Psychiatry* 34, 1365–1385.
Prins, F. E. (1990). Southern-Bushman descendants in the Transkei—rock art and rainmaking. *South African Journal of Ethnology* 13(3), 110–116.
Prinz, J. (2006). Putting the brakes on enactive perception. *Psyche* 12, 1–19.
Protsch von Zieten, R. R. R. (1973). *The dating of Upper-Pleistocene Subsaharan fossil hominids and their place in human evolution: With morphological and archaeological implications.* PhD thesis, University of California, Los Angeles.
Protsch, R. (1975). The absolute dating of Upper Pleistocene sub-Saharan fossil hominids and their place in human evolution. *Journal of Human Evolution* 4, 297–322.
Protsch, R., and Glowatzki, H. (1974). Das absolute Alter des paläolithischen Skeletts aus der Mittleren Klause bei Neuessing, Kreis Kelheim, Bayern. *Anthropologischer Anzeiger* 34, 140–144.
Protsch, R., and Semmel, A. (1978). Zur Chronologie des Kelsterbach-Hominiden. *Eiszeitalter und Gegenwart* 28, 200–210.
Provine, R. (2009). Self and other: A ticklish solution. *Edge, http://www.edge.org/3rd_culture/rama08/rama08_index.html*. Retrieved 2012-1-14.
Radin, P. (1937). *Primitive religion.* New York: Viking.
Rajkowska, G. (2009). Reductions in neuronal and glial density characterize the dorsolateral prefrontal cortex in bipolar disorder. *Biological Psychiatry* 49(9), 741–752.
Ramachandran, V. S. (2009a). Mirror neurons and imitation learning as the driving force behind "the great leap forward" in human evolution. *Edge, http://www.edge.org/3rd_culture/ramachandran/ramachandran_index.html.* Retrieved 2012-1-14.

Ramachandran, V. S. (2009b). Self-awareness: The last frontier. *Edge, http://www.edge.org/3rd_culture/rama08/rama08_index.html*. Retrieved 2012-1-14.

Rapacholi, B. M., and Gopnik, A. (1997). Early reasoning about desires. Evidence from 14- and 18-months-olds. *Developmental Psychology* 33(1), 12–21.

Riley, B., and Kendler, K. S. (2006). Molecular genetic studies of schizophrenia. European Journal of Human Genetics 14*, 669–680.*

Rizzolatti, G., and Arbib, M. A. (1998). Language within our grasp. *Trends in Neurosciences* 21(5), 188–194.

Rizzolatti, G., Fadiga, L., Gallese, V., and Fogassi, L. (1996). Premotor cortex and the recognition of motor actions. *Cognitive Brain Research* 3, 131–141.

Rodman, K. E. (2003). Asperger's syndrome and adults… Is anyone listening? *London: Jessica Kingsley Publishers.*

Rodriguez-Trelles, F., Tarrio, R., and Ayala, F. J. (2001). Erratic overdispersion of three molecular clocks: GPDH, SOD, and XDH. *Proceedings of the National Academy of Sciences, USA* 98, 11405–11410.

Rodriguez-Trelles, F., Tarrio, R., and Ayala, F. J. (2002). A methodological bias toward overestimation of molecular evolutionary time scales. *Proceedings of the National Academy of Sciences, USA* 99, 8112–8115.

Roginsky, Ya. Ya., Gerasimov, M. M., Zamyatnin, S. N., and Formozov, A. A. (1954). Zaklyuchenie po nakhodke iskopaemogo cheloveka v peshchernoi stoyanke Starosel'e bliz g. Bakhchisary. *Sovetskaya Etnografiya 1954*, 39–41.

Rouget, G. (1980). *La musique et la transe*. Paris: Gallimard.

Rubinsztein, D. C., Amos, W., Leggo, J., Goodburn, S., Ramesar, R. S., Old, J., Dontrop, R., McMahon, R., Barton, D. E., and Ferguson-Smith, M. A. (1994). Mutational bias provides a model for the evolution of Huntington's disease and predicts a general increase in disease prevalence. *Nature Genetics* 7(7), 525–530.

Rupert, R. (2004). Challenges to the hypothesis of extended cognition. *The Journal of Philosophy* 101, 1–40.

Sabbagh, M. A., and Moses, L. J. (2006). Executive functioning and preschoolers' understanding of false beliefs, false photographs, and false signs. *Child Development* 77(4), 1034–1049.

Saito, T., Guan, F., Papolos, D. F., Lau, S., Klein, M., Fann, C. S., and Lachman, H. M. (2001). Mutation analysis of SYNJ1: A possible candidate gene for chromosome 21q22-linked bipolar disorder. *Molecular Psychiatry* 6, 387–395.

Samson, D., Apperly, I. A., Chiavarino, C., and Humphreys, G. W. (2004). The left temporoparietal Junction is necessary for representing someone else's belief. *Nature Neuroscience* 7(5), 499–500.

Sanjuan, J., Tolosa, A., Gonzalez, J. C., Aguilar, E. J., Perez-Tur, J., Najera, C., Molto, M. D., and Frutos, R. (2006). Association between FOXP2 polymorphisms and schizophrenia with auditory hallucinations. *Psychiatric Genetics* 16, 67–72.

Sautuola, M. Sanz de (1880). *Breves appuntes sobre algunos obietos prehistóricos de la Provincia de Santander*. Santander: Martínez.

Saxe, R., and Kanwisher, N. (2003). People thinking about people: The role of the temporo-parietal junction in "theory of mind." *Neuroimage* 19, 1835–1842.

Scheff, T. J. (1970). Schizophrenia as ideology. *Schizophrenia Bulletin* 1, 15–19.

Schuldberg, D. (1988). Creativity and schizotypal traits: Creativity test scores and perceptual aberration, magical ideation, and impulsive nonconformity. *Journal of Nervous and Mental Disease* 176, 648–657.

Schuldberg, D. (2000). Six subclinical spectrum traits in normal creativity. *Creativity Research Journal* 13, 5–16.

Schulz, H.-P. (2002). The lithic industry from layers IV–V, Susiluola Cave, western Finland, dated to the Eemian interglacial. *Préhistoire Européenne 16–17*, 7–23.

Schulz, H.-P., Eriksson, B., Hirvas, H., Huhta, P., Jungner, H., Purhonen, P., Ukkonen, P., and Rankama, T. (2002). Excavations at Susiluola Cave. *Suomen Museo 2002*, 5–45.

Schulz, M. (2004). Die Regeln mache ich. *Der Spiegel* 34(18 August), 128–131.

Schulze, T. G. (2010). Genetic research into bipolar disorder: The need for a research framework that integrates sophisticated molecular biology and clinically informed phenotype characterization. *Psychiatric Clinics of North America* 33(1), 67–82.

Schwartz, M., and Vissing, J. (2002). Paternal inheritance of mitochondrial DNA. *New England Journal of Medicine* 347, 576–580.

Searle, J. R. (1995). *The construction of social reality*. London: Allen Lane.

Seeley, W. W., Carlin, D. A., and Allman, J. M. (2006). Early frontotemporal dementia targets neurons unique to apes and humans. *Annals of Neurology* 60(6), 660–667.

Selfe, L. (1977). *Nadia: A case of extraordinary ability in an autistic child*. New York: Harcourt Brace Jovanovich.

Selfe, L. (1983). *Normal and anomalous representational drawing ability in children*. London: Academic Press.

Semendeferi, K., Armstrong, E., Schleicher, A., Zilles, K., and Van Hoesen, G. W. (2001). Prefrontal cortex in humans and apes: A comparative study of area 10. *American Journal of Physical Anthropology* 114(3), 224–241.

Semon, R. (1904). *Die Mneme*. Leipzig: W. Engelmann.

Semon, R. (1921). The mneme. *London: George Allen and Unwin.*

Sestieri, C., Corbetta, M., Romani, G. L., and Shulman, G. L. (2011). Episodic memory retrieval, parietal cortex, and the default mode network: functional and topographic analyses. *Journal of Neuroscience* 31(12), 4407–4420.

Seyfarth, R. M., and Cheney, D. L. (2000). Social awareness in monkeys. *American Zoologist 40*, 902–909.

Sforza, C., Laino, A., d'Alessio, R., Grandi, G., Binelli, M., and Ferrario, V. F. (2009). Soft-tissue facial characteristics of attractive Italian women as compared to normal women. *The Angle Orthodontist* 79(1), 17–23.

Shackelford, T. K., and Larsen, R. J. (1997). Facial asymmetry as an indicator of psychological, emotional, and physiological distress. *Journal of Personality and Social Psychology* 72(1), 456–466.

Sherwood, C. C., Gordon, A. D., Allen, J. S., Phillips, K. A., Erwin, J. M., Hof, P. R., and Hopkins, W. D. (2011). Aging of the cerebral cortex differs between humans and chimpanzees. *Proceedings of the National Academy of Sciences, USA*, DOI: 10.1073/pnas.1016709108.

Shimamura, A. P. (2000). Toward a cognitive neuroscience of metacognition. *Consciousness and Cognition* 9, 313–323.

Shimamura, A. P., Janowsky, J. S., and Squire, L. R. (1990). Memory for the temporal order of events in patients with frontal lobe lesions and amnesic patients. *Neuropsychologia* 28(8), 803–813.

Shipman, M. D. (1988). *The limitations of social research*. London: Longman.

Silberman, N. A. (2000). Promised lands and chosen peoples: The politics and poetics of archaeological narrative. In P. L. Kohl and C. Fawcett (Eds.), *Nationalism, politics, and the practice of archaeology* (pp. 249–262). Cambridge, UK: Cambridge University Press.

Silverman, J. (1967). Shamans and acute schizophrenia. *American Anthropologist* 69(1), 21–31.

Simonton, D. K. (2004). Psychology's status as a scientific discipline: Its empirical placement within an implicit hierarchy of the sciences. *Review of General Psychology* 8, 59–67.

Smail, L. M. (2007). *On deep history and the brain*. Berkeley: University of California Press.

Smith, F. H., Janković, I., and Karavanić, I. (2005). The assimilation model, modern human origins in Europe, and the extinction of Neandertals. *Quaternary International* 137, 7–19.

Smith, F. H., Trinkaus, E., Pettitt, P. B., Karavanić, I., and Paunović, M. (1999). Direct radiocarbon dates for Vindija G_1 and Velika Pećina Late Pleistocene hominid remains. *Proceedings of the National Academy of Sciences, USA* 96(22), 12281–12286.

Smith, W. G. (1894). *Man the primeval savage: His haunts and relics from the hill-tops of Bedfordshire to Blackwall*. London: E. Stanford.

Snyder, A. W., and Thomas, M. (1997). Autistic artists give clues to cognition. *Perception* 26, 93–96.

Spikins, P. (2009). Autism, the integrations of "difference" and the origins of modern human behaviour. *Cambridge Archaeological Journal* 19(2), 179–201.

Spinks, R., Sandhu H. K., Andreasen N. C. and Philibert, R. A. (2004). Association of the HOPA12bp allele with a large X-chromosome haplotype and positive symptom schizophrenia. *American Journal of Medical Genetics, Part B: Neuropsychiatric Genetics* 127, 20–27.

Solomon, A. (1999). Meanings, models and minds: A reply to Lewis-Williams. *South Africa Archaeological Bulletin* 54, 51–60.

Solomon, A. (2000). On different approaches to San rock art. *South African Archaeological Bulletin* 55, 77–78.

Somerville J. A., and Decety, J. (2006). Weaving the fabric of social interaction: Articulating developmental psychology and cognitive neuroscience in the domain of motor cognition. *Psychonomic Bulletin and Review* 13, 179–200.

Sterling, T. D. (1959). Publication decisions and their possible effects on inferences drawn from tests of significance—or vice versa. *Journal of American Statistical Association* 54(285), 30–34.

Stopkova, P., Vevera, J., Paclt, I., Zukov, I., and Lachman, H. M. (2004). Analysis of SYNJ1, a candidate gene for 21q22 linked bipolar disorder: A replication study. *Psychiatry Research* 127, 157–161.

Stringer, C. B., and Andrews, P. (1988). Genetic and fossil evidence for the origin of modern humans. *Science* 239, 1263–1268.

Stuss, D. T., Picton, T. W., and Alexander, M. P. (2001). Consciousness, self-awareness and the frontal lobes. In S. Salloway, P. Malloy and J. Duffy (Eds.), *The frontal lobes and neuropsychiatric illness* (pp. 101–109). Washington (DC): American Psychiatric Press.

Suddendorf, T. (1999). The rise of the metamind. In M. C. Corballis and S. Lea (Eds.), *The descent of mind: Psychological perception on hominid evolution* (pp. 218–260). London: Oxford University Press.

Suddendorf, T., and Busby, J. (2003). Mental time travel in animals? *Trends in Cognitive Sciences* 7, 391–396.

Swartz, K. B. (1997). What is mirror self-recognition in nonhuman primates, and what is it not? In J. G. Snodgrass and R. L. Thompson (Eds.), *The self across psychology: Self-recognition, self-awareness, and the self-concept* (pp. 65–71). New York: New York Academy of Sciences.

Szasz, T. (2006). The pretense of psychology as science: The myth of mental illness in statu nascendi. *Current Psychology* 25, 42–49.

Templeton, A. R. (1992). Human origins and analysis of mitochondrial DNA sequences. *Science* 255, 737.

Templeton, A. R. (1993). The "Eve" hypothesis: A genetic critique and re-analysis. *American Anthropologist* 95, 51–72.

Templeton, A. R. (1996). Gene lineages and human evolution. *Science* 272, 1363.

Templeton, A. (2002). Out of Africa again and again. *Nature* 416, 45–51.

Templeton, A. R. (2005). Haplotype trees and modern human origins. *Yearbook of Physical Anthropology* 48, 33–59.

Terberger, T., and Street, M. (2003). Jungpaläolithische Menschenreste im westlichen Mitteleuropa und ihr Kontext. In J. M. Burdukiewicz, L. Fiedler, W.-D. Heinrich, A. Justus and E. Brühl (Eds.), *Erkenntnisjäger: Kultur und Umwelt des frühen Menschen* (pp. 579–591). Veröffentlichungen des Landesamtes für Archäologie Sachsen-Anhalt, Vol. 57/2, Halle: Landesmuseum für Vorgeschichte.

Thakkar, K. N., Nichols, H. S., McIntosh, L. G., and Park, S. (2011). Disturbances in body ownership in schizophrenia: Evidence from the rubber hand illusion and case study of a spontaneous out-of-body experience. *PLoS ONE* *6*(10), e27089. doi:10.1371/journal.pone.0027089.

The Human Microbiome Jumpstart Reference Strains Consortium (2010). A catalog of reference genomes from the Human Microbiome. *Science* 328(5981), 994–999.

Thiessen, D. D. (1997). *Bittersweet destiny: The stormy evolution of human behavior.* Piscataway, NJ: Transaction Publishers.

Thioux, M., Stark, D. E., Klaiman, C., and Schultz, R. T. (2006). The day of the week when you were born in 700 ms: Calendar computation in an autistic savant. *Journal of Experimental Psychology: Human Perception and Performance* 32(5), 1155–1168.

Torroni, A., Lott, M. T., Cabell, M. F., Chen, Y.-S., Lavergne, L., and Wallace, D. C. (1994). MtDNA and the origin of Caucasians: Identification of ancient Caucasian-specific haplogroups, one of which is prone to a recurrent somatic duplication in the D-loop region. *American Journal of Human Genetics* 55, 760–752.

Treffert, D. (2010). *Islands of genius: The bountiful mind of the autistic, acquired, and sudden savant.* London and Philadelphia: Jessica Kingsley Publishers.

Trehub, A. (2009). Comment on Ramachandran 2008b. *Edge, http://www.edge.org/3rd_culture/rama08/rama08_index.html.* Retrieved 2012-1-14.

Trigger, B. G. (1984). Alternative archaeologies: Nationalist, colonialist, imperialist. *Man* 19, 355–370.

Trigger, B. G. (1989). *A history of archaeological thought.* Cambridge, UK: Cambridge University Press.

Trut, L. N. (1999). Early canid domestication: The farm-fox experiment. *American Scientist* 87(2), 160–169.

Tsuang, M. T., Stone, W. S., and Faraone, S. V. (2001). Genes, environment and schizophrenia. *The British Journal of Psychiatry* 178, s18–s24.

Turner, M. A. (1999). Generating novel ideas: Fluency performance in high-functioning and learning disabled individuals with autism. *Journal of Child Psychology and Psychiatry and Allied Diseases* 40, 189–201.

Varella, M. A. C., Souza, A. A. L. de, and Ferreira, J. H. B. P. (2011). Evolutionary aesthetics and sexual selection in the evolution of rock art aesthetics. *Rock Art Research* 28(2), 153–186.

Velly, L., Rey, M. F., Bruder, N. J., Gouvitsos, F. A., Witjas, T., Regis, J. M., Peragut, J. C., and Gouin, F. M. (2007). Differential dynamic of action on cortical and subcortical structures of anesthetic agents during induction of anesthesia. *Anesthesiology* 107(2), 202–212.

Vigilant, L., Stoneking, M., Harpending, H., Hawkes, K., and Wilson, A. C. (1991). African populations and the evolution of human mitochondrial DNA. *Science* 253, 1503–1507.

Vishnyatsky, L. B. (1994). "Running ahead of time" in the development of Palaeolithic industries. *Antiquity* 68, 134–140.

Voight, B. F., Kudaravalli, S., Wen, X., and Pritchard, J. K. (2006). A map of recent positive selection in the human genome. *PLoS Biology* 4(3), e72.

Walberg, M. W., and Clayton, D. A. (1981). Sequence and properties of the human KB cell and mouse L cell D-loop regions of mitochondrial DNA. *Nucleic Acids Research* 9, 5411–5421.

Walker, L. C., and Cork, L. C. (1999). The neurobiology of aging in nonhuman primates. In R. D. Terry, R. Katzman, K. L. Bick and S. S. Sisodia (Eds.), *Alzheimer's disease*, 2nd edn (pp. 233–243). New York: Lippincott Williams and Wilkins.

Ward, R. H., Frazier, B. L., Dew-Jager, K., and Pääbo, S. (1991). Extensive mitochondrial diversity within a single Amerindian tribe. *Proceedings of the National Academy of Sciences, USA* 88, 8720–8724.

Waterhouse, L. (1988). Extraordinary visual memory and pattern perception by an autistic boy. In L. K. Obler and D. Fein (Eds.), *The exceptional brain* (pp. 325–338). New York: Guilford.

Watson, E., Bauer, K., Aman, R., Weiss, G., Haeseler, A. von, and Pääbo, S. (1996). MtDNA sequence diversity in Africa. *American Journal of Human Genetics* 59, 437–444.

Weakland, J. H. (1968). Shamanism, schizophrenia and scientific unity. *American Anthropologist 70*, 356.

Weiner, W. S., Oakley, K. P., and Le Gros Clark, W. E. (1953) The solution of the Piltdown problem. *Bulletin of the British Museum (Natural History) Geology* 2(3), 141–146.

Weintraub, K. (2011). Autism counts. *Nature* 479(7371), 22–24.

Weiss, M. L., and Mann, A. E. (1978). *Human biology and behavior: An anthropological perspective*. Boston: Little, Brown and Co.

Wellman, H., and Liu, D. (2004). Scaling theory of mind tasks. *Child Development* 75(2), 523–541.

Wellman, H., and Wooley, J. (1990). From simple desires to ordinary beliefs: The early development of everyday psychology. *Cognition 35*(3), 245–275.

Wendt, W. E. (1974). Art mobilier aus der Apollo 11 Grotte in Südwest-Afrika. *Acta Praehistorica et Archaeologica* 5, 1–42.

Whitley, D. (2009). *Cave paintings and the human spirit.* Amherst, NY: Prometheus Books.

Williams, J. H. G., Whiten, A., Suddendorf, T., and Perrett, D. I. (2001). Imitation, mirror neurons and autism. *Neuroscience and Biobehavoural Reviews* 25, 287–295.

Williams, R. S. (2002). Another surprise from the mitochondrial genome. *New England Journal of Medicine* 347, 609–611.

Wimmer, H., and Perner, J. (1983). Beliefs about beliefs: Representation and constraining function of wrong beliefs in young children's understanding of deception. *Cognition* 13, 103–128.

Woodhouse, H. C. (1997). Ostrich eggshell beads in southern Africa. *Rock Art Research* 14, 41–43.

Woodward, A. (1999). Infants' ability to distinguish between purposeful and non-purposeful behaviors. *Infant Behavior and Development* 22(2), 145–160.

Wynn, T. (2002). Archaeology and cognitive evolution. *Behavioral and Brain Sciences* 25(3), 389–438.

Xu, M., St Clair, D., and He, L. (2006). Meta-analysis of association between ApoE epsilon4 allele and schizophrenia. *Schizophrenia Research* 84, 228–235.

Yakimov, V. P. (1980). New materials of skeletal remains of ancient peoples in the territory of the Soviet Union. In *Current argument on early man: Report from a Nobel Symposium* (pp. 152–169). Oxford: Pergamon Press.

Yoshikawa, T., Kikuchi, M., Saito, K., Watanabe, A., Yamada, K., Shibuya, H., Nankai, M., Kurumaji, A., Hattori, E., Ishiguro, H., Shimizu, H., Okubo, Y., Toru, M., and Detera-Wadleigh, S. D. (2001). Evidence for association of the myo-inositol monophosphatase 2 (IMPA2) gene with schizophrenia in Japanese samples. *Molecular Psychiatry* 6, 202–210.

Zaitchik, D. (1990). When representations conflict with reality: The preschooler's problem with false beliefs and "false" photographs. *Cognition* 35, 41–68.

Zebrowitz, L. A., Andreoletti, C., Collins, M. A., Lee, S. Y., and Blumenthal, J. (1998). Bright, bad, babyfaced boys: Appearance stereotypes do not always yield self-fulfilling prophecy effects. *Journal of Personality and Social Psychology* 75, 1300–1320.

Zhang, J., Webb, D. M., and Podlaha, O. (2002). Accelerated protein evolution and origins of human-specific features: FOXP2 as an example. *Genetics* 162, 1825–1835.

Ziegert, H. (2007). A new dawn for humanity: Lower Palaeolithic village life in Libya and Ethiopia. *Minerva* 18(4), 8–9.

Zischler, H., Geisert, H., Haeseler, A. von, and Pääbo, S. (1995). A nuclear "fossil" of the mitochondrial D-loop and the origin of modern humans. *Nature* 378, 489–492.

In: The Psychology of Human Behavior
Editor: Robert G. Bednarik
ISBN: 978-1-62257-901-3

Chapter 2

DIFFERENCES BETWEEN ORAL AND LITERATE CULTURES: WHAT WE CAN KNOW ABOUT UPPER PALEOLITHIC MINDS

Patricia A. Helvenston*
Diplomate, American Board of Professional Neuropsychology,
Historical Neuropsychological Researches Flagstaff, AZ, US

ABSTRACT

When speaking of the modern human mind and modern consciousness, too many cognitive archaeologists and neuropsychologists conflate the mind of people in oral culture with that of the mind of people in literate culture, unaware of the large corpus addressing this issue in literary criticism from the 1960s to 1980s. This is an almost ubiquitous attitude of specialists in literate cultures and is another example of what Bednarik (this volume) describes as faulty methodology in psychology and archaeology. This is a major mistake as the minds of people in the two cultures are significantly different due to writing and computational methods. Political correctness has too long discouraged and denigrated this information. Understanding the oral Paleolithic mind is not possible by referring to modern cognitive capacities as measured by modern neuropsychological testing techniques because they are all normed on people who are highly literate, thus reducing their usefulness as a means of studying the oral mind. As to the content of the oral mind, including the medieval mind, we have significant evidence of the importance of animals to the minds of people in agricultural and pastoralist cultures and of hunting-gathering peoples, including Upper Paleolithic peoples by virtue of the art they created. So, we know much of the content of their minds was concerned with all aspects of animal behavior and how to celebrate, capture, domesticate or hunt them. Through ethnological studies on oral cultures from the 17th to 21st centuries and ancient and medieval historical documents, we can gain some insight into the cognitive capacities of the people as well as examples of what some of the content of their minds would have been like, such as assorted mystical beliefs in myriad spirits who visually or

* Diplomate, American Board of Professional Neuropsychology, Historical Neuropsychological Researches, 1407 N. Aztec St., Flagstaff, AZ 86001, U.S.A, Patscholar@aol.com

verbally communicate with humans and who cause all misfortune or beneficence in nature.

Introduction

To explain human behavior through its present-day manifestations is rather like considering illness through its symptoms instead of its causes (Robert G. Bednarik, this volume)

Explaining Upper Paleolithic cognitive capacities through present-day manifestations of mentalities is characteristic of the work of many neuropsychologists, psychologists, cognitive archaeologists and paleoneurologists, who confuse cognitive characteristics of literate cultures with those of Paleolithic cultures, which were oral. Thus conflating the characteristics of both cultures without realizing how written technology changes brains and minds (Wynn and Coolidge 2010: S5–16). As Wynn and Coolidge state on p. S6:

> Modern cognitive science is replete with well-defined cognitive abilities, many of which can now be tentatively linked to specific neural substrates. Because these abilities have been isolated experimentally and confirmed through a variety of protocols, they have tremendous interpretative power. Cognitive science does, in fact know something about the *modern mind* (my italics, highlighting that the *modern mind* of Wynn and Coolidge is a conflation of mental abilities possessed by people in oral and literate cultures).

What Wynn and Coolidge fail to fully appreciate is that current cognitive science is based upon the mental abilities of highly literate peoples. Thus they conflate the capabilities of literate and oral cultures. They appear unaware of the vast differences in the minds of people in oral versus literate cultures. Speaking of working memory, a concept hypothesized based upon memory capacities of people in modern literate cultures and normed on thoroughly literate, modern minds implicitly assumes that our modern literate mind is similar in cognitive traits to the minds of people from the Upper Paleolithic who are often said to possess a *modern mind*. In this chapter I will refer to the modern literate mind as possessing modern consciousness because it is literate. Oral cultures do not possess *modern consciousness* because they are not literate. I will endeavor to show that there are marked differences between literate and oral cultures and the minds of the people inhabiting each culture are also different, thus revealing a serious epistemological error being perpetuated by too many specialists who are making the same error as Wynn and Coolidge. By studying the oral mind we come closer to understanding the Paleolithic mind than we do by conflating modern literate capabilities with the potential of that mind. In other words, “The past is a foreign country, they do things differently there” (Hartley 1953: 1).

For example, *Working Memory and the Evolution of Modern Thinking* was the 139th Wenner-Gren Symposium held in 2010, and represented a major attempt to understand the role of working memory in the evolution of *modern human consciousness* but the importance of writing in the construction of modern consciousness was never mentioned in any of the papers, although references to highly literate texts such as Shakespeare and abstraction as an attribute of literate cultures were discussed. Many excellent papers were included in a consideration of whether working memory rather suddenly became enhanced about 50 ka (thousand years) ago due to some mutation or whether its evolution was much more gradual (see Bednarik, this volume). Although there was not a consensus, the authorities I found most persuasive concluded that the evolution of working memory was very gradual and extended back into the material record considerably earlier than 50 ka (Ambrose 2010: S135–147; Belfer-Cohen and Hovers 2010: S167–175; Martín-Loeches 2010: S67–75), a position with which I agree. One powerful piece of evidence for this is that working memory as conceived by Wynn and Coolidge (2010: S5–15) involves much of the frontal lobe, which reached its gross morphological appearance and has remained stable since about 300,000 years BP (Bookstein et al. 1999: 217–224.) The more general purpose of the Symposium as stated by Wynn and Coolidge was an attempt to understand the *modern mind.*

Wynn and Coolidge do not define what they refer to as the modern mind but in the context of their paper and previous work they seem to be referring to the mind of *Homo sapiens sapiens* in Europe beginning 37–50 ka ago (Coolidge and Wynn 2005: 5–26; 2006: 18–21; Wynn and Coolidge 2003: 1–16, 2007: 79–90), long after the modern human morphology evolved about 200,000 years ago. The papers in the Supplement represent some of the very interesting work being done in the new discipline of cognitive archaeology; however, in discussing complex cognitive processes none of them discuss the effect of writing on human consciousness. Wynn and Coolidge argue that modern cognitive science should be utilized to understand the modern mind by archaeologists, but nowhere do they discuss the importance of writing in understanding that mind. They constantly conflate oral and literate cultures, as do most in the field of cognitive archaeology. As the name implies, the field attempts to ascertain the cognitive properties possessed by ancestral humans as evidenced from the material record and is quite concerned with the evolution of the human brain and mind. Much effort recently has gone into trying to ascertain what "modern" skills and behaviors can be implied by the assorted artifacts in the archaeological record (McBrearty and Brooks 2000: 453–563). *What is often ignored is the importance of the technology of writing which seems to be taken for granted, but it should not be since oral and literate cultures produce different kinds of minds.* Thus, the minds of Paleolithic peoples would have been characterized as oral minds; whereas, the minds of modern humans in our highly Westernized culture are literate minds with a *modern consciousness.* There are still small, traditional cultures that are oral but that is rapidly changing and soon writing will be a pan-human trait or cultural universal.

As a neuropsychologist and amateur archaeologist and paleoneurologist, having spent considerable time digesting these new disciplines, I have been distressed to see that the cognitive capacities, such as working memory, of modern highly literate peoples are being ascribed to Upper Paleolithic peoples as shown by the Wenner-Gren symposium papers—more as an implicit assumption than an explicit attribution because it seems clear to me that to understand the Paleolithic mind one must understand the preliterate mind. The research on working memory and other cognitive capacities discussed by Wynn and Coolidge (2010) derives from psychological and neuropsychological research on highly literate, scientifically sophisticated people largely in Western cultures and all the norms for tests of these abilities that they refer to are characteristic of that group of people, although this may be changing (Scribner and Cole, 1981, rpt. 1999). Wynn and Coolidge (ibid.) habitually conflate oral and literate cultures in their discussion of working memory.

Many of these cognitive abilities however, are a product of literate culture and not an indigenous property of the modern human brain without the technology of writing. Thus,

Paleolithic peoples, completely pre-literate, had brains similar to our modern brain albeit slightly larger, but without the benefit of written technology their minds were quite different than ours and it is the aim of this chapter to point out some of those differences. Although the differences between cognitive styles and abilities between individuals from oral-aural cultures and those from literate cultures was a topic of literary criticism in the 1960s–80s I think some of those findings need to be introduced into cognitive archaeology, paleoneurology, and neuropsychology because I have seen no references to this large body of work when attempting to understand the mind of Upper Paleolithic peoples and how that mind would differ from that of modern literate peoples as I first suggested it did (Helvenston and Bahn 2003: 213–224).

For example, Walter Ong (1982, rpt. 1997: 1) encapsulates it well when he states:

> In recent years certain basic differences have been discovered between the ways of managing knowledge and verbalization in primary oral cultures (cultures with no knowledge at all of writing) and in cultures deeply affected by the use of writing. The implications of the new discoveries have been startling. Many of the features we have taken for granted in thought and expression in literature, philosophy and science, and even in oral discourse among literates, are not directly native to human existence as such, but have come into being because of the resources which the technology of writing makes available to human consciousness. *We have had to revise our understanding of human identity* (italics mine).

This quotation has direct implications for understanding the oral Paleolithic mind.

In other words, what literate scholars had been assuming to be universal human cognitive attributes of contemporary humans, including scientific thinking and analysis, abstract thinking, logic, etc., depended on whether or not that individual came from an oral versus a literate culture. Cognitive archaeology has yet to come to terms with the effects of literacy on the cognitive capacities of contemporary peoples and it is the purpose of this chapter to explore this issue in order to redress this deficiency and gain some clearer insight into the mind of Upper Paleolithic peoples. Literacy itself confers a technology which enhances communication and cognitive abilities (Ong 1967, 1982, rpt 1997; Goody 1968 rpt. 2005, 1977, 1987; Fox 2000). All of these authors conducted numerous studies on the effects of literacy and their work needs to be incorporated into cognitive archaeology, neuropsychology and paleoneurology. Dean Falk (2011: 83), a paleoneurologist is one of the few to recognize the differences between oral and literate cultures and the uselessness of IQ tests normed on literate cultures to the understanding of the few oral hunting and gathering societies left on the planet.

I - Differences in Minds of People in Oral vs Literate Cultures

First I want to emphasize that the focus on the difference between the minds of people in oral cultures versus literate cultures does not mean to imply a crystallized categorical difference between the two minds that cannot be broached by education in literacy. The brains of infants at birth are the same in both cultures. The minds differ with exposure to oral or literate culture. *In fact, Upper Paleolithic peoples likely had a mind similar to the mind of persons who have not been part of a literate culture in our contemporary world.* This does not mean that the oral mind cannot develop the characteristics of the literate mind through education. The purpose of this chapter will be to discuss the differences in cognitive capacities between individuals in oral as opposed to literate cultures with an eye toward better understanding the mind of Upper Paleolithic peoples. Not that the examples given will directly apply to Paleolithic peoples, but rather that they will illuminate the oral mind and show that understanding oral minds will bring us much closer to understanding the Paleolithic mind than will modern neuropsychological studies of cognitive capacities based upon the normal literate mind. It will not be an exhaustive survey of the many issues involved but rather the goal is to stimulate an active discussion and inquiry into the nature of the preliterate mind. I believe this is necessary because cognitive archaeologists are busily attributing cognitive capacities inherent in the literate mind to the minds of Paleolithic peoples and referring to *their* mind as *modern* and I hope to show this is a major epistemological error. The modern mind is the literate mind with *its modern consciousness*.

Some key differences between oral-aural and literate thought and expression are *summarized* by Terrence Hawkes, editor of Ong's *Orality and literacy*, 1982 rpt. 1997: i. (We will continue with more detail subsequently.)

> Thought and expression in oral cultures is often highly organized but calls for organization of a sort unfamiliar to and often uncongenial to the literate mind. This organization is basically formulaic, structured in proverbs and other set expressions. It is aggregative rather than analytic, participatory rather than distanced, situational rather than abstract. Literacy it is now clear, transforms consciousness, producing patterns of thought which to literates seem perfectly commonplace and "natural" but which are possible only when the mind has devised and internalized, made its own, the technology of writing.

Anticipating the comments of the politically correct with their exquisite sensitivity to any inference that people from oral cultures are inferior or more primitive in mind than people from literate cultures, let me hasten to add, I too am sensitive to the use of categories such as oral versus literate and the potential for denigration of people from one or the other culture. That is not my aim: there is simply no way to discuss differences in experience and how they effect the development of the brain (thus creating the mind) other than by contrasting the two types of culture. Studies comparing and contrasting oral and literate cultures have been denigrated and suppressed for too long, and it is time to move into this fruitful area of research again more vigorously. Moreover, the effects of literacy can be seen imprinted upon the human brain. For example, it is possible to see the brains of 3–4th graders change in the temporal-occipital regions as the children learn to read and calculate, leaving an irreversible imprint of that learning in their brain (Dehaene 2005: 133–158, 2009). Those brain changes are not present in the brains of non-literate peoples although they can be with education, preferably at youth when it is easier to learn to read.

Here I am speaking of a highly plastic human brain with a basic template. The mind of humans in various societies differs considerably because of experience. *The combination of experience acting on the brain and causing it to develop in certain directions constitutes what I refer to as the mind in this chapter.* The literate culture surrounds the young child with many different experiences than encountered in the oral culture and thus fosters different cognitive habits and abilities and vice versa. One major difference is that poetic language, emotionality and empathy are enhanced in oral cultures, whereas scientific language, rationality and objectivity are enhanced in literate cultures.

Some may suggest oral culture is "superior" to literate culture or vice versa but this is an empirical question and depends upon the criteria used—in this example poetic versus scientific language. I am not making any universal value judgment as to which type of culture is best, although it can certainly be said that it is advantageous to success in the modern world to be literate. Indeed many traditional cultures are at a distinct disadvantage to Western culture because they have not had a tradition of literacy (Sowell 2012). It all depends on what is best for who and why, for what purpose. People in oral cultures are said to have enhanced memory capacities as opposed to those in literate cultures—again this is an empirical question that can be determined by research. When considering the pros and cons of literacy the early Greeks felt that literacy would deprive people of their memory capacities and literacy was thought by some to be inferior to oral memory techniques based upon that criterion. A similar argument was made in the Middle Ages to advancing literacy.

Although there may be something of a continuum from oral to literate culture as some cultures are partially literate (the medieval period was an example of a largely oral culture with a very small literate faction and the mind of medieval people was in many respects quite different from the modern mind [see Huizinga 1996]). People from oral cultures begin with a human brain—identical to the human brain of infants in literate cultures. People born into oral cultures can become literate when exposed to literate culture and educated in it—it happens all the time. People in literate cultures can learn to speak in mytho-poetic, beautifully descriptive language, learn the interconnectedness of animistic thinking, how to produce rock paintings, and how to track animals, etc. etc. No incontrovertible difference in the brains exists between people in oral versus literate cultures except that which is acquired and acquirable by experience and writing and shapes the different human minds. But having said this there is a difference in the minds of those who have never been exposed to literate culture as we will consider subsequently. First I would like to discuss Huizinga's interpretation of oral medieval culture in more detail as it enables us to understand a basically oral culture from actual medieval texts written by the few intellectual elites.

The Oral Culture of the Middle Ages

Let us begin with a general description of the cultural milieu of the high and later Middle Ages as regards heightened emotional affectivity which is one of the characteristics of oral cultures. Another characteristic is that whether animistic or Christian or otherwise, oral cultures tend to be highly "spiritual". The cultural milieu of medieval Europe is best described for our purposes by Johan Huizinga's impressionistic intuition based upon the exhaustive research of a lifetime (1996: 1). He tells us that:

> When the world was half a thousand years younger all events had much sharper outlines than now. The distance between sadness and joy, between good and bad fortune, seemed to be much greater than for us; every experience had that degree of directness and absoluteness that joy and sadness still have in the mind of a child.

In fact, many persons studying oral cultures have said the people have a childlike quality about them. In experiencing this passage both intellectually and emotionally, contrast affective associations elicited by representations of angel-filled heavens with horrific, stomach-wrenching visions of hell by placing yourself in the medieval context. Differentiate your emotional reaction to the golden, luminous, *Enthroned Madonna* by Giotto (1310) and the hideous, grotesque demons torturing, devouring and excreting sinners as depicted in *The Last Judgment* by Giselbertus, or the popular *Mouths of Hell*.[1] If such was the experience of medieval people, as Huizinga has suggested, they habitually experienced more frequent and intense mood swings than we do today.

Furthermore, this emotional reactivity occurred in a cultural milieu where all the emotionally intense aspects of life were experienced within a sacred and ritualized society. As Huizinga (p. 174) put it:

> Every event, every deed was defined in given and expressive forms and was in accord with the solemnity of a tight, invariable life style. The great events of human life—birth, marriage, death—by virtue of the sacraments, basked in the radiance of the divine mystery. But even the lesser events—a journey, labor, a visit—were accompanied by a multitude of blessings, ceremonies, sayings, and conventions.

These contrasting religious tones suffusing medieval life with the duality between heaven and hell are ubiquitous and formed important staples of medieval artistic efforts. All of the arts were sacralized because as the reader must remember, during medieval times the enjoyment of music and the fine arts was considered sinful. Only the service of the artistic work to faith alone was recognized as good. Thus, the entire sector of art and literature was sanctified and put into the service of the Christian faith, just as the art and literature in oral cultures that are animistic are put into the service of that mystical system. Indeed, as Huizinga pointed out, the entire life of "medieval Christendom is permeated in all aspects by religious images. There is nothing and no action that is not put into its relationship to Christ and faith". This process by which all nature is imbued with religious faith is what I refer to as the sacralization of the world. One means of doing this was to overlay all of reality with symbolic interpretations. For instance, Huizinga gives the following example. The walnut signifies Christ; the seed kernel is his divine nature, the outer shell is his human nature, and the woody membrane in between is the cross. In this way the walnut assumes a beauty and meaning because of the sacred connotation and thus all nature has a much greater value and meaning than is possible in our secular world.

In the eloquent words of Huizinga, p. 174,

> All things offer support and stability to the mind as it climbs to the eternal; all things lift each other to the heights. Symbolic thought causes the continuous transfusion of the feeling

[1] This work is located in the Uffizi Gallery, Florence, and is reproduced in Medieval art, painting, sculpture, architecture 4th–14th Century by James Snyder, New York, Prentice Hall, 1989, color plate 73. Consider the "The Dragon and The Beasts cast into Hell", wherein the gigantic mouths of brutes are seen swallowing sinners, grisly beasts, demons and dragons. This enthralling illustration is from the Cloisters Apocalypse, fol. 35r, Normandy, France, 1300-25, which is now housed in the Cloister's Collection, The Metropolitan Museum of Art, New York. This illumination is reproduced in Benton, Janetta Rebold, The medieval manageria: Animals in the art of the Middle Ages, New York, Abbeyville Press, 1992, p. 63.

for God's majesty and for eternity into everything that can be perceived and thought. It never allows the fire of the mystic life to be extinguished.

Reflect for a moment on a time when the viewing of a fragrant white rose misty with dew, with its own inherent aesthetic appeal, signified the Virgin Mary and a myriad of virginal saints, all with their own multiple symbolic affective and visual artistic associations. In this world every symbol, by virtue of the fact that all of them are ultimately aligned around the central miracle of the life of Christ, attains a super-value, a much stronger degree of reality. Thus, "symbolic thinking yields to that intoxication of thought, leads to that pre-intellectual obscuring of the definition of things, that muting of rational thought, which lifts the intensity of the feeling for life to its very peak" (Huizinga p. 239). The visual sensory images associated with viewing the walnut and the rose were thus accompanied by intense emotional reactions elicited because of the sacralized view of nature. When the sensory and affective associations are combined, they provide the foundation for a highly imaginative perception of the world that is one of the major conditions necessary to induce altered states of consciousness in individuals and groups today. In such a world as this, imbued with fantasy, we moderns can only strain to imagine the "unrestrained extravagance and inflammability of the medieval heart" (Huizinga p. 15).

I presented this extended series of vignettes regarding medieval culture because it was primarily an oral culture. We know a great deal about medieval culture, however, because a tiny percentage of intellectual elites described it for us and we have those written texts, along with the living archaeology of many English and European medieval chapels and other buildings. Much of the art of medieval Europe remains quite well preserved, including the music in chants and folksongs. The visual, musical and literary arts were highly developed in the service of Christianity as I will maintain the arts during the Paleolithic were imbued with animism and animal or therianthropic worship (a therianthrope is a part-human, part-animal figure). Mysticism also imbues the world with sacredness, a topic we will return to in greater detail subsequently for other oral cultures.

Is Oral Culture Synonymous With Primitive or Savage Categories and Literate Culture with Scientific Modernism?

Jack Goody (1977) examined the characteristics that Levy-Strauss and Lévy-Bruhl (authors whose works have been criticized according to today's standards, the essence of anachronism, but who still have a great deal to contribute regarding oral cultures) and others have regarded as marking the distinction between primitive and advanced, between wild and domesticated thinking, between pre-logical and logical thinking to suggest that many of the valid aspects of these somewhat vague dichotomies can be related to changes in the mode of communication, especially the various forms of writing. *The advantage of this approach lies in the fact that it does not simply describe the differences (as Lévy-Bruhl and Levy-Strauss did) but relates them to a third set of facts, and thus provides an explanation, some kind of mechanism for the changes that are shown to occur*. That mechanism of course is education in literacy: It changes brains.

Many fine minds of the 19th and 20th centuries have made extensive study of "primitive" or "barbaric" or "savage" cultures and described them in contrast to scientific modernism or *modern consciousness* as seen in highly developed literate cultures. Of course, now we know that these cultures were oral cultures fostering the habits of mind of peoples in those cultures. Following is a small selection of a number of older works that contain a great store of ethnographic description detailing the functioning of the preliterate mind for the interested reader. These texts provide examples of the content of pre-literate cultural minds and their beliefs and are an extremely valuable source of information regarding the Paleolithic mind, which would have been far more similar to the oral mind than to our own modern mind. These works demonstrate unquestionably the incredible complexity of the world of the oral mind and anyone interested in the differences between oral and literate minds should study them. For example, Sir James George Frazer (1907, 1923) illuminates the archaic mind (oral mind) beautifully. Unfortunately his work, while still published is largely forgotten today in archaeological circles but could prove very useful in understanding the content of the mind of ancient Greeks and others. I would argue that their mind, as is the case with the medieval mind, is far more similar to the Paleolithic mind than the mind of modern scientifically oriented humans.

Edward Tylor (1871), to whom we will return shortly, discussed primitive culture with research into the development of mythology, philosophy, religion, language, art and custom, in two volumes, the second of which contains a marvelous discussion of animism which in the original work is still fresh and current today in spite of recent critiques (Bird-David 1999: 67-41). Claude Lévi-Straus (1966) presents a fascinating discussion in his study *The savage mind*. Bronislaw Malinowski (1948 rpt. 1992) discussed magic, science and religion among the Trobriand Islanders and presents many insights into the non-literate mind. For example, the Trobriand Islanders exercised rational, logical thought when it came to constructing homes, boats, planting crops, all practical matters in which they were highly skilled. But for all unknowns such as illness, invasions, sailing far out to sea, they resorted to magic. The Egyptians resorted to magic when dealing with death and other *unknowns*, but when building pyramids, which they knew how to construct, their thoughts were very logical and scientific.

And last, but not least, Lucien Lévy Bruhl's works (1910, rpt 1984; 1923, 1926, 1928, 1935, 1949) go into great depth on the participation of the human in the entire animistic universe and contains volumes of ethnographic descriptions of preliterate cultures. All of these works, no matter what critics say about the methods or problems in various analyses, include descriptions of non-literate thinking and ideas that must speak volumes about the type of thought representative of ancient peoples. In other words, when the ethnographic descriptions are viewed from the phenomenological point of view critiques of method and errors of analysis need not cause a complete rejection of the basic observations themselves. Indeed, in a foreword to *How natives think*, originally published in 1910, and reprinted in 1985, C. Scott Littleton (v–lviii) forms a similar conclusion. For example, he says that after rereading Lévy-Bruhl he is convinced that he

> thoroughly deserved to be recalled from the intellectual limbo into which he has been consigned. Moreover it is possible to suggest that in *How natives think* and elsewhere, he managed to adumbrate a great many ideas that have only recently been put forward, in many cases by people who do not consider themselves to be in his intellectual debt (Lévy-Bruhl 1985: p. v–vi).

Littleton continues stating that:

> Many of these ideas involve what may be called for lack of a better term, *cognitive relativity*, that is, the notion that the logic we bring to bear in our descriptions of the world is not universal, but rather a function of our immediate techno-environmental circumstances and our particular and ideological heritage [whether we are *literate* or not, my italics and parentheses], and that no one logic is necessarily superior to any other logic.

This viewpoint is consistent with the theme I have been explicating that oral culture differs from literate culture but neither is inherently superior to the other in all aspects. There is an irony here as Lévy-Bruhl has been criticized for being ethnocentric for *apparently* insisting that the Western thought mode or logic is superior to that of what he identified as primitive societies. This criticism as well as many others is unfounded as Evans-Prichard (1934, 1965, 1981), Rodney Needham (1972), Jan de Vries, (1961 rpt. 1977), Robin Horton (1973), and other contemporary scholars have found and as I argue in this chapter.

Lévy-Bruhl's descriptions will not exactly equal what Upper Paleolithic peoples believed but they will provide an insight into the types of belief they most likely held so we will know something more about their minds than any theory of enhanced memory, normed by neuropsychological tests on highly literate, modern minds, can tell us. We will return to specific examples illustrating the oral mind's content shortly. From that knowledge we will be in a position to consider the likely content of the Paleolithic mind.

Most of these authors considered that there were differences between primitive and modern minds in some degree but literacy was not recognized as the responsible agent for the difference. Hence their use of terms like "savage" or "primitive" or "pre-logical" have been universally criticized because these terms are thought to infer an inferior mind in oral cultures. Today we know the "inferior" or "savage" or "traditional" mind is simply a mind which is shaped by oral rather than literate culture. Lévy-Bruhl initially believed that the mind of the "primitive" was "pre-logical" whereas the mind of the modern was logical. Under withering criticism, he subsequently rejected this position and stated there was no difference (1949). Modern scholarship as exemplified by Ong (1967; 1982 rpt. 1997); supports differences in the minds of pre-logical versus logical peoples that can be attributed to literacy, so the brains of pre-logical and logical peoples would have been the same at birth, but their minds would have been different because one group learned to write. Thus, in spite of his critics, Lévy-Bruhl was correct after all, there are differences in the logical capacities of people in oral versus literate cultures. For example, Jack Goody (1977) has convincingly shown how shifts hitherto labeled as shifts from magic to science, or from the so-called "pre-logical" to the more and more "rational" state of consciousness or from Levi-Strauss's "savage" mind to domesticated thought, *can be more economically and cogently explained as shifts from orality to various stages of literacy* (my italics).

Cognitive Characteristics of the Oral Human Mind

It is so difficult for most literate peoples to imagine what people in a non-literate culture would be like, how their minds would function, that I must first ask the reader to imagine there is no such thing as looking anything up. There are no calendars as we know them. Think about this for a few moments to let the full impact sink in. Human experiences that have been memorized in specific rituals, living human experience recalled for a brief period of time and rituals as a memory device to facilitate hunting, making clothing, etc. are the only means of remembering. Indeed, much of ritual is aimed to help remember the "correct" way to carry out certain special activities as well as how to think and feel about them. The art created in the Upper Paleolithic could have served as memory storage for certain highly important events as rugs with woven or painted symbols served as histories for Native Americans prior to the incursion of Euro-American culture. It seems likely that the geometric and abstract markings in Upper Paleolithic art indicate a symbolic representation of events and Von Petzinger has compiled a detailed listing of the non-figural images from 153 different sites in France, and when seen assembled all together, they definitely look like precursors of writing (see G. von Petzinger, cited by Shipman 2011: 145–6. We think they had meaning but we cannot decipher them. We can only do that when writing becomes more fully developed thousands of years later and persists among larger cultures.

Sound is paramount and very ephemeral; there is no calling it back. We can freeze a visual image on film but we cannot freeze the sound. Sound is considered very powerful in oral cultures, which is largely why great attention to the format of rhetoric was practiced in Greece and Rome, partially literate cultures (Ong 1982 rpt. 1997: 32). Indeed the sound of particular sacred names carries so much power that people like the San of the Kalahari are forbidden to utter the name of certain Gods or animals with supreme powers, as Jewish people were forbidden to utter the name of Ywh (Yaweh). The San use another word, less powerful to refer to the not-to-be-named God or animal. There are strict punishments meted out to those who transgress this stricture. Sound and words have great "medicine", great significance and power. The buffalo and the bear, the wolf and the lion all are conveying their strength in various roars, howls, cries and vocalizations and the human is conveying his strength in the power and beauty of his language. The hunter can see the buffalo sleeping or dead or in far off herds, but when he hears its roar he had better watch out. Sound conveys the imminence of the meeting between animal and man—crucial information for adaptive evolution in capturing prey and avoiding predators.

In an oral culture when one tries to recall sound or thoughts one has to rely on memory, mnemonics and formulas. It is difficult to rely on sustained, lengthy thought to solve problems, because there is no referring back to anything. Memory aids such as notched sticks or a series of carefully arranged objects will not in and of themselves retrieve a complicated series of assertions. How, in fact could a lengthy, analytic solution ever be assembled in the first place. An interlocutor is virtually essential; it is hard to talk to yourself for hours on end. The Greeks like Socrates and Plato engaged in debates or symposia to assist them in their thought processes, but these oral productions subsequently were written down as well as could be remembered and further refined from texts. How could you ever recall a lengthy series of thoughts and problem solving strategies without writing?

Formulas help cement *rhythmic* discourse which is important in oral language, as mnemonic aids in their own right. "Red in the morning, the sailor's warning; red in the night, the sailors delight". "Divide and conquer". "To err is human, to forgive is divine". These phrases are found in written discourse and can be looked up in literate culture, but they help people remember certain salient experiences and knowledge. They are ubiquitous in oral discourse, to the point that it can become annoying and frustrating to people from literate cultures to listen because they cannot wait for the speaker to "get to the point!" Literacy fosters brevity of expression.

"In an oral culture to think through something in non-formulaic, non-patterned, non-mnemonic terms, even if it were possible, would be a waste of time, for such thought once worked through, could never be recovered with any effectiveness as it can with writing. It would not be abiding knowledge, simply a passing thought" (Ong p. 35). The significance of memory as one of the *most important functions* of mind in oral culture was emphasized by Augustine of Hippo because it literally was true in his world, less so for those who were partially literate and could rely on writing to some extent to preserve written memories. Indeed there is a large body of research regarding various memory systems and mnemonic devices from the classical and medieval periods (see Carruthers 2008; and Yates 1974).

In oral cultures words are not separated as fully as in literate cultures, since writing itself facilitates such a separation. Of course, the approach to memorizing a poem was different than memorizing a text. The bard deliberately waited a day or so before incorporating new material into his oral poem as he integrated it into all his own stock phrases and rhymes, he did not attempt to memorize the text as we might. "Poets had thousands of metrically tailored formulas" (Ong p. 59). They simply added these into their oral presentations. Indeed, oral poets who learn to read often have trouble composing orally again as the left hemisphere inhibits their poetry making (a right hemispheric function). In oral cultures there are long segments of text that contain many contradictions (see Ong p. 37 for biblical examples). Once these contradictory statements were written down they could be subjected to analysis that led many to question the accuracy of the biblical texts and led to modern literary criticism as a discipline. Much of oral thought is aggregative rather than analytic, filled with expressions that include clusters of parallel terms or phrases or clauses, antithetical terms or phrases or clauses and epithets. Oral folk prefer, especially in formal discourse, phrases like the brave soldier instead of the soldier, the beautiful maiden instead of the maiden, etc. Oral expression thus carries a load of epithets and other formulary baggage which literacy rejects as cumbersome and unpleasantly redundant or copious. In other words people in oral cultures seem far more verbose, loquacious, and expansive emotionally than people in literate cultures (Ong p. 39–40).

Oral societies must invest great energy in saying over and over again what has been learned arduously over the ages. This need establishes a highly traditionalist or conservative set of mind that with good reason inhibits intellectual experimentation. Knowledge is very hard to come by and precious; and society highly values those who have taken the time to memorize many thoughts, experiences, and events. Oral cultures do not take changes to a memorized sequence lightly, thus change is slower than in literate cultures. Literacy can be conservative too, but by taking on the conservative functions itself, the text frees the mind of conservative tasks, that is, of its memory work, thus enabling the mind to turn itself to new speculation (Havelock 1963: 354–395).

Oral culture is much closer to the human life-world than literate culture, that is to ordinary activities of daily living. In the absence of elaborate analytic categories that depend on writing to structure knowledge at a distance from lived experience, oral cultures must conceptualize and verbalize all their knowledge with close reference to the human life-world, assimilating the alien, objective world to the more immediate, familiar interaction of human beings, i.e. the world is peopled with spirits who have similar motivations to human beings so nature is understood as possessing a "mind" similar to that of the human and therefore understandable and potentially controllable. This is why oral cultures seem to be highly personal, subjective and emotionally involving, in contrast to literate cultures which appear more distanced from emotion and less concerned with single episodes of experience. Writing fosters abstractions that disengage knowledge into abstract categories, far from the subjective arena where human beings struggle with one another (Ong p. 42–46).

In other words oral culture is more empathetic and participatory, rather than objectively distanced. Primary orality fosters personality structures that in certain ways are more communal and externalized, and less introspective than those common among literates. Many authors who have studied the oral or "primitive" mind have commented that asking a person from an oral culture about his or other individual's personalities results in utter confusion (Lévy-Bruhl 1928 transl. 1965). Most all events are communal and the individual is defined by his community. Oral communication unites people in groups. Writing and reading are solitary activities that throw the psyche back on itself. People in oral cultures tend to be much less introspective than literate peoples.

Oral culture can be categorized as homeostatic. That is to say, oral societies live very much in a *present* which keeps itself in equilibrium or homeostasis by sloughing off memories which no longer have present relevance (Ong p. 46–47). Oral culture has a much greater intensity of and attention to the ongoing present than does literate culture and seems more absorbed in the present. Finally, all conceptual thinking is to a degree abstract, but oral cultures tend to use concepts in situational, operational frames of reference that are minimally abstract in the sense that they remain close to the human living life-world (Ong p. 49–57). Hence oral peoples seem less abstract in their conceptualizations than literate peoples and sometimes this has been referred to as "pre-rational" or "pre-logical" versus the rational thought of literates. Literacy encourages rationality, not that oral people cannot also be rational; they can but not to the same extent and in different ways. Their world is peopled with many kinds of spirits of humans, animals, inanimate objects such as rocks, streams, forests, etc. forming very complex interconnected nets of interaction among all these supernatural beings and the human social world. Given the presumption of the power of invisible forces to act on humans and the natural world, oral cultures' reasoning makes complete sense to them in a way it does not to people in literate cultures.

In addition to these habits of mind and communication let us consider some general cognitive capacities of modern oral humans as cited by Amati and Shallice (2007: 358–385). (They do not specify these characteristics as primarily true of oral cultures because they conflate oral with literate cultures.) *I am contending that these cognitive capacities form a basis for literate cultures to teach writing, which changes the human brain and mind.*

1. Language. This is obviously the most frequently discussed basic human capacity with a complex underlying structure, which goes far beyond any communication system used by other animals. I add the following abilities characteristic to language of pre-literate peoples: language is often poetic, metaphorically laced with proverbs and sayings to enhance memory capabilities. Verbalizations are cumulative rather than analytic, paratactic without subordinate clauses, thus giving rise to an aggregative accumulation of contradictory statements which are obvious when studied after they are written down. People in oral cultures may rely more heavily on the right hemisphere than people in literate cultures. Right hemispheric functions include holistic analysis of events, creativity, visual symbolism, heightened affective

reactions. In literate cultures the left hemisphere inhibits the right hemispheric functions (Springer and Deutsch 1993).

2. I add this ability to the list. Oral cultures are dominated by ritual as it helps people remember special occasions and how to perform ceremonies for many activities.
3. The ability to use tools and instruments of advancing sophistication.
4. Signs, signals and other homomorphic representations. Humans have the ability to visually represent aspects of reality for a particular purpose such as indicating something for future use. Thus, a bifurcation or a cross can be used to indicate the correct direction or route.
5. The capacity for conceptualization, including the formation of dynamic concepts such as cause and effect relationships. The following statements are true of oral cultures, where causes are personified spirits, i.e. supernatural spirits cause the phenomenon of nature. Cause and effect relationships are highly affective because all causes are from the spirit world, which can harm or help humans. In oral cultures cause and effect is very different from that of literate cultures where we think in terms of laws of nature to explain cause and effect relationships, but the oral mind thinks in terms of cause as supernatural forces leading to effect. Other than supernatural causes, often referred to as primary causes by Lévy-Bruhl, oral culture is uninterested in secondary causes (natural causes). When you already know the reason for various events (mystical forces) that can harm you, why bother with other causes.
6. Aesthetic sense. It enables other capacities to be sublimated for a further function. (To this I would add Dissanayake's sense of "artification" and perfectionism, which is a human universal.)
7. Meta-representational. Humans are capable of using representations not only of directly perceived things, but also as a second or higher-level interpretation of "mental, public or abstract" entities. This description conflates meta-representational in oral culture with that in literate culture.
8. Algorithmic capacity. Modern humans have this capacity. But advanced algorithms such as arithmetic, geometry, and advanced mathematics are only true in literate cultures, another area of conflation between literate and illiterate cultures.
9. Categorization and organization. Traditional societies have systems for organizing their knowledge, for example they know the properties of the animals and plants of their world.
10. Theory of mind. Humans have the ability to infer or perceive the attitudes or intentions of others of their species. Self-consciousness develops to self-inspection or self-reflection in literate cultures.
11. Anticipatory planning, which includes the use of watercraft. Human behavior is often directed explicitly toward the attainment of some explicitly represented future state of affairs although futurity is not as precisely defined in oral languages as in literate ones.
12. I would add the *animal connection* (Shipman 2010: 519–532), i.e., the importance of animals to human evolution from about 2.6 Mya. Humans have evolved to need animals and rely upon them.

To this list I have added No. 2 as ritual is a mnemonic device for remembering the proper sequence to "make special", and occasions more memorable. To No. 6, I have added Dissanayake's sense of artification (1992, 2008: 241–263, 2009: 148–173, 2010), as well as a sense of perfection (Helvenston 2012), which is a universal human trait (Brown 1991; Pinker 2002: 435–449). Pat Shipman (ibid.), in what I consider to be a very important paper and book (2011), suggested that a crucial pan-human trait she referred to as the *animal connection*, i.e., the importance of animals to human evolution should be added to other characteristics of human behavior, so I add No. 12 to Amati and Shallice's list, the *animal connection*. Thus all of these abilities would have characterized the Upper Paleolithic mind, possibly along with enhanced memory by means of metaphors, analogies, proverbs, repetitive phrases, rhyming oral verse. This brain with its capacities forms the template for the modern human brain, which is then immersed in literate culture except for a few traditional, oral cultures that are rapidly becoming literate or being assimilated into literate cultures.

Cognitive Capacities of the Literate Human Mind

In addition to all the cognitive capacities elucidated for oral cultures, let us now review some cognitive habits of mind and characteristics of the literate mind to contrast with the oral mind and to add to its capabilities. Amati and Shallice (ibid.) are characterizing oral cultures that have all the above characteristics but they are ignoring the extreme importance of the technology of writing on the human mind in modern literate civilizations. They are assuming the cognitive characteristics of contemporary Western civilization are simply pan-human characteristics when they are not. They are present in literate cultures and include such capacities as follows (this is not an exhaustive list):

1. Writing, printing and mathematical computation of an increasingly complex nature. The written word permeates literate culture and the left hemisphere dominates the right.
2. The beginning of Greek philosophy (the origin of disciplines of knowledge in the modern world) is directly tied in with the restructuring of thought brought about by writing (Ong ibid.). The Greeks began to explain cause and effect relationships in nature and to discount supernatural intervention as a primary cause and substituted natural event sequences for it, leading to modern science.
3. Scientific methodology and increasingly complex and perfected scientific hypotheses and theories, giving rise to new sorts of technologically-advanced tools such as automobiles, airplanes, high-speed rail, nuclear bombs, magnetic resonance imaging, computers, cell phones and other sophisticated technical devices, satellite technology, etc. etc., unimaginable in a strictly oral culture. Indeed some technical advances seem like magic to those in oral cultures who do not understand the technology; this is true of many people in literate cultures also, but a small group of people do understand and produce all these creations.
4. Characteristically more objective, distanced verbalization in literate culture almost from the point of view of a third party and less emotional investment in situations and events. A more abstract attitude to reality, not so involved emotionally in discrete events and situations. There is a tendency to recall events in abstract

categories, rather than situationally. Indeed Luria (1976) who made an excellent study of oral versus literate culture found that when non-literate people were asked to name a circle they replied "the moon", when asked to name a square they replied "house" or "barn", a triangle they named "a hill or mountain", showing the concrete, non-conceptual nature of their thought. When asked to define a "tree" a subject replied "why should I, everyone knows what a tree is". Why define when a real life situation, such as pointing to a tree is much more satisfactory than a definition (Ong p. 53–55). Oral cultures simply do not deal in such items as geometrical figures, abstract categorization, formal logical reasoning processes, definitions, or even comprehensive descriptions or articulated self-analysis, all of which does not derive simply from thought itself but from *text-formed thoughts*. These are all legitimate types of questions to be asked of oral and literate cultures but they come from a world the oral respondent does not share (Luria 1976). Attempts at testing oral peoples with highly literate neuropsychological tests reveal major cognitive differences between oral and literate people. Ordinary intelligence test questions are tailored to a special kind of consciousness, one deeply conditioned by literacy and print—i.e., *modern consciousness* (Berger 1978).

5. A hugely expanded vocabulary over oral culture, with an aggregate collection written down that is much larger than the number of words most frequently used is characteristic of literate culture.
6. People in literate cultures may have decreased memory capacities compared to people in oral cultures because oral cultures use metaphors, repetitive phrases, and other mnemonic devices that enhance memory including ritual, which is becoming increasingly rare in literate culture.
7. Writing greatly enhances the ability to sort out contradictions in documents, along with the ability to refine literary scientific writings thus enhancing logical "rational" thought and forming the basis for the construction of scientific methodology.
8. Havelock (1976) attributes the ascendancy of Greek analytical thought to the Greek's introduction of vowels to the Greek alphabet. Thus the sight of words could more directly convey the sound of the words. In introducing vowels into the alphabet the Greeks reached a new level of analytic visual coding of the elusive world of sound, thus leading to increasingly abstract scientific thought.
9. Dominant left hemisphere, with detailed, analytic, rational thought processes related to verbal and textual materials, often dominating consciousness and inhibiting the right hemispheric functions. Literacy enhances the strength of the left hemisphere which may be *one* reason people do not hear the gods in literate culture as often as in oral and ancient cultures. Of course a widespread disbelief in supernatural forces is another.
10. In literate cultures we have detailed calendars that show us a continuum of time (time is spatialized) from the distant past, the present and into the distant future. Our languages also contain words for this continuum but many oral cultures do not have such precise designations for arbitrary segments of time; they focus more on the present, and the future is often vaguely imagined.
11. Cause and effect relationships are understood as intellectual questions and viewed with dispassionate interest, they are not suffused with emotion as in oral cultures

where cause is through the agency of a myriad of supernatural beings who can harm or help humans.

12. Self-consciousness, self-awareness and introspection are more highly developed in literate culture.

II - Content of Upper Paleolithic Minds

The Importance of Animals to Oral and Paleolithic Minds

I would like to shift our attention now, to begin a consideration of examples of the actual content of oral minds as an illustration of what the content of the Upper Paleolithic mind may have been concerned with. By referring to the characteristics of the pre-literate mind, we can reconstruct many likely aspects of the Upper Paleolithic mind. Not that our reconstruction will be identical to the mind of Upper Paleolithic peoples, but it will be more similar to them than modern neuropsychological studies of cognitive capacities. Klingender (1971) has shown the importance of animals in art and thought from the Paleolithic to the end of the Middle Ages, and Rowland (1973) has discussed animals with human faces, showing the tendency of humans to view themselves as part animal, part human (or as a therianthrope) out of a reverence and/or worship for the traits that many animals possess that are seen as admirable. Anati (2010), discussing hunting and gathering peoples, estimates that about 70% of the rock art of the world is devoted to depictions of animals. Given the importance of animals to hunting, gathering, pastoral and farming communities since ancient times, we now turn our attention to them.

Images of animals were predominant in Mesolithic and Neolithic art from Saharan Africa, namely in the Tadrart Acacus and Tassili regions, the earliest of which are believed to have been painted by hunters, followed by animal depictions made by hunters who were developing pastoral strategies. The latter are believed to have created paintings in the so-called "round heads" style (di Lernia 1999). There is a pastoral (Neolithic) petroglyph from Ti-n-lalam, Tadrart Acacus, Libya, that depicts a therianthropic figure, with the head of a dog or jackal and an enormous phallus, graphically penetrating a woman of high status, a priestess perhaps, judging from the adornments she was wearing (Mori 1975: 356). Clearly, this figure must be a supernatural figure to the people who created the drawing. Some of the therianthropic figures from the "round head" paintings, and the pastoral petroglyph just referred to, appear to have some convergences with Egypt, such as the cult of the ram, or the jackal-headed therianthropes which bring to mind the Pharaonic god, Anubis, or the horned goddesses that evoke the Egyptian Hathor (Muzzolini 2001: 605–636). Wilkinson (2003), although by no means the first, pointed out that pre-dynastic Egypt had a very widespread interest in animals and Egyptian funerary priests, donning jackal heads, served in ceremonies linking the living with the dead.

Certainly, animals as the material representation of deities are enshrined in the art and literature of the earliest civilizations of Sumer and Egypt. From the dawn of recorded history we have written evidence that humans seriously pondered their relationship to both animals and supernatural beings. From the third millennium BCE, a Sumerian tale referred to as *The Epic of Gilgamesh* related the life and adventures of the ruler, Gilgamesh of Uruk. Gilgamesh was a half-man, half-god figure whose daemonic energy exhausted his subjects. They prayed to the gods to provide a companion for him and not long thereafter, Gilgamesh encountered Enkidu, who represented the "natural man". Enkidu was covered with hair, reared with animals, and appears to have been part man, part beast, in other words a therianthropic figure. Gilgamesh and Enkidu became like brothers and Enkidu was gradually civilized (Sanders 1960). A similar motif of human/animal combination dates back thousands of years into the Upper Paleolithic.

Based upon the studies of Joseph Campbell (1988, Volumes I and II), hunter-gatherers were very likely to represent animal deities, and there are few depictions of plants in pre-Historic or modern hunter-gatherer cultures. On the other hand, although plants were worshipped in agriculturally based societies, they were associated with human or animal deities, for example ancient depictions of Jesus Christ as wheat. This raises the question of whether or not an empathic connection between humans and the divine is a prerequisite for deification and the Paleolithic art suggests it may be, which one can argue may be more potent in the case of animals than plants. I would suggest the hypothesis that even when plants are deified, they must be materially represented by animal or human "manifestations" which serve to provide the empathic connection. An in-depth, cross-cultural study of the representation of deities in hunter-gatherer societies versus agricultural societies throughout history could test this hypothesis.

If the empathic relationship between humans and animals is as strong as I maintain, there should be evidence from folk tales from around the world that elaborate the link. A preliminary survey from early Greek mythology (Bullfinch 1970; Thompson 1975; Propp 1968) through the Brothers Grimm (Zipes 1987) emphasizes the wisdom (Aesop's fables) and affective lives of animals. Throughout the ancient Middle East, and in ancient Greece and Rome, there are many artistic depictions of humans copulating with animals or therianthropes. In fact, bestiality, or zoophilia, was apparently practiced in the ancient world, as it was prohibited in *Leviticus* for Jewish men or women to defile themselves with animals (19: 23) and such intercourse was punishable by death for both human and beast (20: 15–16). The importance of animal images with human faces, or vice versa, was stressed throughout ancient Near Eastern art and religious beliefs where one sees countless examples of therianthropic figures, (Klingender 1971). Animals remained dominant images throughout the classical (Toynbee 1973) and medieval period (Klingender op cit.; Flores 2000; Hassig 2000) and even today, they are one of the most popular subjects depicted by artists, and animal cartoons mimic human foibles and behavior.

The explicit relationship between knowledge of animal behavior, hunting, and folk tales is provided in sophisticated studies of the stories told by the Kalahari San (Ju/'hoan), a hunting-gatherer society. As Biesele has demonstrated, many folk tales of hunter-gatherers around the world are concerned with presenting, in oral form, a great deal of information about the plant and animal resources upon which the people depend. The stories are enjoyable, memorable, and packed with relevant detail which facilitates more effective hunting and gathering. Indeed Biesele sees these stories as enabling a more effective adaptation to the specific environment (1993: 42) by enhancing hunting skill. We know that contemporary Kalahari San, primarily oral until very recently, are preoccupied with animals to a great extent as shown in their myths, stories and hunting practices (Biesele 1976, 1993; Katz 1982; Lee 1966; Lee and DeVore 1968; Lewis-Williams 1977; Orpen 1874; Solomon 1997, 1999, 2008; Stow 1905; Thackeray 1993, 2005; Vinnicombe 1972, 1975, 1976).

For example, in a significant creation myth of the Maluti Bushmen of South Africa it was believed that men and animals had once been brothers during primal time (that is, they were one and the same creature, not animals, not men and these creatures are depicted in San art as therianthropic figures), long before the world of the civilized modern San was created by Cagn (aka Kaggen, Kagn), their creator god (Orpen 1874: 1–13). For example, one myth tells how Cagn told his son to collect sticks for bows. The baboons killed this youth and hung his body in a tree because they thought the bows would be used against them. Cagn tracked the baboons and found them singing and dancing of their triumph and he was enraged, so he collected a bag of wooden pegs and drove them into the back of each dancer, thus giving baboons their characteristic posture. Then he banished them to the mountains to live on roots, beetles and scorpions. The Bushmen enjoyed enacting a baboon dance in which "the performers imitated all the actions and droll grimaces of rival baboons, springing, gamboling and running on all fours" (Stow 1905: 117). There is a rock art painting of an animated dance showing human figures carrying weapons, leaping and somersaulting, with one participant wearing what appears to be a baboon tail, located in the Drakensberg Mountains in South Africa. Another painting in the same locale shows armed human figures and therianthropic figures dancing around a large centrally positioned baboon (Vinnicombe 1976: 309a). All of these rituals, dances, stories, and artistic depictions present many details based upon keen observation of baboons.

The Bushmen of South Africa, in the 19th and early 20th century employed various animal skins, most particularly the skin of an ostrich, and there are artistic depictions of such figures in Bushmen art (Vinnicombe 1976). By this period, however, a million or so years after our early ancestors probably used disguises, the therianthropes depicted in Bushmen art have assumed a complex mythical status, above and beyond simply referring to actual hunting practices. Wearing buffalo skins during the hunt was a practice that was still carried out until quite recently by some North American plains Indians during the late 19th early 20th century. In addition to animal skins, other assorted disguises such as masks may have been employed. The "sorcerer" figure found in the cave of Les Trois Frères in the French Pyrenees wears animal accoutrements with which he may have been hunting and/or or possibly re-enacting a myth.

Rock paintings from the Drakensberg depict many scenes with human figures carrying weapons and hunting accoutrements, as well as numerous therianthropic figures (Vinnicombe 1976). Most of these paintings date to the last 600 years (Mazel and Watchman 1997: 445–449), although some may be up to 2000 years old (Mitchell 2002: 192–206). It is believed that the therianthropic figures represent ancestral San, who during the first creation (before the creation of the San living today) were brother to an eland, the San creator deity's favorite son (Wilmsen 1986: 347–372). These therianthropes are highly significant in San mythology and their spirits, although long dead, can still mix with, and affect the living (Solomon 1997: 3–13).

Shipman (2010, 2011) and Bahn and Vertut 1997: 170–211) show the Upper Paleolithic mind was also dominated by sights and sounds of the animals of its world as evidenced by the beautiful depictions of animals in the caves of France and Cantabrian Spain. This is a large corpus of archaeological evidence confirming Shipman's hypothesis of the *animal connection* and the importance of animals to human evolution. She suggests that with domestication of animals humans had developed a living tool: transforming the concept of tool making and tool using from inanimate stone or wood to live animals was a fundamental advance in human evolution, predicated on knowledge of biology, ecology, physiology, temperament, intelligence and behavioral characteristics of target species for selective breeding and communication techniques based on the *animal connection*. These activities were beginning in the Upper Paleolithic, although they became predominant in the Neolithic. Writing has contributed to the increased domestication of animals through history, archaeology, genetic studies, ethology, veterinary medicine, etc., although Shipman ignores writing in her book and paper, focusing instead upon the complexity of human language.

As living "tools", animals provide valuable new resources and at least ten examples can easily be identified: 1. muscular power beyond human strength; 2. rapid transport of goods or people; 3. raw material wool or hair for making fabric, etc.; 4. useful fertilizer, fuel, building material; 5. disposal of refuse; 6. mobile wealth and storage for excess grain crops (which can be retrieved via slaughter); 7. high fat and high protein food, milk and milk products; 8. protection for people, possessions and dwellings; 9. tracking and killing of game or pests; 10. combined traits that enable humans to live in new habitats. With just a little imagination one can see how artification or "making" special according to Dissanayake (2008: 241–263, 2009: 148–173, 2010) would have been important in a number of these ways of exploiting animals. For example, special techniques involved in processing wool or hair in the making of fabric, special ceremonial clothing, advances in storage mechanisms leading to special containers and later kitchen utensils, ceremonial cooking involving special recipes, special ritualized methods of processing meat and animal products such as milk, cheese, cream, special breeding programs for desirable traits, special ceremonies accompanying the hunting and killing of animals, animal fables, myths and stories, etc.

Moreover, the intensive handling and observation of animals led to their domestication. It has been suggested that domestication of animals arose from the human tendency to adopt baby wild animals. Clearly the magnificent depictions of horses in Upper Paleolithic French caves, shows their importance to the humans. The relative absence of their bones in cave refuse suggests they were rarely eaten and were not a major source of food, unlike reindeer, which appear to have been the predominant animal hunted for that purpose (Bahn and Vertut 1997: 170–211). However, horses may have been hunted at certain sites where they were butchered in groups and the bulk of bones left at the site, never having been brought into the cave dwelling at all (Olson 1989: 295–327). Interestingly, artistic depictions of reindeer are relatively scarce, suggesting that animals portrayed may have been admired or even worshipped, but not necessarily hunted for food or other resources (Hayden 2003: 20–122).

There is other empirical evidence suggesting the importance of animals to human beings. For example, one piece of evidence for this is that children the world over evince an unusual interest in animals, whether they live in rural areas or urban locales where they rarely ever come in contact with them. Many fairy tales focus on animals, from *Aesop's Fables* (2007) to the *Brothers Grimm* (Zipes 1987). This motive to learn and know about animals appears to be an innate predisposition whose survival value was of primary importance in early childhood for the acquisition of knowledge about the behavior of predators and other dangerous fauna, as well as acquiring knowledge about prey animals. Indeed, classification of fauna is a human universal.

We can gain some insight into the evolution of this process by studying the developing child's category knowledge of animals from the perspective of evolutionary psychology. Barrett (2004) has suggested that humans have a multi-faceted "agency intelligence" (ability to detect animals that behave versus those that do not; as well as the capacity to distinguish living from inanimate objects by means of several variables; prey animals from predator animals, etc.) that allows them to predict and understand both human and non-human animal behavior. This ability is observable in children two years of age and has had significant adaptive advantages over the course of hominin evolution as is evidenced in a number of ways. Infants as young as nine months are able to make inferences about intentional schemas that afford predictions about the behavior of animals (Gergely et al. 1995: 165–193; Csibra et al. 1999: 237–267). By doing so they are in a better position to avoid and evade dangerous animals as soon as they are perceived.

On the Rorschach Test (a projective psychological test, popularly known as the Ink Blot Test), people see animals as the most frequent category and the same applies to hallucinatory states induced by psychoactive substances (Shannon 2002). This is true whether the subjects are Amerindians or individuals from industrial societies with little previous contact with animals. Many present-day rural communities in Asia, Africa, South America and other places around the world still display an extraordinary closeness to their domesticated animals as shown by direct observation, myths and stories that surround these animals.

In 2011, further evidence regarding the importance of animals was derived from neuroscientific studies. For example Mormann and colleagues (pp. 1–3) studied 41 people undergoing surgery for drug-resistant epilepsy. Prior to surgery, doctors needed to map their brains, a task performed by inserting electrodes into different parts of their brains, then measuring neuron by neuron responses to stimuli. Mormann et al. showed the patient pictures of animals, people, landmarks and objects. When patients saw animal pictures neuronal activity spiked in the right amygdala. As the finding extends across many patients it implies something universal—as universal as the much better known brain asymmetry for reading text and for comprehending and producing language, which is located in the left hemisphere. The researchers suspect that animals were *so important during evolutionary history as to merit a dedicated processing area in the brain* (my italics). The amygdala is a relatively ancient structure phylogenetically, developing during the evolution of mammals.

Mormann et al.'s (ibid.) empirical findings suggest that the right hemisphere may have been more dominant in pre-literate peoples because writing enhances the functions of the dominant cortex and to some extent inhibits the artistic expression of the right hemisphere, which is typical of literate culture. Indeed, Julian Jaynes (1977) hypothesized that pre-literate peoples might be more prone to mistake internal thoughts for hallucinated voices and images of the gods as exemplified by the minds of the poets who created and performed the Iliad centuries before Homer wrote it down. Jaynes suggested that the voices originated in the speech areas of the right hemisphere, were communicated to the left hemisphere and heard as commands from the gods. Much neurological evidence supports this hypothesis from modern fMRI studies (Kuijsten 2012: 1–22). Also, the presence of auditory hallucinations in "normal" adults is very widespread (Kuijsten 2006). The phenomenon of imaginary companions in children is now a popular research area and a recent study of 1800 children (Pearson et al. 2001: 401–407) found that 46% described imaginary companions and that this involved hallucinations and not merely imagination (Sidhu and Dickey 2010: 53–62). The reader will recall that most of the activities described in the Iliad were instigated or influenced or commanded by various gods and goddesses, in other words the poets routinely resorted to supernatural causation. The Odyssey coming a few hundred years later, after some literacy was becoming a routine part of education for the elite, still resorts to supernatural forces but much less frequently. It is with the advent of literacy that Jaynes sees *modern consciousness* (i.e. literate culture) finally developing. He puts the date around 1200 BCE, but circa 800 BCE seems more likely as literacy was becoming firmly established in Greece at that time.

Plato's exclusion of poets from his Republic was in fact his rejection of the pristine aggregative (cumulative rather than analytical) paratactic oral style of thinking perpetuated in Homer (Ong ibid.: 28). (Paratactic is Greek meaning to place or arrange side by side; the juxtaposition of clauses or phrases without the use of coordinating or subordinating conjunctions as *It was cold; the snows came*). Without writing, an active right hemisphere might be more prone to hearing voices or seeing images such as medieval saints did. Of course some used altered states of consciousness, hypnosis, meditation, prayer, others were frankly mentally ill, but many appeared to hear voices easily or see images often during contemplation (Helvenston 1999). Medieval culture was largely an oral culture with only the highly educated few literate in writing, the rest literate in Christian art which told picture stories that were read by medieval peoples as pictorial texts. The dominance of the right hemisphere may be under appreciated in medieval history as it is in Paleolithic times. Certainly the visual arts of the Middle Ages are truly spectacular in comparison to our modern visual arts in my view. Our ancestors may have been more creative in many respects than we are on average today, although lacking the rational and analytic skills that we possess that require varying elements of creativity also.

The mind of Upper Paleolithic peoples may have been even more receptive to the sounds and visual perceptions related to animals than our literate mind today. Indeed, with the enhanced development of the left cerebral hemisphere due to language, writing and computational development, the right hemisphere has even become known as the silent hemisphere, because until recently many of its functions were masked by the dominant hemisphere's inhibition of it, so dominated were we in literate Western culture by writing and literate modes of thinking that are left hemispheric functions. We now know that functions of the right hemisphere include holistic appraisal of situations, creativity, dominance of visual images, visual language, visual symbolism, heightened affect, music, etc. (Springer and Deutsch 1993). Indeed Marshall McLuhan (1962) said that involvement, participation and expression in oral cultures was obliterated by print culture. Today we know that much of human creativity, including "artification", the making special of ordinary objects, because someone cared enough to transform them into extraordinary items and continue to perfect them (Dissanayake 1992, 2008, 2009, 2010), relies upon the frontal lobes and temporal-occipital-parietal functions of the right hemisphere.

Hodgson and Helvenston (2006: 3–40) proposed that the emergence and dominance of animals in paleoart, as exemplified by the art of French and Spanish caves, likely evolved from hunting practices wherein early hominins learned to use hunting disguises to fool predators and prey. Such disguises enabled our ancestors to come closer to game, including large game such as elephants, rhinos, aurochs, reindeer, ibex, horses, bison, extinct megaloceros, and extinct mammoths.

Extraordinary evidence regarding hunting disguises comes from a photograph taken by W. H. C. Taylor in 1934, of an individual from the San "Bushmen" wearing the skin of an antelope (Thackeray 2005: 5–18). The use of an animal skin costume and the adoption of a quadrupedal posture by a human figure bending forward with two sticks is strongly similar to the imagery of more ancient Melikane rock art therianthropes of South Africa, considered to be disguised hunters. The use of animal skins in these instances is thought to take advantage of curiosity behavior that encourages an animal to walk towards the hunter to within range of weapons. It would only have been a short step to improving the look of animal skins so that they appeared more like hunted animals, thus leading to the procurement of greater amounts of protein-rich meat, with all the advantages arising there from. More ancient evidence derives from the semi-nomadic hunter/gatherer community of Starr Carr, Yorkshire, England, dating to around 10,000 BP, where antler "frontlets" have been found which were probably worn during rituals and used as a disguise in the hunting of animals (Laing 1982). Also, a triangular cobble from La Madeleine, France (c. 13,000 BP) has engraved upon it a human figure in upright position with two heads, one thought to be a human, the other an animal-like mask (White 2003).

The emotions experienced during the proximity to these animals would have included fear, awe, dread, wonder, reverence, and admiration (all emotions reportedly experienced when humans have felt they were in the presence of supernatural beings) and may have led to crude depictions of animals or their tracks being scratched in the earth. Moreover, the experience of such emotions, coupled with keen observations of animal behavior, probably contributed to the view that the large and powerful prey and predator animals hunted during the Upper Paleolithic were potent deities with supernatural powers, such that these animals came to symbolize traits venerated, admired, and feared by humans, as well as providing a practical solution to hunger and a source of clothing and other goods. Rowland expresses these sentiments very eloquently when she says that the ancients assumed that animals exemplified human and/or divine traits which they admired, feared, or disliked. In time these ideas about animals were confirmed in religious rituals, literature, and art. Humans worshiped the bull or goat because the qualities which they attributed to them seemed divine. The ancient Greeks believed the animal was a symbol, a word taken from the Greek word *συμβαλλειν*, meaning "to throw together". Animals became symbols of qualities admired by man, and animal figures were depicted with human faces (Rowland 1973: XV–XVI) or vice versa. Certainly Greek deity Zeus was often viewed as a bull, or ram, while Hera was a cow.

Upon returning from the chase, the hunters may have recreated the hunt through mimesis of the behavior of animals hunted, through imitating their calls, through scratching their tracks and salient visual characteristics in sand, while singing and dancing around a communal camp fire. We know that in many hunter-gatherer societies complex imitations of animal behavior occur in popular dances. For example, the importance of mimesis to hunting societies is clearly illustrated by the activities of hunter-gatherers in the 1930s that imitated animal and human behaviors in dances and ritual. Pygmies of the African rain forest performed a chimpanzee dance in which men and boys proceeded through the entire camp with slow, serpentine movements, their facial expressions all the while consisting of weird grimaces. The eldest of the group, who represented the hunter lurking behind a bush or a tree, took aim at the revelers with a bow and arrow and when the arrows were launched the participants all rolled on the ground grinning and roaring to the accompaniment of roaring drums (Shebesta 1933: 100). It appears that the group was portraying chimpanzees who have terrifying facial grimaces known as "grins" that express fear and/or excitement, and which are accompanied with vocalizations such as "wraa" and "roar pant-hoot" the second of which is accompanied by aggressive displays (Goodall 1986: 199–136). Also, dances, mimes, and singing games of many kinds were still prominent in the Kalahari Bushmen of the 1970s and many dances were "based upon episodes in the lives of animals, when the hunters' inborn talent for mimicry and imitation is vividly displayed" (Vinnicombe 1976: 307).

These activities may well have led to altered states of consciousness as healing dances do with the Kalahari San today. The trance would have bound the community together and led to group cohesion and solidarity, thus conferring ultimate survival value on those groups who exploited these activities (Lex 1979: 117–151). These initially spontaneous behaviors eventually became ritualized (made special) and may have ultimately been recreated before the hunt as a mechanism for insuring a successful chase. The ritual would have become a memory device for "perfection" of behavioral sequences leading to the anticipated increase of animals that were routinely hunted. All the emotions associated with worship of animals, hunting them, killing them, processing them and cooking and eating them would have been recalled during the ritual. This could have involved the creation of animal costumes, masks, special drawings in sand, special songs and dances, etc., in other words elaborate rituals were developed utilizing the arts, i.e., making special of important events (Dissanayake 2008, 2009, 2010). Thus, from hunting practices and finally the domestication of animals, the predisposition to create cultural rituals evolved that included scratching pictures of animals or their tracks in soil, with increasing demands for more perfect i.e., realistic depictions, along with the accompanying emotional responses, which gradually evolved into the production of exograms (see Bednarik this volume for extended definition of exograms), that include symbolic material and paleoart in French and Spanish caves—now viewed as a singular florescence of artistic activity and not just a stage in the development of artistic expression (Hayden 2003: 20–122).

In this way, artistic depictions of animals, or making animals special, may be looked upon as an exaptation (the use of a biological function for a purpose other than it was evolved for, i.e. where an adaptive hunting activity becomes converted into artification; a culturally adaptive behavior. The human tendency toward artification, as discussed above, including perfectionism, began to exert an increasingly large role in human culture, as the power and perfection of many of the Upper Paleolithic animal depictions suggests. This would have included preparing the animal depictions and the special rituals accompanying the artistic process which may have included musical accompaniment as musical instruments have been found in the Upper Paleolithic caves (Waller 2000: 85–94, 2002, 2003: 31–38). Moreover, studying the acoustics of the caves Waller has found that where large herbivores are depicted, the cave echoes and sounds resemble thundering hooves, whereas feline depictions are in areas that are silent, supporting the hypothesis that location for paintings is affected by acoustic properties.

As Hayden explains (2003: 20–122), small groups of people probably created the Upper Paleolithic art in caves lit by torches during religious rituals that may have included trance-inducing experiences because much of the art is in locations that can be viewed by only a few people at a time, deep in caves. This does not mean that the cave paintings were done while in trance—we simply do not know, except as Bednarik (this volume) points out we lack documentation of shamans painting rock art in contemporary or historical ethnographies. Hayden suggests that these rituals probably included some "coming of age" initiations, as well as rituals intended to increase the herds of animals typically hunted. Some rituals intended to increase the supply of hunted animals may have also been used as fertility insurance for the increase in the human group. In fact he suggests shamanism was a part of Upper Paleolithic religion but it seems more likely that animistic beliefs were predominant (Helvenston and Hodgson 2010: 61–94). Indeed shamanism may be the more highly developed accompaniment of other religious beliefs found in stratified societies and evolving from animistic practices in certain locales.

We have some evidence of ceremonial perhaps mythic human or therianthropic figures from the Upper Paleolithic. For example the "shaft scene from Lascaux Cave" (Bahn and Vertut 1997: 178–179) is a depiction of a human figure next to a bison whose entrails are depicted spilling forth with a shaft in the wound. The human figure, with an erect penis, is believed to be a healer because it has a bird head on a human body (therianthrope) and is accompanied by a bird on a staff, the bird perhaps being a sacred spirit that enabled the healer, in an altered state of consciousness, to travel to the spirit world and assist in ensuring a successful hunt, as is characteristic of animistic or shamanistic practices today. Whether the human figure is dead, or depicted next to the bison as a symbol of a ceremonial ritual aimed to achieve a successful hunt is unknown, but the fact of the figure strongly suggests that the depiction as a whole is "mythic" in nature. The Trois Frères composite figure known as the "sorcerer" (Bahn and Vertut 1997: 165) also suggests some type of healer, again supporting some sort of religious function for the art. The figure appears to be a mythical figure or a deity, or perhaps the "master of the hunt", and it has the antlers and tail of a reindeer on the body of a human—another good example of a therianthrope.

Significantly, the earliest descriptions of shamanism occur in the 16th century CE where it appears highly developed and hierarchical, probably indicating an evolution of thousands of years, but perhaps not 15,000 years (Eliade 1964). Eliade found some evidence of shamanistic practices described by the early Greeks at about 600 to 800 BCE) but not the highly developed type of shamanism first described from northern Eurasia in the 16th century (see Bednarik for an excellent discussion of shamanism and rock art, this volume). According to Winkelman (2002: 71–101) shamanism includes visionary experience, soul journey, guardian spirit quest, healing practices, and self-transformation experiences such as death and rebirth, but these are also characteristics of animistic belief systems and their rituals and ceremonies.

Grossman et al. (2008: 17665–69) found a burial in Israel that they labeled "shamanistic" because the human skeleton was accompanied by skeletal remains of different animals from 12,000 years BP, but the find is just as consistent with animistic beliefs as it is with shamanism which may have evolved from it. Animism is more typical of smaller, egalitarian hunter-gatherer societies such as the Kalahari San where it can permeate nearly all aspects of life (see Helvenston and Hodgson 2010). At the very least, we can state that both animistic and shamanistic belief systems place a great importance on animals, which was certainly true of the Upper Paleolithic, such that the Upper Paleolithic mind would have been dominated by them.

Thus, animals, their behavior, appearance, edible properties, potential for domestication, were clearly one of the contents that occupied the Upper Paleolithic mind, along with ritual development to create art, tools, clothes, adornments, commemorate important aspects of life such as coming of age, marriage, birth of children, and death. These activities would have been common in Paleolithic culture and what we know of oral cultures strongly suggests that they were highly ritualized. We can be confident that Upper Paleolithic peoples engaged in ritualistic behavior, as did earlier hominins because even chimpanzees have some rudiments of religious expression. Thus, we should look for evidence that they possess some simple rituals that may form the basis for human rituals such as birth rites, marriage rites, mortuary rites, etc. Based on a detailed summary of the observational literature of chimpanzee communities, Harrod (2012) has suggested that chimpanzees have birth practices, mortuary practices, consortship practices, culinary practices, initiation practices and medicinal-healing practices. For example, there are specific calls that announce a death, there is some form of group silence and visitation around the corpse, some chimps may keep vigil for long periods of time. Moreover, there are specific patterns of behavior that characterize a hunt and the distribution and eating of meat that follows. This is clearly an area that requires further observational study.

Animism in Oral Cultures

Having mentioned animism and suggested that it was probably an endemic belief in the Upper Paleolithic, I need to explore some of the basics of animism in this chapter. Animism is a very broad based term for a number of different but related beliefs, that Eliade suggested formed the ancient foundational matrix of most, if not all of the world religions (Eliade 1964). Students of animism accentuate different aspects of these assorted beliefs and I will discuss the views of a number of different scholars of animism subsequently. The anthropological concepts associated with my definition of animism were first systematically elucidated by E. B. Tylor in 1871 (reprinted 1958)—though later criticism led to the concept being generally condemned mainly due to the notion that early forms and tribal ways of thinking were held by Tylor to be more "primitive" than so-called civilized Western modes of thought, but Tylor was studying oral cultures and thus the lack of writing was responsible for a more "primitive" or earlier understanding of the world as highly dominated by multiple spirit beings. Most anthropologists, whether they characterize themselves as scholars of animism or not, think animistic beliefs are likely the earliest manifestation of "religion" and may have a very archaic provenance in the biological and cultural evolution of *Homo sapiens*, although speculations as to their earliest inception vary. I choose to select a definition consistent with elements of Tyler and Hallowell, as well as Bird-David, wherein animism is the view that all human beings (believed to be possessed of a soul or spirit) live in community with others labeled "not-human-beings" that also possess a soul or spirit. These invisible but real forces animate the universe and influence all human endeavors. To animate (endow with movement) is thus to "make alive". Indeed, a recent study by a biologist considers the perception of biological motion to be a manifestation of a perceptual "life" detector (Johnson 2006: R37). And the most fundamental category that divides the living from the non-living appertains to movement, the perception of which in humans is multi-faceted especially with regard to discriminating the animate from the inanimate. The ability to perceive animate objects, however, can also be modified, or transferred/projected onto inanimate objects that are perceived as moving (Barrett 2004: 438). In addition to animal and human movement other aspects of the natural world "move" and thus may be endowed with spirits, such as wind, plants, clouds, thunder, water, fire, volcanic action, and assorted other natural processes. Also, "supernatural beings" such as gods, goddesses, genies, angels, ghosts, and demons are believed to possess a spirit. All of these myriad spirits constantly interact with the human world.

From as early as 1919, Gilmore suggested that animism was characterized by a vast interconnected community of "beings" described by the motto "Each for all and all for each" (Gilmore 1919: 2). This general idea can be rephrased such that, just as in the case of fellow humans, animists believe the entire universe is "alive". As will be discussed, however, some contemporary writers on animism believe that such earlier accounts failed to stress certain reciprocal social relationships between human and "other than human persons" in association with how these various communities interacted with the perceived universe.

Some of the many concepts associated with animism, historically and contemporaneously, include the idea that in all cultural systems people experience phenomena such as dreams, visions, sudden insights, out-of-body experiences, and trances that simultaneously conjoin perceptions of being "elsewhere" with the knowledge of being "here". In some cultures everything is deemed to have a soul, including inert matter, though of a lower order due to a lack of "liveliness" (Kingsley 1899: 199).

Other beliefs and practices characteristic of animism include the idea that *what is human is not separate* from animals and other objects of the universe. For example, "a central Australian pointing to a photograph of himself will say, 'That one is just the same as me, so is a kangaroo' " (his totem, or sacred animal). We say the central Australian "belongs to the kangaroo tribe"; "he knows better, *he is a kangaroo*" " [my emphasis] (Harrison 1912: 121; see Ingold 2000: 111, for a detailed discussion of the differences between totemism and animism). Such concepts give rise to the belief that humans and animals can exchange forms or merge together (therianthropes), that there are many varieties of shape-shifting, including animals that contain attributes of two or more different species—moreover, any physical similarity between objects may give rise to the notion that the same essential essence and identity is shared. For example, a recent study of the Baka (forest Pygmies in the north-western Republic of Congo) and their neighbors, a Bantu-speaking group of farmers, demonstrates how, because the Baka observe similarities between gorilla behavior and that of their Bantu neighbors, the Bantu are therefore referred to as gorillas. In contrast, the Bantu view the Baka's behavior as similar to chimpanzees and label them accordingly (Kohler 2005: 407).

Another fundamental animistic belief concerns the idea that the soul exists both prior to and after death. Because the soul of the dead is believed to survive (a topic we will return to shortly), various funerary practices result in favorite objects being placed in the grave with the deceased person and food and drink may be located near the dead person for use in the afterlife. In addition, the soul may inhabit specialized regions varying from a shadowy afterlife, to one where the best things of worldly life, experienced during the individual's lifetime are readily available. The soul is thereby held to be capable of traveling from life in the existing world to other realms or to ancestral souls of the dead, to heaven per se, occasionally to and from an underworld, or can take extended flights to other locations and relocate in animals or other people, rocks, pools, and mountains of the real world. Moreover, a common word characterizes both soul and breath in many languages whereby the soul is associated with the breath of the living (Latin, *spiritus*, *anima*, *animus*; Sanskrit *atman*, Greek *psyche*, *pneuma*, *thumos*, German *Geist*, English ghost, Hebrew *nephesh*, *ruah*; Sumerian *zid*, Egyptian *ka*, etc). This linguistic evidence also suggests that the terms "living" and "breathing" in relation to humans and animals can be regarded as synonymous.

Animal and ancestor worship, as well as reincarnation, can also be viewed as animistic, as are beliefs that free "spirits", not characterized as dead humans or animals, can also exist and inhabit the world of humans. Such spirits might consist of the spirits of the forest, the lake, spring, caves, etc. These spirits may be beneficial or malevolent as in black magic, witchcraft or sorcery, but they must be both attended to and respected. In many animistic communities, death is not believed to be a natural phenomenon but rather thought to be caused by evil spirits and sickness is believed to be a punishment for some unknown "crime" against conspecifics or the spirits, which may require the services of a healer in order to discover the cause and provide appropriate treatment.

Irving Hallowell (1975: 141) carried out a number of ethnographic studies of the Ojibwe—investigations that were to have significant implications for understanding animism. Many scholars of animism had previously assumed that the prevailing "spirits or souls" of the cosmos were identical to human souls, but Hallowell augmented that view and maintained that the Ojibwe recognized a universe composed of both human and other-than-human persons, including animals, plants, trees, rocks, clouds, thunder, stars and other inanimate structures or processes. These other-than-human persons were relational, intentional, conscious and communicative beings and possessed of a soul or spirit. Ethnographer Thomas Blackburn reached similar conclusions in relation to the Chumash Indians, whose cosmos was said to be composed of an "interacting community of sentient creatures" (Blackburn 1974).

Hallowell stressed that other-than-human persons could be helpful, harmful, callous, malicious, indifferent, or tricky, as is the case with living humans. Furthermore, Hallowell reported that it may be helpful or necessary to enter into personal relationships with such entities that could lead to comforting, demanding or dangerous experiences. Hallowell stated that the Ojibwa did not necessarily believe that a "person" had to have anthropomorphous traits, although most spirits inhabiting non-human objects did, suggesting that in some instances, at least, personhood in non-human persons was not "human". Moreover, the Ojibwa believed some stones had spirits whereas others did not. Thus, only certain stones possessed spirits, namely those that had been seen to move or possess other animate qualities, i.e. some resemblance, whole or in part, to humans or animals. Interestingly, Bird-David documented a similar phenomenon in relation to the Nayaka of southern India (1999: 6)

Recently, Bird-David (ibid.) has emphasized that animism consists of a large network of social activities and relational personhoods, between humans, humans and animals, humans and rocks, hills, forces of nature, etc., referred to as *devaru* by the Nayaka, a hunting-gathering people of south India. To Bird-David *devaru* is a Nayaka concept that "objectifies" the relationship between human persons and other-than-human persons as defined by Hallowell. In this respect, Tyler's conception of animism is criticized as failing to take account of the sociality and relational nature of human persons and other-than-human persons that lead to numerous examples of *devaru* by the Nayaka. I would maintain that reading Tyler in the original reveals the incredible complexity of his understanding of animism and the huge network of interacting spirits he describes, so I cannot agree entirely with Bird-David.

Oral Mentalities as Described by Lévy-Bruhl

Next I will consider other oral mentalities to gain more insight into the type of thinking characteristic of oral or "primitive" minds. I am not suggesting any of these examples are exactly like what Paleolithic peoples thought, but that the examples can illuminate the *type of thinking* that most likely characterized their cognition better than erroneous assumptions of literate skills in people who did not possess them. I will be discussing the work of Lévy-Bruhl whose corpus is brilliant, highly complex and subtle. He cites ethnographic material from missionaries, travelers, sailors, pioneers. I can only select a few from many examples in several volumes and thus do not really begin to do justice to his corpus. I highly recommend the interested reader obtain his works and read them in the original format. In *Primitive mentality*, 1923 (all examples in this section, unless otherwise noted, will be taken from this particular volume), Lévy-Bruhl stressed that the mind of the "primitive" (person in oral culture) was a mystic mind so characterized because "mystic" implies belief in forces and influences and actions which, though imperceptible to sense are nevertheless real. In other words, the reality that "primitives" live is itself mystical (p. 7). Not a single being or object or natural phenomena in their group idea (collective representation) is what it appears to be to our minds. The collective representation of certain animals is mystic in character, as is the case with plants. Certain parts of animals and plants are believed to contain specific virtues. Regions in space and the cardinal directions have their mystic significance. This should all sound reminiscent of what we know of oral medieval cultures. Even objects made and used by man have their beneficent or horrific qualities depending on circumstances, as we will see shortly.

If we consider the human body, we will see that each organ of it has its mystic significance as widespread cannibalism and the rites accompanying human sacrifice attest in Mexico. The heart, liver, kidney, eyes, fat, marrow, etc. are all reputed to assure such and such an attribute for those who feed on them. The orifices of the body, the excreta of all kinds, the hair, the nails, the placenta, the umbilical cord and the various fluids of the body can all exercise magic influences (Lévy-Bruhl 1910: 39–40, quoting Preus 1904). Group-ideology attributes mystic influence to all these things. So too, certain parts of plants and animals have specific virtues. "*Badi* is the name given to the evil principle which attends (like an evil angel) … everything in his life." Von der Wallen describes it as the enchanting or destroying influence which issues from anything; for example from a tiger which one sees, from a poisonous tree that one walks under, from the saliva of a mad dog, from an action which one has performed (Lévy-Bruhl 1910: 40, quoting Skeat 1900).

Since everything that exists possesses mystic properties and these properties, from their very nature, are much more important than the attributes of which our senses inform us, the difference between animate and inanimate things is not the same interest to primitive mentality as it is to our own. Thus rocks, according to the form they assume if it strikes the primitive's imagination, readily assumes a sacred character in virtue of their supposed mystic power (Lévy-Bruhl ibid.).

Even things made and constantly used by man have their mystic qualities and can become beneficent or terrifying according to circumstances. Cushing who had lived among the Zunis and had become one of them, says that they,

> No less than primitive peoples elsewhere, conceive of everything made whether structure or utensil or weapon ... as living ... a still sort of life, but as potent and aware nevertheless and as capable of functioning not only obdurately and resistingly, but also actively and powerfully in occult ways, either for good or for evil. As for living things they observe every animal is formed, and acts or functions according to its form—the feathered and winged bird flying, because of its feathered form, the furry four-footed animal running and leaping, and the scaly and finny fish swimming ... So the things made or born in their special forms by the hands of man also have life and function variously according to their various forms. The forms of these various things not only give their power but restrict their power, so if properly made, that is if shaped strictly as other things of their form are made, they will perform only such safe uses as their prototypes have been known to perform. It is therefore of the utmost importance that

> they shall be faithfully reproduced so that one may not have to fear the unknown, "powers" which a fresh form might possess (Lévy-Bruhl ibid. p. 41, quoting Cushing prior to 1900).

In this way we can account for the extraordinary persistence of the same forms among "primitive" peoples, including even the most minute details of the ornamentation by which they decorate the products of their industries and arts. The Indians of British Guiana show extraordinary skill in many of the things they manufacture but they never improve upon them. This is not merely the force of habit or the spirit of conservatism peculiar to these people. It is a direct result of active belief in the mystic properties of the things, properties connected with their shape, and which can be controlled by this, but which would be beyond the powers of man to regulate if there were the slightest change of form. The most apparently trifling innovation may lead to danger, liberate hostile forces and finally bring about the ruin of its instigator and all dependent on him (Lévy-Bruhl ibid. p. 43).

He goes on to say that primitives see nothing in the same way we do. The social milieu which surrounds them is different from ours and precisely because it is different, the external world which they perceive is different from that which we apprehend. Undoubtedly they have the same senses as we do, rather more acute than ours in a general way, and their cerebral structure is as our own. But we have to bear in mind that which their collective representations (culture-specific ideas) instill into all their perceptions. Whatever the object presented to their minds it implies mystic properties which are inextricably bound up with it and the "primitive", in perceiving it, never separates them from it. "Traditionals" see with eyes like ours but they do not perceive with the same minds.

The spirit of conservatism (described earlier as a hallmark of oral cultures) is the direct result of the mystic qualities belonging to objects and connected with their form, through which they may be controlled though the slightest deviation from a formulaic response would enable the object to resist human intervention. An apparently quite insignificant innovation may release hostile forces and finally prove the ruin of the instigator and all his family. Now we see why conservatism in oral cultures is so crucial. (In other words any change from a traditional way of doing things or making things can bring ruin on the perpetrator as all disasters, of which there are always many, suffered by anyone in the group following the innovation *can or may* be ascribed to the deviation from tradition which has displeased the spirits).

To the "primitive" (oral) mind the mystic properties of things and beings form an integral part of their group-ideas, which is at that moment a synthetic whole. In other words, the "primitive" perceives an object along with all the mystic and affective associations that object may conjure for him/her. What Lévy-Bruhl means by representations of "primitives" requires some explanation. Collective representations, also known as group ideas or tribal-concepts passed on through special ceremonies and education of the young, can be characterized by the following signs. They are common to the members of a given social group; they are transmitted from one generation to another within it; they impress themselves upon its individual members and awaken in them sentiments of respect, fear, adoration, etc. according to individual circumstances.

Very often these collective ideas are acquired by the individual in circumstances likely to make the most profound impression upon his sensibility. This is particularly true of these transmitted at the moment when he becomes a man, i.e., initiation ceremonies, a conscious member of the social group the moment when the initiation ceremonies cause him to undergo a new birth, when the secrets upon which the very life of the group depends are revealed to him, amid tortures which subject his nerves to the most severe test. It would be difficult to exaggerate the intense emotional forces of these types of collective representations (Lévy-Bruhl 1910: 36–37). For example,

> The object is not merely discerned by the mind in the form of an idea or image; according to the circumstances of the case, fear, hope, religious awe, the need and the ardent desire to be merged in one common essence, the passionate appeal to a protecting power—these are the soul of these representations, and make them at once cherished, formidable and really sacred to the initiated. We must add too that the ceremonies in which these representations are translated into action, so to speak, take place periodically; consider the contagious effect of the emotional excitement of witnessing the movements which express them, the nervous exaltation engendered by excessive fatigue, the dances, the phenomena of ecstasy and of possession—in fact everything which tends to revive and enhance the emotional nature of these collective representations. Though in a lesser degree, the same character pertains to other collective representations—such as for instance, as those transmitted from generation to generation by means of myths and legends, and those which govern manners and customs.

Representation for us in literate culture is primarily an intellectual and cognitive phenomenon, but this is not true for oral cultures because they do not regard the ideas or images devoid of passion, sentiments and emotions. Thus the affective lability of oral medieval culture and oral culture in general is inevitable. Just as oral medieval culture can not view a white rose as simply that flower because of the emotions associated with its symbolic meanings, neither can people in oral cultures dissociate the emotion aroused by an object from the image of the object itself (p. 6). What to us is strictly a cognitive problem, i.e., identification of a rose, is to the "primitive" (oral culture) a representation plus elements of an emotional or motivating character, colored and imbued by them and therefore implying a different attitude with regard to the objects they represent. In other words, the "primitive" has an image of an object, imbued with fear or awe of all parts or some parts of the object, and expects the object to do something to him/her or expects s/he will be able to control the object for some purpose if only the right formula can be created. Hence, in oral culture a great deal of thought and effort centers around developing effective rituals and incantations that will induce certain spirits to grant the wishes of the petitioner.

After discussing African tribes as described by the missionary, W. H. Bentley, in 1901, Lévy-Bruhl (1923: 27) summarizes the traits of the African thusly:

> An African, whether Negro or Bantu does not think, reflect or reason if he can help it. He has a wonderful memory, has great powers of observation and imitation, much freedom in speech and very many good qualities; he can be kind, generous, affectionate, unselfish, devoted, faithful, brave, patient, and persevering, but the reasoning and inventive faculties remain dormant. He readily grasps the present circumstances, adapts himself to them and provides for them, but a cleverly thought out plan or piece of induction escapes him.

When confronted with something that interests it, disturbs it or frightens it, the "traditional" mind does not follow the same course of reasoning as our literate minds do. For example for literates the uninterrupted feeling of intellectual security is so thoroughly established in our minds that even if we were brought face to face with an unknown phenomenon, we would assume that we were only temporarily ignorant of its causes, because we know that such causes exist and we are secure in the fact that we can sort them out scientifically, according to the laws of nature. However, to the "primitive" (oral mind) all its objects and entities are involved in a system of mystic participation and exclusion (i.e. social intercourse between spirits and humans) and it is to these mystic entities that his/her mind will immediately turn, not to the phenomenon but the cause which will automatically be ascribed to witchcraft or other evil forces. These supernatural forces and means of appeasing them or defying them will become the total object of the "primitives" concern. Indeed, the supernatural is such a constant feature of his life that it furnishes to the "traditional" mind explanations that are as automatic as our recourse to "the laws of nature" (Lévy-Bruhl 1923: 35–36). For example Lévy-Bruhl cites missionary John Phillips who studied South Africans in 1828 speaking of Bechuan superstition as follows:

> Everything in a state of ignorance which is not known and is a mystery is the object of superstitious veneration where second (natural) causes are unknown. The immediate recourse to supernatural powers is the primary cause of anything mysterious, secondary causes are not sought.

Imagine the heightened anxiety and insecurity of the oral mind as opposed to the literate mind in the face of the unknown. There is no understanding of natural causes or laws of nature such as we learn in literate culture. Where we seek for such causes, the "primitive" is uninterested as it is the supernatural powers that concern him because they are the bearers of good or evil fortune, which can have such disastrous effects upon him/her.

The mentality of the natives of the Solomon Islands suggests a similar reflection as Lévy-Bruhl, 1923, quotes Thurwald (p. 36):

> In considering any matter they never go beyond the facts. The profound causal connection is, in theory, entirely lacking. The non-comprehension of the connection between phenomena is the source of their fears and superstitions.

The fact is the primitive, whether he be an African or any other, does not trouble to inquire into causal connections which are not self evident but straightaway refers them to a mystic power. From this it follows that the causal connections, which are so important to us, the very framework of Nature, the basis of its reality and stability are of very little interest in their eyes. On the other hand, he has a huge vocabulary and storage of knowledge about manifold evil and helpful spirits that he *knows* cause everything.

For example, in all uncivilized (oral cultures) races everywhere it is necessary to account for death by other than natural causes. Lévy-Bruhl, 1923, summarizes a number of ethnographers in discussing the fact that when "primitives" see a man die they act as if it were the first time such a thing had ever happened and grieve accordingly. The European asks, "is it possible they don't know this fate must befall everyone sooner or later". But the "traditionalist" has not considered things in this light. To him/her what we knows to be the causes of death such as illness, failure of bodily organs, senility, diminution of functional power, are not connected with death. He can see such people still living. To him, death, as well as senility is caused by a mystic force and there is no reason to suspect any other active force. Lévy-Bruhl (ibid.: 38) cites Jamieson (describing Australian Aborigines from Victoria discussing death) who says that

> To them there is no death other than by human agency. When any black whether young or old dies, it is supposed that an enemy came to them in the night made an incision and removed their kidney fat. Although there is never found any such incision on the corpse, the fact of death itself is seen as proof that such a nefarious deed took place.

Generally speaking, when a man dies it is because he has been doomed by a sorcerer. The predestined victim (Lévy-Bruhl 1923: 39, citing Roth 1907)

> may depart as usual on some hunting expedition … when he suddenly feels something at his leg or foot and sees [*hallucinates*] a snake in the act of biting him. Strange to say this kind of snake will immediately disappear from sight. … By this very process of invisibility the person realizes that some enemy has been pointing a *Mangani* [sorcerers tool] at him and that through this he is sure to die, nothing can possibly save him. He makes no effort to apply a remedy, loses heart, gives way, and lies down to die.

Lévy-Bruhl (1923: 49) similarly quotes Spencer and Gillen on tribes of central Australia in 1899 as saying

> All ailments of every kind from the simplest to the most serious, are without exception attributed to the malign influence of an enemy in either human or spirit shape.

Similarly, death by accidents is attributed to spiritual causes as are all manner of illness to spirits, including the god of smallpox or other diseases, etc. All deaths, except murder, are ascribed to evil forces, and the murderer himself may be said to be possessed of an evil spirit that is the motive for the murder. Sometimes the gods of one's enemies are said to harm one. To "traditionalists" there is no such thing as a natural cause of death, illness or accident. What appears accidental to us Europeans is in the reality of the oral culture always the manifestation of a mystic power. An example can make this point very sharply. Lévy-Bruhl (1923: 49–50) cites Monteiro from Angola, 1875, as follows:

> I was at Ambrizette when three Cabinda women came to the river to fetch water. All three were filling their pots when the middle one was snapped up from the stream by an alligator, seized and drowned. The relatives of the deceased at once accused the relatives of the other two of bewitching her, and causing the alligator to remove her from their midst. When I remonstrated with them and attempted to show them the utter absurdity of the charge their answer was "why did not the alligator take one of the end ones then and not the one in the middle?" And out of this idea it was impossible to move them and the poor women were both obliged to take *casca* (an ordeal poison). I never heard the result but probably one or both were killed or passed into slavery.

Lévy-Bruhl (1923: 50) summarizes the thinking of the natives thusly: What has occurred cannot be accidental. First of all alligators would not have attacked these women of their own accord. Therefore, someone must have incited this one to do it. Then, too, it knew exactly which one to drag under the water. She was "delivered to him" the only thing to find out is who bewitched the alligator. The alligator did not touch the woman on either side, he took the one in the middle, therefore they caused the alligator to drown the middle woman. The ordeal they underwent was not for clearing up a doubt as to who caused the disaster but of revealing the actual origin of the witchcraft in them and of exerting upon it a mystic influence which would render it incapable of injuring others.

Further exploration into the thinking of the "primitives" reveals that whereas we would consider alligators and crocodiles to be vicious predators and dangerous to human beings, these natives believed they were completely harmless by nature and only under the influence of witchcraft would they kill a human. Thus, because so many people fell prey to them there was believed to be a lot of witchcraft going on and every new death confirmed the seriousness of the threat of *witchcraft*, not the alligators! Even after a crocodile was shot for invading a pigsty and cut down the middle wherein were revealed the anklets of two women who had disappeared fetching water, the natives would not believe the crocodiles ate the women. They said that crocodiles had given the women to witches and kept the anklets as their prerogative. No amount of persuasion could shake them from these beliefs. In other regions the crocodiles may have been witch crocodiles or alligator crocodiles according to local belief systems.

Mystic and Invisible Forces in Oral Culture: Spirits

We have seen that the "primitive" does not seek for the causes of phenomena as we do, because he knows all the causes—witchcraft or intervention by malevolent spirits and they occupy his total interest. This is because "primitives" live, think, feel, move and act in a world which in a great many ways does not coincide with ours. The intervention of spirits or mystical forces is an intuitive connection that arises in the "primitive" mind at the beginning of certain kinds of events, just as other causes are intuitively sought by us in response to various natural phenomena (Lévy-Bruhl 1923: 59–61). To the person in oral culture, the crop failure is due to the intervention of evil spirits because someone has violated some cultural norm; to us the crop failure is due to a pestilence, or lack of rain, or too much rain, etc.

To the oral mind life, success, health, the order of nature, everything depends upon mystic forces. The invisible forces that preoccupy the "primitives' " mind can be divided into three categories which frequently overlap. First there are the spirits of the dead. Second there are the spirits that animate the natural world (animals and plants); the spirits that animate the physical world or inanimate objects (lakes, streams, mountains, and manufactured things, including tools made by man), which we discussed under animism above. Third, charms or spells due to the agency of sorcerers. Thus the person in oral culture must constantly be aware of all of these spirits, potential charms and spells and they form a large part of the content of his mind, for there is a perpetual possibility of sorcery which is ever present waiting to manifest itself on the hapless victim. The anxiety engendered by the constant presence of potential witchcraft helps explain the rage with which "primitives" act when the witch or sorcerer is finally revealed. The only recourse is to kill the evil one, either by throwing him/her into water or by burning, thus destroying the evil spirit once and for all so that it cannot bewitch anyone else.

The bewitching is believed to be accomplished by the witch acquiring some part of the victims body, hair, nail clippings, feces, urine, footprints, shadow, name, and so on and then casting a spell on the victim by bewitching these objects which *are* the individual to the oral mind. The list of misfortunes that can be caused the victim by spells cast upon his parts is endless. The wizard can sink his canoe, cause a rock to fall on him, cause an animal to seize and kill him, etc. If necessary the wizard can change himself into an animal to inflict death upon the victim. For example, Lévy-Bruhl (ibid.) cites Latcham (before 1923) describing the Araucans:

> If they notice any peculiar action of bird or beast immediately conclude that it is possessed. A fox or puma that prowls around their hut by night is a witch who has come to see what she can steal. On driving it away they take great care to see they do it no bodily harm for fear of reprisals. ... Everything not immediately explicable by natural and visible agency is put down either to evil spirits or to witchcraft.

Describing the observations of Father Lette on the Ten'a of Canada, Lévy-Bruhl (1923: 66) cites him saying:

> The Ten'a may be said to have an almost continual intercourse with the unwelcome denizens of the spirit world. They hold themselves liable *to see or hear them at any time* [i.e., hallucinations, my italics]. Any unusual noise, any fancy of their imagination [thought] quickly assumes the shape of a devil manifestation. If a black, water-soaked log, under the action of the current, bobs up within their view and then disappears, they have seen a *nekedzaltura* [devil, evil spirit]. If they hear a whistling in the woods somewhat unlike the cries of birds that are familiar to them a *nekedzaltura* is calling them. No day passes in an Indian camp without someone reporting that he or she has heard something of the kind. ... The manifestations of the devil's presence are as familiar to the Ten'a as the blowing of the wind or the singing of the birds. ... The intensity as well as the extent of their devil belief is beyond our conceptions. Their imagination is always on the alert to decry some evil moving about in the dark or the broad daylight and no caprice of their unruly fancy is too strange for them to believe.

This specific quotation highlights the fact of hallucinated voices and images appearing to humans from the spirit world.

Spirits of the Dead

Lévy-Bruhl (1923), citing Hobley, speaking of a Bantu tribe, says:

> It is the utmost importance of people speaking of the sociology of the Bantu, to try and realize the reality and closeness of the ancestral spirits upon the daily life of the native, and unless an ethnologist has been in daily contact with the people and striven to understand their point of view it is difficult for the weight of this to be felt to the full extent.

In other words the dead directly communicate with the living through aural and visual hallucinations, as well as omens and dreams.

Codrington, speaking of Melanesians and cited by Lévy-Bruhl (1923: 67–68) notes that

> When a native says that he is a man, he means he is a man and not a beast. The intelligent agents in this world are to his mind the men who are alive and the ghosts, the men who are dead. When white men first appear to Melanesians they are taken as ghosts, dead men come back. When white men ask the natives what *they* are, they proclaim themselves to be men, not ghosts.

In short, the dead are alive, at least for certain amounts of time (usually until the body is thoroughly decomposed). They are living beings of a different kind from ourselves, beings in whom certain relationships or activities are ruptured or at least impaired. But they have their own social group that they belong to now in death, even though they are still related to the living group from which they came. Eventually, they cease to stimulate much thought about them on the part of the living. The actual moment of death to the "primitive" is not the same as it is to us, which is when the heart stops beating and breathing stops completely. Most "traditional" (oral) races believe that death occurs when the soul leaves the body even if the physical life is not yet extinct, which may be many hours prior to what we would term death. For example in the Fiji Islands Lévy-Bruhl (1923: 68) quotes Williams (1858) as saying

> The process of laying out is often commenced several hours before the person is actually dead. I have known one to take food afterwards and another to live for some 18 hours longer. All this time, in the opinion of the Fijian the man is dead. Eating, drinking, talking, he says, are the involuntary actions of the body—of the empty shell as he calls it, the soul having taken its departure.

And Lévy-Bruhl (1923: 68–69), quoting Nassau (1904) speaking of the Negroes of West Africa, states:

> It has frequently occurred that even intelligent natives, standing by me at the side of a dying person have said to me: "He is dead". The patient was indeed unconscious, lying stiff, not seeing, speaking, eating, or apparently feeling: yet there was a slight heartbeat. I would point out to the relatives these evidences of life, but they would say: "No he is dead, his spirit is gone, he does not see nor hear nor feel, that slight movement is only the spirit of the body shaking itself".

Following death it is customary to render to the dead certain dues that are theirs because they are as a rule evil disposed and ready to do harm to the survivors. The dead appear to the living for some time after death, gradually fading from the consciousness of the living. Indeed, uncivilized races have an almost universal custom of destroying a dead man's weapons, his clothes, the things he used, even his house and occasionally his wives and slaves are killed (Lévy-Bruhl 1910 rpt. 1985: 21). It matters not that they have been amiable and pleasant when alive; their entire disposition after death has now changed. They are irritable and vindictive probably because they are weak, unhappy and suffering as their bodies are decomposing. For example, Lévy-Bruhl (1923: 70) cites Verguet discussing natives of Melanesia as follows:

> Ouasinpareo was one of those men who have such a happy disposition that they live peaceably with everybody. According to the natives he had never killed anyone and if he had eaten human flesh his spear had never dealt the victim his death blow. What conclusion did the "savages" (oral culture) draw from that? Exactly the opposite of what would occur to our minds. They thought that he, having been kindly during his life, would necessarily be malicious after death. Events soon confirmed this superstition of theirs for 2 or 3 natives overcome by age and disease, died shortly after him. "You see", said the natives to us "how bad Oausinpareo has become". Immediately two native priests in the district made it their duty to chase to the open sea the *ataro*, the phantom, soul, spirit of Oausinpareo which they said was prowling about the shore.

The malevolent influence of the ghost may be manifested in hundreds of different ways. The survivors have a special dread that he will try to carry off one or more of them with him; he feels lonely and forsaken; he misses his own friends and therefore wants to have them near him. At this time, should one of them fall ill and die, everyone knows from whence this fresh blow comes. Moreover, those newly dead have a mystical influence on all natural phenomena. If a storm should occur at death, or during burial or shortly thereafter it is attributed to the spirit of the deceased. Therefore when the funeral rites are not performed entirely to specification, the spirit of the deceased can wreak havoc upon the entire group. At all costs, then the ghost must be placated. His demands on the living differ with the social group and his status in it. Young children, ordinary people, women, slaves, a young man not initiated may all be viewed as harmless after death. But medicine men, chiefs or other very important people during life continue to be important after death and can do much harm to a social group so they must be placated. Such placation may involve prayers at the grave, offerings of food and other goods, mourning rituals that should guarantee the dead spirit will not harm the living. Gradually, these propitiating rituals are seen to have appeased the deceased and they fade out for that given individual.

Among the Australian Aborigines and a great many other "traditional oral cultures" the person causing the death of the ghost must be sought, found and punished. In these small tribes, with low birth rates, such seeking for the death of whoever caused another death is often reconciled by "mock" hunts for the evildoer, wherein a group of hunters leave the village to seek the death of the doomsday bringer. They return without a death, but that is often accepted as the ritual of seeking the culprit is deemed as having been enough to propitiate the dead person. Unfortunately, in other cultures, actual victims from other tribes are sought and their heads taken as evidence that the murderer who placed an evil spell upon the deceased has been killed. It is above all the spirits of the dead who are feared because of the evil they can wreak on a community. Thus we can understand the elaborate rituals of burial, funerals, grave ceremonies, praying and giving offerings at the grave—it is all to assure the dead spirits do no harm to the living.

Communing with the Spirits: Dreams

It should be evident now that the world of experience as a whole is very different for us than it is for members of "oral" cultures. Its framework differs from ours because time, space and causation are *imagined and above all felt* in a different way. Also, its data (the entire spirit world, world of the dead etc.) are more complex and copious than ours. When the wind can signify evil spirits, or a bird's unusual call can be the sign of a devil, all reality is imbued with complex forces, many of which are malignant or at best benign and proper methods and ceremonies of detection and then propitiation must be developed. These methods and rituals may be extremely complex and require great creativity. As Lévy-Bruhl says (1923: 97):

> The world we see provides "primitives" as it does us, with a collection of realities perceptible to sense, but in their minds others are added or rather intermingled with these—data arising out of the mystic forces always and everywhere present and these are by far the most important. How are the data about all these mystic forces to be collected. How must they be deduced if they don't immediately seem forthcoming. How are they to be interpreted and

> classified? These are functions which the primitive mind must perform and their collective representations show us how complex they are. We perceive then that the intellectual torpor, the lack of curiosity and indifference which many investigators have reported as existing in primitive communities are nearly always more apparent than real. As soon as the agency of mystic powers is invoked, these dormant minds awake. They are no longer indifferent or apathetic; you find them alert, patient, and even ingenious and subtle. ...
>
> What it behooves the primitive to understand above all is the agency of the mystic forces by which it feels itself surrounded. These forces, by their very nature are invisible and imperceptible. They only reveal themselves by more or less explicit manifestations, and these vary both in their significance and their frequency. ... We have already seen that all which appears unusual, fortuitous, extraordinary, striking or unforeseen is interpreted, as a manifestation of occult powers. But there are other means, more direct and certainly more regular, by which these powers make known what is going to happen, and as it were, warn the individual or social group. Of such a nature are *dreams and good and bad omens* [my italics]. When these manifestations are not forthcoming of themselves, the "primitive" mind exercises its ingenuity to produce them.

Dreams have, since early antiquity, been seen as having the ability to prophesize coming events, to prescribe solutions to problems and answers to questions, because they are a means of communicating with the spirit world. Techniques of inducing dreams have been known for thousands of years if not more. Sleep deprivation, food deprivation, injuries, self-inflicted injuries, such as blood letting, cutting the penis, scarification, dance, ritual, prayer, contemplation, self-hypnosis all are means of inducing altered states of consciousness which in oral cultures may be easier to induce due to the lesser influence of the left hemisphere. To the primitive mind, as we know, the seen and the unseen worlds form one and there is uninterrupted communication between what *we* call *obvious reality* and the mystic powers of the "primitive". Such in fact is the ordinary idea of the dream to "primitive" peoples. The soul leaves its home for the time being, often traveling great distances in order to commune with spirits or with ghosts. At the moment of awakening it returns to the body once more. At other times it is the spirits of the dead or even other powers who come to visit in the dream.

To the "primitive", when a sleeping man dreams his soul leaves his body and until it returns his soul is exactly like that of a person recently dead. The Homeric idea that sleep is the twin-brother of death no doubt has an extremely ancient origin. For example in west Africa, to dream means to be half-dead. In the dream the soul leaves the body and goes away to the land of fantasy where in a moment it seems to see and possess things; but these do not allow themselves to be retained. Nevertheless these spirits are regarded as real. For instance, if anyone has seen in a dream a person who has been dead for a long time, he really has been in communication with him. In a dream we see real objects, happenings, which pass for "real" and the soul which is temporarily freed from the body speaks as it does in the day time when it is in the body. "The sole difference lies in this: in the dream it has its being not in the seen but in the unseen world" (Lévy-Bruhl 1923: 100, citing Spieth in German West Africa). What is seen in dreams is believed to be true by the "primitive". Once having accepted the idea that dreams are a communication with the spirit world during sleep, since nothing seems more natural to him than communication between the seen and the unseen worlds, why should he mistrust what he sees in dreams any more than he mistrusts what he sees with his eyes wide open? He would be more inclined to believe in dreams because of the mystic origin of these data, which makes them all the more valuable and reliable. In Gaboon "a dream is more conclusive than a witness" to the Nyanga (Lévy Bruhl 1923: 101, citing Le Testu).

As an example of the power of dreams to the "primitive" Lévy-Bruhl (1923: 102) cites Taplin speaking of the Narrinyeri tribe:

> One day I heard a great cry at the Huts. I went up and found the women wailing with their faces blackened and their hair shorn off. An old man sat in their midst with a despairing look on his face. I inquired the reason for all this and learned that the old man had dreamed that someone at Tipping had put a sorcerer's tool to the fire to work his death. ... Some of the young men assured me that he would die unless someone went to Tipping to stop the sorcery, so I sent off a party in a boat to comply with their wishes. Next day they returned and said they could find no sorcery, and so it was concluded that there was none, and the old man got well.

According to Lévy-Bruhl (1923: 103) in New Zealand in 1830 a missionary, Williams, relates that

> a man and a woman were just murdered under the pretext that they had bewitched several persons who had died recently. Some other woman dreamed that this was the case and this dream was sufficient in the eyes of the native who committed the murders.

In central Africa, Arnot is cited by Lévy-Bruhl (1923: 103) as stating:

> In central Africa a voyage undertaken as a dream is believed to be an actual voyage. I visited the chief and was surprised to find that he was sitting outside his hut in European clothes. He explained that during the night he dreamed he was in Portugal, England and a few other places, so on rising he had dressed up in European fashion and told his people he had just returned from the white-man's country. All who went to see him, young and old had to shake his hand and bid him welcome back home again.

In the French Congo Le Testu cited by Lévy-Bruhl (ibid.) says that

> A man against whom trial by ordeal has been pronounced, and who does not imagine that it can fail in its finding, admits that he may have committed the act imputed to him in a dream. The man who was accused said "I will pay, because as a matter of fact I may have killed him when I was asleep but I have no conscious knowledge of it".

In New Guinea, the actions a man dreams of can haunt him if they become known. If he reveals he has dreamed of being with another man's wife, he can be held accountable for adultery and fined accordingly. The next example shows that a person can dream someone stole some pumpkins and travel 150 miles to where the thief lives to collect the compensation for them. The accused is baffled and explains he was nowhere near the accuser's village for at least two months but the accuser insists he saw the man in his garden in a dream. The accused continues to deny he took the pumpkins and the accuser says he knows the accused did not take the pumpkins. The accused is puzzled by the contradiction but deeply interested in this native's story so he continues to interrogate him. Finally, the accuser said the accused must have been in two places at once as he had seen the accused in the garden in a dream, but also knew the accused did not take the pumpkins. Lévy-Bruhl (ibid. p. 105), quoting Grubb, cites this incident as one of the reasons missionary observers of many natives felt that they were pre-rational. But the real reason is that the native believes his dream to be true. He also believes it when the accused says he did not do it, that he was nowhere near the pumpkins. In the face of this contradiction the native chooses to believe that the accused was in two places at once.

Dreams played an incredibly important role among Native Americans as described by *Relations des Jésuits* (1636) cited by Lévy-Bruhl (1923: 114). Why is it so necessary that the Native American fulfill the prescriptions of the dream? Simple. If what he has seen in a dream is not realized, he will die. Not only when the dream has suggested some action of his own but also if he has been merely a spectator and others have done the deed, for then these must carry it through. However extraordinary or exacting the demand of the dream may be, they have no choice but to submit to it. It has happened that some unscrupulous natives have enriched themselves at the expense of others by dreaming that they are owed such and such goods by others. Most are too conscientious to consider this route because "The dream is a divinity to savages, and their respect for it is no less than ours for the most sacred things" but it seems that sociopathic behavior is pretty much a pan-human trait.

One final example demonstrates the importance of faithfully carrying out the instructions of a dream. First let us define totem to the Indian. The Indian stands in an unvarying and permanent relationship with his totem (a specific animal, in this instance a bear). He must respect it, merit its favor and follow its advice, put his whole confidence in it and dread the effects of its wrath if he neglects to carry out his duties to it. With this in mind let us consider the story of a Chippeway Indian as cited by Lévy-Bruhl (1923: 119) who describes a tale by John Long (alias Beaver to the Indians) in 1791.

> The evening previous to the departure of the band, one of them, whose Totem was the bear, dreamed that if he would go to a piece of swampy ground, at the foot of a high mountain, about five days' march from the wigwam, he would see a large herd of elk, moose and other animals; but that he must be accompanied by at least ten good hunters. When he awoke he acquainted the band with his dream, and desired them to go with him. They all refused, saying it was out of their way and their hunting grounds were nearer. The Indian, having a superstitious reverence for his dream, thinking himself obliged to do so, as his companions had refused to go with him, went alone and coming near the spot, saw the animals he dreamed of; he instantly fired, and killed a bear. Shocked at the transaction and dreading the displeasure of the Master of Life whom he conceived he had highly offended, he fell down and lay senseless for some time; recovering from his state of insensibility he got up and was making his way to my house when he was met in the road by another large bear, who pulled him down, and scratched his face. The Indian relating this event at his return added in the simplicity of his nature that the bear asked him what could induce him to kill his totem; to which he replied that he did not know he was among the animals when he fired at the herd, that he was very sorry for the misfortune and hoped he would have pity on him; that the bear suffered him to depart, told him to be more cautious in future and acquaint all the Indians with the circumstances, that their totems might be safe, and the Master of Life not angry with them. As he entered my house, he looked at me very earnestly and pronounced these words, "Beaver my faith is lost my totem is angry and I shall *never to able to hunt any more* [my italics].

Today we know, through modern scholarship, that dreams of the ancients are different than our dreams, and that dreams of children follow a developmental path changing from when the child was strictly oral until after he has acquired a great familiarity with literacy. In modern conscious dreams (of people in literate cultures), we see ourselves acting out events in other places and from various perspectives. "By contrast the earliest recorded dreams completely lack these features. They typically consist of the dreamer having the feeling of being asleep in bed and then being visited by a god or spirit who issues a warning or command" (Kuijsten 2012: 12). The content of dreams changes as consciousness develops. Thus, dreams provide another way of gauging the level of consciousness in a given culture or individual (Harris 2009).

Harbingers of Good and Bad Luck: Omens

After dreams which form one of the most important mental experiences for the person in oral culture, bringing him as they do into the direct relationship with the unseen world, come omens. Omens are revelations which are produced spontaneously and enable the primitive to interpret them at once without needing to reflect upon them. Omens announce whether a contemplated endeavor will succeed or fail, or may give warning of a more imminent danger he is unaware of. Of course, as we have seen, anything out of the ordinary is a *revelation* to the "primitive". But those revelations are after the fact. For example, every accident is a revelation, for nothing is fortuitous and the slightest deviation from the ordinary indicates that occult forces are at work. They make known that magical practices have been directed at an individual or group, that taboos have been infringed, that the dead are dissatisfied because their wishes have been disregarded, etc.

Omens are *revelations* that refer to future events. The mentality of "traditional" or oral cultures, just like ours, starts as a rule with the sense data, but it immediately abandons what we call objective reality in search of the mystic cause, the occult, invisible power manifested by a change in the sense impression. Many oral cultures do not have a lot of words describing the future, it is not seen as a line on a continuum from the past to the present to the future (i.e., spatialized), but is vaguely thought about as only something to come. This is one of the reasons why people in oral cultures seem to lack foresight as many people describing them claim. They have few definite terms for degrees of futurity as we do and as their languages show. Hence arises a type of myopia which prevents them from clearly discriminating what is in the near future and can be prepared for as opposed to what is so far distant no preparation makes any sense or is deemed worth the effort.

Lévy-Bruhl (1923: 124) emphasizes that to minds like ours, accustomed to perceiving a fixed order in nature, to reckon upon and deal with this order, to make their hopes and fears depend on it, what on earth can omens be? To us, they are merely signs indicating beforehand what this order of nature will assuredly bring about by virtue of that determinism which regulates the series of cause and effect. Supposing these signs should not occur or if they did occur but nobody should see them, or notice them, there would be no change in the events, the effects would be the same, provided the causes still obtained. Primitive mentality, however, is thus not equilibrated by the conception of a fixed order of the universe. The type of causality which it conceives is quite different. Therefore, for the primitive, omens will assume a different importance. As the manifestations of mystic and occult powers, which alone are causes, they play an essential part in the production of that which they announce. It is not their function to only reveal what will happen, because *what they reveal will not take place without them*.

The study of omens and the custom of noting omens are met with in many cultures but nowhere most propitious for our studies than among the Dayaks of Borneo. The power attributed to omens by native tribes is formidable and described in detail by Perham (cited by Lévy-Bruhl 1923: 126). Among the natives of Sarawah there are omens for every circumstance of life. These omens are furnished by seven different birds, a number of mammals (stag, moose-deer, armadillo, gazelle), three kinds of insects, the lizard, bat, python and cobra, sometimes also the rat. All these creatures may provide omens in different ways and because they have this power they are called *burongs* (birds). Omens are derived from the flight of birds, the cries of animals, the direction whence they come or which they follow and so on. In this respect these omens are very much like the auguries of the Romans.

Many witnesses confirm that in the absence of favorable omens or in the presence of sinister ones an enterprise will not be undertaken, or if already underway it will be abandoned. For instance the Kenyah of Tanah Putih wished to build a boat. But on entering a forest to fell a tree they heard the *hisit* (bird) whistle to the left of them and they turned right around. Half an hour later they returned and felled a tree, but at the moment it fell they again detected an unfavorable augury. They left the tree lying and gave up all idea of constructing their boat. This example comes from Neuwenhuis in Borneo, cited by Lévy-Bruhl (1923: 127).

In the same way the idea of starting a journey is avoided unless the omens are good. The more dangerous the journey the more propitious must be the omens. Several villages wanted to start on a journey including some 500 men. It was necessary for each village to study the birds of their area for omens. For an expedition of this kind it was necessary to have some 10 positive auguries. Since most of the villages found something or other unfavorable the entire expedition was abandoned (Neuwenhuis, cited by Lévy-Bruhl ibid.).

If the decree which the omens yield is thus supreme, it is not only on account of their being considered infallible predictions. The reason goes deeper yet. A favorable omen is a positive support with which one cannot dispense. It does not simply announce success, it *insures* it. It is an indispensable guarantee for it, a *sine qua non*. It is not enough that there should be no unfavorable augury, there must be some favorable omens presenting themselves. Lacking these, nothing can be done even if doing nothing spells disaster. Thus, before beginning to sow the seed it is absolutely necessary to have heard a certain bird on the right, or to have seen another on the left, etc. If it were only a matter of being informed of whether the harvest would be good, one might resign oneself to work on in uncertainty especially when time is pressing, and the season for sowing will soon be over. Nevertheless, the natives will not begin as long as the necessary auguries are not forthcoming, and this is because the bird omens of themselves have a magic virtue which assures a good harvest at the same time they predict it. If these omens have not made their appearance neither will the good crop.

According to Perham (cited by Lévy-Bruhl 1923: 128) it may take about a month to obtain all those augury predictions which are to give them confidence in the results of their labors. The augur now has the same number of twigs or sticks as he has heard birdcalls of the right kind. He takes these to the land selected for farming and plants them in the ground, saying a short form of address to the birds. The magic virtue of the birds has been transferred to the land. It is because the magic virtue of the birds is indispensable to the fertility of the soil that the natives are obliged to await their good pleasure before beginning to cultivate. The native is assured a bountiful crop now. If such a crop is not forthcoming, the native will resort to supernatural interventions to explain the failure.

The bird or other animal furnishing the omen is not viewed simply as the bearer of good tidings, it is to be sought, adored and thanked as the dispenser of gifts which are indispensable and which can be procured from it alone. To a mind of this sort the omen is not a mere sign, it is also a cause. The worst of all omens is a dead beast, especially those included in the omen list, found anywhere on the farm. It infuses a deadly poison into the whole crop and will kill someone or other of the owner's family within a year. When this terrible thing happens they test the omen by killing a pig and examining the appearance of the liver right after death. If the prediction of harm were confirmed all the rice grown on that ground must be sold; and if necessary other rice bought for the family's own consumption. Other people may eat it because the omen only affects those to whom it is directly pointed (Perham cited by Lévy-Bruhl 1923: 112). Thus in the upper Congo the landing of a hippopotamus in one town might be an omen of war for one family and have no significance for another. A huge tree floating freely down the river might be an augury to one town of sickness and many deaths, and be entirely disregarded by another (Weeks, cited by Lévy-Bruhl ibid).

It is possible to defeat an evil omen. For example, a wise-man is hired to eat a sample of the crops, corn or mustard or a few cucumber shoots, for a consideration of compensation and by doing so he takes upon himself the evil omen which in him becomes innocuous and thus delivers the other one from the ban of the taboo. To one mystic power the Dayak opposes another mystic power superior to it. The omen is not averted; it is fought and overcome. But the most usual method employed when circumstances permit of it is the prevention of the sinister omen from making its appearance in the first place. In order not to hear the cry of a bird of evil omen, for instance, the natives will make such a commotion that the bird's cry, even if uttered, will not be heard by anyone.

> In New Zealand, if a traveler should see a lizard in the path before him, he would know it had not come of its own accord but had been sent by an enemy as an evil omen to cause his death. He therefore immediately kills the reptile and craves a woman to step over it as it lies in the path. By this means the evil omen is averted (Lévy Bruhl p. 146 citing Goldie 1904).
>
> In Kamchatka, the Natives regard the lizards as spies and emissaries sent by the ruler of the lower world to seek out men and tell them they are about to die. Therefore they notice lizards carefully, and when they see one they spring upon it with their knives and cut it in pieces so that it may not make any report about them. If it should escape them they are greatly concerned and expect death at any moment, and as this may, indeed, sometimes happen as the result of imagination, or even as a mere coincidence, this belief of theirs gains ground (Lévy-Bruhl 1923: 147 citing Steller).
>
> In the upper Congo the mournful hooting of the owl, heard at midnight by a villager, is a message that death is stealing silently towards the huts waiting to select a victim, and all who hear the call will hasten to the neighboring wood and drive the messenger of ill tidings away with sticks and stones (Lévy-Bruhl ibid. citing Glave).

In nearly all "traditional" (oral cultures) communities observers have noted a special type of omen that proves very alarming to primitives and causes them to make the most desperate efforts to combat the disaster its appearance seems to threaten. Such omens are to be found in facts or events which seem unusual or in individuals who are more or less teratological. These omens are distinguished by a special word in each language which means strange, unwonted or bizarre. This word is used for an omen when the spirits who desire to produce a certain effect or kill a certain man send their messengers to announce the fact. For example,

> in the Waschamba tribe, if a child presents itself feet first in childbirth, it is killed. If a child is born with teeth it is killed. If a goat is seen to be devouring its excreta, a fact so extraordinary it is the work of a wizard and the animal must be sacrificed. Again, if a goat in first giving birth has twins, there is witchcraft in it, and both goat and kids must be destroyed. Should a dog devour his excreta he must be killed for he is the prey of a sorcerer (Lévy-Bruhl 1923: 149 citing Karasek-Eichhorn 1911).
>
> Hobley has described in some detail how the Kikuyu of East Africa act in many similar circumstances. If a cow in grazing happens to twist her tail round a tree, she is possessed of evil powers and must be killed at once. Her owner offers her in sacrifice, the older men receive the backbone, and the young warriors the neck (Lévy-Bruhl ibid. p. 149).
>
> There is a white bird called *nyangi*. ... If one is seen to settle on a cow, and the cow is not killed, the owner of the cow will be *thahu* [possessed of evil spirits] and will die. The cow must be killed, there and then and the meat divided up ... no person belonging to the village must eat of the meat. ... The herd of cattle also need to be purified. ... If a cow's horn comes off in a person's hand, the animal is *thahu* and is slaughtered. ... If a bull or bullock leaves the herd while it is grazing and comes home alone, and stands outside the village digging at the refuse heap with its horns, it is seen to be *thahu* and is forthwith killed by the owner. ... If a goat is giving birth to a kid, and the head appears first and the body is not born quickly, it is said to be *thahu* and is slaughtered by the owner. ... If a woman bears twins the first time she has children, the twins are *thahu* and an old woman of the village, generally the midwife, stuffs grass in their mouths until they are suffocated, and throws them into the bush. . . If a cow or goat bears twins the first time, the same practice is observed (Hobley cited by Lévy-Bruhl 1923: 150).

The abnormalities of man or beast presented by the monsters or unusual behavior are thus omens portending evil, sometimes for the whole village. There is a direct connection between the abnormal child (twin or monster) and the misfortunes it will cause later on should it survive. These abnormalities are associated with certain crop failures in the future, sometimes because of too much rain, sometimes because of too little rain. And just as the omen bird by its mystic agency produces the benefits expected from his song, or his lucky flight, so the cock which crows at the wrong time or the child who is born with teeth, or as twins, is a "harbinger of woe" in the full sense of the word. His abnormality has revealed the malevolent principle with which he is imbued. His "transgression, as manifested in certain circumstances" has betrayed this indwelling evil, which is a constant menace to his family and to the entire social group.

Thus we see that much of the content of the minds of people in oral culture focuses on myriad spirits (human, animal, and inanimate), ghosts, (spirits of the dead), gods and goddesses and other deities. The importance of the spirits of the dead in the living human community cannot be overstated. One of the major means of communing with the spirits is through dreams. All of life is suffused with omens which not only herald, but cause events helpful and/or harmful to human society.

Conclusion

In this chapter we have considered in both summary and detailed exploration the major differences between oral and literate cultures. This has included medieval culture and Upper Paleolithic culture, as well as the importance of 17th to early 20th century ethnographies of oral cultures to aid in our understanding of the differences in the two cultures. We have considered the content of mental activities through an examination of the importance of animals to human beings from Upper Paleolithic times to the present and note animals have been a major portion of the content of human minds for about 2.6 million years according to Shipman (2010 and 2011). This exploration has led to a consideration of the animistic nature of oral cultures and by analogy to the mind of Paleolithic peoples. Their entire world was probably populated by spirits of the dead, animal spirits, spirits of the trees, forest, lakes, etc. in a complex, interconnected, interacting net of beings. I emphasize I am not saying the examples are identical to the thought of the Paleolithic mind but they provide insight into the probable nature of much mental content from that time period.

The language used by Upper Paleolithic peoples would have been flowery, repetitive, full of metaphor and analogy patterned after oral traditions handed down for generations. Mnemonic devices, including ritualization, would have been devised to assist in remembering special events and occasions. Calendars such as notches on bone may have been used to keep track of the moons, or days per moon (Marshack 1972). Using microscopic analysis Marshack showed that seemingly random or meaningless notches on bone were sometimes interpreted as structured series of numbers. For instance, Marshack hypothesized that notches on the bone plaque from Grotte de Thais in southern France, which dates to approximately 12,000 BP, were structured in subsets of 29 notches, thus suggesting that they were used to mark the duration between two lunations (see Bahn 2009, and Robinson 1992 for different perspectives on Marshack's work).

There would be no looking anything up and concepts of the future would have been vague, with the focus of attention on the present. Mimesis would have still been a large part of training young people in the fine points of hunting, gathering, food preparation, clothing preparation, although language certainly played a vital role. All of these activities would have involved rituals to assure the success of the endeavor. Visual artistic rituals would have been very important and as a result the cave paintings were likely produced with just a few participants such as for rituals of hunting success and rituals for "coming of age" ceremonies. More than likely there were rituals for birth, marriage, and death as well as for a plethora of "special occasions" such as meetings between neighboring societies, celebrations of the hunt, etc. Animistic beliefs would have permeated the entire culture and some therianthropic figures may have been worshipped as important deities or mythological heroes, just as the Kalahari San origin myths believe that in mystic time, before the present, animals and men were brothers. As an Inuit legend says, "I who was born to die shall live, so the world of animals and the world of men can come together, I shall live" (from the movie *The Iceman* released in 1984).

All would have been intimately involved in the activities of the present, including emotionally arousing situations and their conceptualizations of cause and effect would have been relatively rudimentary in contrast to those in literate culture. People would have seemed quite concrete in their thinking by today's literate standards. People would have been very conscious of their membership in a tribe or larger confederation of tribes with perhaps special groupings within each tribe as characterized by totemic animals or special animal representatives of each clan. Personal identity would have been derived largely from the group or special subdivisions of it. Introspection as we know it would have been unknown, and the idea of personality would probably not exist.

The right hemisphere may have been more dominant than it is today when it is inhibited by the dominant left hemisphere rendered so through language and writing. Thus, it is possible that the spirits communicated directly with humans via hallucinations, visual or auditory as elaborated by Jaynes theory and supported by current neurological data. Altered states of consciousness may have been typical of much ritualistic behavior, especially that involving mimesis of animal behavior, singing and dancing (Hayden 2003). Animistic beliefs would have permeated the entire culture and some therianthropic figures may have been worshipped as important deities or mythological heroes (Bahn and Vertut 1997).

Myths and stories about the plants, animals and spirits of the world would have been told to the young and perhaps acted out in special ceremonies. Dreams and omens of all kinds would have provided important information to people from the spirit world. Healing ceremonies and dances such as the San engage in would have been common, with a designated healer officiating. Reindeer were one of the most common larger animals consumed, and gathering of smaller animals probably comprised a significant amount of active daily living, especially for females and youth. Reindeer skins were surely used for clothing and hunting disguises. Indeed, "the sorcerer" of Trois Fréres could either be a mythical figure and/or a hunter in reindeer disguise. Horses may have been hunted at certain famous hunting sites such as Solutré where hunters took advantage of the seasonal migration routes to kill groups of horses, butchering them on site and carrying the meat back to cave sites. The Upper Paleolithic peoples would have been undergoing some stratification of society with more freedom to pursue activities less directly related to subsistence such as paleoart, enhanced tool production and clothing, and ritual for special occasions such as hosting nearby tribes with feasts as the huge reindeer herds provided a stable diet and human populations in the area of the Dordogne River valleys in France expanded (Hayden 2003), thus giving rise to increasing trading networks and inter-tribal communication.

REFERENCES

Aesop (1887 rpt. 2007). *Aesop's fables: Complete original translation from Greek.* Transl. G. F. Townsend. Charleston, SC: Forgotten Books Publishers.

Amati, D., and Shallice, T. (2007). On the emergence of modern humans. *Cognition 103*, 358–385.

Ambrose, S. H. (2010). Coevolution of composite-tool technology, constructive memory, and language: Implications for the evolution of modern human behavior. *Current Anthropology* 51, Supplement 1, 135–147.

Anati, E. (2010). *World rock art: The primordial language.* Oxford: Archaeopress.

Bahn, P. G. (Ed.) (2009). *An enquiring mind: Studies in honor of Alexander Marshack.* Oxford: Oxbow Books.

Bahn, P. G., and Vertut, J. 1997. *Journey through the Ice Age*. Berkeley: University of California Press.

Barrett, H. C. (2004). Cognitive development and the understanding of animal behavior. In B. J. Ellis and D. Bjorklund (Eds.), *Origins of the social mind: Evolutionary psychology and child development* (pp. 438–467). New York: Guilford Press.

Bednarik, R. G. (2012). The origins of modern human behavior. In R. G. Bednarik (Ed.), *The psychology of human behavior*. Hauppauge, NY: Nova Science Publishers, Inc.

Belfer-Cohen, A., and Hovers, E. (2010). Modernity, enhanced working memory, and the Middle to Upper Paleolithic record in the Levant. *Current Anthropology 51*, Supplement 1, S167–175.

Berger, B. (1978). A new interpretation of the IQ controversy. *The Public Interest 50*: winter 29–44.

Biesele, M. (1976). Aspects of !Kung folklore. In R. B. Lee and I. DeVore (Eds.), *Kalahari huntergatherers* (pp. 302–324). Cambridge, MA: Harvard University Press.

Biesele, M. (1993). *Women like meat: The folklore and foraging ideology of the Kalahari Ju/'hoan*. Bloomington, IN: Indiana University Press.

Bird-David, N. (1999). Animism revisited: personhood, environmental and relational epistemology. *Current Anthropology* 40, 67–91.

Blackburn, T. (1974). *Chumash oral traditions: a cultural analysis*. Unpublished doctoral dissertation, Department of Anthropology, Los Angeles: University of California.

Bookstein, F., Schaeffer, K., Prossinger, H., Seidler, H., et al. (1999). Comparing frontal cranial profiles in archaic and modern *Homo* by morphometric analysis. *The Anatomical Record (New Anat.)* 257, 217–224.

Brown, D. E. (1991). H. U. M. A. N. UNIVERSALS. Boston: McGraw Hill Publishers.

Bullfinch, T. (1970). *Bullfinch's mythology: The age of fable, the age of chivalry, legends of Charlemagne*. New York: Crowell.

Campbell, J. (1988). *Historical atlas of world mythology*, Vol. 1, Part 1, *Mythologies of the primitive hunters and gatherers: The way of the animal powers*. Volume I, Part 2: Mythologies of the great hunt. Volume II, Part 1, *The way of the seeded earth: The sacrifice*. Volume II, Part 2: *Mythologies of the primitive planters: The North Americas*. Volume II, Part 3, *The Middle and Southern Americas*. New York: Harper and Row Publishers.

Carruthers, M. (2008). *The book of memory: A study of memory in medieval culture*. Cambridge, UK: Cambridge University Press.

Coolidge, F. L., and Wynn, T. (2005). Working memory, its executive functions, and the emergence of modern thinking. *Cambridge Archaeological Journal* 15, 5–26

Coolidge, F. L., and Wynn, T. (2006). The role of enhanced working memory in the production of therianthropic art. *Rock Art Research* 23, 18–21.

Csibra, G., Gergely, G., Koos, G., and Brockband, M. (1999). Goal attribution without agency cues. The perception of 'pure reason' in infancy. *Cognition* 72, 237–267.

Dehaene, S. (2005). Evolution of human cortical circuits for reading and arithmetic: The "neuronal recycling" hypothesis. In S. Dehaene, J. R. Duhamel, M. Hauser and G. Rizzolatti (Eds.), *From monkey brain to human brain* (pp. 133–158). Cambridge, MA: MIT Press,

Dehaene, S. (2009). *Reading in the brain: The new science of how we read*. New York: Penguin Group.

di Lernia, S. (Ed.) (1999). *The Uan Afuda Cave: Hunter-gatherer societies of central Sahara.* Arid Zone Archaeology Monographs 1, Rome: Edizioni All'Insegna del Gigli.

de Vries, J. (1971, rpt. 1977). *Perspective in the history of religion* (transl. K. W. Bolle). Berkeley: University of California Press.

Dissanayake, E. (1992). *Homo Aestheticus: Where art comes from and why.* Seattle: University of Washington Press.

Dissanayake, E. (2008). The arts after Darwin: Does art have an origin and Adaptive function? In K. Zijlmans and W. van Damme (Eds.), *World art studies: Exploring concepts and approaches* (pp. 241–263). Amsterdam: Valiz.

Dissanayake, E. (2009). The artification hypothesis and its relevance to cognitive science, evolutionary aesthetics, and neuroaesthetics. *Cognitive Semiotics Special Issue on Aesthetic Cognition* 5, 148–173.

Dissanayake, E. (2010). The deep structure of Pleistocene rock art: the "artification" hypothesis. *Prè-actes du Congrés IFRAO. Ariège 2010. Pleistocene Art of Europe*, DVD. Terascon-sur-Ariège: Lacombe.

Eliade, M. (1964). *Shamanism: Archaic techniques of ecstasy* (transl. W. R. Trask). Princeton, NJ: Princeton University Press.

Evans-Pritchard, E. E. (1934). Lévy-Bruhl's theory of primitive mentality. *Bulletin of the Faculty of Arts, Cairo, Egyptian University V2*, 1–26.

Evans-Pritchard, E. E. (1965). *Theories of primitive religion.* Oxford: Oxford University Press.

Evans-Pritchard, E. E. (1981). *A history of anthropological thought* (Ed. A. Singer). New York: Basic Books.

Falk, D. (2011). *The fossil chronicles: How two controversial discoveries changed our view of human evolution.* Berkeley: University of California Press.

Flores, N. C. (2000). *Animals in the Middle Ages.* New York: Routledge.

Fox, A. (2000). *Oral and literate culture in England 1500–1700.* Oxford: Clarendom Press.

Frazer, J. G. (1907). *Adonis, Attis, Osiris: Studies in the history of oriental religion.* London: McMillan and Co.

Frazer, J. G. (1923). *The golden bough: A study in magic and religion*, Vol. 1–4. London: McMillan and Co.

Gergely, G., Nadasdy, Z., Csibra, G., and Biro, S. (1995). Taking the intentional stance at 12 months of age. *Cognition* 56, 165–193.

Gilmore, W. (1919). *Animism: Or, thought currents of primitive peoples.* Boston, MA: Marshall Jones. *<http://www.sacred-texts.com/sha/anim/anim01.htm>*.

Goodall, J. (1986). *The chimpanzees of Gombe.* Cambridge, MA: Harvard University Press.

Goody, J. (1968, rpt. 2005). *Literacy in traditional societies.* Cambridge: Cambridge University Press.

Goody, J. (1977). *The domestication of the savage mind.* Cambridge: Cambridge University Press.

Goody, J. (1987). *The interface between the written and the oral.* New York: Cambridge University Press.

Grossman, L., Monro, N. D., and Belfer-Cohen, A. (2008). A twelve thousand year old shaman burial from the southern Levant. *Proceedings of the National Academy of Science, USA* 105, 17665–69.

Hallowell, A. I. (1975). Ojibwe ontology, behavior and world view. In D. Tedlock and B. Tedlock (Eds.), *Teachings from the American earth: Indian religion and philosophy* (pp. 141–178). New York: Liveright Press.

Harris, W. B. (2009). *Dreams and experience in classical antiquity*. Cambridge, MA: Harvard University Press.

Harrison, J. E. (1912). *Themis: a study of the origins of Greek religion*. Cambridge, UK: Cambridge University Press.

Harrod, J. B. (2012). The case for chimpanzee religion. *Journal for the Study of Religion, Nature, Culture*. In Press.

Hartley, L. P. (1953). *The go-between*. New York: Stein and Day.

Hassig, D. (2000). *The mark of the beast*. New York: Routledge.

Havelock, E. A. (1963). *Preface to Plato*. Cambridge: Belknap Press of Harvard University Press.

Havelock, E. A. (1976). *Origins of Western literacy*. Toronto: Toronto Institute for Studies in Education.

Hawkes, T. (1983, rpt. 1997). Orality and literacy. In T. Hawkes (Ed.), *Orality and literacy: The technologizing of the word* (p. I). New York: Routledge.

Hayden, B. (2003). *A prehistory of religion: Shamans, sorcerers and saints*. Washington, DC: Smithsonian Books.

Helvenston, P. A. (1999). *Concepts regarding melancholia and mania in medieval Europe with an emphasis on England*. M. A. in History, Flagstaff, AZ, University of Northern Arizona, V2.

Helvenston, P. A. (2012). "Artification": Examples of human perfectionism from deep in the archaeological record. *Rock Art Research* 29(1) in press.

Helvenston, P. A., and Bahn, P. G. (2003). Testing the three stages of trance model. *Cambridge Archaeological Journal* 13(2), 213–224.

Helvenston, P. A., and Hodgson, D. (2010). The neuropsychology of animism: Implications for understanding rock art. *Rock Art Research* 27(3), 61–94.

Hodgson, D., and Helvenston, P. A. (2006). The emergence of the representation of animals in Paleoart: Insights from evolution and the cognitive, limbic and visual systems of the human brain. *Rock Art Research* 32(1), 3–40.

Horton, R. (1973). Lévy-Bruhl, Durkheim and the scientific revolution. In R. Horton and R. Finnegan (Eds.), *Modes of thought: Essays on thinking in Western and non-Western thought* (pp. 249–305). London: Faber.

Huizinga, J. (1996). *The autumn of the Middle Ages*. Chicago: University of Chicago Press.

Ingold, T. (2000). Totemism, animism and the depiction of animals. In T. Ingold (Ed.), *The perception of the environment: Essays on livelihood, dwelling and skill* (pp. 111–131). London: Routledge.

Jaynes, J. (1977). *The origin of conscientiousness in the bicameral mind*. Boston: Houghton Mifflin.

Johnson, M. (2006). Biological motion: A perceptual life detector. *Current Biology* 16, R376–377.

Katz, R. (1982). *Boiling energy: Community healing among the Kalahari Kung*. Cambridge, MA: Harvard University Press.

Kingsley, M. H. (1899). West African studies. New York: McMillan and Co. Ltd.

Klingender, F. 1971. *Animals in art and thought to the end of the Middle Ages*. Cambridge, MA: MIT Press.

Kohler, A. (2005). Of apes and men, Baka and Bantu attitudes to wildlife and the making of eco-goodies and baddies. *Conservation and Society* 3, 407–435.

Kuijsten, M. (Ed.) (2006). *Consciousness, hallucinations and the bicameral mind: Three decades of new research*. Henderson, NV: Julian Jaynes Society.

Kuijsten, M. (Ed.) (2012). *The Julian Jaynes Collection*. Henderson, NV: Julian Jaynes Society.

Laing, J. (1982). *The origins of Britain*. London: Granada.

Lee, R. B. (1966). The sociology of Kung Bushman trance performances. In R. Prince (Ed.), *Trance and possession states* (pp. 35–57). Montreal: R. M. Bucke Memorial Society.

Lee, R. B., and DeVore, I. (Eds.) (1968). *Man the hunter*. Chicago: Aldine Press.

Lévy-Bruhl, L. (1910 rpt. 1985). *How natives think* (transl. L. A. Clare). Princeton, NJ: Princeton University Press.

Lévy-Bruhl, L. (1923). *Primitive mentality* (transl. L. A. Clare). New York: The McMillan Co.

Lévy-Bruhl, L. (1926 rpt 1985). *How natives think* (transl. L. A. Clare). Princeton, NJ: Princeton University Press.

Lévy-Bruhl, L. (1928, rpt. 1965). *The soul of the primitive* (transl. L. A. Clare). London: George Allen and Unwin Ltd.

Lévy-Bruhl, L. (1935, rpt. 1973). *Primitives and the supernatural* (transl. L. A. Clare). New York: Haskell House Publishers Ltd.

Lévy-Bruhl, L. (1949, rpt. 1975). *The notebooks on primitive mentality* (transl. P. Rivière). New York: Harper and Row.

Levi-Strauss, C. (1966). *The savage mind*. Chicago: University of Chicago Press.

Lewis-Williams, J. D. (1977). *Believing and seeing: An interpretation of symbolic meanings in southern San rock paintings*. Doctoral dissertation, University of Natal.

Lex, B. W. (1979). Neurobiology of ritual trance. In E. G. d'Aquili, C. D. Laughlin, and J. McManus (Eds.), *The spectrum of ritual: A biogenetic structural analysis* (pp. 117–151). New York: Columbia University Press,

Luria, A. R. (1976). *Cognitive development, its cultural and social foundations* (Ed. M. Cole, transl. M. Lopez-Morillas and L. Solotaroff). Cambridge, MA: Harvard University Press.

Malinowski, B. (1948, rpt. 1992). *Magic, science and religion and other essays*. Long Grove, IL: Waveland Press.

Marshack, A. (1972). *The roots of civilizations: The cognitive beginnings of man's first art, symbol and notation*. New York: McGraw Hill.

Martín-Loeches, M. (2010). Uses and abuses of the enhanced-working-memory hypothesis in explaining modern thinking. *Current Anthropology* 51, Supplement 1: S67–75.

McBrearty, S., and Brooks, A. S. (2000). The revolution that wasn't. *Journal of Human Evolution* 39, 453–563.

McLuhan, M. (1962). *The Gutenberg galaxy: The making of typographic man*. Toronto: University of Toronto Press.

Mazel, A. D., and Watchman, A. L. (1997). Accelerator radiocarbon dating of Natal Drakensberg paintings: Results and implications. *Antiquity* 71, 445–449.

Mitchell, P. (2002). *The archaeology of southern Africa*. Cambridge, UK: Cambridge University Press.

Mori, F. (1975). Contributo allo studio del pensiero magico-religioso attraverso l'esame di alcune raffigurazioni upestri preistoriche del Sahara. In E. Anati (Ed.), *Les religions de la préhistoire* (pp. 343–366). Valcamonica, Italy: Valcamonica Symposium.

Mormann, F., Dubois, J., Kornblith, S., Milosavljevic, M., et al. (2011). A category-specific response to animals in the right human amygdala. *Nature Neuroscience Online publication* August 28. doi: 10.1038/nn.2899.

Muzzolini, A. (2001). Saharan Africa. In D. S. Whitley (Ed.), *Handbook of rock art research* (pp. 605–636). Walnut Creek, CA: Altamira Press.

Needham, R. (1972). *Belief, language, and experience*. Oxford: Basil Blackwell.

Olson, S. (1989). Solutré: A theoretical approach to the reconstruction of Upper Paleolithic hunting strategies. *Journal of Human Evolution* 18, 295–327.

Ong, W. J. (1967). *The presence of the word*. Minneapolis, MN: University of Minnesota Press.

Ong, W. J. (1982 rpt. 1997). *Orality and literacy: The technologizing of the word*. New York: Routledge.

Orpen, J. M. (1874). A glimpse into the mythology of the Maluti Bushmen. *Cape Monthly Magazine* 9, 1–13.

Pearson, D., Burrow, A., Fitzgerald, C., Green, K., et al. (2001). Auditory hallucinations in normal child populations. *Personality and Individual Differences* 31(3), 401–407.

Pinker, S. (2002). *The blank slate: The modern denial of human nature*. New York: Penguin Books.

Propp, V. (1968). *Morphology of the folk tale*. Austin: University of Texas Press.

Robinson, J. (1992). Not counting on Marshack: A reassessment of the work of Alexander Marshack on notation in the Upper Paleolithic. *Journal of Mediterranean Studies* 2(1), 1–16.

Rowland, B. (1973). *Animals with human faces: A guide to animal symbols*. Knoxville: University of Tennessee Press.

Sanders, N. K., (Transl.) (1960). *The Epic of Gilgamesh: An English version with an introduction by N. K. Sanders* (rpt.1980). New York: Penguin Books.

Scribner, S., and Cole, M. (1981, rpt. 1999). *The psychology of literacy*. Cambridge, MA: Harvard University Press.

Shannon, B. (2002). *The antipodes of the mind: Charting the phenomenology of the ayahuasca experience*. New York, NY: Oxford University Press.

Shebesta, A. P. (1933). *Revisiting my Pygmy hosts* (transl. G. Griffin). London: Hutchinson Publishing.

Shipman, P. (2010). The animal connection and human evolution. *Current Anthropology* 52(4), 519–532.

Shipman, P. (2011). *The animal connection*. New York: W.W. Norton and Co.

Sidhu, K. A. S., and Dickey, T. III. (2010). Hallucinations in children: Diagnostic and treatment strategies. *Current Psychiatry* 9(10), 53–62.

Solomon, A. (1997). The myth of ritual origins? Ethnography, mythology and interpretation of San rock art. *South African Archaeological Bulletin* 52(June), 3–13.

Solomon, A. (1999). Thoughts on therianthropes, myth and method. *Pictogram* 10(2), 10–16.

Solomon, A. (2008). Myths, making and consciousness. *Current Anthropology* 49(1), 59–86.

Sowell, T. (2012). The way that history went down. *National Review Online*, January 21. *http://www.nationalreview.com/articles/288547/way-hist.*

Springer, S., and Deutsch, P. (1993). *Left brain, right brain.* San Francisco: W. H. Freeman and Company.

Stow, G. W. (1905). *The native races of South Africa.* London: Swan Sonnenschein and Co. Ltd.

Thackeray, J. F. (1993). New directions in the study of southern African rock art. *African Arts* 26(1), 74–75, 102.

Thackeray, J. F. (2005). The wounded roan: a contribution to the relation of hunting and trance in southern African rock art. *Antiquity* 79, 5–18.

Thompson, S. (1975). *Motif index of folk literature.* Bloomington: Indiana University Press.

Toynbee, J. M. C. (1973). *Animals in Roman life and art.* London: Thames and Hudson.

Tylor, E. B. (1871, 1874). *Primitive culture: Researches into the development of mythology, philosophy, religion, language, art and custom.* Vol. I and II. Boston: Estes and Lauriat.

Vinnicombe, P. (1972). Myth, motive, and selection in southern African rock art. *Africa* 42(3), 192–204.

Vinnicombe, P. (1975). The ritual significance of eland (*Taurotragus oryx*) in the rock art of southern Africa. In E. Anati (Ed.), *Les religions de la préhistoire* (p. 397). Valcamonica, Italy: Centro Camuno di Studi Preistorici.

Vinnicombe, P. (1976). *People of the eland: Rock paintings of the Drakensberg Bushmen as a reflection of their life and thought.* Pietermaritzburg: University of Natal Press.

Waller, S. J. (2000). Spatial correlation of acoustics and rock art exemplified in Horseshoe Canyon. *American Indian Rock Art* 13, 85–94.

Waller, S. J. (2002). *Rock art acoustics.* Available from *http://www.geocities.com/Cape Canaveral/ 9461.*

Waller, S. J. (2003). Conservatism of rock art acoustics "unexpected" echoes at Petroglyph National Monument. *Rock Art Papers* 41(16): 31–38.

White, R. (2003). *Prehistoric art—the symbolic journey of humankind.* New York: Harry N. Abrams.

Wilkinson, T. (2003). *Genesis of the Pharaohs.* London: Thames and Hudson.

Wilmsen, E. W. (1986). Of paintings and painters in terms of Zu/'hoansi interpretations. In R. Vossen, and K. Keuthmann (Eds.), *Contemporary studies on Khoisan: In honour of Oswin Kohler on the occasion of his seventy-fifth birthday*, Volume 2 (pp. 347–372). Hamburg: Helmut Buske Verlag.

Winkelman, M. (2002). Shamanism and cognitive evolution. *Cambridge Archaeological Journal* 12(1), 72–101.

Wynn, T., and Coolidge, F. L. (2003). The role of working memory in the evolution of managed foraging. *Before Farming* 2, 1–16.

Wynn, T., and Coolidge, F. L. (2007). Did a small but significant enhancement in working memory capacity power the evolution of modern thinking. In P. Mellars, K. Boyle, O. Bar-Yosef, and C. B. Stringer (Eds.), *Rethinking the human revolution* (pp. 79–90). Cambridge, UK: McDonald Institute for Archaeological Research.

Wynn, T., and Coolidge, F. L. (2010). Beyond symbolism and language: An introduction to supplement 1. Working memory. *Current Anthropology* 51, Supplement 1, S5–15.

Yates, F. A. (1974). *The art of memory.* Chicago, IL: The University of Chicago Press.

Zipes, J. (transl.) (1987). *Complete fairy tales of the Brothers Grimm.* New York: Bantam.

In: The Psychology of Human Behavior
Editor: Robert G. Bednarik
ISBN: 978-1-62257-901-3

Chapter 3

THE COMPARATIVE PSYCHOLOGY OF HUMAN UNIQUENESS: A COGNITIVE BEHAVIORAL REVIEW

Robert A. Dielenberg*
Australian Rock Art Research Association, VIC, Australia

ABSTRACT

The dominant paradigm of comparative psychology is that nonhuman primate cognitive abilities differ from humans in degree, not kind. In broadly reviewing the human-nonhuman research landscape, including two areas still well under-represented—volitional control and innovation, it was found that while nonhuman primates (and apes in particular) demonstrate flexible physical adeptness, this flexibility does not extend to the realm of imagination and ideas. Specifically, apes were found to have "first order awareness of the unseen world", that is, the ability to infer some physical unseen causation, but lack "second order awareness of the unseen world"—the ability to infer properties of things based purely on observational knowledge of internal structure derived from primary experience of simple elements. It is argued that second order unseen awareness emerges from self-reflective consciousness. Access to unseen worlds of imagination and ideas allows humans to create cumulative culture through a process of renewed hybridization of form and function. Nonhuman primate culture by comparison lacks hybridization and therefore displays a general paucity of cumulative traditions.

INTRODUCTION

Ever since Darwin (and probably before) we have looked at the great apes and wondered how we got from sharing a common ancestor with them, to being us. What distance lies between them and us—in time, anatomy and especially, cognitive ability. The current consensus in evolutionary psychology is that we are not different from them in kind, only "in degree" (Darwin 1874/1896: 101). On the face of it, it would appear that all that remains to be

* Australian Rock Art Research Association, 3 Buxton Street, Elsternwick, VIC 3185, Australia, robertad@tpg.com.au

done is to specify what magnitude of degree we are talking about. The working assumption is of a monadic linear progression from a "less" evolved to "more" evolved cognitive dimension. If true, then over half a century of evolutionary psychology has taught us that the great ape-human dimension is a multi-stranded one, with each strand representing a degree and each degree possessing a discontinuity somewhere along its length. Imagine, if you will, a rope with strands that have been cut at different points along its length. If you tease out the strands and lay them flat on a 2-dimensional plane you will get a picture like the one depicted in Figure 1. We will call this the Multi-Stranded Variable Discontinuity Model.

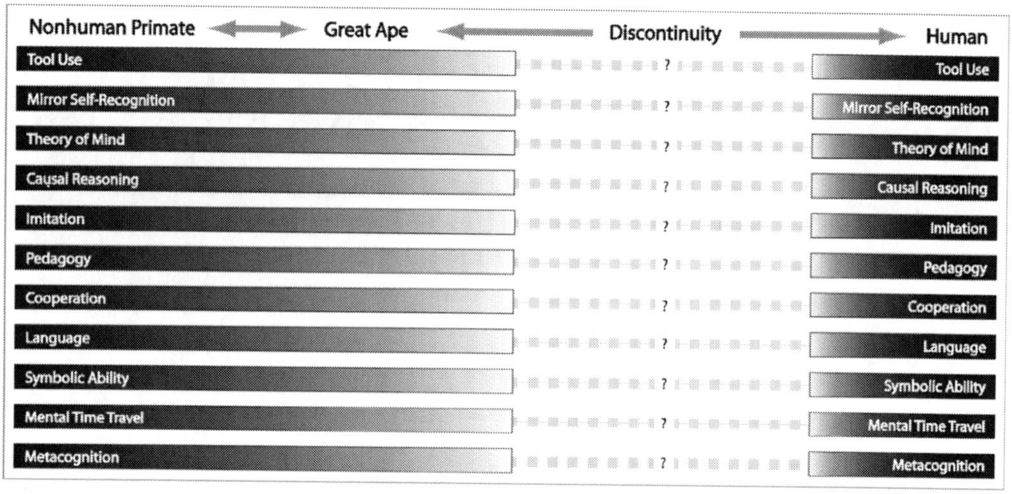

Figure 1. The Multi-Stranded Variable Discontinuity Model. No assumptions are made as to the exact magnitude of each discontinuity; the gaps are for visualization purposes only. Also, the categories depicted are by no means exhaustive. They are merely representative of the literature. For example we could add "intentionality" and "innovation."

The assumptions of the model are:

1. Each strand is viewed as a network of interconnected fibers.
2. Discontinuities are viewed as boundaries with potentially permeable thresholds.
3. The number of strands is potentially indeterminate.
4. Humans, great apes and other nonhuman primates evolved strands of cognitive abilities sufficient and necessary for the needs of their species.
5. The goal of the model is to help identify where discontinuities—if any—occur.

The over-arching assumption of a monadic dimension is maintained because we share a common ancestor with the great apes, which implies a common root of cognitive abilities. This assumption, however, has the potential to lull us into thinking that there is a ladder or pyramid of progress between us and them (Bickerton 2009). This could not be further from the truth. Point four (4) above asserts that evolution is blind. Humans are not the purpose of evolution, but merely one of the players. We would like to believe that evolution has produced a species that for the very first time has the ability to step outside the evolutionary process itself and modify it, but this too may turn out to be just another step in evolution. In this view, there is no stepping outside of evolution, no super-species. There are only more or less evolved species. What we would like to know then is how did we transition to this point in our existence? What were the milestones? What can we learn by looking at our genetic cousins? What can they tell us about our uniqueness?

Convention holds that the main transition began with the split away from chimpanzees (*Pan troglodytes*) approximately 6–10 mya (Scally et al. 2012; Wilkinson et al. 2011) and made its presence fully felt in *Homo erectus* and so-called archaic *Homo sapiens*. Both of these species can be tied to the emergence of human uniqueness. In line with our preamble, we will argue for "behavioral variability" as opposed to a linear, non-overlapping progression (de Waal and Ferrari 2010; Shea 2011a). This will allow us to ask what factors were necessary and sufficient for apes, *Homo erectus* and archaic *Homo sapiens* to adapt to the environment, rather than impose unnecessary constraints based on preconceived notions of a "general purpose" cognitive apparatus (Gallistel 2000). Finally, by unpacking the strands of our model, we will be able to revisit the definition of culture, the keystone of human uniqueness, which in evolutionary psychology is often fleetingly defined as "socially transmitted information" (Alvard 2003; Boesch and Tomasello 1998; Boyd and Richerson 1985; Cronk 1999; Durham 1991; Flinn 1997; Whiten et al. 1999). As we shall see, variations of this form persist due to different perspectives and agendas (Byrne et al. 2004). Ideally, we would like to update the definition of human uniqueness by integrating the strands of our model.

Some Preliminary Remarks

Gene-Evolution Interaction

When we said that *Homo erectus* adapted to the environment, we meant both to its own genetic changes and the external environment. For a long time, evolutionary scientists have been uneasy about the relationship between organisms and the environment. The relationship was thought to be tightly coupled, so that the organism always adapted to environmental shifts. However, this idea is losing traction in the face of mounting data. There are two new ideas that need to be taken into consideration. The first is that the organism-environment relationship is non-linear (Bennet 2010). Specifically, evolutionary biologists need to take into account the fact that species may show no evolution of morphological characteristics despite major environmental changes (both short and long-term). Interestingly, the shift from forest to savanna has been long touted as a dominant driving factor of hominin evolution. But recent studies of modern forest communities have shown that distinctive mixes of species, such as boreal, deciduous, and aspen parkland, are often in fact just temporary groupings. Multi-species communities do not shift their distributions in a coordinated way in response to climatic change. Rather, trees respond individually (Davies 1983). In another example, using a molecular clock approach to determine rates of speciation in birds, it has been shown that these animals appeared more or less continuously in the Quaternary and the longer cooling period that preceded it regardless of the dramatic climate oscillations that occurred over this epoch (Lovette 2005). Similarly, in human populations in the last 50–100,000 years, it turns out that the genome actually contains few examples of very strong natural selection. Instead, what seems to have happened is that once a beneficial mutation occurred it was rapidly carried to faraway locales as the population expanded into new territories, thereby producing evolutionary change independent of environment (Pritchard 2010). "Neutral theory" is a new area of research that is attempting to come to grips with these phenomena—namely that speciation appears to be driven more by genetic drift and mutation than natural selection (Kimura 1968; King and Jukes 1969). It is a complicated area of research and going into it deeply here would take us too far away from our main thrust. Suffice to say that neutral theory does not discount the environment or natural selection as a core Darwinian mechanism; rather, it shifts the effects from the macro world to the micro world.

Which leads to the second idea: epigenetics; for a review see (Nelson and Nadeau 2010). Several interesting findings have challenged the central dogma that DNA alone acts as the arbiter of an organism's destiny. Pembrey and Bygren in a Swedish study found that men who had experienced famine when they were aged around ten had paternal grandsons who lived much longer than their grandfathers, who had experienced times of plenty (Pembrey et al. 2006). On the other hand, women who experienced famine while they were in the womb had paternal granddaughters who died on average far earlier. Granddaughters were affected by their grandmother's prenatal experience, while grandsons were affected by their grandfather's peri-pubertal food consumption. Intrigued by this finding, researchers have sought to replicate it in animals. Mice genetically engineered to have memory problems were raised in an enriched environment—given toys, exercise, and social interaction—for two weeks during adolescence. The animals' memories improved, an unsurprising finding, given that enrichment has for a long time been known to boost brain function (Altman and Das 1964; Rosenzweig et al. 1962). The mice were then returned to normal conditions, where they grew up and had offspring. This next generation of mice also had better memory, despite having the genetic defect and never having been exposed to the enriched environment (Arai et al. 2009). In a pattern typical in science, a study was rediscovered from over 20 years ago that supported this finding, showing pregnant rats exposed to an enriched environment enhanced the maze learning abilities of their offspring, even if the offspring were raised by non-enriched foster mothers (Kiyono et al. 1985). The mechanisms of epigenetic inheritance are slowly being uncovered. Histone methylation is one of the main molecular species involved. In the cell nucleus, DNA is wound around histones. Methylation and demethylation of histones turns the genes "on" and "off" respectively, either by loosening their tails, thereby allowing transcription factors and other proteins to access the DNA, or by encompassing their tails around the DNA, thereby restricting access to the DNA. In empirical support of this, a recent study found that a single 30-minute episode of acute stress causes a rapid histone methylation in the rat hippocampus, a brain region known to be especially susceptible to the effects of stress in both rodents and humans (Hunter et al. 2009). Thus, researchers are honing in on the specific biochemical pathways that subserve epigenetic effects and in the coming years this new knowledge will infiltrate evolutionary psychology and broaden its horizon.

Putting these two effects together, we are left with a potentially contradictory situation. On the one hand, an organism may respond more to its own internal milieu than the environment; that is, while large environment shifts are occurring outside its body boundary, it may continue on unchanged, or change in unexpected ways. On the other hand, certain environmental events may seep into the genome through the germ line, occurring in females prenatally and males peri-pubertally, which then precipitate knock-on effects generations down the line. Finally, any genomic changes that do occur may spread through a population via emigration. Newcomers to a region may change the genome of the native population in ways that are independent of other environmental shifts. And these effects are just the ones we know about. There are probably many others waiting to be discovered. The upshot of all this for evolutionary psychologists is that it will force the field to reconsider its views on gene-environment interactions, which according to Darwinian theory are supposed to occur in lockstep, but which now appear to be less tightly coupled than once thought. It is almost as if evolutionary psychology is on the verge of entering a similar phase that physics did at the turn of the 19th century, when atomic theory separated the Newtonian macro world from the micro world of non-linear quantum indeterminacy. We would hope that such a development will not impede evolutionary psychology from developing a new synthesis of its data.

Conscious versus Unconscious Cognition

One of the key debates in primatology is the question of whether great apes and other nonhuman primates (henceforth "apes" and "monkeys") have self-reflective consciousness and conceptual thought. A large amount of ambiguity surrounds these terms in the literature. For the present, when using the term "self" we will try to limit it to situations referencing humans, not other animals. For animals, we will assume body awareness, whereas the question whether they have mind awareness will be left open to debate. Body awareness, which refers to both humans and animals, is the ability to focus attentional resources on the body, and includes behaviors that are intentionally directed at the body. Excluded from this definition are instinctual routines such as scratching, grooming, and excreting. The second, mind awareness, which here only refers to humans, involves consciously focusing attentional resources on mental events, such as mental representations, thoughts, and language. However, because mental representations are also used in relation to animals in the comparative psychology literature, its use has become somewhat confused. By definition, a mental representation is precisely what it is: a *re-presentation* of content previously subserved by a dynamical brain state. Typically, these will be fragments of percept data and/or memories, and their knock-on associations and hybridization products (the latter is commonly referred to as "concepts"). Two commonly held assumptions are applied to *re-presented* mental contents: 1) they are intentional, and 2) they are conscious. In fact, most mental representations are unintentional and occur outside the field of conscious awareness (Bargh and Chartrand 1999; Kihlstrom 1987). Moreover, attentional processing and situational awareness can occur completely independent of each other (Hsieh et al. 2011; Watanabe et al. 2011). The evolution of this ability for the importance of survival in the wild (for example against predators) cannot be overstated (Lin et al. 2009). However, primate research literature, while aware of the role of intentionality in the cognitive economy (Horowitz 2003), generally fails to distinguish between conscious and unconscious mental representations (hence the confusion in the literature). Here we take a more explicit stance. When the term "mental representation" is used in relation to animals, we will assume it to be *unconscious*. This is not a trivial distinction. It means that it is perfectly sensible to ascribe mental representations to apes and monkeys. What is contested, what is regarded as the Holy Grail for some primate researchers is to prove beyond reasonable doubt that apes (at least) have *intentional conscious* mental representations, that is, "thinking about thinking." The section on theory of mind (ToM) will attempt to address some of these issues.

COMPARATIVE PRIMATE RESEARCH

Our discussion begins with ape-monkey cognitive abilities. This will provide us with a baseline perspective from which to view evolutionary transitions related to *Homo erectus* and archaic *Homo sapiens*. Evolutionary psychology seeks to explain how we evolved vis-à-vis primate cognition and behavior (note: "primate/s" refers to apes and monkeys collectively). As with any research subject, ideological divisions arise through a combination of culture, data bias, and life philosophy. On one side, you have staunch behaviorists, who view animal behavior through the lens of association learning and reductionism. This group also includes hardline geneticists who believe genes are dominant over individual innovation. On the other hand, you have the humanists, who see emotions and motivations in animals and are not afraid to engage in anthropomorphic projection. It is interesting that often field researchers, who generally spend the longest time with the subjects they study, fit into this camp. In between, you have the middlemen, who think they see the merits and failings of both approaches. The fact is, we are now deep into the details of primate research. The number of papers published is enormous and growing at a rapid rate. It is impossible for one reviewer to absorb all the facts and so biases, as always, will remain inevitable. The goal however is noble: find the pivotal cognitive factors that separate humans from their close animal cousins and from this deduce what it is that is unique about humans. Despite a hundred years or more of research into this endeavor, one thing remains unchallenged: even though apes and monkeys clearly possess a rich and diverse behavioral repertoire, no one can deny that there is a gap between us and them. Accordingly, whenever we compare their cognitive abilities with ours, we shall adhere to Morgan's Canon: "In no case is an animal activity to be interpreted in terms of higher psychological processes, if it can be fairly interpreted in terms of processes which stand lower in the scale of psychological evolution and development" (Morgan 1903). A further interpretative distinction that permeates the comparative psychology literature will be useful: ultimate versus proximal explanations (Dewsbury 1984). To give an example, an animal that hoarded food with the intention of recovering it for later consumption would be using a proximal cognitive mechanism. It may possess an ability to mentally time travel. Alternatively, the ultimate explanation argues that an animal with acquired genes that control a tendency to hoard and recover food will have a survival advantage causing its genes and its behavior to spread throughout its species and its descendants; it hoards food with no awareness of why it does it.

TOOL USE

Paleoanthropology has a long tradition of drawing conclusions about hominin cognitive abilities from the stone tools they used and created (McPherron 2000). Some commentators have raised justifiable criticisms of this tradition (Bednarik 2006), in that we cannot say any more about early hominin culture than we can say about our own culture if we happened upon a giant ceramic vase. We would think we had stumbled upon a culture of giant vase worshippers. Our culture is obviously so much more than that. The same must apply for hominins. Nevertheless, techniques in neuroscience married with established techniques in ethnology have shown the potential to reveal new insights into the relationship between stone tools and imagined hominin brains (Geribàs et al. 2010; Stout et al. 2008). The key issue that we have to be careful about is extrapolating behavior from lithic assemblages:

> The most surprising aspect about the debate regarding when *Homo sapiens* became human is that archaeologists have not tested the core hypothesis that there were significant behavioral differences between the earliest and more recent members of our species. [...] For example, expedient and opportunistic flintknapping of river pebbles and cobbles by living humans often creates stone tools indistinguishable from the pebble tools knapped by *Homo habilis* or *Homo erectus*. This similarity reflects the nature of the tool-making strategies, techniques and raw materials, not the evolutionary equivalence of the toolmakers (Shea 2011b).

What, therefore, can primate tool use tell us about hominin behavioral differences? In Byrne's (Byrne 2004) comprehensive study of tool use among apes (*Pan troglodytes*, *Pan paniscus*, *Gorilla gorilla*, *Gorilla beringei*, *Pongo p. pygmaeus*, and *Pongo p. abelii*), which emphasized that manual skills required for stone tool use are just one subset of a more fundamental skill base, it was found that all of these apes had "precision handling" ability; i.e., tip-to-tip precision grips, rather than whole-hand power grips useful only in rough and ready manipulation (Christel 1993; Marzke and Wullstein 1995). But more specifically, in chimpanzees, the species we share the closest common ancestor with, they were also found to possess the ability for:

- Accurate aiming of powerful blows: e.g., to detach a useful flake, blows must be highly accurate in placement, yet still forceful (Inizian et al. 1999).
- Bimanual role differentiation: e.g., holding a stone securely while aiming a blow at it with a hammer—the two hands perform different actions but in a complimentary way, so that they work together to achieve a single purpose (Connolly 1998; Elliott and Connolly 1984).
- Regular and sequential plan: e.g., in percussion flaking, the order of detachments is normally crucial to the final result (Inizian et al. 1999; Pelegrin 2000).

In an interesting development, a bonobo (*Pan paniscus*) named Kanzi was given a demonstration by an experienced flint knapper on how to create flakes (Schick et al. 1999; Toth et al. 1993). Bonobos have received far less research attention compared to chimpanzees, but as Savage-Rumbaugh has pointed out, they may be bipedally closer to humans in that they possess a somewhat more upright posture than chimpanzees. Tempering this view somewhat is a study that found bonobos differed only in degree of their use of bipedalism, showing more bipedality for carrying and vigilance, while chimpanzees showed more bipedality for display (Videan and McGrew 2001). This finding seems to go hand-in-hand with the preliminary view that bonobos are generally more socially accommodating; their societies are controlled by females and sex, whereas chimpanzee societies are controlled by males and political infighting. Savage-Rumbaugh had this to say about Kanzi's ability to knap stone tools:

> Kanzi makes fine Oldwan type cutting knives from a variety of stone materials. He learned to do this by observing the archeologist Dr. Nicholas Toth. Nick showed Kanzi what to do in a single encounter and after a few brief demonstrations, Kanzi began to utilize a rock

> as cutting edge. He tested different flakes for sharpness and easily chose the best one. He attempted to knap without success. But he continued to attempt what he had seen Nick do, long after Nick left. Kanzi's first flake was not produced for several months and a number of years were required before he was able to perfect his technique. Similar amounts of time have been required for some adult human subjects to become equally adept (Savage-Rumbaugh et al. 2005).

Contrary to most reports, Kanzi did progress beyond merely throwing stones to create flakes. He learned to hold the blank in one hand, and using a hammer stone in the other, knap flakes which he seemed to test with his tongue before using them to cut rope and animal hide to get at hidden food (Savage-Rumbaugh 2009).

Kanzi is an interesting case, because under the tutelage of Savage-Rumbaugh, he did not learn language or flint knapping formally. Rather, he was immersed in a *Pan-Homo* social setting from birth, where humans invested just as much time learning about bonobo culture as bonobos about humans. The basis of this "joint" society was imitation, a fundamental driver of learning (see "Imitation" below). The important feature here is that expert flint knapping requires years of practice. In a study conducted on human expert and novice flint knappers, three key technical gestures over and above others were found to differentiate the two groups: "percussion support", "position of the blank," and "angle of percussion" (Geribàs et al. 2010). We note that these three "gestures" map reasonably well (with some overlap) onto Byrne's "bimanual role differentiation," "accurate aiming of powerful blows," and "regular and sequential plan," and avail themselves to be broken down into a sequence of movements that can be measured and classified as belonging to one class or another. In a natural setting, where knappers must find their own raw material, analysis would extend to object relations: where, how and why knappers choose certain rocks.

Figure 2. The top row of flakes were collected from Olduvai Gorge by Lewis Leaky and Desmond Clark and date to approximately 1.9 mya. The bottom row were made by Kanzi and were used to cut ropes off boxes concealing food. Image copyright Pete Bostrom, 1994. Source: University of California-Berkeley and Craft Research Center Collection.

What is going on in Kanzi's mind during the knapping act? We have no insight into Kanzi's planning abilities, which on the face of it appear present. Savage-Rumbaugh pre-supplied Kanzi's materials which were collected from Olduvai Gorge, the namesake of the technological industry associated with the hominins (including *Homo*) that made them. So Kanzi's relationship to the stone materials is somewhat artificial. Nevertheless, Kanzi produced flakes with surprising similarities to those found at Olduvai Gorge (Figure 2). The evidence requires us to infer a feedback process in Kanzi's cognition, which in turn suggests the use of motor and mental imagery, where stored representations of actions (models) can be compared with incoming sense and proprioception data vis-à-vis a goal. Mental imagery have the potential to be accessed via functional imaging (Kosslyn 2005). While functional imaging research with modern humans cannot directly reveal the cognitive capacities or neural organization of extinct hominin species, it can clarify the relative demands of specific, evolutionarily significant behaviors, which in turn can be imputed into extinct species. What is striking about these studies is not which areas are activated, but which areas are not. It was expected that the prefrontal cortex, an area important in planning (i.e., required for mental models) would be activated, but this was not the case (Stout and Chaminade 2007; Stout et al. 2008). Instead, prehensive motor and visual areas were activated, with strong overlap of Broca's area (language function). The implication is for a more intimate connection between grasp and gestural communication (Arbib 2008), and allows us to speculate that stone tool use may have helped facilitate the development of articulated language.

What we can say with surety is that Kanzi is acting in accordance with the configuration of local environmental cues; i.e., being placed in an arena with plenty of stones, a food source requiring a sharp implement to access it, and past experience in flint knapping. The confluence of these elements sets in motion the appropriate behavior by triggering motor areas without involving metacognitive processes residing in prefrontal cortical areas. This view asks us to rethink what is required for complex activities. Simple technological advances in hominins may not have occurred as a result of a progression to more conscious, planned acts, but as sensorimotor routines that are triggered through environmental feedback and basic biological drives (such as hunger). Referred to as "situatedness" or "embeddedness," it is a concept that has gained increased currency in the cognitive sciences over the last decade (Lakoff and Johnson 1999). Embededness includes the idea that an organism not only changes the environment, but is changed by it in turn—a process known as "niche construction" (Odling-Smee et al. 1996). In Savage-Rumbaugh's words:

> Kanzi's own experiences in becoming an excellent knapper suggest that the changes are hewn from the fabric of engagement. Kanzi's affair with stone has changed the structure of his musculature and wiring of his brain, for it takes two hands, operating simultaneously but nonsymmetrically, to produce stone flakes. Kanzi did not change simply by watching us. He changed through the physicality of knapping (Savage-Rumbaugh et al. 2005).

If Kanzi can produce Oldowan-type stone tools, what does this say about our multi-stranded variable discontinuity model when comparing apes with humans? Are we to conclude that this strand is continuous, that there are essentially no differences between apes and humans? To answer this we will have to examine another example of primate tool use. Primatologists recently found wild chimpanzees using not one, but two tools for a specific task, and furthermore, evidence of planning—in that they often brought tools with them from a different location (Sanz and Morgan 2010). The behaviors include honey gathering, leaf sponging, and termite fishing at elevated and subterranean nests. Most previous studies of chimpanzee tool use have defined a tool by a general description of its use, rather than analyzing the actual sequence of actions involved in its use. But Sanz and Morgan found "multiple-function" tools with single tools having relationships with multiple targets and different functions in each of the many contexts they observed. This suggests a degree of behavioral sophistication and flexibility not previously associated with chimpanzees.

As evocative as these findings are, we are not yet ready to remove the discontinuity between nonhuman primate and human tool use. One factor that still separates us from them is that we don't just make more complex tools, but we also hybridize them; i.e., combine different elements to produce objects greater than the sum of their parts. At its core, the difference appears to be that apes and monkeys still live in a *subtractive* world, whereas humans also exploit *additive* technologies. Examples of primate subtractive behavior include stripping twigs off branches to make fishing tools, peeling skins of fruits, cracking nutshells to extract nuts and so forth. For example, even though orangutans display engineering-like skills in making nests, which are combined from various plant materials (van Casteren et al. 2012), the elements are not fused or permanently conjoined to produce a new or extended concept. Nut-cracking, which has been observed across a range of primate species including the wild bearded capuchin monkey (*Cebus libidinosus*) (Liu et al. 2011), also does not count. On the face of it, the use of a hammer and anvil appears to be additive. However, it is not a true conjoining of objects to produce a new or extended concept that is then *kept and maintained beyond its immediate use.* The elements, if anything, are smashed together. The conjoint moment is extremely brief and forgotten as soon as the nut is cracked open.

Mirror Self-Recognition (MSR)

While not exhaustive, the discussion on primate tool use is for the present comprehensive enough to explore the next strand: mirror self-recognition (MSR). The "mirror test," as it is known, began with a simple presentations of mirrors to chimpanzees (Gallup 1970). After observing a range of interesting reactions, the chimpanzees' responses were manipulated by placing two odorless marks on their body, one visible in the mirror, the other occluded by their body. The chimpanzees consistently reacted to the visible mark but not the occluded one. (It should be noted that the chimpanzees had to be anaesthetized in order to place the marks.) The test, now standardized across species, requires the subject to respond unambiguously to the "other" as itself, not as a threat. In humans, an additional requirement is that subjects must attempt to remove the mark. Besides chimpanzees, bonobos (Westergaard and Hyatt 1994), orangutans (Miles 1995) and some gorillas have passed the test (Patterson and Gordon 1993). Findings are by no means secure, and numerous qualifications appear in the literature. The main requirements appear to be good psychological health and enriched rearing alongside humans (Ujhelyi et al. 2000). When these two factors are taken into account, claims have also been made for primate mirror self-recognition (Heschl and Fuchsbichler 2009; Rajala et al. 2010; Ujhelyi et al. 2000).

Alongside primates, several other species appear to have MSR-like abilities: Asian elephants (*Elephas maximus*) (Plotnik et al. 2006), four marine mammals—the bottlenose dolphin (*Tursiops truncates*) (Marten and Psarakos 1995), killer whale (*Orcinus orca*), false killer whale (*Pseudorca crassidens*) and California sea lion (*Zalophus californianus*) (Delfour and Marten 2001)—and the Eurasian-African magpie (*Pica pica*) (Prior et al. 2008). In an extended analysis of human subjects undergoing the test (Asendorpf et al. 1996) it was noted that only children who correctly recognized the mark were also motivated to remove it. Removal of the mark involves motor coordination that some children may not have; but they may still recognize its presence. Accordingly, in its most truncated form the MSR test at its very minimum requires some sort of pointing to, or touching of the mark (in animals altered/unusual bodily gestures directed at the mark), but not necessarily the removal of it (Heschl and Burkart 2006). This levels the playing field between animals and humans, but admittedly makes it much harder to determine MSR abilities in animals, since they cannot verbalize their knowledge, while children may babble something to the effect that they recognize the presence of the mark.

These issues aside, what does the test reveal? It has been pointed out that MSR is not required for survivability, since many species lack it (de Waal 2008). Rather, it has been tied to social cognition (Gallup 1983). Social cognition rests on a whole gamut of factors, the most important of which is objective self-awareness. Objective self-awareness can occur unconsciously but can also regulate subjective self-awareness (Bargh 1984; Damásio 1994). The former implies bodily processes—physiological, sensorimotor, emotional, spatial—while the later implies an ability for self-reflective consciousness, a term we circumscribed earlier. When we read reports of chimpanzees inspecting body parts in mirrors previously out of range of their vision, such as teeth, tongue, lips, anogenital region, and so forth, we might be inclined to see ourselves in those actions. It looks like they have a sense of "self." After all, such actions look very human. In humans, the act of looking in the mirror prompts internal dialogue: Is that a liver spot forming there? Are those bags under my eyes? Am I getting old? And a host of other vain questions related mostly to the way we think of ourselves *in the eyes of others* (Epley and Whitchurch 2008). There is a major social component to our mirror-self investigations. Of course, sometimes there are more important reasons for using a mirror, such as when we need to find out if we are healthy: Is that mole cancerous? Is that an abscess in my mouth? Does my tongue look off-color? Great apes have been observed eating medicinal plants in the wild (Cousins and Huffman 2002; Gustafsson et al. 2011; Huffman and Wrangham 1994; Masi et al. 2011; Ohigashi et al. 1994; Wrangham and Nishida 1983) and chimpanzees have been observed to "dab" leaves on wounds, inspecting the leaves afterwards (Boesch 1995; Goodall 1986; Sanz and Morgan 2007), and performing actions such as "penis wipe" after copulation (Goodall 1986; Quiatt, 2006; Sanz and Morgan 2007; Watts 2008). These are just some examples of a whole range of personal care behaviors reported of apes in the wild that fall within the scope of objective self-awareness. In most cases they occur in association with discomfort, pain, irritation, or just plain curiosity. From this we could conclude that they possess mental representations of their own bodies, but MSR doesn't on its own prove the more elusive claim that they are also aware of those mental representations (Barth et al. 2004).

Notwithstanding, because apes and monkeys are adept at identifying conspecifics, researchers have asked whether MSR also reveals processes important for social interaction. More specifically, does it tap into mental events used for predicting intentions, even thoughts of others? The human ability to judge what others think and feel is so automatic that few question its reliability. In apes and monkeys we hesitate to impute this ability. Looking at this question leads to an entirely new field of research called theory of mind (ToM). We shall turn to it now.

Theory of Mind (ToM)

ToM refers to the stage in development when a subject becomes aware that an "other" possesses attentional behavior and that such behavior can be directed, indicating that the other is thinking about something—has knowledge of something. In that moment, the subject recognizes that, while it cannot experience what the other is thinking, it can infer from the other's behavior ideas about what the other is thinking. In this sense, the subject has developed a theory of the other's mind based on awareness of the way their *own* mind works, knowing what they do when they themselves express attentional behavior. The question is not whether apes and monkeys can predict others' behavior; they certainly can. The issue is whether this means they can also infer mental processes in the other. The following is an anecdotal example of a bonobo called Panbanisha putatively demonstrating ToM:

> Bill was fixing lunch and Panbanisha was using an old non-talking keyboard to tell him something. Bill feeling rushed and busy responded, "Panbanisha, I can't see what you're saying. Please use the talking keyboard." Panbanisha knocked on the glass and signaled for him to come over to her. As Bill approached, she held the keyboard out so Bill could see it clearly and uttered "GRAB" and then pointed to his glasses on the washing machine. The clear implication is, of course, you cannot see because you don't have your glasses on. Then Panbanisha uttered "KEYBOARD." Bill could immediately see he had not turned the keyboard on so that it would talk. (Savage-Rumbaugh et al. 2005)

This example involves the basic building blocks of the standard ToM test called "false-belief-task" (Wimmer and Perner 1983). In this task, children observed how a protagonist put an object into location X and then witnessed, in the absence of the protagonist, the object transferred from location X to a new location, Y. When asked where the protagonist would look for the object when they came back, if the answer was X, they would be correct, as they demonstrated the protagonist's belief *against* their own knowledge that the object was now at location Y. In other words, the bonobo Panbanisha appears to have a theory of Bill's mind. Up until about four years of age, most children fail this test.

Successful ToM demonstrates a subject's awareness of a boundary between themselves and others. It goes hand-in-hand with a sense of using their own knowledge as an instrument, as the subject must co-existentially hold two items of contradictory information in memory. When the subject deliberately withholds this dual knowledge from the other, it marks the birth of deception. Apes and monkeys typically engage in deception over food (Kirkpatrick 2007). For example, chimpanzees have been observed to approach a contested food item via a route hidden from human view (Hare et al. 2006); free-ranging rhesus monkeys alter their food-calling rates depending on who is around (Hauser and Marler 1993), and in a test with two experimenters, one facing towards the subject and the other with back-turned, the same species steal grapes from the back-turned experimenter (Flombaum and Santos 2005). As evocative as these findings are, they might have to be tempered by recent findings of deception behavior in the barnyard chicken (*Gallus gallus*) (Gyger and Marler 1988; Smith et al. 2011). Male domestic chickens regularly produce food-associated calls even when no food is available. Such deceptive food calling benefits the caller by attracting potential female mates to the area. While the barnyard chicken has not yet been tested for ToM, and it is doubtful they would ever pass, the fact that they employ deception deepens the mystery of how such a "simple" creature is able to employ seemingly "complex" behavior. At the very minimum, it asks us to re-evaluate the natural tendency to associate complex behavior with complex mental abilities.

The evidence to date is that chimpanzees can predict the actions of others in many situations based on past experience, but they do not go beneath the surface to an understanding of the goals, perceptions, knowledge and beliefs that guide action (Call and Tomasello 2008). Povinelli has reached this conclusion after putting his chimpanzees through a comprehensive test battery (Povinelli 2000, 2004, 2012; Povinelli and Dunphy-Lelii 2001; Povinelli and Vonk 2003; Povinelli and Vonk 2004). Two examples from his studies are representative: juvenile chimpanzees gesturally begged food from a human even when the human was blindfolded or had a bucket covering their head (Povinelli and Eddy 1996); when chimpanzees saw two humans pointing to different locations to indicate the location of a single piece of hidden food—and one of those humans had watched the original hiding process whereas the other had not—they followed the knowledgeable and ignorant humans' pointing gestures indiscriminately (Povinelli et al. 1994). These results were taken to show that chimpanzees do not draw inferences from gaze or pointing behavior. More subtle experiments later revealed that chimpanzees *can* follow directed gaze, even to locations outside their own field of view (Barth et al. 2005; Bräuer et al. 2005; Okamoto-Barth et al. 2007; Povinelli and Eddy 1996), but are not good at following pointing (Bräuer et al. 2006; Kirchhofer et al. 2012). This, however, is not the last word on "declarative communication"—Menzel's studies of an enculturated chimpanzee Panzee demonstrated robust responses to human pointing coupled with a vocalized question (Menzel 1999). Panzee watched from her outdoor enclosure while an experimenter hid two food objects in the woods at locations that varied by at least 25 degrees as measured from the indoor testing room. Panzee was then brought indoors to the testing room, where no view of the outdoor enclosure or woods was possible, and kept there for up to 30 minutes. Whereupon a caregiver, who knew the location but not the type of object, extended an arm toward the location of one of the objects (literally pointing at an opaque wall) and said, "What is out there?" Panzee touched the name of the hidden object on her lexigram keyboard, and the caregiver was able to correctly deduce the food item at the pointed location for 19 of 20 locations. These results prompted the authors to wonder why so many zoo and laboratory-raised adult chimps should perform barely better-than-chance at declarative communication tests. Environmental conditions—including spatially constrained apparatus, less-than-obvious procedures, and rearing experience—have all been cited as possible causative factors (Lyn et al. 2010).

Another issue raised was that begging food from "an experimenter that can see you" does not reflect the natural behavior of chimpanzees in the wild. Food competition rather than food sharing governs chimpanzee lives. In an alternate experimental method (Hare et al. 2000), subordinate and dominant chimps were allowed to access an arena where food had previously been hidden. The subordinate chimp could see both pieces of food, whereas the dominant chimp could only see one. Dominant chimpanzees tend to monopolize any food they see first; the only way a subordinate chimp could get some of the food was approach the hidden piece first. Therefore, the subordinate's decision about which piece to approach first should have been dictated by its understanding of what the dominant could or could not see. Experimenters released the subordinate a few seconds before the dominant to eliminate the possibility that the subordinate might only respond to the approach behavior or gaze direction of the dominant. Sure enough, the subordinates on average chose the concealed piece over the visible one and this was taken as evidence that the subordinate had a ToM of the dominant chimpanzee. Unfortunately, in a replication of the study, Povinelli found that although the subordinate chimpanzees tended to retrieve the hidden rather than the visible food, they did not selectively reach or move toward the hidden piece of food *first* (Karin-D'Arcy and Povinelli 2002). In counter-response, Tomasello's group re-jigged the experiment and found that the space where the animals competed was critical in determining the appropriate level of competition to reveal positive results (Bräuer et al. 2007). They concluded that chimpanzees do indeed take into account the perspective of the dominant competitor. Thus, chimpanzees know what others currently see, and what they saw just a few minutes before. Ironically, this should come as no surprise. Field researchers showed that chimpanzees were more likely to alarm call in response to a snake in the presence of unaware group members than in the presence of aware group members, unambiguously demonstrating they recognize knowledge and ignorance in others (Crockford et al. 2011).

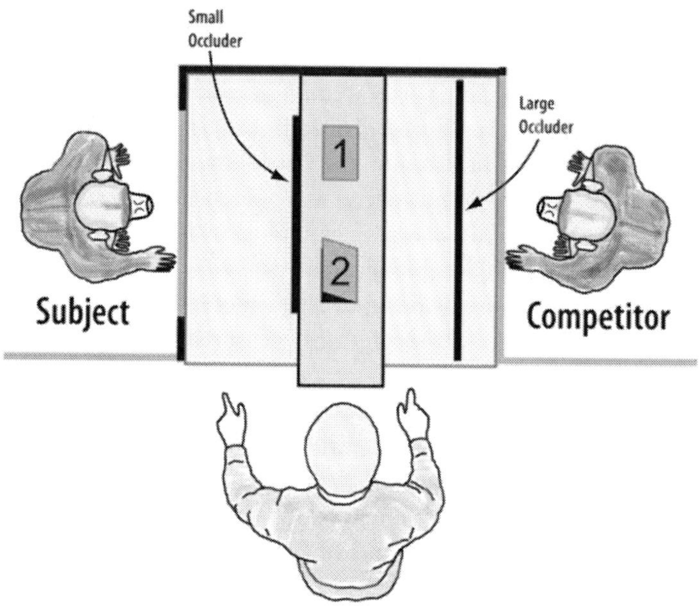

Figure 3. Schematic of the inference test. Board #1 covers a secret compartment in the table so that it lies flat, while board #2 acquires a slant when food is placed beneath it. The Subject is ignorant of whether the Competitor knew a hole was in the table. Subjects and Competitors alternatively chose "first" and "last." In the "Subject chooses last" procedure, the experimenter places food under both boards allowing the Subject to see (the siding panel is absent) while the Competitor's view is blocked by the occluder (which also prevents the Subject from seeing the Competitor). The sliding panel is then introduced on the Subject's side, the occluder is removed from the Competitor's side and positioned flush against the Subject's cage, now fully blocking the Subject's view. The table is slid over to the Competitor's side and the Competitor is allowed to choose (typically the slanted board). After receiving a reward, the Competitor's view is blocked again by the occluder and the table is slid to the Subject's side and the Subject pushes the sliding panel aside to choose a board (typically the board with the secret compartment). Adapted from (Schmelz et al. 2011). Reprinted with permission from PNAS.

In the lab Tomasello's group performed two more studies to tease out chimpanzees' putative ToM abilities. Both involved a "subject" and a "competitor." Three opaque cups randomly hid food. The subject witnessed the competitor see the experimenter hide food under one cup, but not another. Invariably, when the subject was allowed to choose first, they always chose food from the cup the competitor had no knowledge about, suggesting that chimpanzees can differentiate between knowledge and ignorance in a competitor (Kaminski et al. 2008). In the same study, however, chimps failed when tested on false belief. The experimenter switched the original cup that the competitor saw without the competitor's knowledge but in full view of the subject. The subject theoretically should have chosen the new location over the old, but did not perform above chance, sometimes still choosing the old location. The second study examined whether chimpanzees could pass the knowledge-ignorance test, not on the basis of visual or auditory perception, but on the basis of inferences alone (Schmelz et al. 2011). The methodology is best understood by referring to (Figure 3). The authors concluded that chimpanzees know that others go beyond direct perception and immediate memory to make inferences about non-perceived realities and emphatically state: "If we define thinking as going beyond the information given in perception to make inferences, we may conclude that not only is thinking not the exclusive province of human beings, but thinking about thinking is not either."

No doubt, this will not be the last word on ToM in chimpanzees. But it does give us a position from which to estimate the size of discontinuity on this strand of cognitive ability. The gap would appear to be quite small, with only a failure in the ability to perceive false belief in others separating us from them. This inability may prove to be telling. What is certain is that researchers will continue to find that apes and monkeys will perform better in problems grounded on causal compared to arbitrary relations (Schrauf and Call 2011)—which is to say, problem solving through goal-directed food acquisition related to "domain specific prior knowledge"—something we will explore in more detail in the next section.

Causal Reasoning

When we talk about causal reasoning, in a strict sense we are talking about *conscious* causal reasoning. As one investigator described it: "... controlled and effortful inferential reasoning" (Beckers et al. 2006). However, most, if not all causal reasoning occurs unconsciously, even in humans (Bechara et al. 1997; Gigerenzer 2007). This becomes even more important when talking about animals. Until such a time that we can secure incontrovertible evidence to the contrary, we must assume *a priori* that all animals perform causal reasoning at an unconscious level. To some commentators, this might seem like an unnecessary stipulation. Most scientists automatically assume animals are not consciously aware of their own mental processes. Phrases such as "situation-bound," "stuck in the here and now" are commonly applied. However, for reasons outlined in the introduction, some researchers are keen to prove that apes have awareness of their own mental acts. It would bring them fully into the human fold.

With that aside, we can state that the simplest causal reasoning involves the drawing of a phenomenological relation between two events. The statement "event A caused event B" rests on the assumption that A and B are self-contained entities, and that A came before B. The first derives from an intact self-world boundary and discrete object perception capability; the second, from the perception that time's arrow always flows in one direction. New assumptions are subsequently formed on this foundation: A is seen as *changing* B in some way, seen or unseen. Change assumes agency. Either A has been moved by an agent (seen or unseen) or A itself is an agent. The complex issue of whether B can become an agent after being changed by A will be omitted (such as an inert egg transforming into an animated object when hatching). For the present, B will be seen as a passive object/event.

Current research on causal reasoning in animals is hotly contested between three approaches: those who maintain learning can be explained in terms of associative principles (i.e., classical and instrumental conditioning) (Barberia et al. 2011), Bayesian logic (Gopnik and Tenenbaum 2007), or domain-specific prior knowledge (Penn and Povinelli 2007). Regardless of the species, humans and all animals learn relationships between events through observation and intervention. Bayesian learning theorists claim that associative learning is incapable of deriving correct predictions for interventions based on observation alone (Hagmayer et al. 2007). However, counter examples are easy to imagine. For example, observing water flowing over a partly submerged rock in a creek leads to the rock getting wet (observation). Splashing water on the rock using one's hand leads to the rock getting wet (intervention). By simple association of seeing the rock getting wet from self-propelled water, one can easily predict splashing water on one's body will make one wet. No loss in reliability of prediction occurs from observation alone. Considering the role of water in all life, we have to assume that apes and monkeys would have no problem drawing inferences about water behavior purely from observation. What this illustrates is that past experience of basic environmental elements must comprise part of the library of predictive templates for decision-making. These templates may be invariant or at least resistive to change in laboratory test conditions. Thus, domain-specific prior knowledge must play an important role in behavior.

Domain-specific prior knowledge can be said to be intuitive knowledge for it is not based on theory-driven mental processes, but a dynamic interaction between innate abilities and sensorimotor feedback learning from the internal and external environment. The interactionist formulation argues that cognitive abilities develop from the periphery inward—physical knowledge depends on internalized sensorimotor structures that arise gradually as perceptions and actions become intercoordinated (Piaget 1952). In contrast, domain-specific prior knowledge rests on highly structured innate mechanisms designed to build representations with specific content—the so-called "core knowledge" hypothesis (Spelke et al. 1992), which can be traced back at least to Helmholtz who spoke of "unconscious inferences" (Hatfield 2002; Helmholtz 1867/1910). In its modern incantation, we acknowledge that the sensorimotor system does more than enable us to move our bodies; it has precisely the right kind of structure to characterize so-called "abstract" concepts that constitute the meanings of grammatical constructions and general inference patterns (Gallese and Lakoff 2005). For example, humans can adopt motor strategies in mental rotation of non-body objects without explicit knowledge (Wraga et al. 2003). Put another way, we use our bodies as a metaphor to comprehend abstract concepts (Amorim et al. 2006). There is no reason to assume primates, who have comparable motor systems, should not process interactions in similar fashion.

To take this further, when one researcher says: "Children appear to learn about the world in much the same way that scientists do—by conducting experiments, analyzing statistics, and forming intuitive theories of the physical, biological and psychological realms" (Gopnik 2010), no one truly believes that children perform these feats based on conscious awareness of their mental representations. Children as young as 6 months old and younger understand fundamental physical relations such as solidity (Spelke et al. 1992), object permanence (Baillargeon et al. 1985), continuity, inertia (Spelke et al. 1994), size, weight, density (Smith et al. 1985), even "straight down belief" (McCloskey et al. 1983). Children also discriminate biological from non-biological motion, animate from inanimate objects (both with and without motion cues) and even perceive self-propelled inanimate objects as having goals (Carey 1985; Gelman et al. 1994; Gergerly et al. 1995; Premack and Premack 1997; Spelke et al. 1995). Perhaps most impressive of all is that children appear to perform inductive reasoning effortlessly. Take the following example of inductive reasoning (of which there are many types): there are 20 balls in a box, either white or red. To estimate their respective numbers you draw a sample of 4 balls and find that 3 are white, 1 is red. A good inductive generalization would result in a prediction of 15 white and 5 red balls in the box. Gopnik performed this test on children: 8-month old babies were shown a box full of mixed up Ping-Pong balls, where the ratio was approximately 80 percent white and 20 percent red. The experimenter would then take out 5 balls, seemingly randomly. The babies were more surprised (that is, they looked longer and more intently at the scene) if the experimenter pulled out 4 red and 1 white ball—an improbable outcome—compared to when the experimenter pulled out the opposite. From this Gopnik concluded that babies perform some sort of unconscious statistical reasoning (she believes they use Bayesian theory). A simplistic conclusion appears to be: *the brain is a kind of computer designed by evolution and programmed by experience*. We should add, *an unconscious computer*. If we are Bayesian calculators, then Gigerenzer proposes we are so only when the problem is presented to us in frequency formats, not probability formats (Gigerenzer and Hoffrage 1995). Probabilities, he points out, are a recent invention on the evolutionary scale. Frequencies, on the other hand, are built into the very fabric of existence. It should come as no surprise then that children can perform operations on reality well beyond their conscious abilities.

Nor should we be surprised that primates do too. Interestingly, a lot of work has been done on monkeys. In a simple tool-using context, cotton-top tamarins (*Saguinus oedipus*), common marmosets (*Callithrix jacchus*), vervet monkeys (*Cercopithecus aethiops*), and lemurs (*Eulemur fulvus* and *Lemur catta*) paid special attention to the size or shape of objects rather than nonfunctional properties such as color or texture (Hauser et al. 2002; Santos et al. 2005; Santos et al. 2003; Santos et al. 2006; Spaulding and Hauser 2005). In addition to this, cotton-top tamarins in particular both differentiated between functional and nonfunctional object properties in a particular setting and also successfully transferred only functionally relevant information to a novel context while ignoring perceptual features that were irrelevant to the solution (Hauser et al. 1999). Like infants tested on expectancy violations using toys (Berthier et al. 2000; Hood et al. 2000), rhesus macaques (*Macaca mulatta*) look longer when an apple appeared to fall through a solid shelf or roll through a solid barrier, but do not use this knowledge when searching for the apple (Santos and Hauser 2002). Referred to as "a dissociation between seeing and acting," monkeys and infants do not take into account the principle of solidity when reaching for objects despite appearing to show observational understanding of solidity in physics violation tests (i.e., after looking longer at anomalous events compared to normal events). Similarly, children (2 years of age) and monkeys over-generalized the prediction that falling objects travel in a straight line in spite of extensive counter-evidence that the object's path had been deviated by an opaque tube to an anomalous location (Hood et al. 2000; Hood et al. 1999). Tamarins tested for reaction to objects appearing in novel locations (the objects were moved while occluded) expressed surprise for all objects except a live mouse, tree frog, and perhaps furry toy mouse (Hauser 1998a), suggesting an ability to differentiate animate from inanimate objects. These studies suggest that infants and monkeys share many "core knowledge" capacities.

Apes are thought to exhibit the highest degree of behavioral flexibility amongst primates (Westergaard 1999), but in a series of comprehensive tests similar to those performed on monkeys showed only marginally greater sophistication of cognitive abilities. These included the trap-tube, trap-table, inverted- and broken-rake, flimsy tool, tool-insertion, rope, hook, touching-stick, cloth support, bendable-tool, tool construction, and tool modification tests (Povinelli, 2000). Each one of these required multiple trials, some of them upwards of 140 before even a single ape succeeded in passing them. As with most tests, numerous methodological flaws have been identified (Call and Tomasello 2005; Girndt et al. 2008; Horner and Whiten 2007; Machado and Silva 2003; Manrique et al. 2010; Martin-Ordas et al. 2008; Mulcahy and Call 2006b; Mulcahy et al. 2005; Silva et al. 2005). However, viewed as a test battery, the pattern of result suggests that while apes have the flexibility to solve a range of problems related to food acquisition, at a deeper level they appear to consistently overlook *unobservable causal mechanisms* (Povinelli 2012). The trap tube test (Figure 4) is emblematic because it highlights both the challenges apes face when confronted with laboratory tests and the potential methodological flaws that can mar a good experiment. The fundamental physical force at stake is gravity, with causal relationships between pushing and retrieving involved. Animals are first trained with a trap-less tube, then a trap is added. There are two conditions: normal and inverted. In the normal condition the trap is facing down so that food falls into it if pushed the wrong way. In the inverted condition, the trap faces up so that it makes no difference which way the food is pushed (basically a trick condition). Both apes and monkeys, on average, transferred the same method they used in the normal condition to the inverted condition. From this it was concluded that apes and monkeys failed to understand the force of gravity. Critics of the method claim that because the specific behavior that would reveal the animal's failure to understand gravity was never formally operationalized—merely inferred *ad hoc* after failure on the test—any claim of a definition of gravity is rendered meaningless. Ethologically, arboreal creatures tempt gravity on a daily basis, swinging from branch to branch, and no doubt they learn the effects of gravity quickly through falls. Considering this, it is surprising that only one visual cliff experiment (Gibson and Walk 1960) has been conducted on monkeys (Rosenblum and Cross 1963), and none yet on any apes. It would seem like an obvious gravity test—or with some inventiveness, a variation that involved accessing food across an elevated span with some depth cues added beneath.

Unsurprisingly, criticisms of the casual relations between pushing and retrieving food in the trap tube have led to variations in its design—this is because except for termite fishing, chimpanzees generally pull and poke things, not push. In one variant, the trap was placed asymmetrically (to one side of the tube) and the reward was placed in the center. This was done in an effort to control for animals' biases for always pushing the food only from one side once they learned the task (Limongelli et al. 1995). However, the experimenters failed to test the inverted condition, so their findings cannot be compared. In another variant, the pushing tool was removed and a slot was created for animals to push food with their fingers. Traps were arranged in various configurations and the authors concluded that without the confounding variable of the pushing tool, their chimpanzees did indeed encode information about the functional properties of the apparatus (Seed et al. 2009). Obviously, you can get different results using different apparatus. Very few laboratories actually perform perfect replications, so results generally can only be interpreted relative to the laboratory's specific set of circumstances (including background history of the animals, which vary considerably between labs). What can be said in favor of Povinelli's work is that he applied a comprehensive test battery, which provides some protection against methodological error variance through sheer number and variety of tests. If apes continue to show similar patterns across all tests, one is forced to conclude that their specific set of adaptive skills differs from ours, and once again we err on the side of caution and invoke a discontinuity on this cognitive strand.

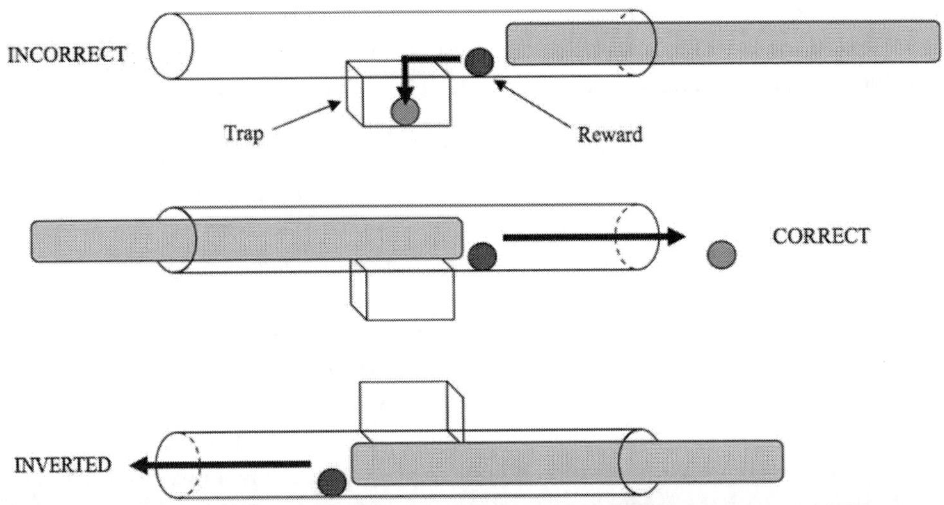

Figure 4. The original trap tube design used by (Visalberghi and Limongelli 1994) adapted from previous tube paradigms introduced by (Ladygina-Kohts and Dembovskii 1969; Lethmate 1977, 1979; Yerkes 1943). Animals are first trained to retrieve food from a cylinder without a trap. Top: Insertion of the tool into the side nearest the reward results in the reward being pushed into the trap. Bottom: Insertion of the tool into the side farthest from the reward results in the food being pushed away from the trap and retrieved. Inverted: pushing the food from either direction makes no difference; the food cannot drop into the trap. Adapted from (Horner and Whiten 2007). Reprinted with permission from APA.

Imitation

The comparative primate literature largely differentiates between imitation and emulation, but also deals with mimicking, and to a lesser extent, mimesis. In behavioral psychology, to mimic means to copy another's behavior, in the sense of mirroring or reflecting. It is primarily a functional behavior in that it serves to facilitate affiliation, and generally operates at an unconscious, instinctive level (van Baaren et al. 2003) while remaining ignorant of the goals or intentions of the model (Zentall 2006). Emulation is invoked when an animal copies the causal structure and results of the model's actions but then uses its own, different set of actions to accomplish the task (Horner and Whiten 2005; Tomasello and Call 1997; Whiten and Ham 1992). For example, one animal may poke an ant nest with a stick to attract ants, while another may pound it. In contrast to this, imitation has been defined by some as the copying of actions and goals of a model without understanding the underlying causal structure of the actions (Carpenter and Call 2002; Tomasello and Call 1997). This is equivalent to pounding the ant nest to attract ants (not in identical fashion, but in one's own style) and doing it not because there is an understanding that pounding causes ants to appear, but because the model did it and succeeded and therefore set a precedent. Mimesis is a specialized word and is reserved for the "invention of intentional representations" (Donald 1991: 169) and accordingly is only applied to hominins.

The debate whether imitation in humans is innate or learned has a long history (Miller and Dollard 1941; Morgan 1896; Piaget 1962; Skinner 1953). Research into neonate responses to adults' facial expressions in the 1970s suggested it was innate (Meltzoff and Moore 1977) and gave rise to the notion of a "body schema" as a way of explaining it (Meltzoff and Moore 1997). Infants' own facial movements are invisible to them, but are not unperceived by them. Infants monitor their unseen facial acts through proprioception. Infants store a representation of the adult's act and subsequently compare their own acts to this internal model. This representation also allows them to correct their imitative movements to more faithfully match the target they see, which infants do when the adult model demonstrates novel actions such as tongue-protrusion-to-the-side (Meltzoff and Moore 1994). The process has been encapsulated as "active intermodal mapping" (AIM). Infants match-to-target via a "supramodel" representation, where imitation, perception and action are coupled by a direct perceptual-motor mapping. While replications of Meltzoff and Moore's work have met with some failures, their model nevertheless has proven quite influential (Wohlschläger et al. 2003). A large number of human imaging studies now indicate bi-directional links between perception and action: visual processing can automatically induce related motor processes, and motor actions can direct future visual processing (Vogt and Thomaschke 2007). Moreover, the AIM model has recently received a boost from the discovery of mirror neurons in the macaque inferior frontal gyrus (region F5) and inferior parietal lobule—so called because neurons in these regions "fire" both during observation and during execution of particular actions (di Pellegrino et al. 1992; Gallese et al. 1996). Claims that humans possess mirror neurons have been made (Iacoboni et al. 1999), but others maintain that a homologous system in humans has yet to be robustly demonstrated (Lingnau et al. 2009; Turella et al. 2009). Single cell recordings in humans have the ability to provide conclusive evidence, but so far only one study has succeeded (Mukamel et al. 2010). Therefore more work is needed to properly establish not just the existence of, but the homology of the human mirror neuron system with apes and monkeys.

The imitation-emulation distinction has provided leverage for researchers investigating social learning in apes. The challenge is devising tests that tease out the differences. One approach is the "two-action" method, where two visibly different techniques result in an identical outcome (Dawson and Foss 1965). The expectation is that by showing two mutually exclusive groups only one or the other method—so long as the individuals of each group remain conformist in their social transmission of the technique—divergent cultures should logically ensue. Primatologist devised the "artificial fruit task" (Whiten et al. 1996)—so named because it comprised a small plastic box containing a food reward held shut by a hinged lid fixed with two latches—an analog of a nut in a shell. The rationale for the design was based on imitative-like behaviors that had been reported in wild primates during foraging and/or cleaning food (Kawai 1965; Marshall-Pescini and Whiten 2008b). Basically a puzzle box, the hinged lid is held closed by two bolts and a T-shaped pin. The bolts could be poked free either inwardly, or pulled or twisted out (a two action technique), while the T-shaped pin could be either rotated or lifted out altogether (also a two action technique), allowing the hinged lid to open. In the original test, children (aged 2–4) and young chimpanzees (mean age 4.5 years) were exposed to a human demonstrator performing only one of the two techniques on each of the latches, and were then presented with the artificial fruit themselves. This permitted subsequent imitation by subjects to be distinguished from emulation; i.e., if an idiosyncratic technique was used, it suggested the subject's attentional resources were focused more on the task goal, not the technique, whereas if the subjects slavishly adhered to the instructed technique, they were focused more on imitating the action—while neither method will have accessed the underlying causal structure of the task. The researchers found that chimpanzees imitated the least faithfully while children imitated more faithfully, and did so with greater fidelity as their age increased. Notwithstanding, chimpanzees did weakly imitate actions demonstrated for the bolts: those who had seen twisting produced more twisting-like actions, while those who had seen poking produced more poking-like actions, suggesting that chimpanzees are capable of imitation, although their default mode is emulation.

More evidence for chimpanzee emulation comes from another puzzle box experiment, this time involving both causally relevant and irrelevant actions (Horner and Whiten 2005). A food reward was placed at the bottom of a box, and could only be pulled out by inserting an aluminum tool through a small trap door (causally relevant condition). Actions directed to the top of the box had no impact on retrieving the reward (causally irrelevant condition). The box was presented in two conditions: opaque and clear. In the opaque condition, causal information about the effect of the tool inside the box was not available, and hence it was impossible to differentiate between the relevant and irrelevant parts of the demonstration. However, in the clear condition causal information was available, and subjects could potentially determine which actions were necessary. When chimpanzees were presented with the opaque box, they reproduced both the relevant and irrelevant actions, thus imitating the overall structure of the task. When the box was presented in the clear condition they ignored the irrelevant actions in favor of a more efficient, emulative technique. In contrast to chimpanzees, children employed imitation to solve the task in both conditions, at the expense of efficiency, that is, they slavishly imitated both the relevant *and* irrelevant actions. The results were interpreted as follows: emulation is the favored strategy of chimpanzees when sufficient causal information is available. However, if such information is not available, chimpanzees are prone to employ a more comprehensive copy of an observed action. A similar conclusion, of switching from imitation to emulation depending on the level of acquired information, was echoed in a controlled experiment examining chimpanzee nut-cracking behavior (Marshall-Pescini and Whiten 2008b). As for the puzzling arbitrary copying behavior of children, researchers have dubbed it "overimitation" (Flynn and Whiten 2010; Lyons et al. 2007; McGuigan et al. 2011; Nielsen and Tomaselli 2010; Whiten et al. 2009). A flurry of research has been carried out on this phenomenon because it is thought to be peculiar to humans and as such might reflect on the social transmission of human culture. Hypothetical mechanisms have been divided into three categories: social, causal, and sensorimotor; for a review see (Kenward 2012). Neither mechanism on its own has been able to explain the phenomenon, suggesting that overimitation is not driven by a unitary process, although recent research suggests that the explanation may lie in the causal domain. In one experimental paradigm where the aim was to actually prevent children from overimitating, the demonstrator pretended to get a call from his mother on his cell phone and "accidentally" flipped a useless lever on a puzzle box while gesturing during the supposed conversation (Lyons et al. 2011). In this case, the children did not include the useless lever, suggesting they do not overimitate to please adults. Rather, it appears that "automatic causal encoding" (ACE) underlies the process, where children assume adults "know better;" i.e., know what they are doing and that each step of the procedure is necessary.

From the preceding evidence, the question is no longer whether chimpanzees can imitate, but what factors other than causal transparency affect their behavior during social transmission. One recently observed factor has been "prestige" (Horner et al. 2010). When given opportunities to watch alternative solutions to a foraging problem performed by two different conspecific models, chimpanzees preferentially copied the method shown by the older, higher-ranking individual with a prior track-record of success. The researchers noted that wild chimpanzees are generally conservative innovators. Even when new behaviors arise, they remain highly conserved (Hrubesch et al. 2009; Whiten et al. 2005) and rarely become established long-term (Nishida et al. 2009). Other evidence suggests that the majority of chimpanzee innovations are performed by low-ranking individuals, most likely as a means of circumventing competition from dominant group mates (Reader and Laland 2001). Naturally, young, low ranking individuals may rise to dominance, so their behaviors may become models for the next generation. A discussion of primate innovation would not be complete without mentioning the famous Japanese macaques of Koshima island that have learned to wash sweet potatoes before consumption (Kawai 1965). We will never know the true circumstances of how the behavior spread, but it almost certainly began as a result of incidental feeding by researchers to gain proximity to the animals for study. Thus, in order to habituate the shy macaques to their presence, the primatologists provisioned them with sweet potatoes, dropping them on the sandy beach. One day, in 1952, an 18-month-old female macaque, whom the researchers had named Imo, carried a sandy potato into the sea shallows and washed it. She taught this trick to her mother. Her playmates subsequently learned the technique and they taught it to their mothers. Before long, the behavior spread, and by 1958 all the young monkeys on the island had joined in on the act. Apart from this striking example, the imitation of innovative behavior in the wild monkeys (and apes) is considered a rare event.

Somewhat conservatively, imitation of non-innovative behaviors in monkeys has also been thought to be rare, even non-existent. Laboratory research, however, is starting to overturn this view (Bugnyar and Huber 1997; Custance et al. 2006; Dindo et al. 2010; Falcone et al. 2012; Subiaul et al. 2004; Voelkl and Huber 2000). Importantly, strong conformity in imitation is observed in chimpanzees when conspecifics are used as model demonstrators (Hopper et al. 2008), but this has not been found in monkeys (Custance et al. 2006), showing that researchers must take into account ethological factors when designing their experiments. The picture that is emerging is that primates are capable of imitation, although it cannot be said to be "pure", and depends on available contextual information, skill level, social hierarchy, arbitrariness, motivation, animal life history, and ethological experimental design factors, among others. When taken into account, the gap between ape, human and other primate imitation blurs. That being said, one significant remaining difference appears to be that humans have a greater ability to read intentions into others' behavior (Blakemore and Decety 2001; Tomasello and Carpenter 2005) and seek out affiliation to a much greater degree than apes and monkeys (Meltzoff 2005; Parker-Rees

2007). Arguably, the ability to read intentionality in another's behavior when observing a technique allows for the learner to acquire non-contextual skills that could play an important role in the subsequent transferal of the skill to an analogous task. Thus, even though human imitation may be more pure than apes', the ability to infer intentions may ultimately afford humans with a greater sense of sharing the learning experience. This additional factor, as we shall see, plays a key role in intentional teaching.

Pedagogy

Pedagogy, the teaching of one individual by another, appears to be an activity largely confined to humans. Premack and Premack have baited the current zeitgeist in an article entitled: "Why animals have neither culture nor history" (Premack and Premack 1994). Despite the fact that we share between 95–98.5% of our genes with chimpanzees and gorillas (Britten 2002; Fujiyama et al. 2002; Gagneux and Varki 2001; Hughes et al. 2010; Scally et al. 2012), they warn us that "a human being is not a chimpanzee to which language has been added." They cogently argue that if chimpanzees possess pedagogy, which they define as intentional feedback to a student *for the benefit of the student*, they do it not for the benefit of the student, but for themselves. They give a detailed account of a chimpanzee social exchange in which a dominant female taught a submissive female to place its arm around her (the dominant female's) shoulders. The training occurred over a period of two hours. Importantly, the training was carried out not for the benefit of the student, but the trainer. This seems to fit the general pattern of chimpanzee behavior, which is highly competitive and self-oriented; for a review see (Mitani 2009). Of course, we cannot rule out long-term effects of such behavioral modification. Chimpanzees have dominance hierarchies which play an important role in maintaining group harmony (de Waal 1992; Mitani 2009). It is not beyond the bounds of possibility that in training a student to behave submissively, even if for self-benefit, such behavior in the long run may serve to promote group harmony. In the Premackian example, the submissive female initially ran off whenever the dominant female approached. Therefore, the dominant female first had to teach the student to stay still and stay calm. In cognitive behavioral psychology, this is referred to as habituation (Smith 1992; Thompson 2009). We might be tempted to conclude that this is evidence of animals acting like behaviorists among themselves, but we would be wrong (Fletcher and Carruthers 2012). Dominance hierarchies in primates is intimately linked to reproduction (Townsend et al. 2008). A careless commentator might write: "The female chimpanzee envisages her future reproductive potential and accordingly moves to secure it." A very human-like response. However, there is a more parsimonious explanation: the female's behavior is triggered by endogenous hormones that are in turn governed by maturational and social factors. Behavioral data—for a review see (Cowlishaw and Dunbar 1991)—and a growing body of data on genetics, for example (Altmann et al. 1996; De Ruiter et al. 1994), support the argument that fostering and maintaining dominance hierarchies, if successful, can yield reproductive payoffs. The dominant female, therefore, wasn't acting like a behaviorist. Rather, her behavior was instinctive.

While intentional feedback training for the benefit of the student is all but absent in other primates, the observation of extensive trial-and-error social learning in chimpanzees has led one researcher to label such learning "education by master-apprenticeship" (Matsuzawa

2002). Young chimpanzees learn skills by carefully observing the behavior of adults for a long time after birth. Learning is a one-way process: adult chimpanzees seldom observe the behavior of the younger members of the community. Evidence for this kind of teaching in the wild is limited to a handful of examples, all involving foraging behaviors of mothers with their infants (Boesch 1991; Greenfield et al. 2000). While not definitive, mother chimpanzees were observed making exaggerated movements while cracking nuts when in the presence of their infants. More recently, observations of mother and infant chimpanzees with respect to termite fishing revealed that the amount of time mothers spent alone or with maternal family members (which is highly correlated with time spent on termite fishing) was related to their offspring's skill at specific components of termite fishing, suggesting that the young animals were, indeed, learning these skills from their mothers (Lonsdorf 2006). However, there was no evidence of active facilitation of the offsprings' actions by the mothers, suggesting that teaching, though possibly practiced by some mothers, is not the primary means by which young chimpanzees learn foraging skills. In an interesting mammalian species comparison, adult wild meerkats (*Suricata suricatta*) were found to teach pups prey-handling skills by providing them with opportunities to interact with live prey (Thornton and McAuliffe 2006). In response to changes in pup begging calls, helpers alter their prey-provisioning methods as pups grow older, thus accelerating learning without the use of complex cognition. The main reason why teaching evolved in meerkats is that young pups very rarely catch difficult prey items themselves. Part of their diet consists of foods such as insect larvae and pupae which are easy to handle. But in order for young pups to survive it is essential that they learn how to handle difficult prey items like scorpions and lizards, a food source high in nutritional value and necessary for survival in the harsh conditions of their environment. Thus, behavioral variability is explained by niche demands but due to the comparative cognitive capacity of this species, should be viewed as an ultimate mechanism.

Figure 5. A left-to-right sequence of video frames showing a young chimpanzee imitating the arm-action of a nut-cracking adult. In frame one, the young chimpanzees' arm follows upward with a slight delay; in frame two, the arm follows downward with a slight delay; in frame three, the arm is simulating the striking action of the adult. This is an example of how chimpanzees learn the components of a more complex behavioral sequences through iterative imitation. Note the asymmetry of arm laterality suggesting mirroring. Adapted from (Marshall-Pescini and Whiten 2008b). Reprinted with permission from APA.

Regardless of the paucity of evidence for intentional teaching in chimpanzees, what is certain is they do not enter life fully equipped to deal with life's challenges, unlike most other species. Like humans, they depend on their mothers to nurture them until they have learned how to forage for themselves, form alliances, and protect themselves from environmental dangers. When it comes to learning how to use tools, young apes attend to the activities of others around them (Figure 5), closely observing numerous details, and in a graded progression spontaneously combine certain objects that resemble what they have just observed (Hauser 2000; Matsuzawa 1996; Matsuzawa and Yamakoshi 1996; Parker 1996). In one case, an older role model has been observed to intervene and demonstrate a correct technique to a juvenile, a behavior suggestive of intentional teaching (Goodall 2011). This pattern of evidence pushes us to reduce the size of discontinuity on this strand of cognitive abilities, but does not allow us to fully close the gap. The reason for this is that in order to attribute intentional teaching to chimpanzees we must also find evidence of cooperative teaching, which in humans produces a culture of accumulation. Humans don't just teach one-on-one, but in groups—a behavior derived from our ability to cooperate. What degree of cooperative behavior, therefore, can we expect to find in apes, and other primate species?

Cooperation

When the first reports of meat-eating chimpanzees came out of the jungle (Goodall 1963), commentators were too surprised to consider that cooperative hunting might play an important role in the behavior (Goodall 1986). Since then, field studies on chimpanzees have unearthed a wealth of data on chimpanzee social lives. Currently, much more is known about wild male chimpanzees than wild female chimpanzees. Females are relatively asocial while males tend to be more gregarious and therefore lend themselves better for study (Mitani 2009). Consequently, it is now well established that male chimpanzees jointly patrol their territories, hunt collectively, share meat, groom one another, form coalitions in aggressive intragroup encounters, and cooperate in mate guarding (Goodall 1986; Muller and Mitani 2002). These behaviors occur within the context of "fission-fusion" communities—groups that vary considerably in size, ranging from 20–50 individuals (Boesch and Boesch-Achermann 2000; Goodall 1986; Nishida 1968; Nishida et al. 2003; Sugiyama 2004). Within communities, chimpanzees form temporary subgroups or parties that fluctuate in size, composition, and duration. Parties include 4–10 individuals on average, and usually contain more males than females (Boesch 1996; Chapman et al. 1995; Matsumoto-Oda et al. 1998; Mitani et al. 2002; Newton-Fisher et al. 2000; Sakura 1994; Wrangham 2000). Membership in chimpanzee communities is open due to dispersal. Female chimpanzees, typically, but not always, disperse from their natal groups after reaching sexual maturity at an age of about 11 years (Boesch and Boesch-Achermann 2000; Nishida et al. 2003; Sugiyama 2004; Williams et al. 2002). In contrast, males are philopatric and remain on their natal territories for life. Except for some minor differences, bonobos follow a similar pattern (Hohmann and Fruth 2002; Stanford 1998; White 1996).

The term cooperation has been used to indicate joint activities that involve active coordination between conspecifics who understand something about the role of others in the interaction; this stands in contrast to "similarity and synchrony" cooperation where simultaneous actions are directed towards the same goal, but without coordination or understanding of how others' actions relate to one's own actions and potential success (Boesch and Boesch 1989). Closer study of the behavior revealed that the style of cooperative hunting varied between different chimpanzee communities (Boesch 1994; Boesch and

Boesch-Achermann 2000; Gilby et al. 2006; Gilby et al. 2008; Gilby 2006; Goodall 1986; Mitani and Watts 1999; Nishida et al. 1992; Nishida et al. 1983; Takahata et al. 1984; Uehara et al. 1992; Watts and Mitani 2002) even though all groups predominantly hunted troops of red colobus monkeys (genus *Procolobus*) (Boesch 2002). Taï and Ngogo chimpanzees were observed to hunt mostly in groups, while Gombe and Mahale chimpanzees hunted primarily as solitary individuals. The level of coordination between hunters also differed, where Gombe and Mahale male chimpanzees hunted at the same time but independent of one another, while Taï male chimpanzees coordinated their actions by predominantly performing different but complementary roles (the Ngogo chimpanzees live in a much larger community and up to 25 males can hunt at the same time, making it difficult to determine the level of coordination between hunters). What drove these differences? Researchers discovered that tree height and density were primary factors, with red colobus response to predation a secondary contributor, so that at Gombe, for example, tree height varied between 8–15 m and red colobus fearlessly defended their positions resulting in quick capture by chimpanzees, whereas at Taï tree heights ranged from 45–55 m and red colobus there are fearful of chimpanzees and climb up high to thin branches that chimpanzees cannot reach which necessitates specialist roles such as "driver" "blocker", "chaser" and "ambusher" to bring them down, suggesting that individuals react opportunistically to the present situation while taking in account the shared goal of the "team" (Boesch 2005).

The savanna hypothesis—for a review see (Potts 1998)—is generally considered a plausible selective mechanism that drove hominins to bipedalism and cooperative behavior, but the Gombe chimpanzees challenge this account. The forest, actually, has its own pressures. For example, gaining visibility of predators and prey on the savanna can be achieved by standing momentarily upright or climbing a tree, whereas this problem is not easily solvable in the dense tropical forest. In forest, social animals are forced to rely on acoustics rather than visual means for group cohesion, group movements, and sometimes for recognition of individuals (Boesch and Boesch 1989). Gombe chimpanzees were also observed to generally only hunt for meat when other foods were in plentiful supply (Mitani and Watts 2001). From a cost-benefit perspective, this makes sense, since hunting is an energy-demanding activity. One group of chimpanzees may be instructive in helping us differentiate forest and savanna impacts on evolution: the Fongoli community in southeastern Sénégal (Pruetz 2006). Inevitably, because of the hot, dry conditions that these chimpanzees live in, they prefer small patches of closed-canopy habitats, such as gallery forest, where they can minimize energy expenditure during the hottest time of day by resting more and traveling less. Uniquely, in the dry season, they use caves as shelters (Pruetz 2007) and forage at night during maximal phases of the moon. In the rainy season, they soak in pools of water. They also exploit protein sources, such as prosimian primates—which chimpanzees at more forested sites ignore—and use tools to hunt these animals (Pruetz and Bertolani 2007). Interestingly, they maintain the largest party sizes of any other wild chimpanzee community; water availability was determined to be the direct cause of this behavior. Given the need to rest during the hottest part of the day, one wonders how this tallies up with another important theory directly related to the savanna hypothesis: "persistence hunting" (Bramble and Lieberman 2004; Carrier 1984). Persistence hunting describes the tracking of prey species over long distances and durations until the animal is exhausted, whereupon killing can be achieved relatively risk-free. The fact that Gombe chimpanzees generally only hunt monkeys when food is plentiful and Fongoli chimpanzees forage during the cooler part of the day suggests that energy conservation is a primary factor in food acquisition. The savanna, if anything, would have pushed hominins to further economize energy expenditure, and this may have been one selective pressure that drove biology, such as thermoregulation (e.g., hair loss) (Ruxton and Wilkinson 2011; Sutou 2012) and cultural innovation (e.g., projectile weapon development).

Another cooperative behavior observed in chimpanzees is meat sharing. With regard to the Taï chimpanzees, those that participated in anticipating prey movement, ambushed it and captured it, received the greatest share of the spoils (Boesch 2002). Thus, certain roles during the hunt were valued more highly by group members than others, and those who performed these roles were allowed access to more meat. This indicates that group members monitor what other individuals are doing during a hunt and can assess the contribution of each hunter. The fieldwork data are supported by recent laboratory tests showing chimpanzees recognize when they need help in solving a problem and to actively recruit good over bad collaborators (Melis et al. 2006a). Using the "baited food platform" paradigm (Hirata and Fuwa 2007), chimpanzees were able to inhibit going for food directly and recruit the more effective of two partners on the basis of their experience with them on a previous day (Figure 6). On that previous day, they were exposed to two conditions: trials where it was possible to retrieve the food alone, and trials where it was impossible to retrieve the food without help. When they could retrieve the food alone, they did so, choosing not to release a partner from an adjacent room. These results reinforce the general pattern of chimpanzee behavior showing they are highly adaptable but that adaptability is foremost pressed into the service of egocentric goals.

In an interesting twist on the baited food platform paradigm, chimpanzees were pitted against bonobos (Hare et al. 2007). Unsurprisingly, bonobos showed greater tolerance of co-feeding when food was placed in a single dish in the middle of the platform and could not be monopolized. In a further study, bonobo test subjects placed in a room with food let in a locked-out conspecific to share food with them, rather than eat it all by themselves (Hare and Kwetuenda 2010). Captive brown capuchins (*Cebus apella*) have also demonstrated paired cooperative behavior in a similar baited platform pulling task (Mendres and de Waal 2000), suggesting that cooperation is not limited to apes, while reinforcing the importance of task type in revealing cooperative behavior, as others in the past have failed to find cooperation in capuchins using a different experimental design (Chalmeau et al. 1997). In the design which failed to show cooperation, both animals could access the reward once it was pulled within reach, which allowed for the monopolization of food by dominant animals. This may have reduced cooperative motivation of some individuals. Furthermore, because the food release was electronically mediated, the task may not have been intuitively understandable to the monkeys. Thus, once again, depending on the experimental configuration, apes and monkeys can be shown to be less cooperative: (Brosnan et al. 2009; Jensen et al. 2006; Silk et al. 2005; Vonk et al. 2008; Yamamoto and Tanaka 2009a, 2009b); or more cooperative: (Barnes et al. 2008; Bovet and Vauclair 2000; Burkart et al. 2007; de Waal et al. 2008; Hattori et al. 2012; Hauser et al. 2003; Hockings et al. 2007; Horner et al. 2011; Lakshminarayanan and Santos 2008; Melis et al. 2006b, 2009; Melis, Schneider et al. 2011; Melis, Warneken et al. 2011; Warneken et al. 2007; Yamamoto et al. 2009; Yamamoto et al. 2012).

Clearly, much work still needs to be done on ape and monkey cooperative behavior research before the degree of discontinuity between them and us can be drawn into sharper focus. Of all the papers reviewed for this section, perhaps the Melis, Hare and Tomasello 2006 paper entitled "Engineering cooperation in chimpanzees: tolerance constraints on cooperation" best sums it up. In that paper, the authors conclude that chimpanzees are capable of spontaneous cooperation in a novel instrumental task, but tolerance acts as a constraint on their problem solving abilities. Chimpanzee pairs that shared food more freely outside the test performed better on the cooperative task in the test than pairs that didn't share previously. In other words, matching up established socially tolerant pairs enhances outcomes in cooperative tests. Similarly, in another study, chimpanzees were better at deducing the location of hidden food when its location was gesturally revealed by a competitor as opposed to a cooperative partner, suggesting that shifting chimpanzees toward situations of unwanted tolerance might actually inhibit their cooperative abilities (Herrmann and Tomasello 2006). Which reveals a subtle but important potential discontinuity on this strand of cognitive abilities. Apes and monkeys may show cooperative behavior under the right conditions, but humans possess a degree of social tolerance that these two species may not possess. One wonders, then, what would happen if apes and monkeys had the kind of articulate language that humans have. Could language have facilitated social tolerance? Robin Dunbar seems to think so and has posited a social grooming hypothesis to explain it (Dunbar 2003). After all, language plays such an all-pervading role in how we come to understand one another that we almost take it for granted. Of course, we can form deep connections through purely non-linguistic interactions, but when it comes to sharing, and a host of other social challenges, it seems more likely that without language relationships we would rely on physical displays and brute strength, neither of which are conducive to smooth social relations, especially when it comes to competing over resources.

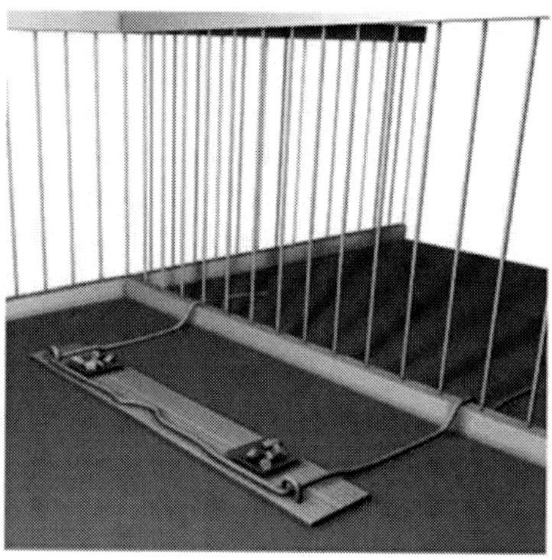

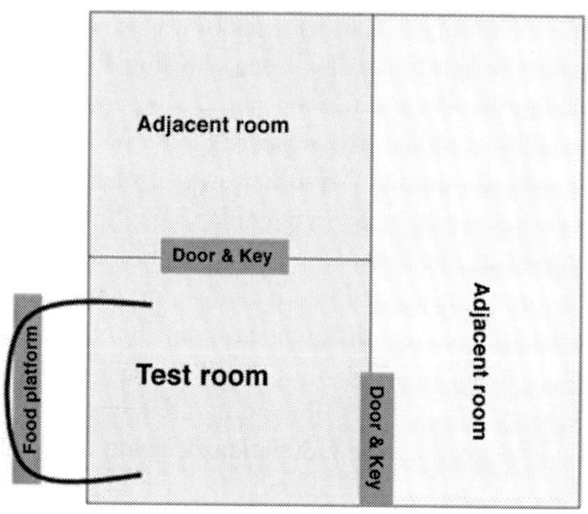

Figure 6. The baited food platform: pulling one end of the rope alone will result in the rope threading through the steel hoops leaving the platform standing where it is leaving the food out of reach. In experiment 1, the subject was released from an adjacent room into the testing room, while the partner was "locked" in another adjacent room that only the subject could open with a key (a wooden peg) from inside the testing room. In experiment 2, the subject was released directly *into* the test room from a third adjacent room not represented here, while two potential partners were each locked in one of two adjacent rooms that the subject could again open with a key. From (Melis et al. 2006a). Reprinted with permission from AAAS.

Language

Studies of wild ape and monkey vocalizations has reached the point where researchers are confident that these species possess greater subtlety of communication than once thought. Thus, adult vervet monkeys differentially produce alarm calls for leopards (*Panthera pardus*), martial eagles (*Polemaetus bellicosus*), and pythons (*Python sebae*) (Seyfarth et al. 1980), rhesus monkeys produce and respond to two functionally different categories of calls based on whether they find high-quality, rare food items, or whether they find low-quality, common food items (Hauser 1998b), and tufted capuchins alter the latency to call as a function of the proximity of other group members (Di Bitetti 2005). In a related study, captive brown capuchins have been observed to call more for larger audiences containing kin (Pollick et al. 2005). Wild chimpanzees, likewise, produce "rough grunts" that vary in acoustic quality depending on whether they find high- or low-quality food items (Slocombe and Zuberbühler 2006). A recent study of alarm calls in free-ranging adult Campbell's monkeys (*Cercopithecus campbelli campbelli*) has demonstrated that this species utilized the same call stems and added a simple suffix rule to modify the call for less specific events (e.g., hok → hok-oo; krak → krak-oo) (Ouattara et al. 2009). Despite these findings, the prevailing hypothesis is that apes and monkeys do not emit such calls intentionally; rather, they are triggered by concrete events occurring in the present that are directly visible or visible through the reactions of conspecifics. This fact becomes more acute when we take into consideration the human ability for displacement (Hockett 1960). Displacement refers to the ability to communicate about things that are not immediately spatially or temporally present. While animals do have the ability to remember food locations spatially and temporally removed from their present circumstances (Menzel 1999), this ability may have more to do with evolved sensitivity to the demands of foraging than manipulation of abstract concepts completely divorced from sensory data.

Language, of course, is not strictly limited to vocalizations; gestures also play an important role. In chimpanzees, a large number of these have now been documented (Nishida et al. 2010). Moreover, in chimpanzees, gestural communication has been found to be far more flexible than its vocal counterpart, and this has led to some attempts at enculturating apes using a system of gestural signs, computer lexigrams, and plastic tokens (Fouts 1973; Gardner and Gardner 1969; Ladygina-Kohts 2002; Miles 1980; Patterson 1978; Premack and Premack 1972; Rumbaugh et al. 1973; Terrace et al. 1979). Using these methods, the hope was to teach chimpanzees syntax. However, at the end of the day, no chimpanzee—let alone other ape—has *consistently* managed to produce more than three "words" sequentially in a given communication event (spontaneous or otherwise). Lack of working memory capacity (or volitional use of) has been hypothesized as the primary factor for this "deficit" (Read 2008). Working memory has been divided into three main components (Baddeley and Hitch 1974), with a fourth recently added (Baddeley 2000): the phonological loop, the visuospatial sketchpad, and the episodic buffer—all three of which are dependent upon a fourth attentionally-limited control system, the central executive. The phonological loop, our main concern here, consists of two parts: a short-term phonological store with auditory memory traces that are subject to rapid decay and an articulatory rehearsal component (sometimes called the articulatory loop) that can revive the memory traces. Minimally, the phonological loop is neuroanatomically supported by Wernicke's and Broca's area, with the arcuate fasciculus linking them together and connecting them to supporting sub-regions (Bernal and Ardila 2009; Catani and Mesulam 2008; Dronkers and Ogar 2004; Dronkers et al. 2004; Ojemann 1991, 2003; Yeatman et al. 2011). Although the human phonological loop may include new cortical areas (in particular Brodmann areas 40 and 39) and a richly collateral arcuate fasciculus, it derives from a preexisting auditory-inferior frontal circuit that is present in apes and monkeys (Aboitiz et al. 2006). Importantly, however, a detailed examination of the arcuate fasciculus in three species (human, chimpanzee and macaque) has revealed that only in humans does it form an uninterrupted pathway between Broca's and Wernicke's area, as well as forming a stronger dorsal route into the temporal lobe (Rilling et al. 2008) (Figure 7). Accordingly, apes' and monkeys' limited language ability may be less about working memory, and more about a lack of neural integration between language areas and prefrontal cortical control.

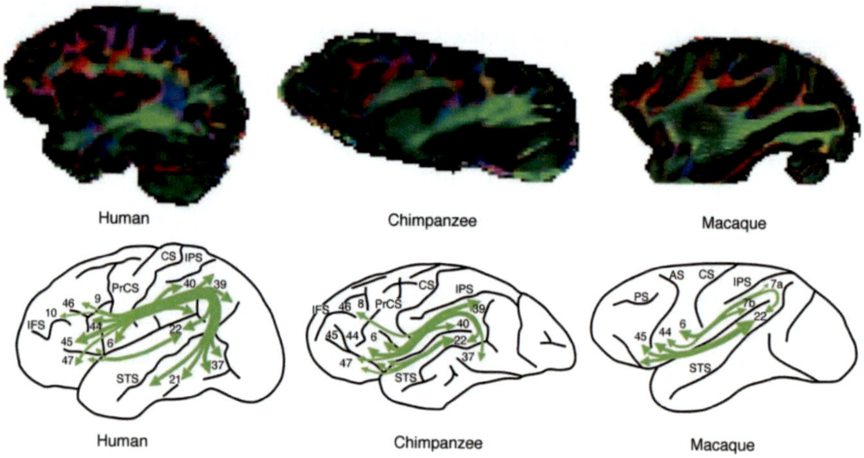

Figure 7. Arcuate fasciculus in three hominid species. Top row: diffusion tensor imaging; Bottom row: AS, arcuate sulcus; CS, central sulcus; IFS, inferior frontal sulcus; IPS, intraparietal sulcus; PrCS, precentral sulcus; PS, principal sulcus; STS, superior temporal sulcus; Broadman's Area 6, ventral premotor cortex, planning of complex, coordinated movements, part of Broca's area; 7b, anterior inferior parietal cortex, plays a role in reaching to grasp an object; 8 in chimpanzees, 9 in humans, the middle frontal gyrus (marks dorsolateral prefrontal cortex), serves as the highest cortical area responsible for motor planning, organization, and regulation. It plays an important role in the integration of sensory and mnemonic information and the regulation of intellectual function and action. It is also involved in working memory; 10, anterior prefrontal, rostral prefrontal cortex and frontopolar prefrontal cortex, involved in strategic processes in memory retrieval and executive function. During human evolution, the functions in this area resulted in its expansion relative to the rest of the brain; 21, middle temporal area, auditory processing and language; 22, part of Wernicke's area, on the left side of the brain this area helps with generation and understanding of individual words. On the right side of the brain it helps tell the difference between melody, pitch, and sound intensity, i.e., prosody; 37, occipitotemporal area, processing of color information, face and body recognition, word recognition, within-category identification; 39, parietal cortex, angular area, damage in humans results in semantic aphasia; 40, parietal cortex (homologue to macaque area 7b, part of the mirror neuron system, and active in humans during imitation); 44, pars opercularis, phonological and syntactic processing, suppression of response tendencies; 45, pars triangularis, semantic processing; 46, middle frontal area, semantic processing; 47, pars orbitalis, musical structure processing, syntax in spoken and signed languages. Image adapted from (Rilling et al. 2008). Reprinted with permission from Macmillan Publishers Ltd.

Further confirmation of differences between chimpanzee and human language cognitive apparatus comes from work done on the FOXP2 gene (Enard et al. 2002). Forkhead box protein P2 is a member of FOX group of transcription factors and is involved in the regulation of gene expression. Mutations of the FOXP2 gene cause a severe form of language impairment and orofacial dyspraxia (MacDermot et al. 2005). It was first discovered after analyzing the genome of an English family that exhibited a common pattern of severe speech and language deficits (Lai et al. 2001). Many of its target genes have since been found to be important for neural connectivity in the central nervous system (Vernes et al. 2011). With the exception of bats (Li et al. 2007)—perhaps due to the sensorimotor demands of echolocation—FOXP2 is relatively well conserved in mammalian species; it differs in humans and chimpanzees by only two amino acids. When a humanized version of FOXP2 was inserted into the mouse genome, the transgenic animals displayed practically completely opposite traits to those carrying a nonfunctional FOXP2 allele modeled on the human mutation associated with speech impairment (Enard et al. 2009). They displayed less exploratory behavior than usual, had elevated levels of dopamine throughout their brains, and in their basal ganglia showed an 80% increase in axonal and dendritic length of medium spiny neurons affording them increased synaptic plasticity, a factor important for flexible learning. The indices of all these traits were reversed in the mutant FOXP2 mice.

The MYH16 myosin gene mutation has also recently been implicated as playing a role in the evolution of language in humans (Stedman et al. 2004). Loss of the protein coded by the MYH16 gene is associated with marked size reductions in individual muscle fibers and entire masticatory muscles. Using the molecular clock technique, the mutation was found to have appeared approximately 2.4 million years ago, occurring around the time when the shift from *Australopithecus* and *Paranthropus* to *Homo erectus* was taking place; for a review see (McHenry and Coffing 2000). It has been hypothesized that the MYH16 mutation set pre-*Homo* skull development on a path towards gracilization. A weakening of the masticatory muscles may have allowed the cranium to widen at the crucial temporal lobe area, thereby facilitating the expansion of a nascent Broca's area as well as changing the articulatory behavior of the jaw, both factors potentially facilitating language development. Speculatively, the mutation appears to have conferred a paradoxical advantage, whereby the physical weakening provided the impetus to solve problems in novel ways suggesting an evolution meditated by behavior independent of environmental change. Without doubt, rapid, articulated language stands as one of the largest discontinuities on the strand of comparative cognitive abilities in humans, apes and monkeys. This is not to say that without such language abilities, apes and monkeys (or other species for that matter) cannot perform complex cognitive tasks—particularly where language has been thought to be mandatory for solving such tasks. Animal studies have taught us that cognition without language is not only possible, but normal. However, when displacement is added to language, as it is in humans, it pushes this cognitive ability into a new realm, and opens the door for symbol use. Some interesting studies have looked at symbol use in animals, and we will turn to those now.

Symbolic Ability

The research landscape is relatively barren when it comes to the study of symbolic ability in animals. At one end of the scale, where animals have been trained to recognize symbols such as alphabets, numerals, pictograms, work has progressed steadily to the point where evidence is gathering of animals' ability to perform conceptual operations on symbolic content. In the semiotics of Charles Sanders Peirce, a symbol is defined as pattern (a marking or behavior) conventionalized as a habit or rule, and involves cross-modal processing between arbitrary signs and their signifiers (Peirce et al. 1998). To grasp a symbol one must move from the particular (concrete) to the general (abstract) (Liberman and Trope 2008). Concrete perception is directly coupled to the contextualized representation of a pattern, where individual features are seen as the thing to be consumed, or acted on. Abstract perception involves decoupling the pattern from its context, causing individual features to recede so that a displaced (i.e., spatially and temporally distant) cluster of associations arises in place of it. The cluster of associations could represent a consumable (or a behavioral pattern), but it could equally be another symbol. With this in mind, a captive-reared Californian sea lion (*Zalophus californianus*) has been shown to form concepts based on alpha-numero-picto symbols (Kastak and Schusterman 2002); captive baboons (*Papio papio*) similarly demonstrated an ability to form concepts based on words they had learned and words they had never seen before shown on a computer screen (Grainger et al. 2012); and one captive-reared chimpanzee in particular (Ayumi) has impressed everyone with her ability to "memorize" sequences of rapidly masked numerals (Inoue and Matsuzawa 2007). Using a touchscreen, "Ayumi" was trained to tap out the sequence "1-9". Later, Aiyumi transferred this ability to non-adjacent sequences such as "2-3-5-8-9". A masking test was then introduced. As soon as Aiyumi tapped the first numeral of the sequence the remaining numerals were covered (masked) with a white square. Aiyumi had to complete the sequence indicating the correct numerical order the squares concealed. To compare humans on the task, an additional level of control was introduced. After tapping the first numeral in the sequence, the numbers would be displayed for 650, 430 and 210 milliseconds before being masked. 210 milliseconds was chosen as the lowest value as this was closely correlated with the frequency of occurrence of human saccadic eye movement (Bartz 1962). What the researchers found, to their astonishment, was that Aiyumi consistently beat humans on the test at 210 milliseconds. They concluded that young chimpanzees have extraordinary eidetic memory, that is, an ability for detailed and vivid recall, particularly of visual images. Children are thought to possess superior eidetic-like ability over adults but there are no peer-reviewed publications to support this claim. Nevertheless, the researchers theorized that humans traded off this ability for language as we diverged from our ancient ancestors. The argument implies that chimpanzees need eidetic imagery for the kind of world they live in—where life is situation-bound and competition for resources is immanent. The ability to memorize a pattern of scattered food would enable faster collection and therefore less risk from competitors and predators. Unfortunately, the Arabic numeral masking test has already invited a detractor. It has been found that Aiyumi had extensive practice on a non-time-pressured version of the task; the human subjects received none. When the test was repeated with human subjects that had adequate training they substantially outperformed Aiyumi (Cook and Wilson 2010).

Convincing demonstrations of picture recognition, where animals' responses to 2D images are spontaneous and often defensive or inquisitive, includes species as diverse as pigeons, sheep, fish and spider; for a review see (Bovet and Vauclair 2000). But "pictorial recognition", where the picture is not immediately recognizable—is missing natural elements—requires "attentional purpose" to start the subject on a search through the image space until a percept settles, is only found in great apes with some glimmers. Persson performed a preliminary investigation, finding that bonobos of the Great Ape Trust, perhaps because of their advanced lexigraph abilities, performed the best of the group in this challenge (Persson 2008). He concluded that much research still needs to be done to convincingly demonstrate pictorial recognition in apes. On the other side of the coin, representational drawing in chimpanzees has been studied (Saito 2010). Chimpanzees were compared to children on two types of tasks: pictorial imitation and pictorial completion. The imitation task was designed specifically with motor control in mind. The subjects were given geometric primitives—lines and simple shapes—and had to imitate a human role model and trace the shapes. Chimpanzees demonstrated fine motor control and were able to achieve the semblance of tracing lines on the simple shapes. In the completion task, the outline of a chimpanzee face was presented, albeit missing certain facial features in a graded sequence of increased deletions. For example, in the easy versions, one of the eyes was missing, whereas in the final version, both eyes, nose and mouth were missing. As children increased in age, they completed the missing parts, however chimpanzees continued to mainly trace the outlines of the face only. With motor control ruled out as a confounding factor in the first task, the results of the second task showed that chimpanzees lacked the ability to draw non-existent things; i.e., they lacked awareness of the unseen world. Thus, at this stage, symbolic ability in animals, like language, appears to cover a large discontinuity, although perhaps with greater variability due to some animals' superior adeptness at visual cognition compared to other sensory modalities. Perhaps most telling of all, is that in making this qualification, we are not just talking about associating a symbol with its meaning, but looking for evidence of generativity in the animal's behavior. We would like to see them spontaneously invent arbitrary signs and utilize them as part of their communicating strategy. A chimpanzee picking up a stick and threatening a conspecific with it as a weapon is not symbolic behavior, since the stick was not invented; it was ready to hand and appropriated for use in a pre-prepared action pattern. It appears to be that humans alone possess the ability to spontaneously generate symbols, and furthermore, manipulate them in almost an infinite variety of ways.

Mental Time Travel

Mental time travel refers to the faculty that allows humans to mentally project themselves backwards or forwards in time to re-live/pre-live events (Suddendorf and Corballis 1997). The different types of temporal information that humans and animals might engage in are: when an event occurred (or is expected to occur) within some time pattern ("temporal locations"), how long ago an event occurred ("temporal distances"), and before–after relations and other relations of the order of events (Friedman 1993). This picture is complicated by the fact that autobiographical memory in humans is not only involved in reconstructing snapshots of personal experiences of the past, but also constructing snapshots of imagined personal experiences of the future—the brain regions that subserve the two functions show very similar patterns of activity (Addis et al. 2007; Szpunar et al. 2007). This fits well with the brain's general ability to perform mental simulations. Mental simulations may be part of a more general process of the brain's ability to decouple from sense perceptions and/or engage in reflection upon its own contents (consciously or unconsciously) (Hopkins et al. 2011). No doubt, we have all seen apes sitting around staring dreamily into space. What are they thinking in these moments? Are they thinking at all? When we capture our own thoughts in these moments, we usually find that we have engaged in fantasy. Ironically, fantasy is a powerful creative force in human beings that accounts for much of our adaptive and maladaptive behavior. When adaptive, it is often involved in the planning of future contingencies. Evidence of planning in apes, therefore, may represent a useful way of operationalizing putative mental time travel in this species.

The Fongoli chimpanzees at Senegal have been observed to hunt and spear prosimian prey with sharpened sticks, providing evidence of foresight and intellectual complexity (Pruetz and Bertolani 2007). Surprisingly, the most frequently observed participants in this activity were juvenile females. Scrub jays (*Aphelocoma coerulescens*)—a member of the crow family, corvids— transport food from old sites and re-cache it in new ones to avoid losing their caches to conspecifics that observed the initial location of the cache sites, thereby saving the items for future consumption (Clayton and Dickinson 1998; Clayton et al. 2001). This has been claimed to fulfill the so-called "what, where, when" criteria (www) first proposed by Tulving to define the function of episodic memory (memory of autobiographical events) (Tulving 1972). This definition has since been updated in light of evidence that humans can mentally revisit an event without accurate information of www, and conversely know www for something that happened without remembering the event itself (e.g., one's birth) (Suddendorf and Busby 2003). Accordingly, episodic memory must be shown not only have www content but also an integrated structure where information is deployed flexibly (Clayton et al. 2003).

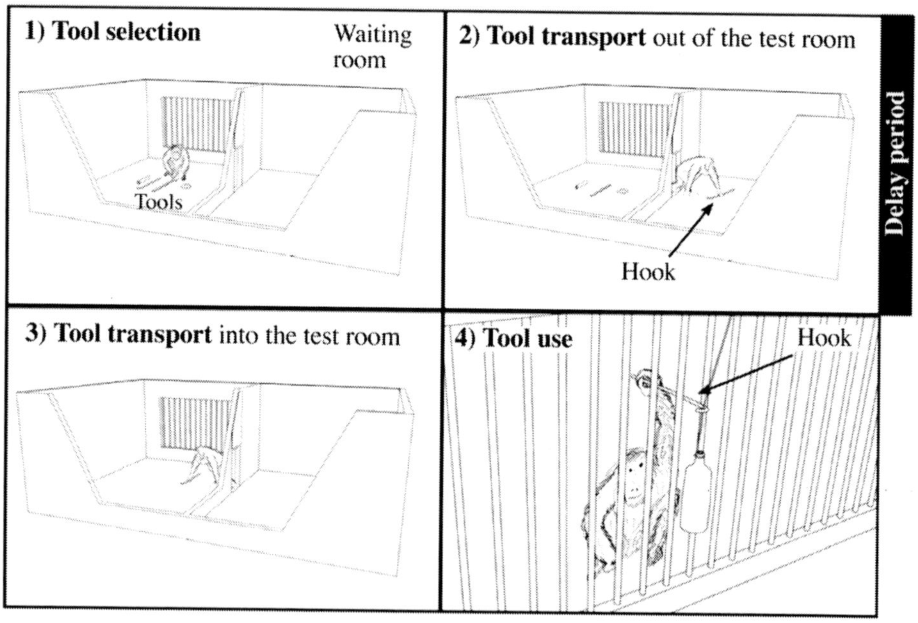

Figure 8. Depiction of the hook version of the "saving a tool for future use" task. Subjects were introduced into the test room while a caretaker baited the apparatus and placed tools in a random order on the floor for use. Access to the apparatus was blocked during this procedure using a sheet of clear Plexiglas. After 5 minutes, subjects (with one or more tools in hand) were ushered outside the test room into a waiting room from where they could see the apparatus and the caretaker removing all remaining tools. After 1 hour, subjects were allowed to return to the test room and were given access to the apparatus. From (Mulcahy and Call 2006a). Reprinted with permission from AAAS.

With these factors in mind, Mulcahy and Call trained orangutans and bonobos to obtain grapes using a tube and diluted grape juice using a hook (Mulcahy and Call 2006a) (Figure 8). Once the apes understood how to get the food reward using the respective tool, they were tested to see if they would pick the right tool from among three other distractor tools and save it for future use. There were strong individual differences in performance, with one orangutan achieving 15 out of 16 correct trials. This orangutan and the best performing bonobo were then tested again, but with an overnight delay between tool selection and return. They still returned with a suitable tool in more cases than expected by chance. A third experiment showed that the apes could pass the task even when they could not see the apparatus during tool selection. The final control study investigated whether the animals merely associated the tool with the reward. Subjects again received a food reward if they returned with the right tool, but were not actually given an opportunity to use the tool. Performance in this condition was poorer, suggesting that they did plan ahead in the other studies.

The authors of the study concluded that apes do indeed plan for the future and, moreover, suggested that it supports the hypothesis that apes and corvids underwent convergent evolution, that is, the process of arriving at the same biological trait through an unrelated evolutionary lineage. One issue the study raised was that subjects in the early phase of the experiment had visual access to the food reward. This, it has been argued, could lead subjects to potentially experience a desire for the reward throughout the experiment (Suddendorf 2006; Suddendorf and Corballis 2007). Therefore it is not considered clear whether the apes only anticipated the future need for the tool or if they also foresaw their future motivational state. This last qualification raises an additional interesting point: the difference between mentally visualizing the concrete need for a tool in a future scenario and visualizing the abstract idea of a hypothetical need in the future (the latter has generalizability). It is a subtle distinction but may be splitting one hair too many and highlights the relatively nascent state of mental time travel theoretical and empirical research.

As if to confuse matters even further, a potential associative learning effect was identified as another caveat in the Mulcahy and Call experiment because the subjects were rewarded with the same tools throughout the experiment (Suddendorf and Corballis 2007). In response to this, Osvath and Osvath re-ran the experiment with some modifications (Osvath and Osvath 2008). They trained their subjects—two female chimpanzees, Linda (22 years old) and Maria Magdalena (6 years old), and a male orangutan Naong (12 years old)—how to obtain a "fruit soup" reward from an apparatus using a plastic hose tool. The demonstrator showed them how to suck up the fruit soup then gave them the tool, which all subjects used successfully. Only one demonstration was given. Theoretically, this kept the opportunity for associative learning at a minimum. Also, it was the only time they were given the tool by the experimenter immediately in association with the food reward. Later, the baited apparatus was installed in a "reward room" adjacent to their indoor cages; the apes were allowed into the reward room, but without any tools. This was done to create a potential incentive for possessing a functional tool in the future. This step was repeated twice in one day. The next day subjects were presented with a tray containing the hose and three non-functional distractor objects while in their indoor cages. The apparatus in the reward room was visible but inaccessible. The distracter objects were objects commonly used by the subjects in different enrichment activities and thus possibly associated with previous rewards. Subjects were permitted to make only one selection among the options. This was the second time they ever saw the hose, yet the three subjects all selected it. Subjects were not allowed into the reward room until 1 hour had passed.

With training complete, the experiment proper began. This time, the subjects were called individually into a "selection room" from where the reward room was not visible. The hose and the three non-functional distractor objects were briefly presented and the subjects were allowed to make their choice. After selection, the subjects returned to their enclosure shared by other group members not participating in the experiment. Thus, the subjects had to maintain interest in their tool despite social distractions while in group housing. 70 minutes later, they were let into the reward room and were given access to the food reward. The results showed that subjects chose the correct tool and obtained the reward most of the time out of 14 trials. The authors concluded that this demonstrated "advanced future oriented cognition" in these animals. Two variations were conducted to flesh out the experiment. A "self-control" task, in which a favorite fruit (a grape) was added among the distractor objects, and a "control for associative learning" task, where in addition to the grape, a second identical hose was added to the distractor objects. Of the second identical hose, the authors reasoned that, "if the tool evoked an immediate craving in the same sense as the grape, then selecting the hose would reduce this drive state and consequently not be part of a planning behavior." The results were that subjects generally resisted the grape and in the self-control task, but took the grape instead of the second identical hose in the prescribed non-associative learning task, thereby passing both tests. In conclusion, the authors stated that their study "shows that great apes are capable of acting towards a future state although experiencing a strong current and competing drive."

While it is true that their apes did indeed perform delayed gratification in selecting the hose over the grape in the self-control task, it is not so clear that they weren't operating under associative learning in the non-associative learning task. Basically, the authors failed to take into account the numerous successful trials each subject experienced in the lead up to the non-associative learning task. By that time, the subjects would have formed very strong associations between the hose and the food reward—so much so, in fact, that the hose would have become a conditioned stimulus representing the food reward itself. The fact that there was a time delay between acquisition of the hose and the food reward is irrelevant. Contiguity in this case, represented by the proximal spatial relation between the hose and the food reward, was more than sufficient to establish an associative learning bond in the subjects' brains. This crucial caveat, however, does not detract from the simple fact that subjects took care of their tool over a period of 70 minutes in anticipation of getting a food reward. It demonstrates that chimpanzees and orangutans are capable of maintaining an associative link with an object and a non-immediately visible food reward over extended periods. Whether this behavior is truly indicative of planning is an open question.

Perhaps an example of planning in humans might go some way towards clearing up the theoretical landscape. When we pack a first-aid kit in preparation to go hiking, we are not necessarily anticipating future harm to ourselves. We reason the crepe bandage in the kit will come in handy if we got bitten by a snake, even though we have never personally experienced a snake bite ourselves. Thus, we plan for hypotheticals. The same way we take out travel insurance when going overseas. We do these things not out of any sense of reward, but, in fact, out of a sense of anticipated aversion. More importantly, we do them through vicarious learning. We take precautions because we have seen others come to harm and act accordingly (with a background memory of our own accident proneness perhaps adding motivation). It is hard to imagine how we could plan for the future based on our limited personal experience alone if we did not have such vicarious experience. Vicarious experience is not the same thing as semantic memory (i.e., concept-based knowledge unrelated to specific experiences). A large part of our episodic memory base, paradoxically, is appropriated from others. Watching others experience something sometimes creates a simulated experience in us—and is facilitated by both episodic and semantic memory. The act of appropriating others' experiences seems to be almost instinctive in us, and no doubt has something to do with theory of mind, imitation, and the mirror neuron system.

Given that apes have been shown to perform emulative behaviors, it might pay to re-investigate their planning abilities vis-à-vis vicarious learning from conspecifics. Observing a conspecific using a tool to achieve an end might be a good place to start. At some point later in the experiment, the test subject is given the opportunity to select the tool for future use. For the ambitious researcher, they might want to provide a different but analogous tool at the selection stage. This might seem like the original experimental design one step removed, however, it has the advantage of completely disassociating the test subject's senses from the reward, thereby further reducing potential associative learning artifacts—although over trials the association will be strengthened again. Notwithstanding, the ape must initially form a conceptual notion of the tool and the reward, and this it can be argued provides a stronger analogy to human planning.

Metacognition

The study of metacognition—literally, "thinking about thinking" (Flavell 1976; Flavell 1979; Koriat 1993; Metcalfe and Shimamura 1994; Nelson and Narens 1990)—is a relatively new field in comparative psychology. Metacognition is widely regarded as the sine qua non of what it means to be human. While the study of metacognition can easily become a nebulous subject in itself—ostensibly because attempts to define it rest on other metacognitive acts (hence leading us into circularity)—at a phenomenological level, at its most basic, metacognition appears to be a retrospective act. It involves retrieving aspects of mental processes that *have already occurred*. The contents of metacognition, therefore, are memories. The process of metacognition is to work on those memories in relation to immediate problems and form new mental contents, some of which in turn become new memories. Many regard the act of retrieving memories and working on them as occurring within the field of conscious awareness, leading some to refer to the process as "self-reflective." This is not to be interpreted as consciousness *reflecting back on itself*—a logical paradox—rather, it should be seen as one part of the brain observing another *different* part of itself, just as the brain can observe parts of the body that houses it. This self-observation process, generally speaking, occurs in near real-time when the object of attention is the corporeal body. However, when the object of attention is the brain's own mental contents, indeterminate delays occur between the instantiation and retrieval of contents due to the linear nature of conscious attention. Moreover, retrieval is not a carbon-copy process, but a reconstructive process, and therefore fallibility is the norm. Inevitably, the quality and quantity of retrieved content decays or changes over time.

Self-reflective cognition is generally considered to have evolved through natural selection and should therefore in principle be identifiable in both humans and nonhuman animals through specifically adapted behaviors without reference to verbal communication (Hampton 2005). Two types of behaviors have been leveraged in nonhuman animal studies and both are based on assessing the quality of memory retrieval: escape behavior (Fujita 2009; Hampton 2001; Shields et al. 1997; Smith et al. 1995; Smith et al. 1998; Suda-King 2008; Washburn et al. 2006) and information seeking (Beran and Smith 2011; Call 2004; Call and Carpenter 2001; Hampton et al. 2004; Kornell et al. 2007; Marsh and Macdonald 2011; McMahon et al. 2010). In escape behavior, animals opt out for a lesser reward in the face of uncertainty, rather than choosing an incorrect answer resulting in a reward-less time out. To elaborate, suppose subjects are given a delayed-matching-to-sample test based on visual imagery. Subjects are shown an image and are allowed to study it as long as they want. Subjects then give a signal whereupon the image disappears and a delay period starts. Once the delay elapses, a choice appears. Subjects can go on to perform a recognition test where the image will be re-presented mixed in with several other distractor images—if the subject picks the correct image it gets a high-quality reward (voluntary choice); or, they can opt out and receive a low-quality reward (escape option); or, on some trials randomly interspersed throughout the session they are forced to do the recognition test—if they answer correctly they get the high-quality reward; if they fail they get a reward-less time out (forced choice). When rhesus monkeys were tested using this paradigm (Hampton 2001), in a certain number of cases they chose the escape option suggesting they felt uncertain about their ability to correctly recognize the image they studied. To control for alternate explanations of forgetting, two variations were introduced: blanks were inserted randomly in place of images on some trials and the delay period was increased over trials. Monkeys responded by opting out on blanks and longer delays, suggesting they knew when their memory was going to be fallible; i.e., they had access their own knowledge states. This was construed as evidence of metacognition.

Recently, the suggestion has been raised that image-based delayed-matching-to-sample paradigms in nonhuman animals may come about as a result of "visual fluency" rather than metacognition (Voss et al. 2008; Voss and Paller 2009). Visual fluency is the phenomenon whereby repeated exposure to an image increases the ease with which the image is processed in the brain. Thus, one can imagine that a nonhuman animal could select the old item simply because repetition enhanced visual processing fluency relative to the new item, and that the subject had learned to associate fluency with a behavior via conditioning. In the rhesus monkey study, while it is true that the subjects performed best when they chose the test themselves, in the forced choice condition they still performed significantly above chance. On the one hand, because only four images were randomly presented on any one testing day, proactive interference (difficulty in learning because of already existing information) is expected. On the other, monkeys still performed well above chance in the forced condition giving greater credence to the visual fluency hypothesis. Moreover, it must be pointed out that animals are extremely sensitive to reward contingencies and so the forced condition may have created motivational conflict in them, where they sensed that their choice was now limited to an all-or-nothing outcome, thereby reducing their performance. Yet even here, such hypothetical motivational conflict was not enough to detract from their well above chance performance in the forced choice condition; it merely dented it.

The information-seeking paradigm seeks a way around some of these limitations. The apparatus used is extremely simple and does not require pre-test training. In its most basic form, when deployed with apes and monkeys, two opaque tubes are oriented perpendicularly toward the subject who is able to access them through the wire mesh of their cage. An experimenter baits one of the tubes in one of two conditions: visible and non-visible. In the visible condition, the subject has full view of which tube is being baited. In the non-visible condition, a screen is interposed between the subject and the tubes so that the subject cannot see which tube is being baited. Subjects typically bend down and inspect tubes to find the food location in the non-visible condition. In order to get the reward, the subject has to touch the baited tube first. Using this paradigm on gorillas, chimpanzees, bonobos, and orangutans, Call found that when he provided indirect auditory information about the food's location or increased the cost of checking (by angling the tubes obliquely making it harder to look inside), subjects reduced their checking behavior before choosing (Call 2010). They were also more likely to check inside the tube after a longer period of time had elapsed between the baiting and retrieval of the reward, or when a high-quality food reward was involved. The increased checking when a high-quality reward was at stake is particularly interesting because it suggests that subjects wanted to make sure they got it right—to excuse the anthropomorphic explanation. Intuitively it makes sense to check more when a high-quality reward is at stake because making an incorrect decision results in greater loss for a given unit of energy expenditure. However, because apes in the wild instinctively pursue high-quality food rewards (foraging hypothesis), the most plausible explanation would seem to be a simple stimulus-response pattern; pre-knowledge of a high-quality reward triggers greater effort because of the greater potential payoff. As an example, orangutans in the wild crave cemengang seeds but the seeds are embedded in a mass of razor-sharp needles (van Schaik 2004). To extract them they use tools (short, straight sticks with the bark stripped off), often making the tool in advance of entering the tree that produces the delicacy. Thus, the high-quality food reward triggers greater effort, including ingenuity and planning. The fact that animals decreased checking behavior when the cost of checking was increased (while offering a low-quality reward) supports this hypothesis.

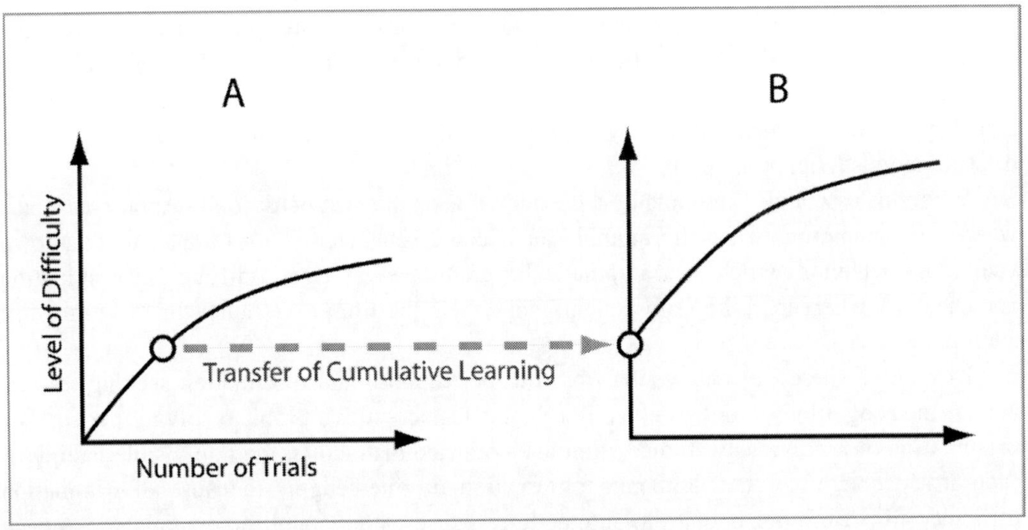

Figure 9. Schematic depicting the transfer of cumulative learning from problem set A to analogous problem set B. Starting at a higher skill level on the first trial in set B requires conscious retrieval of cumulative learning from set A. The likelihood that retrieval becomes conscious varies as a function of the analogous "distance" between problem domains.

It would have been interesting to see if they maintained reduced checking in the obliquely angled condition using a high-quality reward, but this was not tested. Applying the foraging hypothesis, one would predict that angling the tubes with high-quality rewards should not significantly limit the checking behavior—this of course depends on the motivational state of the ape, which is extremely hard to measure. Progressive ratio paradigms are typically used to measure motivation in animals, but may not be accepted in ape research on ethical grounds.

Several other paradigms for testing metacognition in animals exist. One of these, the retrospective gambling paradigm, is interesting in that it forces subjects to make a bet (i.e., take a risk) *after* experiencing a psychophysical test but *before* they receive feedback on their performance. In an example implementation of the test, rhesus monkeys were trained to touch a video screen to pick out the longest of nine lines (Son and Kornell 2005). For a correct "high-risk" bet monkeys received two tokens that, after accumulating to a sufficient amount, could be cashed out for a food reward. An incorrect choice on a high-risk bet resulted in a decrement of two tokens. The same procedure was applied to "low-risk" bets except only one token incremented or decremented depending on the correctness of choice. Training monkeys on a difficult paradigm like this involving secondary rewards understandably takes an enormous amount of researcher persistence, as monkeys do not learn such tasks easily. It takes years of training to achieve results with just one animal, so experimental numbers are typically low and have no statistical power. Nevertheless, the monkeys did eventually learn to take high-risk bets when their "confidence" judgments were high, and low-risk bets when they were low. But this is when things just got interesting. Researchers then put the monkeys through a transfer test presenting them with yellow squares containing varying numbers of black dots.

Previous to this, they had learned to discriminate these geometric pictures by pressing on them in order of their numerosity. Now they were presented with nine of them and asked to identify the one with the most dots (an analogous task to the nine lines test). Unlike the laborious learning that was required to teach them the line-risk task, the monkeys took to this test quickly, and sure enough, showed the same risk-taking behavior as the line-risk test, suggesting that they did indeed transfer their cognitive judgments to the new test. It is difficult to interpret these findings, however, since the monkeys received so much training that they could have been primed by response latency as an autobehavioral cue on difficult discriminations (Hampton 2009).

What this essentially amounts to is the animal takes its own behavioral response as a cue, where over numerous trials the animal can become sensitized, for example, to their own vacillating behavior (which they automatically produce every time a difficult discrimination is presented), whereupon they subsequently take their cue from *that*, rather than from the test stimulus.

Despite all these caveats, results from escape response and information seeking tests of animal metacognition do not completely rule out metacognitive problem solving per se. The presentation of a previously studied stimulus alongside distractors, the non-visible baiting of food in opaque tubes, the deliberate obfuscation of line lengths to cause discrimination difficulty all perturb behavior from automatic response patterns and force animals to engage in cognitive deliberation. The most parsimonious explanation is that animals act on "sensed" uncertainty in the face of automonitoring of memory-stimulus comparisons.

However, as hinted at earlier, this is only one component of the metacognitive *process*. The other component can be described as achieving a level of competency on a current problem set that can be transferred to an analogous problem set which, most importantly, *starts at a level of competency achieved on the prior set* (see Figure 9. Note: this two-component model can be seen as an extension of Nelson-Narens' 1990 model of "monitoring" and "control"). Just think of video games. Call it "transfer of cumulative learning." To achieve a smooth transition the subject must create a mental/body schema solution of the problem space. This allows the subject to start at a much higher level of competency than would be otherwise allowable if the subject had started on the new set de novo. Transfer of cumulative learning has been experimentally tested on sanctuary-housed chimpanzees (Marshall-Pescini and Whiten 2008a).

The experiment, which was based on the reliable puzzle box method, was designed in such a way that learning could be divided into two phases. The box contained a special lid that contained a small sliding trapdoor. In the first phase, a demonstrator showed chimpanzees individually how to pull back the sliding trapdoor and insert a rod tool and extract honey.

The chimpanzees were allowed to get as close to the apparatus as they wanted. Only chimpanzees that succeeded in this task went on to the transfer of cumulative learning phase, where this time the demonstrator showed the chimpanzees how to open the lid by first pushing a catch bolt through a hole then, *critically*, pulling back the sliding trapdoor and using the rod tool *as a lever* to open the lid to get honey as well as peanuts. Thus to lever the lid open, a variation of the dipping technique was incorporated, making the probing technique one that could be built upon cumulatively once the dipping technique was already in the subject's repertoire. Only one chimpanzee succeeded at transferring cumulative learning, however, the experimenters noted that this subject had already discovered the probing technique during baseline trials through social learning. Thus, no subjects actually demonstrated transfer of cumulative learning, which corroborates comparative studies where chimpanzees failed to switch to a novel behavior after learning an already successful technique (Hrubesch et al. 2009; Tennie et al. 2009).

Arguably, the more "distant" analogous problem sets are, the higher the likelihood that *conscious* retrieval of cumulative learning takes place. This is the essence of metacognition in humans and is one of the reasons why we have cumulative culture. Given that large amounts of cognitive processing occur unconsciously in both humans and animals, there is no a priori reason why animals cannot achieve the first requirement of metacognition: they retrieve memories and use them to solve current discrimination problems (albeit *unconsciously*). We could call this "metarecognition." What is not clear is whether they can pass the second requirement: transfer of cumulative learning to analogous problem domains at elevated levels of competency. More testing is required before conclusions can be drawn, however, considering the strong claims against metacognition in animals on the first requirement (Carruthers 2007; Staddon et al. 2007), it seems less likely that they will display abilities of the second. In drawing a discontinuity on this strand of cognition, we would obviously like to know how conscious metacognition works its magic in humans. Unfortunately, this would encompass an entire investigation on its own. Suffice to say that conscious awareness has the curious effect of supercharging cognitive processes in a way that elevates them from the ordinary to the extraordinary. The role of volitional control in this process cannot be over-stated.

Additional Strands of Interest

Volitional Control

Humans have the uncanny ability to step outside the stream of events and dispassionately examine their circumstances. This process is intimately linked with conscious volitional control. Very few people would go so far as to ascribe such an ability to an ape, let alone a monkey. In one anecdotal example, however, Kanzi the bonobo exhibited behavior suggestive of this ability (Savage-Rumbaugh et al. 2005). One day, the journalist Paul Raffaele visited the Great Ape Trust Research Facility in Iowa where Kanzi is the dominant male in a matriarchal society:

> I'd told Savage-Rumbaugh about some of my adventures, and she invited me to perform a Maori war dance. I beat my chest, slapped my thighs and hollered. The bonobos sat quiet and motionless for a few seconds, then all but Kanzi snapped into a frenzy, the noise deafening as they screamed, bared their teeth and pounded on the walls and floor of their enclosure. Still calm, Kanzi waved an arm at Savage-Rumbaugh, as if asking her to come closer, then let loose with a stream of squeaks and squeals. "Kanzi says he knows you're not threatening them," Savage-Rumbaugh said to me, "and he'd like you to do it again just for him, in a room out back, so the others won't get upset." I'm skeptical, but I follow the researcher through the complex, out of Kanzi's sight. I find him, all alone, standing behind protective bars. Seeing me, he slapped his chest and thighs, mimicking my war dance, as if inviting me to perform an encore. I obliged, of course, and Kanzi joined in with gusto (Raffaele 2006).

Intuitively, the ability to step outside the stream of events seems like a comprehensible act, however, when put under the scrutiny of the neuroscientist's microscope, it rapidly dismantles into unconscious antecedents that threaten to relegate conscious awareness to a mere epiphenomenon:

> Freely voluntary acts are preceded by a specific electrical change in the brain (the "readiness potential", RP) that begins 550 ms before the act. Human subjects became aware of intention to act 350–400 ms after RP starts, but 200 ms before the motor act. The volitional process is therefore initiated unconsciously. But the conscious function could still control the outcome; it can veto the act. Free will is therefore not excluded (Libet 1999).

Libet naturally goes on to ask: "Does the conscious veto have a preceding unconscious origin?" His answer is no. He believes that the vetoing process is a matter of control and does not require unconscious antecedents. In his words: "The awareness of the decision to veto could be thought to require preceding unconscious processes, but the content of that awareness (the actual decision to veto) is a separate feature that need not have the same requirement." What Libet is saying is that by the time we become aware of the need to make a decision, all the choice options are already arrayed before our field of conscious awareness; all we have to do is pick out the best option. Unfortunately, this naïve view overlooks the fact that even if all choice options are present, the actual choice (and moment of choice) still rests on a bed of unconscious impulses over which we do not have full control. That some control exists in humans is undoubted. But this is not because it exists over each choice; rather, it exists because over time we build up a catalogue of experience that guides us at the unconscious moment. Otherwise known as heuristics, it has been proposed that we evolved an "adaptive toolbox" that allows us to make most of our decisions within a framework of "bounded rationality" (Gigerenzer 2001). Generally speaking, humans have recourse to only two methods when making choices: either learn from their mistakes, or mentally simulate the problem before deciding. In time-critical tasks, the former is the only method available. If time then permits, reflection (i.e., mental simulation) can be used to facilitate error correction during the next attempt. It would appear that the only thing that separates us from apes and monkeys at this level is that we generally require fewer trial-and-error attempts before succeeding at a particular task. In other words, our reflective function has developed to a more sophisticated degree than our animal cousins. We are able to intentionally recollect both mental contents and life experience to form our choices—even choices that negate our own biological drives.

Christensen sees the origins of cognition in problems of complexity, and identifies the major functional benefit as flexibility (Christensen 2007). But whereas most accounts focus on external complexity (environmental or social), Christensen proposes a prominent role for internal functional complexity, and identifies the evolution of the fundamental mechanisms of cognition as beginning much earlier than most accounts, and in response to much more general complexity problems. Indeed, he proposes that the evolutionary process that has given rise to advanced cognition can be traced back to early metazoan evolution. Further, he proposes that the core trait under selection in the evolution of cognition is high order control capacity, rather than more specific abilities such as spatial cognition, tool use or theory of mind. Many specific abilities have played a role in the evolution of cognition, but the deepest level of organization is shaped by problems of control that are common across many abilities.

A graphic example of the importance of intentionality in nonhuman primates comes from this anecdotal description—also of the Great Ape Trust (and here we stand to undo all our good work)—by Bickerton, where he discusses the use of lexigrams by the bonobos there:

> ... these sheets were scattered here and there in the ape's enclosures so they would be available any time a bonobo felt like using them spontaneously. Which was hardly ever. Far from treating them as keys to a new, richer world, the bonobos totally ignored them, except when cajoled by their keepers. For the rest of the time, these plastic dictionaries, piss-stained, fouled with the dirt that accumulates, no matter how often and diligently you clean up, wherever animals (including us) are trapped in confined spaces, were trampled under foot ... (Bickerton 2009: 90–91).

The use of the word "cajole" is not derogatory. It simply states the fact that nonhuman primates, like all other animals, are primarily motivated by instinctual drives. Humans by comparison, while equally driven by instinctual needs, also have the exceptional gift of volitional control that drives them to excel, often beyond what is necessary for survival. The reason for this, intuitively, is that humans have evolved a self-reflective function not only of themselves and their peers, but of nature, resulting in the experience of a separation between psyche and matter. No animal we are aware of has stopped and asked: "What is this stuff that I am made of?" Or if they have asked it, they do not have the means to implement an answer. The need to answer the psyche-matter question is the engine that drives humans to greater accomplishments. And we have the means. Whether our driving intentionality gave us the means, by acting as a catalyst on our nascent cognitive abilities, or whether it happened the other way around, is an empirical question. What is certain is that while cognitively adept animals have the drive to meet their physical and emotional requirements, they do not go beyond those needs and strive toward seen and unseen goals with the long-term aim of deciphering the psyche-matter enigma. Furthermore, it may be precisely *because* of intentionality (i.e., volitional control) that we are able to bring representational contents into the field of conscious awareness via attention. This may in turn allow us to build up a self-construct, which through internal and external feedback inevitably drives us to further divide psyche and matter.

Very few ape and monkey experiments test directly for volitional control. Two areas touch on the subject: facial expressions-vocalization, and delayed gratification (patience). A recent review found that apes do appear to have some control over facial expressions and vocalizations, with the former slightly more prevalent than the latter (Hopkins et al. 2011). Two major findings were summarized. First, most of the studies reported in the review were situated in laboratories where apes had to interact with humans. In this case, apes commonly deploy acoustic signals to instrumentally manipulate humans to obtain food that is otherwise not available. In other words, what exerts stimulus control over the sound is the human not the food, or primary reinforcer. This led the reviewers to conclude that the development and use of their vocalizations is under the social control as opposed to non-social stimuli. Second, because the described "attention-getting" sounds are, at least in some instances, not what might be considered species-typical; there is the suggestion that their production may be mediated by a degree of intentionality. The reviewers hypothesized that our ancestors may have faced a similar challenge moving from the forest to the savanna, where selection pressure may have shifted communication strategies due to environmental factors such as visibility and auditory range.

Delayed gratification and patience experiments study what has been technically termed "intertemporal choice" (Berns et al. 2007). In animal studies, because food is generally offered as the reward, intertemporal choice has been cast in the form of "temporal discounting" where the subject is hypothesized to perceive a decrease in the value of the reward as the time delay to receiving the reward increases (Stevens and Mühlhoff 2012). Anthropomorphized, temporal discounting can be formulated as: "Should I eat now while I've got the chance, or take a risk and wait till later and get more, even though it may not be around?"

In a review of humans and nonhuman animals (Hayden and Platt 2007), it was found that humans may be patient when it comes to money, but of all the animals, chimpanzees are capable of waiting longer for food than humans, suggesting that patience in the form of delayed gratification may have evolved in different species depending on distinct behavioral contexts, and is not something specifically innate to humans. In summarizing the findings of these reviews, what is not clear is whether apes and monkeys exert the kind of vetoing power described by Libet above. Also, the fact that apes and monkeys *do* show some form of volitional control in specific circumstances does not imply that such behavior is generalizable across other behaviors, as is clearly the case in humans. More research needs to be done in this all-important area, particularly if it is true that volitional control exerts such a widespread influence on all other cognitive abilities.

Creativity, Innovation

Perhaps no factor is greater in our driving intentionality than creativity. It is generally accepted now that the lives of cognitively adept creatures do not just revolve around fixed action patterns, but also depend on novel problem solving. As we have seen, the monkeys of Koshima spontaneously began washing sweet potatoes in seawater after one individual first began the behavior. Driven by imitation and the saliency of better tasting vegetables, the behavior spread rapidly through the community. The monkeys also learned to separate seeds from sand by throwing seeds on water; the sand sank allowing them to scoop up the seeds sand-free. But these are rare examples. We also learned that apes and monkeys tend to be quite conservative. Many innovative behaviors initiated by individuals rapidly fade away as members return to group norms. Humans are no different. In fact, the same time we consciously say we desire and value creativity, we actually unconsciously reject it (Mueller et al. 2012). The tension between exploration and neophobia (the aversion to new things) is common among all animals—including humans—the classic study of which is Barnett's experiments on neophobia in rats (Barnett 1958). Creativity in societies tends to emerge in bursts, pushed by environmental shifts. Once a new solution is found, everything settles back to a status quo. Sometimes creative solutions are adopted for a while, then are replaced by new ones, only to re-emerge later when environmental conditions force their return.

Biologically, play could be construed as a precursor to creativity. Many species of juvenile animals play as a way of preparing them for their adult futures. For example squirrel monkeys (genus *Saimiri*) engage in play fighting which prepares them for dominance hierarchy fights as adults (Biben 1998). In a study of New World and Old World monkeys infant play vocalizations were found to correlate with maternal retrieval (Masataka and Kohda 1988), representing a case where play serves an immediate functional benefit. Juvenile chimpanzees develop future skills in imitative play such as sponge making from leaves or preparing sticks for digging termites (Goodall 1968). These are just some examples which, if looked at from the point of view of creativity, represent instances of nascent skills iterating towards mature behavioral forms. It is in those iterations that small deviations take place due to individual differences. Behind individual differences in the developing juvenile is a brain governed by the competing forces of hard-wired instinct and neural plasticity. Neural plasticity is the brain's variable ability to dynamically rewire itself via learning or after injury (Pascual-Leone et al. 2011). Neural plasticity is offset by synaptic pruning, a general feature of the mammalian brain, which in humans starts around birth and completes around sexual maturity (Huttenlocher 1979). This shift parallels the transformation of juvenile play into established survival repertoires of adult behavior and increased behavioral inhibition.

The most striking difference between juvenile nonhuman primates and human children is the latter engage in fantasy play in addition to social carousing (for a review of fantasy play in apes see Gómez and Andrade 2005). Generally, girls will play with dolls and create imaginary conversations with them; boys with vehicles and superheroes. While such play obviously prepares children for adult responsibilities, it also opens a door into parallel, imaginary worlds that stay with individuals throughout their lifespan. Imaginary worlds become an endless source of creative ideas, where fantasy and reality intersect, partly a product of driving intentionality, partly the synergistic energizer of intentionality itself. The confluence of these forces undoubtedly separates humans from their genetic cousins by a wide margin even though their evolutionary roots are deeply connected.

DISCUSSION

Re-Evaluation of the Comparative Cognitive Strands

The preliminary survey of the comparative psychology literature on nonhuman primate and human cognitive abilities now complete, we are in a position to summarize the key findings and see if we can draw out a pattern in the data. As stated in the preamble, it is not possible to turn over every stone, however, we hope that we have at least turned over all the big ones, and if there are a few remaining, they should not significantly impact our overall findings. To forestall any dissatisfaction, we should add that some additional stones will be turned over in the final discussion, and will bring us back full circle to our original aim of using the multiple stranded variable discontinuous model to deepen our understanding of the phenomenon of human uniqueness in the animal kingdom.

For a quick summary, refer to Figure 10. Here we will confine ourselves mostly to apes, the species closest to us genetically, while making passing references to other species. The theme that most strikingly emerges from the human-ape comparative experiments is that apes, while physically quite adept, overall lack *awareness of the existence of a parallel world of imagination and ideas*. This theme runs through the comparative cognitive strands like Ariadne's thread, tying them together into a unified whole, supporting the original idea of a branching away from a monadic dimension based on a common ancestor. Thus, apes have direct physical awareness of most things—in mirrors (awareness of their own body but doubtfully their own mind), in theory of mind (predicting an agent's physical behavior, but not their planned behavior including false belief), of causality (they know what the world does, but not how it does it), in imitation (they're expedient copiers, but are blind to others' intentions), in pedagogy (teaching occurs incidental to their own pursuits; they rarely perform intentional instruction), in cooperation (they're opportunistic collaborators triggered by local stimuli; they don't plan for future events together), in language (they're situation-bound; they don't utter vocalizations for displaced events), in using symbols (they can learn symbols and perform some abstract reasoning, but do not generate their own symbols), in mental time travel (they can plan for short-term concrete goals, but show no evidence of planning for hypothetical situations), in metacognition (they deliberate when sensing a discrepancy between memory and ambiguous stimuli, but do not appear to be able to transfer cumulative learning to analogous tasks).

In running through this list, it is hard not to get the impression that the root cause behind apes' cognitive limitations is their putative lack of self-awareness. This finding may disappoint some. To be fair, in certain situations apes *do* show awareness of the unseen world. For example, an ape can discriminate the weight of an object based on kinesthetic information (Schrauf and Call 2011). At the very minimum, they have access to a relative sense of "heavier/lighter." But to achieve it, they need to have direct physical contact with the objects of interest. This suggests they have what we might call "first order unseen awareness." Humans by comparison are able to infer that something is heavy based purely on observational knowledge of internal structure. To illustrate this point, take a car battery. Even if we have never lifted it, we know it is very heavy for its size because it contains a lot of lead—the heaviness of which we have learned independently. In this respect, we have "second order awareness of the unseen world." We are able to generate theoretical knowledge about things based on first order experiences. It would be interesting to see if apes could infer the second order concept of weight after acquiring the first order experience of a heavy element.

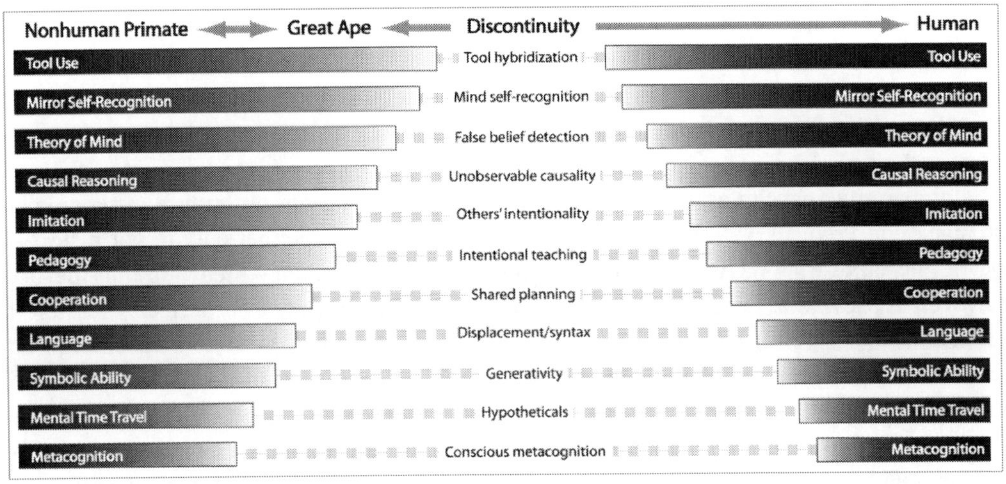

Figure 10. The Multi-Strand Variable Discontinuity Model revised based on the review of the comparative strands.

Arguably, second order awareness of the unseen world emerges only once the brain has achieved self-reflective consciousness. This is because self-awareness instantiates an experience of the unseen world in the subject's mind. Working memory and automonitoring play a pivotal role in this process. Baddeley's phonological loop/visual scratchpad exemplifies the experience, where replay of previously heard or seen auditory/visual stimuli occurs *decoupled* from the external world. To the person experiencing it, it has ultimate intimacy, *yet its location is unseen.* A parallel world of imagination has sprung into existence, one that is not concrete, not "here-and-now," yet resembles the world in many fleeting aspects. To take our car battery again, we are able to simulate its weight in our minds using a representation of the heaviness of lead. And we can do this not just with a real battery, but with a symbolic representation of it, and seamlessly transfer that knowledge to analogous domains. For example, if we are shown two bell shaped objects that are identical in all respects and pick them up discovering that one is made of steel, the other wood, before we have even struck them, we will know they will make two completely different sounds.

The first hominids that experienced self-awareness most probably were not aware of the fact. Dreams for example, which are completely decoupled from the external world, if recollected upon waking may have appeared as journeys into the real world unawares—ghost walking so-to-speak—and not until much later as the automonitoring function and causal reasoning more fully integrated would an inkling have occurred that some things in dreams simply don't make sense and could never happen in the real world. Given the long gestation period of human consciousness, we would have to conclude that differentiation of this sort probably didn't take place until very recently in human history, as diverse remnants of magical thinking still dominate much of human cognition. It is this latter archaic vestige of the human mind, *the proclivity to attribute causation to unseen agents that is the hallmark of our species.* On the one hand, it makes us realize how close we (still) are to our genetic cousins in terms of emerging from our distant animal past. On the other hand, when those attributions get out of control, we fall victim to mental disorders. It may be that mental disorders are the price we pay for an overwrought self-aware function. It is here that volitional control plays such an important role, as regulator of self-awareness. It is what allows us to leverage self-awareness for the benefit of ourselves and society.

Revisiting the Definition of Culture

Comparative psychology has struggled with the definition of culture. In one case (Premack and Premack 1994) it has been argued that apes have neither culture nor history. If you define culture as having only one component—accumulation—then this may be true. However, if viewed as "tradition" (Whiten et al. 2003), then it may be perfectly feasible to talk about apes having culture. Even though it is rare for new behaviors to emerge and become established in wild chimpanzee communities, studies show local differences in behavioral patterns and these are not dependent on genes (Lycett et al. 2009). Local variations arise through individual responses and through intergroup migration and can even differ between neighboring communities (Luncz et al. 2012). Vertical transmission appears to be the best account of how they become established. African elephants (*Loxodonta africana*) are well known in this respect, relying on the memory and experience of the female matriarch who gained her knowledge from previous generations of role models (McComb et al. 2011). It is this generational passing on of learned behavior that gives it the appearance of tradition. However, in humans, something else happens. Humans willfully manipulate the environment resulting in the production of myriad artificial traditions that, in many cases, are propagated long after the initial reasons for their invention have been forgotten. The learned behavior has become divorced from its environmental circumstances. In chimpanzees it can be seen that the adoption of a probing tool for termite fishing occurs because of the contiguous relationship between foraging and a local resource. The reason for adopting the behavior is constantly refreshed and present.

The divorcing of tradition from its immediate environmental stimuli leads to another very important development allied to cumulative culture: specialization. Specialization goes hand in hand with self-awareness because in order to specialize, one must have imagination. And to have imagination, one must have access to the parallel world of imagination that self-awareness affords. This is where human tool making far outstrips that of apes. Humans hybridize. We take two simple components and marry them in a unique way to produce an object greater than the sum of its parts. Moreover, once a hybridized tool is made, it is not just used once and forgotten. It is kept for long periods, modified, repaired, even traded. All of this is due to imagination, which is founded on the brain acquiring the ability to observe different parts of itself consciously. Here we should add: parts that are often a complete mystery to itself, but as a force of nature express themselves adaptively, sometimes maladaptively, regardless.

Hybridization is so ubiquitous in human culture, that a definition of culture without it would not be complete. Hybridization is the content of cumulative culture. If culture accumulated the same things over and over again, it would stagnate and collapse under its own weight. Thus, renewal of ideas and objects is vital for accumulation to function properly. From this standpoint, it is interesting to note that because ape cultures are essentially conservative and do not accumulate, they don't suffer the potential catastrophe that stagnation brings. As territorial nomads, they are constantly on the move. Humans by comparison settle down, which facilitates specialization and trade. But these are epiphenomena of culture and do not define it. Hybridization, on the other hand, is the lubricant of progress, and progress is the engine of human culture. So much so that it has almost become its raison d'être.

It is incredible to think that hybridization, which at its most basic level involves the associational linking of two seemingly independent mental representations, should have become such a powerful force in human evolution. The Sphinx is a hybridized icon. A human head on a lion's body. Two independent ideas linked together and physically impressed into matter out of pure imagination. Going back, microliths hafted onto wooden spears produced a major revolution in hunting technology. Going back even further, the symmetrical knapping of hand-axes exemplified the hybridization of form and function and proved so useful that it lasted over a million years with little change. Thus, culture in its broadest sense can be encapsulated as *the cumulative social transmission of renewed hybridization of form and function*. This definition captures the critical factors: accumulation, non-genetic transmission, and renewed hybridization of the two fundamental aspects of reality—the shape of things and the way they work.

In closing, we find that apes, while possessing social transmission of form and function, do not engage in renewed hybridization. Knowledge and skills that have accumulated in individuals must be passed on to conspecifics within their own lifetimes or become lost. The ability of humans to record information outside the brain has overcome this limitation and is another advance that owes its genesis to the hybridization of mental representations and physical expression. This fantastic ability and many more like it probably derived from a self-reflective function born out of a brain that grew, not necessarily larger, but more interconnected (Liu et al. 2012). The causal antecedents of this process is a question for another review—but there are some contenders: meat eating, gracilization, delayed maturation. Once the journey began, the *Pan-Homo* comparative psychology literature points to a watershed event: the birth of self-awareness, which, together with volitional control, supercharged our cognitive abilities, transforming them from the ordinary into the extraordinary.

REFERENCES

Aboitiz, F., García, R. R., Bosman, C., and Brunetti, E. (2006). Cortical memory mechanisms and language origins. *Brain and Language* 98(1), 40–56.

Addis, D. R., Wong, A. T., and Schacter, D. L. (2007). Remembering the past and imagining the future: Common and distinct neural substrates during event construction and elaboration. *Neuropsychologia* 45(7), 1363–1377.

Altman, J., and Das, G. D. (1964). Autoradiographic examination of the effects of enriched environment on the rate of glial multiplication in the adult rat brain. *Nature* 204(4964), 1161–1163.

Altmann, J., Alberts, S. C., Haines, S. A., Dubach, J., Muruthi, P., et al. (1996). Behavior predicts genetic structure in a wild primate group. *Proceedings of the National Academy of Sciences, USA* 93(12), 5797–5801.

Alvard, M. S. (2003). The adaptive nature of culture. *Evolutionary Anthropology* 12(3), 136–149.

Amorim, M.-A., Isableu, B., and Jarraya, M. (2006). Embodied spatial transformations: "Body analogy" for the mental rotation of objects. *Journal of Experimental Psychology: General* 135(3), 327–347.

Arai, J. A., Li, S., Hartley, D. M., and Feig, L. A. (2009). Transgenerational rescue of a genetic defect in long-term potentiation and memory formation by juvenile enrichment. *The Journal of Neuroscience* 29(5), 1496–1502.

Arbib, M. A. (2008). From grasp to language: Embodied concepts and the challenge of abstraction. *Journal of Physiology - Paris* 102(1-3), 4–20.

Asendorpf, J. B., Warkentin, V., and Baudonniere, P.-M. (1996). Self-awareness and other awareness II: Mirror self-recognition, social contigency awareness, and synchronic imitation. *Developmental Psychology* 32(2), 313–321.

Baddeley, A. D. (2000). The episodic buffer: A new component of working memory? *Trends in Cognitive Sciences* 4(11), 417–423.

Baddeley, A. D., and Hitch, G. J. (1974). Working memory. In G. A. Bower (Ed.), *The Psychology of Learning and Motivation: Advances in Research and Theory* (pp. 47–89). New York: Academic Press.

Baillargeon, R. e., Spelke, E. S., and Wasserman, S. (1985). Object permanence in five-month-old infants. *Cognition* 20(3), 191–208.

Barberia, I., Baetu, I., Murphy, R. A., and Baker, A. G. (2011). Do Associations Explain Mental Models of Cause? *International Journal of Comparative Psychology* 24, 365–388.

Bargh, J. A. (1984). Automatic and conscious processing of social information. In R. S. J. Wyer and T. K. Srull (Eds.), *Handbook of Social Cognition* (Vol. 3, pp. 1–43). Hillsdale, NJ: Lawrence Erlbaum Associates, Inc.

Bargh, J. A., and Chartrand, T. L. (1999). The unbearable automaticity of being. *American Pyschologist* 54(7), 462–479.

Barnes, J. L., Hill, T., Langer, M., Martinez, M., and Santos, L. R. (2008). Helping behaviour and regard for others in capuchin monkeys (Cebus apella). *Biology Letters* 4(6), 638–640.

Barnett, S. A. (1958). Experiments on 'neophobia' in wild and laboratory rats. *British Journal of Psychology* 49(3), 195–201.

Barth, J., Povinelli, D. J., and Cant, J. G. H. (2004). Bodily origins of self. In D. Beike, J. Lampinen and D. Behrend (Eds.), *The Self and Memory*. New York: Psychology Press.

Barth, J., Reaux, J. E., and Povinelli, D. J. (2005). Chimpanzees' (*Pan troglodytes*) use of gaze cues in object-choice tasks: different methods yield different results. *Animal Cognition* 8(2), 84–92.

Bartz, A. E. (1962). Eye-movement latency, duration, and response time as a function of angular displacement. *Journal of Experimental Psychology* 64, 318–324.

Bechara, A., Damásio, H., Tranel, D., and Damásio, A. R. (1997). Deciding advantageously before knowing the advantageous strategy. *Science* 275(5304), 1293–1295.

Beckers, T., Miller, R. R., De Houwer, J., and Urushihara, K. (2006). Reasoning rats: Forward blocking in Pavlovian animal conditioning is sensitive to constraints of causal inference. *Journal of Experimental Psychology General* 135(1), 92–102.

Bednarik, R. G. (2006). The Lower and Middle Palaeolithic origins of semiotics. In A.V. Yevglevsky (Ed.), *Structural and Semiotic Investigations in Archaeology* (pp. 89–106). Donetsk: Donetsk University Press.

Bennet, K. (2010). The chaos theory of evolution. *New Scientist,* 16 October, 28–31.

Beran, M. J., and Smith, J. D. (2011). Information seeking by rhesus monkeys (*Macaca mulatta*) and capuchin monkeys (*Cebus apella*). *Cognition* 120(1), 90–105.

Bernal, B., and Ardila, A. (2009). The role of the arcuate fasciculus in conduction aphasia. *Brain* 132(9), 2309–2316.

Berns, G. S., Laibson, D., and Loewenstein, G. (2007). Intertemporal choice – toward an integrative framework. *Trends in Cognitive Sciences* 11(11), 482–488.

Berthier, N. E., DeBlois, S., Poirier, C. R., Novak, M. A., and Clifton, R. K. (2000). Where's the ball? Two- and three-year-olds reason about unseen events. *Developmental Psychology* 36(3), 394–401.

Biben, M. (1998). Squirrel monkey play fighting: Making the case for a cognitive training function for play. In M. Bekoff and J. A. Byers (Eds.), *Animal Play: Evolutionary, Comparative, and Ecological Approaches* (pp. 161–182). New York: Cambridge University Press.

Bickerton, D. (2009). *Adam's Tongue: How Humans Made Language, How Language Made Humans*. New York: Hill and Wang.

Blakemore, S.-J., and Decety, J. (2001). From the perception of action to the understanding of intention. *Nature Reviews Neuroscience* 2(8), 561–567.

Boesch, C. (1991). Teaching among wild chimpanzees. *Animal Behaviour* 41(3), 530–532.

Boesch, C. (1994). Cooperative hunting in wild chimpanzees. *Animal Behaviour* 48(3), 653–667.

Boesch, C. (1995). Innovation in wild chimpanzees (Pan troglodytes). *International Journal of Primatology* 16(1), 1–16.

Boesch, C. (1996). Social grouping in Taï chimpanzees. In W. McGrew, L. Marchant and T. Nishida (Eds.), *Great Ape Societies* (pp. 101–113). Cambridge, MA: Cambridge University Press.

Boesch, C. (2002). Cooperative hunting roles among Taï chimpanzees. *Human Nature* 13(1), 27–46.

Boesch, C. (2005). Joint cooperative hunting among wild chimpanzees: Taking natural observations seriously. *Behavioral and Brain Sciences* 28(5), 692–693.

Boesch, C., and Boesch, H. (1989). Hunting behavior of wild chimpanzees in the Taï National Park. *American Journal of Physical Anthropology* 78(4), 547–573.

Boesch, C., and Boesch-Achermann, H. (2000). *The Chimpanzees of the Taï Forest: Behavioural Ecology and Evolution*. Oxford: Oxford University Press.

Boesch, C., and Tomasello, M. (1998). Chimpanzee and human cultures. *Current Anthropology* 39(5), 591–614.

Bovet, D., and Vauclair, J. (2000). Picture recognition in animals and humans. *Behavioural Brain Research* 109(2), 143–165.

Boyd, R., and Richerson, P. J. (1985). *Culture and the Evolutionary Process*. Chicago: University of Chicago Press.

Bramble, D. M., and Lieberman, D. E. (2004). Endurance running and the evolution of *Homo*. *Nature* 432(7015), 345–352.

Bräuer, J., Call, J., and Tomasello, M. (2005). All Great Ape species follow gaze to distant locations and around barriers. *Journal of Comparative Psychology* 119(2), 145–154.

Bräuer, J., Call, J., and Tomasello, M. (2007). Chimpanzees really know what others can see in a competitive situation. *Animal Cognition* 10(4), 439–448.

Bräuer, J., Kaminski, J., Riedel, J., Call, J., and Tomasello, M. (2006). Making inferences about the location of hidden food: Social dog, causal ape. *Journal of Comparative Psychology* 120(1), 38–47.

Britten, R. J. (2002). Divergence between samples of chimpanzee and human DNA sequences is 5% counting indels. *Proceedings of the National Academy of Sciences, USA* 99(21), 13633–13635.

Brosnan, S. F., Silk, J. B., Henrich, J., Mareno, M. C., Lambeth, S. P., et al. (2009). Chimpanzees (Pan troglodytes) do not develop contingent reciprocity in an experimental task. *Animal Cognition* 12(4), 587–597.

Bugnyar, T., and Huber, L. (1997). Push or pull: An experimental study on imitation in marmosets. *Animal Behaviour* 54(4), 817–831.

Burkart, J., Fehr, E., Efferson, C., and van Schaik, C. (2007). Other-regarding preferences in a non-human primate: Common marmosets provide food altruistically. *Proceedings of the National Academy of Sciences, USA* 104(50), 19762–19766.

Byrne, R. W. (2004). The manual skills and cognition that lie behind hominid tool use In A. E. Russon and D. R. Begun (Eds.), *The Evolution of Thought: Evolutionary Origins of Great Ape Intelligence* (pp. 31–44). Toronto: Cambridge University Press

Byrne, R. W., Barnard, P. J., Davidson, I., Janik, V. M., McGrew, W. C., et al. (2004). Understanding culture across species. *Trends in Cognitive Sciences* 8(8), 341–346.

Call, J. (2004). Inferences about the location of food in the great apes (Pan paniscus, Pan troglodytes, Gorilla gorilla, Pongo pygmaeus). *Journal of Comparative Psychology* 118(2), 232–241.

Call, J. (2010). Do apes know that they could be wrong? *Animal Cognition* 13(5), 689–700.

Call, J., and Carpenter, M. (2001). Do chimpanzees and children know what they have seen? *Animimal Cognition* 3(4), 207–220.

Call, J., and Tomasello, M. (2005). Reasoning and thinking in nonhuman primates. In K. J. Holyoak and R. G. Morrison (Eds.), *The Cambridge Handbook of Thinking and Reasoning* (pp. 607–632). Cambridge, MA: Cambridge University Press.

Call, J., and Tomasello, M. (2008). Does the chimpanzee have a theory of mind? 30 years later. *Trends in Cognitive Sciences* 12(5), 187–192.

Carey, S. (1985). *Conceptual change in childhood*. Cambridge, MA: MIT Press.

Carpenter, M., and Call, J. (2002). The chemistry of social learning. *Developmental Science* 5(1), 22–24.

Carrier, D. R. (1984). The energetic paradox of human running and hominid evolution. *Current Anthropology* 25(4), 483–495.

Carruthers, P. (2007). Meta-cognition in animals: A skeptical look. *Mind and Language* 22(1), 58–89.

Catani, M., and Mesulam, M. (2008). The arcuate fasciculus and the disconnection theme in language and aphasia: History and current state. *Cortex* 44(8), 953–961.

Chalmeau, R., Visalberghi, E., and Gallo, A. (1997). Capuchin monkeys (Cebus apella) fail to understand a cooperative task. *Animal Behaviour* 54(5), 1215–1225.

Chapman, C., Wrangham, R., and Chapman, L. (1995). Ecological constraints on group size: An analysis of spider monkey and chimpanzee subgroups. *Behavioral Ecology and Sociobiology* 36(1), 59–70.

Christel, M. (1993). Grasping techniques and hand preferences in Hominoidea. In H. Preuschoft and D. J. Chivers (Eds.), *Hands of Primates* (pp. 91–108). New York: Springer Verlag.

Christensen, W. (2007). The evolutionary origins of volition. In D. Spurrett, H. Kincaid, D. Ross and L. Stephens (Eds.), *Distributed Cognition and the Will: Individual Volition and Social Context* (pp. 255–288). Cambridge, MA: MIT Press.

Clayton, N. S., Bussey, T. J., Emery, N. J., and Dickinson, A. (2003). Prometheus to Proust: The case for behavioural criteria for "mental time travel". *Trends in Cognitive Sciences* 7(10), 436–437.

Clayton, N. S., and Dickinson, A. (1998). Episodic-like memory during cache recovery by scrub jays. *Nature* 395(7130), 272–274.

Clayton, N. S., Yu, K. S., and Dickinson, A. (2001). Scrub jays (*Aphelocoma coerulescens*) form integrated memories of the multiple features of caching episodes. *Journal of Experimental Psychology: Animal Behavior Processes* 27(1), 17–29.

Connolly, K. J. (1998). *The psychobiology of the hand*. Cambridge: Mac Keith Press.

Cook, P., and Wilson, M. (2010). Do young chimpanzees have extraordinary working memory? *Psychonomic Bulletin and Review* 17(4), 599–600.

Cousins, D., and Huffman, M. A. (2002). Medicinal properties in the diet of gorillas: an ethno-pharmacological evaluation. *African Study Monographs* 23(2), 65–89.

Cowlishaw, G., and Dunbar, R. I. M. (1991). Dominance rank and mating success in male primates. *Animal Behavior Monographs* 41(6), 1045–1056.

Crockford, C., Wittig, R. M., Mundry, R., and Zuberbühler, K. (2011). Wild chimpanzees inform ignorant group members of danger. *Current Biology* 22(2), 142–146.

Cronk, L. (1999). *That Complex Whole: Culture and Evolution of Behavior*. Boulder: Westview Press.

Custance, D., Prato-Previde, E., Spiezio, C., Rigamonti, M. M., and Poli, M. (2006). Social learning in pig-tailed macaques (*Macaca nemestrina*) and adult humans (*Homo sapiens*) on a two-action artificial fruit. *Journal of Comparative Psychology* 120(3), 303–313.

Damásio, A. R. (1994). *Descartes' Error: Emotion, Reason and the Human Brain*. New York: Putnam.

Darwin, C. (1874/1896). *The Descent of Man and Selection in Relation to Sex* (2nd ed.). New York: D. Appleton and Company.

Davies, M. B. (1983). Quartenary history of deciduous forests of Eastern North America and Europe. *Annals of the Missouri Botanical Garden* 70(3), 550–563.

Dawson, B. V., and Foss, B. M. (1965). Observational learning in budgerigars. *Animal Behaviour* 13(4), 470–474.

De Ruiter, J. R., Van Hooff, J. A. R. A. M., and Scheffrahn, W. (1994). Social and genetic aspects of paternity in wild long-tailed macaques (*Macaca fascicularis*). *Behaviour* 129(3/4), 203–224.

de Waal, F. (1992). Coalitions as part of reciprocal relations in the Arnhem chimpanzee colony. In A. H. Harcourt and F. B. M. de Waal (Eds.), *Coalitions and Alliances in Humans and Other Animals*. Oxford: Oxford University Press.

de Waal, F. B. M. (2008). The thief in the mirror. *PLoS Biology (Public Library of Science)* 6(8), e201.

de Waal, F. B. M., and Ferrari, P. F. (2010). Towards a bottom-up perspective on animal and human cognition. *Trends in Cognitive Sciences* 14(5), 201–207.

de Waal, F. B. M., Leimgruber, K., and Greenberg, A. R. (2008). Giving is self-rewarding for monkeys. *Proceedings of the National Academy of Sciences, USA* 105(36), 13685–13689.

Delfour, F., and Marten, K. (2001). Mirror image processing in three marine mammal species: killer whales (Orcinus orca), false killer whales (Pseudorca crassidens) and California sea lions (*Zalophus californianus*). *Behavioural Processes* 53(3), 181–190.

Dewsbury, D. A. (1984). *Comparative Psychology in the Twentieth Century*. Stroudsburg, PA: Hutchinson Ross.

Di Bitetti, M. S. (2005). Food-associated calls and audience effects in tufted capuchin monkeys, *Cebus apella nigritus*. *Animal Behaviour* 69(4), 911–919.

di Pellegrino, G., Fadiga, L., Fogassi, L., Gallese, V., and Rizzolatti, G. (1992). Understanding motor events: a neurophysiological study. *Experimental Brain Research* 91(1), 176–180.

Dindo, M., de Waal, F. B. M., Thierry, B., and Whiten, A. (2010). Conditional copying fidelity in capuchin monkeys (*Cebus apella*). *Journal of Comparative Psychology* 124(1), 29–37.

Donald, M. (1991). *Origins of the Modern Mind: Three Stages in the Evolution of Culture and Cognition*. Cambridge: Harvard University Press.

Dronkers, N. F., and Ogar, J. (2004). Brain areas involved in speech production. *Brain* 127(7), 1461–1462.

Dronkers, N. F., Wilkins, D. P., Van Valin, R. D. J., Redfern, B. B., and Jaeger, J. J. (2004). Lesion analysis of the brain areas involved in language comprehension. *Cognition* 92(1–2), 145–177.

Dunbar, R. I. M. (2003). The social brain: Mind, language, and society in evolutionary perspective. *Annual Review of Anthropology* 32, 163–181.

Durham, W. (1991). *Coevolution: genes, culture and human diversity*. Palo Alto: Stanford University Press.

Elliott, J. M., and Connolly, K. J. (1984). A classification of manipulative hand movements. *Developmental Medicine and Child Neurology* 26(3), 283–296.

Enard, W., Gehre, S., Hammerschmidt, K., Holter, S. M., Blass, T., et al. (2009). A humanized version of FOXP2 affects cortico-basal ganglia circuits in mice. *Cell* 137(5), 961–971.

Enard, W., Przeworski, M., Fisher, S. E., Lai, C. S., Wiebe, V., et al. (2002). Molecular evolution of FOXP2, a gene involved in speech and language. *Nature* 418(6900), 869–872.

Epley, N., and Whitchurch, E. (2008). Mirror, mirror on the wall: Enhancement in self-recognition. *Personality and Social Psychology Bulletin* 34(9), 1159–1170.

Falcone, R., Brunamonti, E., Ferraina, S., and Genovesio, A. (2012). Monkeys monitor human goals in a nonmatch-to-goal interactive task. *PLoS ONE (Public Library of Science)* 7(2), e32209.

Flavell, J. H. (1976). Metacognitive aspects of problem solving. In L. B. Resnick (Ed.), *The Nature of Intelligence* (pp. 231–236). Hillsdale, NJ: Erlbaum.

Flavell, J. H. (1979). Metacognition and cognitive monitoring: A new area of cognitive-developmental inquiry. *American Psychologist* 34(10), 906–911.

Fletcher, L., and Carruthers, P. (2012). Behavior-reading versus mentalizing in animals. In J. Metcalfe and H. Terrace (Eds.), *Agency and Joint Attention*. Oxford: Oxford University Press.

Flinn, M. (1997). Culture and the evolution of social learning. *Evolution Human Behavior* 18(1), 23–67.

Flombaum, J. I., and Santos, L. R. (2005). Rhesus monkeys attribute perceptions to others. *Current Biology* 15(5), 447–452.

Flynn, E., and Whiten, A. (2010). Studying children's social learning experimentally "in the wild". *Learning and Behavior* 38(3), 284–296.

Fouts, R. S. (1973). Acquisition and testing of gestural signs in four young chimpanzees. *Science* 180(4089), 978–980.

Friedman, W. J. (1993). Memory for the time of past events. *Psychological Bulletin* 113(1), 44–66.

Fujita, K. (2009). Metamemory in tufted capuchin monkeys (*Cebus apella*). *Animal Cognition* 12(4), 575–585.

Fujiyama, A., Watanabe, H., Toyoda, A., Taylor, T. D., Itoh, T., et al. (2002). Construction and analysis of a human-chimpanzee comparative clone map. *Science* 295(5552), 131–134.

Gagneux, P., and Varki, A. (2001). Genetic differences between humans and great apes. *Molecular Phylogenetics and Evolution* 18(1), 2–13.

Gallese, V., Fadiga, L., Fogassi, L., and Rizzolatti, G. (1996). Action recognition in the premotor cortex. *Brain* 119(2), 593–609.

Gallese, V., and Lakoff, G. (2005). The brain's concepts: The role of the sensory–motor system in conceptual knowledge. *Cognitive Neuropsychology 22*(3), 455–479.

Gallistel, R. (2000). The replacement of general-purpose learning models with adaptively specialized learning modules. In M. Gazzaniga (Ed.), *The New Cognitive Neurosciences* (2nd ed.). Cambridge, MA: MIT Press.

Gallup, G. G. J. (1970). Chimpanzees: Self recognition. *Science* 167(3914), 86–87.

Gallup, G. G. J. (1983). Toward a comparative psychology of mind. In R. L. Mellgren (Ed.), *Animal Cognition and Behavior* (pp. 473–510). New York: North-Holland.

Gardner, R. A., and Gardner, B. T. (1969). Teaching Sign Language to a Chimpanzee. *Science* 165(3894), 664–672.

Gelman, S. A., Coley, J. D., and Gottfried, G. M. (1994). Essentialist beliefs in children: The acquisition of concepts and theories. In L. A. Hirschfield and S. A. Gelman (Eds.), *Mapping the Mind: Domain Specificity in Cognition and Culture* (pp. 341–366). New York: Cambridge University Press.

Gergerly, G., Nadasdy, Z., Csibra, G., and Biro, S. (1995). Taking the intentional stance at 12 months of age. *Cognition* 56(2), 165–193.

Geribàs, N., Mosquera, M., and Vergès, J. M. (2010). The gesture substratum of stone tool making: an experimental approach. *Museologia Scientifica e Naturalistica* 6, 155–162.

Gibson, E. J., and Walk, R. D. (1960). The "visual cliff". *Scientific American* 202, 64–71.

Gigerenzer, G. (2001). The Adaptive Toolbox: Toward a Darwinian rationality. In J. A. French, A. C. Kamil and D. W. Leger (Eds.), *Evolutionary Psychology and Motivation*

(Nebraska Symposium on Motivation) (Vol. 48, 113–143). Lincoln: University of Nebraska Press.

Gigerenzer, G. (2007). *Gut Feelings: The Intelligence of the Unconscious*. New York: Viking Adult.

Gigerenzer, G., and Hoffrage, U. (1995). How to improve Bayesian reasoning without instruction: Frequency formats. *Psychological Review* 102(4), 684–704.

Gilby, I., Eberly, L., Pintea, L., and Pusey, A. (2006). Ecological and social influences on the hunting behaviour of wild chimpanzees, *Pan troglodytes schweinfurthii*. *Animal Behaviour* 72(1), 169–180.

Gilby, I., Eberly, L., and Wrangham, R. (2008). Economic profitability of social predation among wild chimpanzees: Individual variation promotes cooperation. *Animal Behaviour* 75(2), 351–360.

Gilby, I. C. (2006). Meat sharing among the Gombe chimpanzees: Harassment and reciprocal exchange. *Animal Behaviour* 71(4), 953–963.

Girndt, A., Meier, T., and Call, J. (2008). Task constraints mask Great Apes' ability to solve the trap-table task. *Journal of Experimental Psychology: Animal Behavior Processes* 34(1), 54–62.

Gómez, J.-C., and Andrade, B. (2005). Fantasy in apes. In A. D. Pellegrini and P. K. Smith (Eds.), *The nature of play: Great apes and humans* (pp. 139–172). New York: Guilford.

Goodall, J. (1963). Feeding behaviour of wild chimpanzees: A preliminary report. *Symposia of the Zoological Society of London,* 10(August), 39–47.

Goodall, J. (1968). The behaviour of free-living chimpanzees in the Gombe Stream area. *Animal Behavior Monographs 1*, 161–311.

Goodall, J. (1986). *The Chimpanzees of Gombe: Patterns of Behavior*. Cambridge, MA: Harvard University Press.

Goodall, J. (2011). 'Learning'. Retrieved April 15, 2012, Web Address *http://www.janegoodall.org/media/videos/learning*

Gopnik, A. (2010). How babies think. *Scientific American* (July), 76–81.

Gopnik, A., and Tenenbaum, J. (2007). Bayesian networks, Bayesian learning and cognitive development. *Developmental Science* 10(3), 281–287.

Grainger, J., Dufau, S., Montant, M., Ziegler, J. C., and Fagot, J. (2012). Orthographic Processing in Baboons (*Papio papio*). *Science* 336(6078), 245–248.

Greenfield, P. M., Maynard, A. E., Boehm, C., and Schmidtling, E. Y. (2000). Cultural apprenticeship and cultural change: tool learning and imitation in chimpanzees and humans. In S. T. Parker, J. Langer and M. L. McKinney (Eds.), *Biology, brains, and behavior: the evolution of human development* (pp. 237–277). Santa Fe, NM: School of American Research Press.

Gustafsson, E., Krief, S., and Saint Jalme, M. (2011). Neophobia and learning mechanisms: How captive orangutans discover novel plants. *Folia Primatologica* 82(1), 45–55.

Gyger, M., and Marler, P. (1988). Food calling in the domestic fowl, *Gallus gallus*: The role of external referents and deception. *Animal Behaviour* 36(2), 358–365.

Hagmayer, Y., Sloman, S., Lagnado, D., and Waldmann, M. R. (2007). Causal reasoning through intervention. In A. Gopnik and L. Schulz (Eds.), *Causal Learning: Psychology, Philosophy, and Computation* (pp. 86–101): Oxford University Press.

Hampton, R. H. (2005). Can rhesus monkeys discriminate between remembering and forgetting? In H. S. Terrace and J. Metcalfe (Eds.), *The Missing Link in Cognition:*

Origins of Self-Reflective Consciousness (pp. 272–295). Oxford: Oxford University Press.

Hampton, R. R. (2001). Rhesus monkeys know when they remember. *Proceedings of the National Academy of Sciences, USA* 98(9), 5359–5362.

Hampton, R. R. (2009). Multiple demonstrations of metacognition in nonhumans: Converging evidence or multiple mechanisms? *Comparative Cognition and Behavior Reviews* 4, 17–28.

Hampton, R. R., Zivin, A., and Murray, E. A. (2004). Rhesus monkeys (*Macaca mulatta*) discriminate between knowing and not knowing and collect information as needed before acting. *Animal Cognition* 7(4), 239–254.

Hare, B., Call, J., Agnetta, B., and Tomasello, M. (2000). Chimpanzees know what conspecifics do and do not see. *Animal Behaviour* 59(4), 771–785.

Hare, B., Call, J., and Tomasello, M. (2006). Chimpanzees deceive a human competitor by hiding. *Cognition 101*(3), 495–514.

Hare, B., and Kwetuenda, S. (2010). Bonobos voluntarily share their own food with others. *Current Biology 20*(5), R230.

Hare, B., Melis, A. P., Woods, V., Hastings, S., and Wrangham, R. (2007). Tolerance allows bonobos to outperform chimpanzees on a cooperative task. *Current Biology* 17(7), 619–623.

Hatfield, G. (2002). Perception as unconscious inference. In D. Heyer and R. Mausfeld (Eds.), *Perception and the Physical World: Psychological and Philosophical Issue in Perception* (pp. 115–143). Chichester, UK: John Wiley and Sons, Ltd.

Hattori, Y., Leimgruber, K., Fujita, K., and de Waal, F. B. M. (2012). Food-related tolerance in capuchin monkeys (Cebus apella) varies with knowledge of the partner's previous food-consumption. *Behaviour* 149(2), 171–185.

Hauser, M., Chen, K., Chen, F., and Chuang, E. (2003). Give unto others: genetically unrelated cotton-top tamarin monkeys preferentially give food to those who altruistically give back. *Proceedings of the Royal Society B: Biological Sciences* 270(1531), 2363–2370.

Hauser, M. D. (1998a). A nonhuman primate's expectations about object motion and destination: The importance of self-propelled movement and animacy. *Developmental Science* 1(1), 31–37.

Hauser, M. D. (1998b). Functional referents and acoustic similarity: field playback experiments with rhesus monkeys. *Animal Behaviour* 55(6), 1647–1658.

Hauser, M. D. (2000). *Wild Minds: What Animals Really think.* New York: Henry Holt and Company.

Hauser, M. D., Kralik, J., and Botto-Mahan, C. (1999). Problem solving and functional design features: Experiments on cotton-top tamarins, *Saguinus oedipus oedipus*. *Animal Behaviour* 57(3), 565–582.

Hauser, M. D., and Marler, P. (1993). Food-associated calls in rhesus macaques (*Macaca mulatta*). II. Costs and benefits of call production and suppression. *Behavioral Ecology* 4(3), 206–212.

Hauser, M. D., Pearson, H., and Seelig, D. (2002). Ontogeny of tool use in cotton-top tamarins, *Saguinus oedipus*: Innate recognition of functionally relevant features. *Animal Behaviour* 64(2), 299–311.

Hayden, B. Y., and Platt, M. L. (2007). Animal cognition: Great apes wait for grapes. *Current Biology* 17(21), R922–R923.

Helmholtz, H. L. (1867/1910). Handbuch der physiologischen optik. In A. Gullstrand, J. von Kries and W. Nagel (Eds.), *Handbuch der Physiologischen Optik* (3rd ed.). Hamburg and Leipzig: L. Voss.

Herrmann, E., and Tomasello, M. (2006). Apes' and children's understanding of cooperative and competitive motives in a communicative situation. *Developmental Science* 9(5), 518–529.

Heschl, A., and Burkart, J. (2006). A new mark test for mirror self-recognition in non-human primates. *Primates* 47(3), 187–198.

Heschl, A., and Fuchsbichler, C. (2009). Siamangs (*Hylobates syndactylus*) recognize their mirror image. *International Journal of Comparative Psychology* 22(4), 221–233.

Hirata, S., and Fuwa, K. (2007). Chimpanzees learn to act with other individuals in a cooperative task. *Primates 48*(1), 13–21.

Hockett, C. F. (1960). The origin of speech. *Scientific American* 203, 88–96.

Hockings, K. J., Humle, T., Anderson, J. R., Biro, D., Sousa, C., et al. (2007). Chimpanzees share forbidden fruit. *PLoS ONE (Public Library of Science)* 2(9), p. e886.

Hohmann, G., and Fruth, B. (2002). Dynamics in social organization of bonobos (*Pan paniscus*). In G. H. L. F. M. C. Boesch (Ed.), *Behavioural Diversity in Chimpanzees and Bonobos* (pp. 138–150). Cambridge, UK: Cambridge University Press.

Hood, B. M., Carey, S., and Prasada, S. (2000). Predicting the outcomes of physical events: Two-year-olds fail to reveal knowledge of solidity and support. *Child Development* 71(6), 1540–1554.

Hood, B. M., Hauser, M. D., Anderson, L., and Santos, L. R. (1999). Gravity biases in a non-human primate? *Developmental Science* 2(1), 35–41.

Hopkins, W. D., Taglialatela, J. P., and Leavens, D. A. (2011). Do chimpanzees have voluntary control of their facial expressions and vocalizations? In A. Vilain, J.-L. Schwartz, C. Abry and J. Vauclair (Eds.), *Primate Communication and Human Language: Vocalisation, Gestures, Imitation and Deixis in Humans and Non-Humans* (pp. 71–88).

Hopper, L., Lambeth, S., Schapiro, S., and Whiten, A. (2008). Observational learning in chimpanzees and children studied through "ghost" conditions. *Proceedings of the Royal Society B: Biological Sciences* 275(1636), 835–840.

Horner, V., Proctor, D., Bonnie, K. E., Whiten, A., and de Waal, F. B. M. (2010). Prestige affects cultural learning in chimpanzees. *PLoS ONE (Public Library of Science)* 5(5), e10625.

Horner, V., and Whiten, A. (2005). Causal knowledge and imitation/emulation switching in chimpanzees (*Pan troglodytes*) and children (*Homo sapiens*). *Animal Cognition* 8(3), 164–181.

Horner, V., and Whiten, A. (2007). Learning from others' mistakes? Limits on understanding a trap-tube task by young chimpanzees (*Pan troglodytes*) and children (*Homo sapiens*). *Journal of Comparative Psychology* 121(1), 12–21.

Horner, V. J., Cartera, D., Suchaka, M., and de Waal, F. B. M. (2011). Spontaneous prosocial choice by chimpanzees. *Proceedings of the National Academy of Sciences, USA* 108(33), 13847–13851.

Horowitz, A. C. (2003). Do humans ape? Or do apes human? Imitation and intention in humans (*Homo sapiens*) and other animals. *Journal of Comparative Psychology* 117(3), 325–336.

Hrubesch, C., Preuschoft, S., and van Schaik, C. (2009). Skill mastery inhibits adoption of observed alternative solutions among chimpanzees (Pan troglodytes). *Animal Cognition* 12(2), 209–216.

Hsieh, P.-J., Colas, J. T., and Kanwisher, N. (2011). Pop-out without awareness: Unseen feature singletons capture attention only when top-down attention is available. *Psychological Science* 22(9), 1220–1226.

Huffman, M. A., and Wrangham, R. W. (1994). Diversity of medicinal plant use by chimpanzees in the wild. In R. W. Wrangham, W. C. McGrew, F. B. M. de Waal and P. G. Heltne (Eds.), *Chimpanzee Cultures* (pp. 129–148). Cambridge: Harvard University Press.

Hughes, J. F., Skaletsky, H., Pyntikova, T., Graves, T. A., van Daalen, S. K. M., et al. (2010). Chimpanzee and human Y chromosomes are remarkably divergent in structure and gene content. *Nature* 463(7280), 536–539.

Hunter, R. G., McCarthy, K. J., Milne, T. A., Pfaff, D. W., and McEwen, B. S. (2009). Regulation of hippocampal H3 histone methylation by acute and chronic stress. *Proceedings of the National Academy of Sciences, USA* 106(49), 20912–20917.

Huttenlocher, P. R. (1979). Synaptic density in human frontal cortex - developmental changes and effects of aging. *Brain Research* 163(2), 195–205.

Iacoboni, M., Woods, R. P., Brass, M., Bekkering, H., Mazziotta, J. C., et al. (1999). Cortical mechanisms of human imitation. *Science* 286(5449), 2526–2528.

Inizian, M.-L., Reduron-Ballinger, M., Roche, H., and Tixier, J. (1999). Technology and technology of knapped stone. *Nanterre: C.R.E.P.*

Inoue, S., and Matsuzawa, T. (2007). Working memory of numerals in chimpanzees. *Current Biology* 17(23), R1004–R1005.

Jensen, K., Hare, B., Call, J., and Tomasello, M. (2006). What's in it for me? Self-regard precludes altruism and spite in chimpanzees. *Proceedings of the Royal Society B: Biological Sciences* 273(1589), 1013–1021.

Kaminski, J., Call, J., and Tomasello, M. (2008). Chimpanzees know what others know, but not what they believe. *Cognition* 109(2), 224–234.

Karin-D'Arcy, M. R., and Povinelli, D. J. (2002). Do chimpanzees know what each other see? A closer look. *International Journal of Comparative Psychology* 15(1), 21–54.

Kastak, R. C., and Schusterman, R. J. (2002). Long-term memory for concepts in a California sea lion (*Zalophus californianus*). *Animal cognition* 5(4), 225–232.

Kawai, M. (1965). Newly-acquired pre-cultural behavior of the natural troop of Japanese monkeys on Koshima islet. *Primates* 6(1), 1–30.

Kenward, B. (2012). Over-imitating preschoolers believe unnecessary actions are normative and enforce their performance by a third party. *Journal of Experimental Child Psychology,* Epub ahead of print.

Kihlstrom, J. F. (1987). The cognitive unconscious. *Science* 237(4821), 1445–1452.

Kimura, M. (1968). Evolutionary rate at the molecular level. *Nature* 217(5129), 624–626.

King, J. L., and Jukes, T. H. (1969). Non-Darwinian evolution. *Science* 164(3881), 788–798.

Kirchhofer, K. C., Zimmermann, F., Kaminski, J., and Tomasello, M. (2012). Dogs (*Canis familiaris*), but Not Chimpanzees (*Pan troglodytes*), Understand Imperative Pointing. *PLoS ONE (Public Library of Science)* 7(2), e30913.

Kirkpatrick, C. (2007). Tactical deception and the Great Apes: Insight into the question of theory of mind. *Totem: The University of Western Ontario Journal of Anthropology* 15(1), p. Article 4.

Kiyono, S., Seo, M. L., Shibagaki, M., and Inouye, M. (1985). Facilitative effects of maternal environmental enrichment on maze learning in rat offspring. *Physiology and Behavior* 34(3), 431–435.

Koriat, A. (1993). How do we know that we know? The accessibility model of the feeling of knowing. *Psychological Review 100*(4), 609–639.

Kornell, N., Son, L. K., and Terrace, H. S. (2007). Transfer of metacognitive skills and hint seeking in monkeys. *Psychological Science* 18(1), 64–71.

Kosslyn, S. M. (2005). Mental images and the brain. *Cognitive Neuropsychology* 22(3/4), 333–347.

Ladygina-Kohts, N. N. (2002). *Infant Chimpanzee and Human Child: A Classic 1935 Comparative Study of Ape Emotions and Intelligence* (B. Vekker, Trans.). Oxford: Oxford University Press.

Ladygina-Kohts, N. N., and Dembovskii, Y. N. (1969). The psychology of primates. In M. Cole and I. Maltzman (Eds.), *A Handbook of Contemporary Soviet Psychology* (pp. 41–70). New York: Basic Books.

Lai, C. S. L., Fisher, S. E., Hurst, J. A., Vargha-Khadem, F., and Monaco, A. P. (2001). A forkhead-domain gene is mutated in a severe speech and language disorder. *Nature* 413(6855), 519–523.

Lakoff, G., P., and Johnson, M. (1999). *Philosophy In The Flesh: the Embodied Mind and its Challenge to Western Thought.* New York: Basic Books.

Lakshminarayanan, V. R., and Santos, L. R. (2008). Capuchin monkeys are sensitive to others' welfare. *Current Biology* 18(21), R999–R1000.

Lethmate, J. (1977). Further studies on manipulation and tool behavior of young orangutans. *Primates* 18(3), 531–543.

Lethmate, J. (1979). Instrumental behaviour of zoo orangutans. *Journal of Human Evolution* 8(8), 741–744.

Li, G., Wang, J., Rossiter, S. J., Jones, G., and Zhang, S. (2007). Accelerated FOXP2 evolution in echolocating bats. *PLoS ONE (Public Library of Science)* 2(9), e900.

Liberman, N., and Trope, Y. (2008). The psychology of transcending the here and now. *Science* 322(5905), 1201–1205.

Libet, B. (1999). Do we have free will? *Journal of Consciousness Studies* 6(8–9), 47–57.

Limongelli, L., T., B. S., and Visalberghi, E. (1995). Comprehension of cause–effect relations in a tool-using task by chimpanzees (*Pan troglodytes*). *Journal of Comparative Psychology* 109(1), 18–26.

Lin, J. Y., Murray, S. O., and Boynton, G. M. (2009). Capture of attention to threatening stimuli without perceptual awareness. *Current Biology 19*(13), 1118–1122.

Lingnau, A., Gesierich, B., and Caramazza, A. (2009). Asymmetric fMRI adaptation reveals no evidence for mirror neurons in humans. *Proceedings of the National Academy of Sciences, USA* 106(24), 9925–9930.

Liu, Q., Fragaszy, D., Wright, B., Wright, K., Izar, P., et al. (2011). Wild bearded capuchin monkeys (*Cebus libidinosus*) place nuts in anvils selectively. *Animal Behaviour* 81(1), 297–305.

Liu, X., Somel, M., Tang, L., Yan, Z., Jiang, X., et al. (2012). Extension of cortical synaptic development distinguishes humans from chimpanzees and macaques. *Genome Research* 22(4), 611–622.

Lonsdorf, E. V. (2006). What is the role of mothers in the acquisition of termite-fishing behaviors in wild chimpanzees (*Pan troglodytes schweinfurthii*)? *Animal Cognition* 9(1), 36–46.

Lovette, I. J. (2005). Glacial cycles and the tempo of avian speciation. *Trends in Ecology and Evolution* 20(2), 57–59.

Luncz, L. V., Mundry, R., and Boesch, C. (2012). Evidence for cultural differences between neighboring chimpanzee communities. *Current Biology* in press.

Lycett, S. J., Collard, M., and McGrew, W. C. (2009). Cladistic analyses of behavioural variation in wild Pan troglodytes: exploring the chimpanzee culture hypothesis. *Journal of Human Evolution* 57(4), 337–349.

Lyn, H., Russell, J. L., and Hopkins, W. D. (2010). The impact of environment on the comprehension of declarative communication in apes. *Psychological Science* 21(3), 360–365.

Lyons, D. E., Damrosch, D. H., Lin, J. K., Macris, D. M., and Keil, F. C. (2011). The scope and limits of overimitation in the transmission of artefact culture. *Philosophical Transactions of the Royal Society B: Biological Sciences* 366(1567), 1158–1167.

Lyons, D. E., Young, A. G., and Keil, F. C. (2007). The hidden structure of overimitation. *Proceedings of the National Academy of Sciences, USA* 104(50), 19751–19756.

MacDermot, K. D., Bonora, E., Sykes, N., Coupe, A.-M., Lai, C. S. L., et al. (2005). Identification of FOXP2 truncation as a novel cause of developmental speech and language deficits. *American Journal of Human Genetics* 76(6), 1074–1080.

Machado, A., and Silva, F. J. (2003). You can lead an ape to a tool, but . . .: A review of Povinelli's folk physics for apes: the chimpanzee's theory of how the world works. *Journal of the Experimental Analysis of Behavior* 79(2), 267–286.

Manrique, H. M., Gross, A. N.-M., and Call, J. (2010). Great Apes select tools on the basis of their rigidity. *Journal of Experimental Psychology: Animal Behavior Processes* 36(4), 409–422.

Marsh, H. L., and Macdonald, S. E. (2011). Orangutans (*pongo abelii*) "play the odds": Information-seeking strategies in relation to cost, risk, and benefit. *Journal of Comparative Psychology,* Epub ahead of print.

Marshall-Pescini, S., and Whiten, A. (2008a). Chimpanzees (*Pan troglodytes*) and the question of cumulative culture: an experimental approach. *Animal Cognition* 11(3), 449–456.

Marshall-Pescini, S., and Whiten, A. (2008b). Social learning of nut-cracking behavior in East African sanctuary-living chimpanzees (*Pan troglodytes schweinfurthii*). *Journal of Comparative Psychology* 122(2), 186–194.

Marten, K., and Psarakos, S. (1995). Evidence of self-awareness in the bottlenose dolphin (*Tursiops truncatus*). In S. T. Parker, R. Mitchell and M. Boccia (Eds.), *Self-awareness in Animals and Humans: Developmental Perspectives* (pp. 361–379). Cambridge, U.K.: Cambridge University Press.

Martin-Ordas, G., Call, J., and Colmenares, F. (2008). Tubes, tables and traps: Great apes solve two functionally equivalent trap tasks but show no evidence of transfer across tasks. *Animal Cognition* 11(3), 423–430.

Marzke, M. W., and Wullstein, K. L. (1995). Chimpanzee and human grips: A new classification with a focus on evolutionary morphology. *International Journal of Primatology* 17(1), 117–139.

Masataka, N., and Kohda, M. (1988). Primate play vocalizations and their functional significance. *Folia Primatologica International Journal of Primatology* 50(1–2), 152–156.

Masi, S., Gustafsson, E., Saint Jalme, M., Narat, V., Todd, A., et al. (2011). Unusual feeding behaviour in wild great apes, a window to understand origins of self-medication in humans: Role of sociality and physiology on learning process. *Physiology and Behavior* 105(2), 337–349.

Matsumoto-Oda, A., Hosaka, K., Huffman, M., and Kawanaka, K. (1998). Factors affecting party size in chimpanzees of the Mahale Mountains. *International Journal of Primatology* 19(6), 999–1011.

Matsuzawa, T. (1996). Chimpanzee intelligence in nature and in captivity: Isomorphism of symbol use and tool use. In W. C. McGrew, L. F. Marchant and T. Nishida (Eds.), *Great Ape Societies* (pp. 196–209). Cambridge: Cambridge University Press.

Matsuzawa, T. (2002). Chimpanzee Ai and her son Ayumu: An episode of education by master-apprenticeship. In C. Allen, M. Bekoff and G. M. Burghardt (Eds.), *The Cognitive Animal: Empirical and Theoretical Perspectives on Animal Cognition* (pp. 189–195). Cambridge, MA: MIT Press.

Matsuzawa, T., and Yamakoshi, G. (1996). Comparison of chimpanzee material culture between Bossou and Nimba, West Africa. In A. E. Russon, K. A. Bard and S. T. Parker (Eds.), *Reaching into Thought: The Minds of the Great Apes* (pp. 211–232). Cambridge: Cambridge University Press.

McCloskey, M., Washburn, A., and Felch, L. (1983). Intuitive physics: The straight-down belief and its origin. *Journal of Experimental Psychology: Learning, Memory, and Cognition* 9(4), 636–649.

McComb, K., Shannon, G., Durant, S. M., Sayialel, K., Slotow, R., et al. (2011). Leadership in elephants: the adaptive value of age. *Proceedings of the Royal Society B: Biological Sciences* 278(1722), 3270–3276.

McGuigan, N., Makinson, J., and Whiten, A. (2011). From over-imitation to super-copying: Adults imitate causally irrelevant aspects of tool use with higher fidelity than young children. *British Journal of Psychology* 102(1), 1–18.

McHenry, H. M., and Coffing, K. (2000). Australopithecus to Homo: Transformations in body and mind. *Annual Review of Anthropology* 29, 125–146.

McMahon, S., Macpherson, K., and Roberts, W. A. (2010). Dogs choose a human informant: Metacognition in canines. *Behavioral Processes* 85(3), 293–298.

McPherron, S. P. (2000). Handaxes as a measure of the mental capabilities of early hominids. *Journal of Archaeological Science* 27(8), 655–663.

Melis, A. P., Hare, B., and Tomasello, M. (2006a). Chimpanzees recruit the best collaborators. *Science* 311(5765), 1297–1300.

Melis, A. P., Hare, B., and Tomasello, M. (2006b). Engineering cooperation in chimpanzees: tolerance constraints on cooperation. *Animal Behaviour* 72(2), 275–286.

Melis, A. P., Hare, B., and Tomasello, M. (2009). Chimpanzees coordinate in a negotiation game. *Evolution and Human Behavior* 30(6), 381–392.

Melis, A. P., Schneider, A.-C., and Tomasello, M. (2011). Chimpanzees, Pan troglodytes, share food in the same way after collaborative and individual food acquisition. *Animal Behaviour* 82(3), 485–493.

Melis, A. P., Warneken, F., Jensen, K., Schneider, A. C., Call, J., et al. (2011). Chimpanzees help conspecifics obtain food and non-food items. *Proceedings of the Royal Society B: Biological Sciences* 278(1710), 1405–1413.

Meltzoff, A. N. (2005). Imitation and other minds: The 'Like Me' hypothesis. In S. Hurley and N. Chater (Eds.), *Perspectives on Imitation: From Neuroscience to Social Science* (Vol. 2: Imitation, Human Development, and Culture, 55–77). Cambridge, MA: MIT Press.

Meltzoff, A. N., and Moore, M. K. (1977). Imitation of facial and manual gestures by human neonates. *Science* 198(4312), 75–78.

Meltzoff, A. N., and Moore, M. K. (1997). Explaining facial imitation: A theoretical model. *Early Developmental Parenting* 6(3–4), 179–192.

Mendres, K. A., and de Waal, F. B. M. (2000). Capuchins do cooperate: The advantage of an intuitive task. *Animal Behaviour 60*(4), 523–529.

Menzel, C. R. (1999). Unprompted recall and reporting of hidden objects by a chimpanzee (Pan troglodytes) after extended delays. *Journal of Comparative Psychology* 113(4), 426–434.

Metcalfe, J., and Shimamura, A. P. (1994). *Metacognition: Knowing about knowing.* Cambridge, MA: MIT Press.

Miles, H. L. W. (1980). Acquisition of gestural signs by an infant orangutan (*Pongo pygmaeus*). Paper presented at the Infant development. *Symposium conducted at the 3rd annual meeting of the American Society of Primatologists*, Winston-Salem, North Carolina.

Miles, H. L. W. (1995). Me Chantek: The development of self-awareness in a signing orangutan. In S. T. Parker, R. Mitchell and M. Boccia (Eds.), *Self-Awareness in Animals and Humans: Developmental Perspectives* (pp. 254–272). New York: Cambridge University Press.

Miller, N. E., and Dollard, J. (1941). *Social Learning and Imitation.* New Haven, CT: Yale University Press.

Mitani, J., and Watts, D. (1999). Demographic influences on the hunting behavior of chimpanzees. *American Journal of Physical Anthropology* 109(4), 439–454.

Mitani, J., Watts, D., and Lwanga, J. (2002). Ecological and social correlates of chimpanzee party size and composition. In C. Boesch, G. Hohmann and L. Marchant (Eds.), *Behavioural Diversity in Chimpanzees and Bonobos* (pp. 102–111). Cambridge, MA: Cambridge University Press.

Mitani, J. C. (2009). Cooperation and competition in chimpanzees: Current understanding and future challenges. *Evolutionary Anthropology* 18(5), 215–227

Mitani, J. C., and Watts, D. P. (2001). Why do chimpanzees hunt and share meat? *Animal Behaviour* 61(5), 915–924.

Morgan, C. L. (1896). *Habit and Instinct.* London: Edward Arnold Publishers.

Morgan, C. L. (1903). *An Introduction to Comparative Psychology* (2nd ed.). London: Walter Scott.

Mueller, J. S., Melwani, S., and Goncalo, J. A. (2012). The bias against creativity: Why people desire but reject creative ideas. *Psychological Science* 23(1), 13–17.

Mukamel, R., Ekstrom, A. D., Kaplan, J., Iacoboni, M., and Fried, I. (2010). Single-neuron responses in humans during execution and observation of actions. *Current Biology* 20(8), 750–756.

Mulcahy, N. J., and Call, J. (2006a). Apes Save Tools for Future Use. *Science 312*(5776), 1038–1040.

Mulcahy, N. J., and Call, J. (2006b). How great apes perform on a modified trap-tube task. *Animal Cognition* 9(3), 193–199.

Mulcahy, N. J., Call, J., and Dunbar, R. I. M. (2005). Gorillas and orangutans encode relevant problem features in a tool-using task. *Journal of Comparative Psychology* 119(1), 23–32.

Muller, M. N., and Mitani, J. C. (2002). Conflict and cooperation in wild chimpanzees. *Advances in the Study of Behavior* 35(5), 275–331.

Nelson, T. O., and Narens, L. (1990). Metamemory: a theoretical framework and new findings. In G. H. Bower (Ed.), *The Psychology of Learning and Motivation* (Vol. 26, 125–173). New York: Academic Press.

Nelson, V. R., and Nadeau, J. H. (2010). Transgenerational genetic effects. *Epigenomics* 2(6), 797–806.

Newton-Fisher, N., Reynolds, Y., and Plumptre, A. (2000). Food supply and chimpanzee (*Pan troglodytes schweinfurthii*) party size in the Budongo Forest Reserve, Uganda. *International Journal of Primatology* 21(4), 613–628.

Nielsen, M., and Tomaselli, K. (2010). Overimitation in Kalahari Bushman children and the origins of human cultural cognition. *Psychological Science* 21(5), 729–736.

Nishida, T. (1968). The social group of wild chimpanzees in the Mahale Mountains. *Primates* 9(3), 167–224.

Nishida, T., Hasegawa, T., Hayaki, H., Takahata, Y., and Uehara, S. (1992). Meat-sharing as a coalition strategy by an alpha male chimpanzee? In T. Nishida, W. C. McGrew, P. Marler, M. Pickford and F. B. M. de Waal (Eds.), *Topics in Primatology* (Vol. 1: Human Origins, 159–174). Basel: Karger AG.

Nishida, T., Matsusaka, T., and McGrew, W. C. (2009). Emergence, propagation or disappearance of novel behavioral pattern in the habituated chimpanzees of Mahale: A review. *Primates* 50(1), 23–36.

Nishida, T., N., C., Hamai, M., Hasegawa, T., Hiraiwa-Hasegawa, M., et al. (2003). Demography, female life history, and reproductive profiles among the chimpanzees of Mahale. *American Journal of Primatology* 59(3), 99–121.

Nishida, T., Uehara, S., and Nyondo, R. (1983). Predatory behavior among wild chimpanzees of the Mahale Mountains. *Primates* 20(1), 1–20.

Nishida, T., Zamma, K., Matsusaka, T., Inaba, A., and McGrew, W. C. (2010). *Chimpanzee Behavior in the Wild: An Audio-Visual Encyclopedia*. Tokyo: Springer.

Odling-Smee, F. J., Laland, K. N., and Feldman, M. W. (1996). Niche construction. *American Naturalist* 147(4), 641–648.

Ohigashi, H., Huffman, M. A., Izutsu, D., Koshimizu, K., Kawanaka, M., et al. (1994). Toward the chemical ecology of medicinal plant-use in chimpanzees: The case of *Vernonia amygdalina Del.*. A plant used by wild chimpanzees possibly for parasite-related diseases. *Journal of Chemical Ecology* 20(3), 541–553.

Ojemann, G. A. (1991). Cortical organization of language. *The Journal of Neuroscience* 11(8), 2281–2287.

Ojemann, G. A. (2003). The neurobiology of language and verbal memory: Observations from awake neurosurgery. *International Journal of Psychophysiology* 48(2), 141–146.

Okamoto-Barth, S., Call, J., and Tomasello, M. (2007). Great apes' understanding of other's line of sight. *Psychological Science* 18(5), 462–468.

Osvath, M., and Osvath, H. (2008). Chimpanzee (*Pan troglodytes*) and orangutan (*Pongo abelii*) forethought: self-control and pre-experience in the face of future tool use. *Animal Cognition* 11(4), 661–674.

Ouattara, K., Lemasson, A., and Zuberbühler, K. (2009). Campbell's Monkeys Use Affixation to Alter Call Meaning. *PLoS ONE (Public Library of Science) 4*(11), e7808.

Parker, S. T. (1996). Apprenticeship in tool-mediated extractive foraging: The origins of imitation, teaching, and self-awareness in great apes. In A. E. Russon, K. A. Bard and S. T. Parker (Eds.), *Reaching into Thought: The Minds of the Great Apes* (pp. 348–370). Cambridge: Cambridge University Press.

Parker-Rees, R. (2007). Liking to be liked: Imitation, familiarity and pedagogy in the first years of life. *Early Years* 27(1), 3–17.

Pascual-Leone, A., Freitas, C., Oberman, L., Horvath, J. C., Halko, M., et al. (2011). Characterizing brain cortical plasticity and network dynamics across the age-span in health and disease with TMS-EEG and TMS-fMRI. *Brain Topography* 24(3–4), 302–315.

Patterson, F. G. (1978). The gestures of a gorilla: language acquisition in another pongid. *Brain and Language* 5(1), 72–97.

Patterson, F. G., and Gordon, W. (1993). The case for personhood of gorillas. In P. Cavalieri and P. Singer (Eds.), *The Great Ape Project: Equality Beyond Humanity*. New York: St. Martin's Griffin.

Peirce, C., Houser, N., and Kloesel, C. (1998). *The Essential Peirce: Selected Philosophical Writings, 1893–1913*: Indiana University Press.

Pelegrin, J. (2000). The knapping methods and techniques practiced at Cambay. In V. Roux (Ed.), *Cornaline de l'Inde: Des Oratiques de Cambay aux Techno-Systemes de l'Indus*. Paris: Editions de la Maison des sciences de l'homme.

Pembrey, M. E., Bygren, L. O., Kaati, G., Edvinsson, S., Northstone, K., et al. (2006). Sex-specific, male-line transgenerational responses in humans. *European Journal of Human Genetics* 14(2), 159–166.

Penn, D. C., and Povinelli, D. J. (2007). Causal cognition in humans and nonhuman animals: A comparative, critical review. *Annual Review of Psychology* 58, 97–118.

Persson, T. (2008). *Pictorial Primates: A Search for Iconic Abilities in Great Apes*. Lund University, Lund.

Piaget, J. (1952). *The Origins of Intelligence in Childhood*. New York: International University Press.

Piaget, J. (1962). *Play, Dreams and Imitation in Childhood* (C. Gattegno and F. M. Hodgson, Transl.). New York: Norton.

Plotnik, J. M., de Waal, F. B. M., and Reiss, D. (2006). Self-recognition in an Asian elephant. *Proceedings of the National Academy of Sciences, USA* 103(45), 17053–17057.

Pollick, A. S., Gouzoules, H., and de Waal, F. B. M. (2005). Audience effects on food calls in captive brown capuchin monkeys, *Cebus apella*. *Animal Behaviour* 70(6), 1273–1281.

Potts, R. (1998). Environmental hypotheses of hominin evolution. *American Journal of Physical Anthropology,* Supplemental 27, 93–136.

Povinelli, D. J. (2000). *Folk Physics for Apes: The Chimpanzee's Theory of How the World Works*. Oxford: Oxford University Press.

Povinelli, D. J. (2004). Behind the ape's appearance: Escaping anthropomorphism in the study of other minds. *Daedalus: Journal of the American Academy of Arts and Sciences* 133(1), 29–41.

Povinelli, D. J. (2012). *World Without Weight: Perspectives on an Alien Mind.* Oxford: Oxford University Press.

Povinelli, D. J., and Dunphy-Lelii, S. (2001). Do chimpanzees seek explanations? Preliminary comparative investigations. *Canadian Journal of Experimental Psychology* 55(2), 93–101.

Povinelli, D. J., and Eddy, T. J. (1996). Chimpanzees: Joint visual attention. *Psychological Science* 7(3), 129–135.

Povinelli, D. J., and Eddy, T. J. (1996). What young chimpanzees know about seeing. *Monographs of the Society for Research in Child Development* 61(3), 1–152.

Povinelli, D. J., Rulf, A. B., and Bierschwale, D. T. (1994). Absence of knowledge attribution and self-recognition in young chimpanzees (*Pan troglodytes*). *Journal of Comparative Psychology* 108(1), 74–80.

Povinelli, D. J., and Vonk, J. (2003). Chimpanzee minds: Suspiciously human? *Trends in Cognitive Sciences* 7(4), 157–160.

Povinelli, D. J., and Vonk, J. (2004). We don't need a microscope to explore the chimpanzee's mind. *Mind and Language* 19(1), 1–28.

Premack, A. J., and Premack, D. (1972). Teaching Language to an Ape. *Scientific American 227*(4), 92–99.

Premack, D., and Premack, A. J. (1994). Why animals have neither culture nor history. In T. Ingold (Ed.), *Companion Encyclopedia Of Anthropology*. London: Routledge.

Premack, D., and Premack, A. J. (1997). Infants attribute value ± to the goal-directed actions of self-propelled objects. *Journal of Cognitive Neuroscience* 9(6), 848–856.

Prior, H., Schwarz, A., and Güntürkün, O. (2008). Mirror-induced behavior in the magpie (Pica pica): Evidence of self-recognition. *PLoS Biology (Public Library of Science)* 6(8), e202.

Pritchard, J. K. (2010). How we are evolving. *Scientific American 303*(4), 22–29.

Pruetz, J. D. (2006). Feeding ecology of savanna chimpanzees (*Pan troglodytes verus*) at Fongoli, Sénégal. In G. Hohmann, M. M. Robbins and C. Boesch (Eds.), *Feeding Ecology in Apes and Other Primates: Ecological, Physical and Behavioral Aspects* (pp. 161–182). New York: Cambridge University Press.

Pruetz, J. D. (2007). Evidence of cave use by savanna chimpanzees (*Pan troglodytes verus*) at Fongoli, Sénégal: Implications for thermoregulatory behavior. *Primates* 48(4), 316–309.

Pruetz, J. D., and Bertolani, P. (2007). Savanna chimpanzees, *Pan troglodytes verus*, hunt with tools. *Current Biology* 17(5), 412–417.

Quiatt, D. (2006). Instrumental leaf use by chimpanzees of the Budongo Forest (Sonso Community). *Primates of Western Uganda,* Developments in Primatology: Progress and Prospects(Section Three), 313–325.

Raffaele, P. (November 2006). Speaking bonobo. *Simithsonian.*

Rajala, A. Z., Reininger, K. R., Lancaster, K. M., and Populin, L. C. (2010). Rhesus monkeys (*Macaca mulatta*) do recognize themselves in the mirror: Implications for the evolution of self-recognition. *PLoS ONE (Public Library of Science)* 5(9), e12865.

Read, D. W. (2008). Working memory: A cognitive limit to non-human primate recursive thinking prior to hominid evolution. *Evolutionary Psychology* 6(4), 676–714.

Reader, S. M., and Laland, K. N. (2001). Primate innovation: sex, age and social rank differences. *International Journal of Primatology* 22(5), 787–805.

Rilling, J. K., Glasser, M. F., Preuss, T. M., Ma, X., Zhao, T., et al. (2008). The evolution of the arcuate fasciculus revealed with comparative DTI. *Nature Neuroscience* 11(4), 426–428.

Rosenblum, L. A., and Cross, H. A. (1963). Performance of neonatal monkeys in the visual cliff-situation. *American Journal of Psychology 76*(2), 318–320.

Rosenzweig, M. R., Krech, D., Bennett, E. L., and Diamond, M. C. (1962). Effects of environmental complexity and training on brain chemistry and anatomy: a replication and extension. *Journal of Comparative and Physiological Psychology* 55(4), 429–437.

Rumbaugh, D., Gill, T. V., and Glasersfeld, E. v. (1973). Reading and Sentence Completion by a Chimpanzee (*Pan*). *Science* 182(4113), 731–733.

Ruxton, G. D., and Wilkinson, D. M. (2011). Avoidance of overheating and selection for both hair loss and bipedality in hominins. *Proceedings of the National Academy of Sciences, USA 108*(*52*), 20965–20969.

Saito, A. (2010). The origin of representational drawing: Drawing behavior of chimpanzees compared with that of human children. *Japanese Psychological Review* 53(3), 367–382.

Sakura, O. (1994). Factors affecting party size and composition of chimpanzees (*Pan troglodytes verus*) at Bossou, Guinea. *International Journal of Primatology* 15(2), 167–183.

Santos, L. R., and Hauser, M. D. (2002). A non-human primate's understanding of solidity: Dissociations between seeing and acting. *Developmental Science* 5(2), F1–F7.

Santos, L. R., Mahajan, N., and Barnes, J. L. (2005). How prosimian primates represent tools: Experiments with two lemur species (*Eulemur fulvus* and *Lemur catta*). *Journal of Comparative Psychology* 119(4), 394–403.

Santos, L. R., Miller, C. T., and Hauser, M. D. (2003). Representing tools: How two non-human primate species distinguish between the functionally relevant and irrelevant features of a tool. *Animal Cognition* 6(4), 269–281.

Santos, L. R., Pearson, H. M., Spaepen, G. M., Tsao, F., and Hauser, M. D. (2006). Probing the limits of tool competence: Experiments with two non-tool-using species (*Cercopithecus aethiops* and *Saguinus oedipus*). *Animal Cognition* 9(2), 94–109.

Sanz, C., and Morgan, D. (2010). Complexity of chimpanzee tool using behaviours. In S. R. R. Elizabeth Lonsdorf, Tetsurō Matsuzawa (Ed.), *The Mind of the Chimpanzee: Ecological and Experimental Perspectives*. Chicago: University of Chicago Press.

Sanz, C. M., and Morgan, D. B. (2007). Chimpanzee tool technology in the Goualougo Triangle, Republic of Congo. *Journal of Human Evolution* 52(4), 420–433.

Savage-Rumbaugh, S. (2009). 'Kanzi the Toolmaker'. Retrieved March 12, 2012, Web Address *http://www.youtube.com/watch?v=1zsSH9UUQtQ*

Savage-Rumbaugh, S., Fields, W. M., Segerdahl, P., and Rumbaugh, D. (2005). Culture prefigures cognition in Pan/Homo bonobos. *Theoria* 20(3), 311–328.

Scally, A., Dutheil, J. Y., Hillier, L. W., Jordan, G. E., Goodhead, I., et al. (2012). Insights into hominid evolution from the gorilla genome sequence. *Nature* 483(7388), 169–175.

Schick, K. D., Toth, N., Garufi, G., Savage-Rumbaugh, E. S., Rumbaugh, D., et al. (1999). Continuing investigations into the stone tool-making and tool-using capabilities of a bonobo (*Pan paniscus*). *Journal of Archaeological Science* 26(7), 821–832.

Schmelz, M., Call, J., and Tomasello, M. (2011). Chimpanzees know that others make inferences. *Proceedings of the National Academy of Sciences, USA* 108(7), 3077–3079.

Schrauf, C., and Call, J. (2011). Great apes use weight as a cue to find hidden food. *American Journal of Primatology* 73(4), 323–334.

Seed, A. M., Emery, N. J., Call, J., and Clayton, N. S. (2009). Chimpanzees solve the trap problem when the confound of tool-use is removed. *Journal of Experimental Psychology: Animal Behavior Processes* 35(1), 23–34.

Seyfarth, R. M., Cheney, D. L., and Marler, P. (1980). Monkey responses to three different alarm calls: evidence of predator classification and semantic communication. *Science* 210(4471), 801–803.

Shea, J. J. (2011a). *Homo sapiens* is as *Homo sapiens* was: Behavioral variability versus "behavioral modernity" in Paleolithic archaeology *Current Anthropology* 52(1), 1–35.

Shea, J. J. (2011b). Refuting a myth about human origins. *American Scientist 99*(2), 128–132.

Shields, W. E., Smith, J. D., and Washburn, D. A. (1997). Uncertain responses by humans and rhesus monkeys (Macaca mulatta) in a psychophysical same-different task. *Journal of Experimental Psychology: General* 126(2), 147–164.

Silk, J. B., Brosnan, S. F., Vonk, J., Henrich, J., Povinelli, D. J., et al. (2005). Chimpanzees are indifferent to the welfare of unrelated group members. *Nature* 437(7063), 1357–1359.

Silva, F. J., Page, D. M., and Silva, K. M. (2005). Methodological–conceptual problems in the study of chimpanzees' folk physics: How studies with adult humans can help. *Learning and Behavior 33*(1), 47–58.

Skinner, B. F. (1953). *Science and Human Behavior*. New York: Macmillan.

Slocombe, K. E., and Zuberbühler, K. (2006). Food-associated calls in chimpanzees: responses to food types or food preferences? *Animal Behaviour* 72(5), 989–999.

Smith, C., Carey, S., and Wiser, M. (1985). On differentiation: A case study of the development of the concepts of size, weight, and density. *Cognition* 21(3), 177–237.

Smith, C. L., Taylor, A., and Evans, C. S. (2011). Tactical multimodal signaling in birds: Facultative variation in signal modality reveals sensitivity to social costs. *Animal Behaviour* 82(3), 521–527.

Smith, J. D., Schull, J., Strote, J., McGee, K., Egnor, R., et al. (1995). The uncertain response in the bottlenosed dolphin (*Tursiops truncatus*). *Journal of Experimental Psychology: General* 124(4), 391–408.

Smith, J. D., Shields, W. E., Allendoerfer, K. R., and Washburn, D. A. (1998). Memory monitoring by animals and humans. *Journal of Experimental Psychology: General* 127(3), 227–250.

Smith, R. (1992). *Inhibition: History and Meaning in the Sciences of Mind and Brain*. Berkeley: University of California Press.

Son, L. K., and Kornell, N. (2005). Meta-confidence judgments in rhesus macaques: Explicit versus implicit mechanisms. In H. S. Terrace and J. Metcalfe (Eds.), *The missing link in cognition: Origins of self-reflective consciousness* (pp. 296–320). New York: Oxford University Press.

Spaulding, B., and Hauser, M. (2005). What experience is required for acquiring tool competence? Experiments with two callitrichids. *Animal Behaviour* 70(3), 517–526.

Spelke, E. S., Breinlinger, K., Macomber, J., and Jacobson, K. (1992). Origins of knowledge. *Psychological Review* 99(4), 605– 632.

Spelke, E. S., Katz, G., Purcell, S. E., Ehrlich, S. M., and Breinlinger, K. (1994). Early knowledge of object motion: Continuity and inertia. *Cognition 51*(2), 131–176.

Spelke, E. S., Phillips, A., and Woodward, A. L. (1995). Infants' knowledge of object motion and human action. In D. Sperber, D. Premack and A. Premack (Eds.), *Causal Cognition* (pp. 44–76). Oxford: Clarendon Press.

Staddon, J. E. R., Jozefowiez, J., and Cerutti, D. (2007). Metacognition: a problem not a process. *PsyCrit*, 1–5.

Stanford, C. B. (1998). The social behavior of chimpanzees and bonobos: Empirical evidence and shifting assumptions. *Current Anthropology* 39(4), 399–420.

Stedman, H. H., Kozyak, B. W., Nelson, A., Thesier, D. M., Su, L. T., et al. (2004). Myosin gene mutation correlates with anatomical changes in the human lineage. *Nature* 428(6981), 415–418.

Stevens, J. R., and Mühlhoff, N. (2012). Intertemporal choice in lemurs. *Behavioural Processes* 89(2), 121–127.

Stout, D., and Chaminade, T. (2007). The evolutionary neuroscience of tool making. *Neuropsychologia* 45(5), 1091–1100.

Stout, D., Toth, N., Schick, K., and Chaminade, T. (2008). Neural correlates of Early Stone Age toolmaking: Technology, language and cognition in human evolution. *Philosophical Transactions of the Royal Society B: Biological Sciences* 363(1499), 1939–1949.

Subiaul, F., Cantlon, J. F., Holloway, R. L., and Terrace, H. S. (2004). Cognitive imitation in rhesus macaques. *Science* 305(5682), 407–410.

Suda-King, C. (2008). Do orangutans (*Pongo pygmaeus*) know when they do not remember? *Animal Cognition* 11(1), 21–42.

Suddendorf, T. (2006). Foresight and evolution of the human mind. *Science* 312(5776), 1006–1007.

Suddendorf, T., and Busby, J. (2003). Mental time travel in animals? *Trends in Cognitive Sciences* 7(9), 391–396.

Suddendorf, T., and Corballis, M. C. (1997). Mental time travel and the evolution of the human mind. *Genetic Social and General Psychology Monographs* 123(2), 133–167.

Suddendorf, T., and Corballis, M. C. (2007). The evolution of foresight: What is mental time travel, and is it unique to humans? *Behavioral and Brain Sciences* 30(3), 299–313; discussion 313–351.

Sugiyama, Y. (2004). Demographic parameters and life history of chimpanzees at Bossou, Guinea. *American Journal of Physcial Anthropology* 124(2), 154–165.

Sutou, S. (2012). Hairless mutation: a driving force of humanization from a human-ape common ancestor by enforcing upright walking while holding a baby with both hands. *Genes to Cells* 17(4), 264–272.

Szpunar, K. K., Watson, J. M., and McDermott, K. B. (2007). Neural substrates of envisioning the future. *Proceedings of the National Academy of Sciences, USA,* 104(2), 642–647

Takahata, Y., Hasegawa, T., and Nishida, T. (1984). Chimpanzee predation in the Mahale Mountains from August 1979 to May 1982. *International Journal of Primatology* 5(3), 213–233.

Tennie, C., Call, J., and Tomasello, M. (2009). Ratcheting up the ratchet: On the evolution of cumulative culture. *Philosophical Transactions of the Royal Society B: Biological Sciences* 364(1528), 2405–2415.

Terrace, H. S., Petitto, L. A., Sanders, R. J., and Bever, T. G. (1979). Can an ape create a sentence? *Science* 206(4421), 891–902.

Thompson, R. F. (2009). Habituation: A history. *Neurobiology of Learning and Memory* 92(2), 127–134.

Thornton, A., and McAuliffe, K. (2006). Teaching in wild meerkats. *Science* 313(5784), 227–229.

Tomasello, M., and Call, J. (1997). *Primate Cognition*. London: Oxford University Press.

Tomasello, M., and Carpenter, M. (2005). Intention reading and imitative learning. In S. Hurley and N. Chater (Eds.), *Perspectives on Imitation: From Neuroscience to Social Science* (Vol. 2: Imitation, Human Development, and Culture, 133–148). Cambridge, MA: MIT Press.

Toth, N., Schick, K. D., Savage-Rumbaugh, E. S., Sevcik, R. A., and Rumbaugh, D. M. (1993). Pan the tool-maker: Investigations into the stone tool-making and tool-using capabilities of a bonobo (*Pan paniscus*). *Journal of Archaeological Science* 20(1). 81–91.

Townsend, S. W., Deschner, T., and Zuberbühler, K. (2008). Female chimpanzees use copulation calls flexibly to prevent social competition. *PLoS ONE (Public Library of Science)* 3(6), e2431.

Tulving, E. (1972). Episodic and semantic memory. In E. Tulving and W. Donaldson (Eds.), *Organization of memory* (pp. 381–403). New York: Academic Press.

Turella, L., Pierno, A. C., Tubaldi, F., and Castiello, U. (2009). Mirror neurons in humans: Consisting or confounding evidence? *Brain and Language* 108(1), 10–21.

Uehara, S., Nishida, T., Hamai, M., Hasegawa, T., Hayaki, H., et al. (1992). Characteristics of predation by the chimpanzees in the Mahale Mountains National Park, Tanzania. In T. Nishida, W. C. McGrew, P. Marler, M. Pickford and F. B. M. de Waal (Eds.), *Topics in Primatology* (Vol. 1: Human Origins, 143–158). Tokyo: University of Tokyo Press.

Ujhelyi, M., Merker, B., Buk, P., and Geissmann, T. (2000). Observations on the behavior of gibbons (*Hylobates leucogenys*, *H. gabriellae*, and *H. lar*) in the presence of mirrors. *Journal of Comparative Psychology* 114(3), 253–262.

van Baaren, R. B., Maddux, W. W., and Chartrand, T. L. (2003). It takes two to mimic: Behavioral consequences of self-construals. *Journal of Personality and Social Psychology* 84(5), 1093–1102.

van Casteren, A., Sellers, W. I., Thorpe, S. K. S., Coward, S., Crompton, R. H., et al. (2012). Nest-building orangutans demonstrate engineering know-how to produce safe, comfortable beds. *Proceedings of the National Academy of Sciences, USA* 109(18), 6873–6877.

van Schaik, C. (2004). *Among Orangutans: Red Apes and the Rise of Human Culture*. Cambridge, MA: Belknap Press.

Vernes, S. C., Oliver, P. L., Spiteri, E., Lockstone, H. E., Puliyadi, R., et al. (2011). Foxp2 regulates gene networks implicated in neurite outgrowth in the developing brain. *PLoS Genetics (Public Library of Science)* 7(7), e1002145.

Videan, E. N., and McGrew, W. C. (2001). Are bonobos (Pan paniscus) really more bipedal than chimpanzees (Pan troglodytes)? *American Journal of Primatology* 54(4), 233–239.

Visalberghi, E., and Limongelli, L. (1994). Lack of comprehension of cause–effect relations in tool-using capuchin monkeys (Cebus apella). *Journal of Comparative Psychology* 108(1), 15–22.

Voelkl, B., and Huber, L. (2000). True imitation in marmosets. *Animal Behaviour* 60(2), 195–202.

Vogt, S., and Thomaschke, R. (2007). From visuo-motor interactions to imitation learning: Behavioural and brain imaging studies. *Journal of Sports Sciences* 25(5), 497–517.

Vonk, J., Brosnan, S. F., Silk, J. B., Henrich, J., Richardson, A. S., et al. (2008). Chimpanzees do not take advantage of very low cost opportunities to deliver food to unrelated group members. *Animal Behaviour* 75(5), 1757–1770.

Voss, J. L., Baym, C. L., and Paller, K. A. (2008). Accurate forced-choice recognition without awareness of memory retrieval. *Learning and Memory* 15(6), 454–459.

Voss, J. L., and Paller, K. A. (2009). Recognition without awareness in humans and its implications for animal models of episodic memory. *Communicative and Integrative Biology* 2(3), 1–2.

Warneken, F., Hare, B., Melis, A. P., Hanus, D., and Tomasello, M. (2007). Spontaneous altruism by chimpanzees and young children. *PLoS Biology (Public Library of Science),* 5(7), e184.

Washburn, D. A., Smith, J. D., and Shields, W. E. (2006). Rhesus monkeys (*Macaca mulatta*) immediately generalize the uncertain response. *Journal of Experimental Psychology: Animal Behavior Processes* 32(2), 185–189.

Watanabe, M., Cheng, K., Murayama, Y., Ueno, K., Asamizuya, T., et al. (2011). Attention but not awareness modulates the BOLD signal in human V1 during binocular suppression. *Science* 334(6057), 829–831.

Watts, D., and Mitani, J. (2002). Hunting and meat sharing by chimpanzees at Ngogo, Kibale National Park, Uganda. In C. Boesch, G. Hohmann and L. Marchant (Eds.), *Behavioural Diversity in Chimpanzees and Bonobos* (pp. 244–255). Cambridge, MA: Cambridge University Press.

Watts, D. P. (2008). Tool use by chimpanzees at Ngogo, Kibale National Park, Uganda. *International Journal of Primatology* 29(1), 83–94.

Westergaard, G. C. (1999). Structural analysis of tool-use by tufted capuchins (*Cebus apella*) and chimpanzees (*Pan troglodytes*). *Animal Cognition* 2(3), 141–145.

Westergaard, G. C., and Hyatt, C. W. (1994). The responses of bonobos (Pan paniscus) to their mirror images: Evidence of self-recognition. *Human Evolution* 9(4), 273–279.

White, F. J. (1996). *Pan paniscus* 1973 to 1996: Twenty-three years of field research. *Evolutionary Anthropology* 5(1), 11–17.

Whiten, A., Custance, D. M., Gomez, J.-C., Teixidor, P., and Bard, K. A. (1996). Imitative learning of artificial fruit processing in children (*Homo sapiens*) and chimpanzees (*Pan troglodytes*). *Journal of Comparative Psychology* 110(1), 3–14.

Whiten, A., Goodall, J., McGrew, W., Nishida, T., Reynolds, V., et al. (1999). Cultures in chimpanzees. *Nature* 399(6737), 682–685.

Whiten, A., and Ham, R. (1992). On the nature and evolution of imitation in the animal kingdom: Reappraisal of a century of research. *Advances in the Study of Behavior* 21(21), 239–283.

Whiten, A., Horner, V., and de Waal, F. B. M. (2005). Conformity to cultural norms of tool use in chimpanzees. *Nature* 437(7059), 737–740.

Whiten, A., Horner, V., and Marshall-Pescini, S. (2003). Cultural panthropology. *Evolutionary Anthropology* 12(2), 92–105.

Whiten, A., McGuigan, N., Marshall-Pescini, S., and Hopper, L. M. (2009). Emulation, imitation, overimitation and the scope of culture for child and chimpanzee. *Philosophical Transactions of the Royal Society B: Biological Sciences* 364(1528), 2417–2428.

Wilkinson, R. D., Steiper, M. E., Soligo, C., Martin, R. D., Yang, Z., et al. (2011). Dating primate divergences through an integrated analysis of palaeontological and molecular data. *Systematic Biology 60*(1), 16–31.

Williams, J. M., Pusey, A. E., Carlis, J. V., Farm, B. P., and Goodall, J. (2002). Female competition and male territorial behaviour influence female chimpanzee's ranging patterns. *Animal Behaviour* 63(2), 347–360.

Wimmer, H., and Perner, J. (1983). Beliefs about beliefs: Representation and constraining function of wrong beliefs in young children's understanding of deception. *Cognition* 13(1), 103–128.

Wohlschläger, A., Gattis, M., and Bekkering, H. (2003). Action generation and action perception in imitation: an instance of the ideomotor principle. *Philosophical Transactions of the Royal Society B: Biological Sciences* 358(1431), 501–515.

Wraga, M., Thompson, W. L., Alpert, N. M., and Kosslyn, S. M. (2003). Implicit transfer of motor strategies in mental rotation. *Brain and Cognition 52*(2), 135–143.

Wrangham, R. (2000). Why are male chimpanzees more gregarious than mothers? A scramble hypothesis. In P. Kappeler (Ed.), *Primate Males. Causes and Consequences of Variation Competition in Group Composition* (pp. 248–258). Cambridge, MA: Cambridge University Press.

Wrangham, R. W., and Nishida, T. (1983). *Asplia spp.* leaves: A puzzle in the feeding behavior of wild chimpanzees. *Primates* 24(2), 276–282.

Yamamoto, S., Humle, T., and Tanaka, M. (2009). Chimpanzees help each other upon request. *PLoS ONE (Public Library of Science)* 4(10), e7416.

Yamamoto, S., Humle, T., and Tanaka, M. (2012). Chimpanzees' flexible targeted helping based on an understanding of conspecifics' goals. *Proceedings of the National Academy of Sciences, USA* 109(9), 3588–3592.

Yamamoto, S., and Tanaka, M. (2009a). Do chimpanzees (*Pan troglodytes*) spontaneously take turns in a reciprocal cooperation task? *Journal of Comparative Psychology* 123(3), 242–249.

Yamamoto, S., and Tanaka, M. (2009b). Selfish strategies develop in social problem situations in chimpanzee (*Pan troglodytes*) mother-infant pairs. *Animal Cognition,* 12(Supplement 1), 27–36.

Yeatman, J. D., Dougherty, R. F., Rykhlevskaia, E., Sherbondy, A. J., Deutsch, G. K., et al. (2011). Anatomical Properties of the Arcuate Fasciculus Predict Phonological and Reading Skills in Children. *Journal of Cognitive Neuroscience 23*(11), 3304–3317.

Yerkes, R. M. (1943). *Chimpanzees: A Laboratory Colony*. New Haven, CT: Yale University Press.

Zentall, T. (2006). Imitation: Definitions, evidence, and mechanisms. *Animal Cognition 9*(4), 335–367.

In: The Psychology of Human Behavior
Editor: Robert G. Bednarik

ISBN: 978-1-62257-901-3

Chapter 4

GRAPPLING WITH AN ENIGMA: THE COMPLEXITY OF HUMAN BEHAVIOR AS A MULTIDIMENSIONAL PHENOMENON

Derek Hodgson*
Palaeocentre, University of York, Heslington, York, England, U.K

ABSTRACT

The issue as to what factors led to the behavioral and associated psychological make-up of modern humans has been beset with controversy over the past two decades. This controversy revolves around two main criteria; first, whether human behavior arrived suddenly and relatively late at the end of the Pleistocene as a result of some decisive neuro-cognitive event or, second, whether it derived from a more protracted process stretching back to the Middle Pleistocene involving a much more convoluted scenario. The intensity of this debate has been inflamed by new findings from various disciplines including archaeology, anthropology, genetics, neuroscience and psychology, which has generally led to advocates of the above approaches selecting those findings that support their particular viewpoint while ignoring insights that may prove contradictory. The aim of this chapter is to show that the reason the debate on this issue has become so polarized is due to the various proponents not taking full account of what the new evidence implies. In what follows, recent research from neuroscience and related disciplines will be explored in a way that will help clarify and hopefully dispel some of the continuing disagreements.

INTRODUCTION

One of the major impediments to understanding when and how so-called "modern human behavior" [MHB] arose has been the quest for a single cognitive attribute that may have made the difference. These have included brain size (Jerison 1973), neural reorganization

* Palaeocentre, University of York, Heslington, York .YO10 5DD England, U.K., derekhodgson@hotmail.com

(Holloway 1966), rapid modal integration (Mithen 1996) etc. At present, working memory is being considered as the single most likely candidate (Coolidge and Wynn 2009, 2011), which is continuing to generate considerable debate. As will be demonstrated, these proposals may contain some truth but because they offer single causative explanations to account for MHB they all fall short of the mark. What has been sorely lacking in these debates is a drawing together of the neuro-cognitive evidence that sees the brain as a complex interactive and flexible organ where each area of the cortex depends upon and works in parallel with others to the extent that no one function should be regarded as having given rise to what is regarded as MHB. What adds an extra layer of complexity to this picture concerns the social and socio-cultural context that impinges on brain function in multifarious ways. It is only by considering these various criteria as interacting on many different levels that any progress on understanding how the cognitive profile that typifies modern humans was arrived at. Notwithstanding these issues, there are also problems concerning how MHB itself is defined. Problems defining MHB have come to the fore now that there is a growing consensus that this is unable to be identified simply by appealing to a trait list that was thought, for example, to provide evidence for the purported appearance of MHB during the European Upper Paleolithic. It is, therefore, now essential to look toward other possible explanations and approaches that will allow a more comprehensive understanding of the evolution of human behavior as it appeared in various locations throughout the world rather than in the limited context of Europe or even South Africa. In order to illustrate the limitations of approaches that depend on single cognitive factors that attempt to account for the appearance of MHB, the first part of this chapter will examine the claim that it was enhanced working memory that made the difference. I will then go on to critically examine other theoretical accounts that have endeavored to interpret the archaeological record in relation to understanding the cognitive profile of humans as a species and attempt to show how a broader interdisciplinary synthesis can provide interesting alternatives that can help elucidate the main criteria that impacted on cognitive evolution.

Enhanced Working Memory

Up until quite recently it was assumed that modern cognition did not begin until quite late in the Upper Paleolithic. Thanks to repeated archaeological finds, this date has been increasingly consigned to the distant past, especially in the light of evidence that has emerged outside Europe (Henshilwood et al 2002; Bednarik 1992, 2003a; McBrearty and Brooks 2000). This suggests that archaeologists and anthropologists have consistently underestimated the abilities of not just *Homo sapiens* but also earlier hominins. In a similar vein, it was once thought the cognitive difference between nonhuman primates and *Homo sapiens* was immense but this gap has narrowed substantially since controlled experiments and detailed observations have demonstrated the relative sophistication of thinking in chimps (Belfer-Cohen and Hovers 2010). This realignment has also led to a reassessment of the abilities of Neanderthals (I will sidestep the controversy regarding whether Neanderthals are a separate subspecies to *Homo sapiens sapiens* [Bednarik, this volume]) with some arguing that their cognitive profile either approached or corresponded to *Homo sapiens sapiens* (d'Errico and Zilhão 1998); a proposition that has recently been confirmed by the finding that the 50,000-

year-old Neanderthal flute from Slovenia is, in fact, a flute and not a consequence of carnivore intervention (Turk and Dimkaroski 2011). As what exists in the archaeological record at any one time has been deemed to depend on, and is closely aligned to presiding cognitive abilities, this has led to the notion that a single neuro-cognitive event could account for the extant material remains. One such idea was put forward by Mithen (1996) who attempted to explain the purported sudden appearance of a suite of different artifacts in the European Upper Paleolithic as a result of a breaking down of the barriers that typified a previous modular, and therefore limited, way of thinking.

A similar reliance on a singular cognitive event relates to working memory. Although working memory is an important factor that underwrites the ability to hold a limited number of items in mind while momentarily reflecting on other things, this ability itself will have evolved as part of and in parallel with other functions. This accords with the fact that each part of the brain evolved in tandem with others, although this is often a haphazard make-and-do process (Allman 1999). Coolidge and Wynn's (2009, 2011) thesis that enhanced working memory can explain the cognitive profile of *Homo sapiens sapiens*, because it relies on a single causative factor, ignores the obvious complexity and interconnectivity of the human brain. They also rely too heavily on Baddeley's (Baddeley and Hitch 1974; Baddeley 2007) approach to working memory. In response to these criticisms Barnard (2010) has formulated a much more interactive model of brain function that sees working memory as one function amongst a set of interrelated cognitive mechanisms. Although Barnard's model is an advance on Coolidge and Wynn's, both depend heavily on the concept of a modular brain, which has been criticized for being overly rigid and mechanistic (Hodgson and Helvenston 2006). As Fuster (2009) states:

> A functional module, as generally understood, is a continuous and circumscribed portion of cortex dedicated to one particular function and not others. In cortical physiology, certain anatomical configurations of neural elements (e.g., microscopic columns) have been identified as functional modules inasmuch as they contain geometrical arrangements of neurons specialized in a particular sensory or motor function.

This statement confirms the fact that modules do exist in the brain but these may be more relevant to the sensory/motor input end of the chain of events than is the case for the later association areas where much integration of information occurs, and will be the focus of concern here.

Other accounts as to the role of working memory do not regard it as such an encapsulated system, rather it is seen as having evolved in tandem with other neural networks or/and as a distributed system implicated in different areas of the cortex. Moreover, some of these alternative approaches do not regard working memory as a completely separate system but rather as intimately connected to long-term memory (Ranganath and Blumenfeld 2005; Cowan 1995, 2005; Fuster 2009) where short-term memory may simply represent a temporary neural signal (Fuster 2003) or is otherwise related to attention (Postle 2006). On this view, a neuron can function as part of many distributed memory networks that are involved in a range of different kinds of knowledge (Constantinidis and Procyk, 2004; Fuster, 2009; Postle 2006). In a review of working memory, Jonides et al. (2008) show that, despite the amount of research stimulated by Baddeley's model, this has only served to hamper a consideration of the available alternatives. In fact, Jonides et al. come down in favor of a more integrated and distributed model of memory that contradicts Baddeley's theory. Baddeley's standard model has also not been without criticism on a number of other counts. Nairne (2002), for example, has emphasized that it is increasingly being accepted that short-term retention is cue driven, as is the case with long-term memory, and neither rehearsal nor decay is able to fully explain how forgetting occurs in short-term memory loss. Baddeley (2012), in response to the neuroimaging results on memory confirming the complexity of the interactive systems involved that contradict the standard model, has, in fact, recently stated that he does not place much store on such findings despite researchers emphasizing their significance (see Jonides et al. 2008). Baddeley even went so far as to admit being "temperamentally skeptical of complex theoretical architectures." Baddeley's inability to accept both the neuroimage findings and complex architectures may stem from the fact that the standard theory derives from computer modeling, which he continues to applaud, and is based on neatly packaged components that seem inappropriate to understanding the evolution of human cognition. One has only to look at Felleman and Van Essen's (1991) wiring diagram of the primate brain, let alone the human brain, to appreciate the intricacy of the neural interconnections that resist being compartmentalized into discrete units. A further criticism of Baddeley's model is that it posits a capacity limit of seven items, give or take one or two, but this has been challenged in that it is now thought that the actual capacity is on average four (Cowan 2000).

Rather than relying on Baddeley's model for understanding both working memory and memory in general, I would recommend that Fuster's (2009) "New Network Paradigm" of memory be favored, not least because it is more in line with how the brain may have evolved. Fuster states that working memory constitutes the active "online" retention of information for a prospective action or to solve a problem or attain a goal where working memory and long-term memory share most of the same cortical structure (Fuster 2006). In order for a sensory stimulus to be retained in working memory, a cortical network is also activated that not only encodes that stimulus but also its past associative context within long-term memory. From an evolutionary point of view, Fuster shows how the brain develops and evolves ontogenetically and phylogenetically; first from the primary concrete sensory and motor areas at lower layers toward ever more complexity and abstract knowledge in the association areas at the topmost level. The implications for understanding the evolution of the brain is that the primary sensory areas appear to have developed first out of which more complex systems concerning the association of information from early areas accrues. Interestingly, Fuster suggests that most if not all the sensory and association systems are based, in a general sense, on memory in one form or another, which is aptly summarized by the phrase "perception is at all stages informed by memory."

In addition to criticisms of Baddeley's approach to working memory, there have also been criticisms of Coolidge and Wynn's reliance on Baddeley's model as a way of understanding cognitive evolution; a criticism which came to the fore at the recently held Wenner-Gren conference on Coolidge and Wynn's thesis (see Welshon 2010 for a summary). A number of participants at this conference including Barnard (2010), Haidle (2010) and Belfer-Cohen and Hovers (2010) highlighted the limitations of employing a unimodal approach to cognitive evolution by stating that there needed to be a more inclusive and wide-ranging consideration of the issue. Coolidge and Wynn's thesis argues that working memory underwent an enhancement with the appearance of more "complex" implements and artifacts from about 40,000 years ago. This explains why *Homo sapiens sapiens* and Neanderthals were unable to produce the same type of objects, including depictions in the form of figurines and two-dimensional representations. The question arises as to whether the evidence from Upper Paleolithic Europe provides a dependable way of gauging the appearance of modern cognitive abilities. It should be remembered that, unlike during the European Upper Paleolithic, even quite recent indigenous groups such as the native Tasmanians survived using a relatively simple technology where representational art was lacking. Similar examples where indigenous groups resorted to using Middle Paleolithic-like technology alongside geometric art bereft of representations can also be cited, such as in the case of the Andamanese (Weber 2009). In fact, representational art seems to be more of an exception than the rule throughout history with many native people relying exclusively on geometric mark-making for realizing "art." Recent research into other isolated island communities in Oceania seems to confirm the fact that reduced and isolated populations give rise to impoverished technologies whereas larger interacting populations produce more complex artifacts through the preservation and cumulative effects of innovation (Kline and Boyd 2010; Powell et al. 2010). Evidence from wide-ranging indigenous groups therefore supports the fact that technologies can "decline" to a subsistence level due to isolation and reduced population levels involving, for example, the loss of the ability to make fire, the use of rudimentary and usually temporary shelters, the employment of basic stone tools kits and implements with bone tools often not exploited, the use of minimal cold-weather clothing, the loss of hafted tools, nets, barbed spears, spear-throwers, and other more complex implements such as boomerangs (the role of population levels will be discussed more fully below).

If representational depictions and more complex technologies of the Upper Paleolithic are cited as a signature of enhanced working memory, then logically we have to assume that more recent and not so recent native peoples were not endowed with enhanced working memory; which is unsustainable as it is universally accepted that, as a species, *Homo sapiens sapiens* share the same type of brain and neural structure. As the human brain is thought to date back 200,000 years, this suggests that it was not some mysterious neural event that led to the complex range of technologies etc., of the Upper Paleolithic but a rise in population numbers and density. Thus, it may have been population that accounts for the variation in technologies and artifacts before and during the Upper Paleolithic. So, enhanced working memory or simple working memory alone is insufficient in the sense that it was population that was the defining factor that mediated material innovation. Having said this, we still need to factor in how neural and cognitive criteria interface with the rise in population levels that underscored the ebb and flow of material culture as it unfolded in the archaeological record. In other words, the cognitive profile of *Homo sapiens sapiens* does not just depend on what occurs cognitively within the brain but the way in which environmental, social, and cultural factors modulate thinking in the context of groups and communities, which is also related to niche construction and how this impacts on behavior and evolutionary parameters through the Baldwin effect (Deacon 1998).

From this perspective, the seeking for the roots of MHB by way of a set of diagnostic traits is too fixed in that such behavior and the related material outcomes can range from not much more than a rudimentary stone age culture to one that is overly complex and convoluted, which is not to say that the cognitive profile of the former is any less sophisticated than the latter. As the signs of human behavior can potentially be indicated by the existence of a range of artifacts from the "rudimentary" to the complex, the cognitive mechanism responsible for this flexibility now needs to be identified. In fact, a mechanism does exist that seems to be able to respond and interface with environmental and socio-cultural dictates according to ongoing needs. Yet, this is also a mechanism that necessarily interrelates with many other aspects of the brain in a flexible and timely way and does not operate as a single entity that determines behavioral outcomes.

Cognition, Neuro-Structure and Population Dynamics

Population dynamics, especially when considered alongside how information is transmitted within and between groups, has provided a useful alternative means of understanding variability in the archaeological record that can, when linked to neuro-cognition, help clarify possible behavioral correlates. In what follows, a more feasible approach to understanding variability in the archaeological record will be set out by showing how population dynamics, transmission effects, and neuro-cognition can be accommodated within a broader theoretical framework that encompasses both embodied and disembodied cognition. It will be argued that such an analysis can provide a more useful way of determining the relationship between archaeology and human behavior.

Controversy has continued over the recent past regarding the relevance of insights into cognition and associated neuro-structures and how these relate to "modern human behavior" and when such behavior might have first arisen. This debate has become particularly engaging thanks to recent important archaeological finds as well as a number of pertinent theoretical insights. In response to this debate, an increasing number of scholars now take the view that the concept of MHB (1) has outlived its usefulness (McBrearty 2007; Barham 2007; Straus 2009; Shea 2011; (2) the evidence from Upper Paleolithic Europe is idiosyncratic (McBrearty and Brooks 2000; d'Errico 2003); (3) population is more informative than brain structure for understanding innovation and change in the archaeological record (Richerson and Boyd 2005; Boyd and Richerson 2005; Shennan 2001; Henrich 2004, 2006; Powell et al. 2009, 2010). In the first part of this section, I will demonstrate that although neuro-structural accounts appear to have failed to explain change in the archaeological record, this does not mean that such accounts should be ignored. Indeed, it will be demonstrated that the organization of the brain continues to be highly relevant to understanding MHB but this needs to be considered within the context of the ability of humans to respond in an informative way to other individuals within socially organized groups. This approach provides a means of understanding the way neuro-structures dynamically interact with culture that accords with dual inheritance theory by describing how certain brain systems provide a means for the individual to become disengaged from actual brain processes through interaction with the socio-cultural world. Despite reservations expressed by some authorities (Grove and Coward 2008; Renfrew and Malafouris 2008), this analysis will therefore show that the neuroscience of the individual brain continues to be crucial to understanding the way brain structure and socio-cultural influences interact that has important consequences for understanding material culture. In this respect, trait lists as a means of defining MHB, especially with regard to the European Upper Paleolithic, will be shown to have led to a biased and misinformed account of behavioral antecedents. Moreover, arguments that depend on trait lists tend to be circular in that the existence of a range of archaeological finds is automatically assumed to be a reliable indication of MHB. In addition, this approach not only appears overly rigid but assumes that

MHB is signified by an increase in complexity or by an accumulation of innovations when, in fact, a decrease in such criteria can be just as diagnostic.

Perhaps the main reason why neuro-structural accounts have increasingly been subject to criticism resides in the fact that much of the variance in the archaeological record, which has come to light since the appearance of anatomically modern humans some 200 ka, can be explained by changes in population densities and the propensity of communities to interact across and within cultural groups (Powell et al. 2009, 2010; Shea 2011). Such population dynamics seem to control the rate and level at which innovation can occur and accumulate, and are therefore governed by social factors rather than being tied to any newly evolved neuro-cognitive components. The influence of population levels on innovation seems to be generic as the principle has been found to apply equally to a number of diverse indigenous groups, which is confirmed by research in this field (Powell et al. 2010; Kline and Boyd 2010; Shennan 2001). This has received further confirmation from the way microlith technology in South Asia seemed to vary in line with population levels and density (Petraglia et al. 2009). The question therefore arises as to whether neuro-cognition can continue to play any meaningful role in understanding human behavior in relation to understanding the variability of the archaeological record. Evidence will, however, be presented demonstrating that neuro-cognitive factors are indeed still relevant to this issue. Thus, although population dynamics may be able to account for a large share of the variance, there must also have been some associated neuro-cogntive substrate involved (Hodgson 2010), which suggests neuro-cognition continues to be relevant to the issue.

Correlating MHB with the artifacts that existed in Europe from 40 ka onwards now appears untenable (Shea 2011; d'Errico 2003), not least because anatomically modern humans appeared long before this date (McDougal et al. 2005). Moreover, as already hinted, indigenous groups from the modern era, such as exist(ed) in Oceania and Tasmania, possessed a subsistence technology more rudimentary than that of the European Upper Paleolithic (Jones 1977, 1995; Diamond 1978; Henrich 2004, 2006; Pardoe 1991; Kline and Boyd 2010; Powell et al. 2010; Hodgson 2010), which points to considerable variability in the degree of complexity attainable by various groups horizontally and vertically through time. Furthermore, some of the artifacts that were once thought to be exclusive to the European Upper Paleolithic have now been found up to 80 ka in South Africa, and there have been claims for the use of ochre, the engagement in funerary activities, and the existence of shell beads at much earlier periods (McBrearty and Brooks 2000; Henshilwood et al. 2009; Barham 2002, 2007; Bednarik 2003a). As a result, it is increasingly accepted that the signature of MHB varies greatly in response to changing population rates, which is a situation that has been further complicated by taphonomy, whereby the archaeological record becomes more impoverished over time (Bednarik 1994), thereby accentuating the observed mosaic effect (Hovers and Belfer-Cohen 2007). One of the important aspects of population density concerns the transmission of ideas and skills that tend to occur more frequently in interacting populations and subpopulations through vertical (in the majority of cases), oblique, or horizontal mechanisms (Shennan and Steele 1999; Kline and Boyd 2010; Powell et al. 2010), which can be either formal or informal (Boyd and Richerson 1985). In order to appreciate the relevance of these issues to understanding behavioral outcomes, it is first necessary to explore the way neural systems determine sociality in relation to population dynamics.

As a population expands the opportunity to engage in social encounters increases, which suggests there is a significant flexibility inherent to cognitive abilities for dealing with such encounters. But what precisely does this cognitive ability consist of? Interestingly, mirror neurons have recently been confirmed in the human brain (Keysers and Gazzola 2011), which are more extensive than in non-human primates, and appear to facilitate social interaction (Rizzolatti et al. 2001). Unlike in nonhuman primates, mirror neurons allow a person to copy the actions of others even when the actions are being pantomimed (Ferrari et al. 2005; Grèzes et al. 1998; Buxbaum et al. 2005). This has allowed humans to engage in unrewarded imitation, a proclivity that is absent in non-human primates (Hill et al. 2009). The ability to imitate seems to derive from a constitutive mirror system as part of a fronto-parietal network which, although shared by non-human primates, operates at a more sophisticated level in humans in not being tied to the prevailing situation (Teufel et al. 2010). The fronto-parietal network is, therefore, functionally complex in humans and, importantly, appears to be directly linked to brain areas mediating theory of mind that allows the world to be seen from the perspective of others (Iriki 2006; Gallese 2007). The mirror/theory of mind system (MToMs) is fundamental to copying actions in an informed way in that a learner needs to put him/herself in the position of the instructor in order for learning to proceed. It has recently been established that the degree to which this system is able to function depends on sustained socially-mediated input in that, even though a skill may be acquired in response to the appropriate level of input, this may be rapidly lost when such input is no longer available (Heyes 2003; Heyes 2010). This is due to the fact that such learning appears to depend on associative processes that require sustained input for skills to be maintained (Catmur et al. 2007; Catmur et al. 2008; Catmur et al. 2009). The mirror system, when considered together with theory of mind, therefore appears to be particular sensitive to, and dependent on, the level of input from others. Thus, the more one engages in visuo-motor skills, the easier it becomes to imitate actions in several domains, which is a tendency that has also been observed in tool-trained macaques where training seemed to facilitate social behavior (Iriki 2006). Accordingly, when there is greater interaction between subgroups, which is more likely with higher population densities (Powell et al. 2009, 2010; Shennan 2001), the potential inherent to the MToMs is more liable to be exploited—which can be further exploited through the dynamic interaction between the MToMs itself and interacting individuals within the group as a result of the "ratchet effect" (Tomasello 1999). As the copying of skills by way of the mirror system derives from associative learning, expertise can therefore be rapidly lost should the socio-ecological situation alter. As most skills are difficult to acquire, not least because of the sophistication that accrues as a result of the ratchet effect, when population rates decline or become more dispersed, skills will be lost due to a lack of input on which the mirror system can act. In addition, the more visuo-motor skills are utilized, the easier it will become to imitate actions in a range of different fields. Note that, especially for those skills involving visuo-spatial/motor capacities (i.e., procedural abilities), considerable training is needed before an individual is able to acquire the necessary skills (Wynn and Coolidge 2010; Stout 2002a, 2002b). This means that, as population levels decline, the opportunity for the mirror system to exploit input will be reduced with a concomitant loss of skills in the general population. This will occur whether learning proceeds through straightforward observation or structured learning, although the latter will entail more serious detrimental effects due to the level of expertise required for such instruction.

We now turn to the important topic of ontogenetic development in humans, as this appears to differ markedly from non-human primates in being much longer in the former and seems to be related to the need to learn socio-cultural skills and may be able to provide evidence as to when such skills began to become important in hominin lifeways. The ability to learn from others develops throughout an extended childhood in *Homo sapiens sapiens,* where neural circuits undergo differentiation according to experience gained through interaction with increasingly extended groups of significant others (from close kin, to extended family and peers) to more detached individuals as part of a wider social interplay. Interaction of this kind requires considerable learning that is acquired implicitly through regular contact and observation, and explicitly through guided instruction that is particularly dependent on various aspects of memory, which is one of the main criteria that gives rise to conscious awareness (i.e., of self and others through theory of mind [Buckner and Carroll 2007; Adolphs 2009]).

Grove and Coward (2008) have shown that the extended immaturity of humans is important for determining when social abilities became important and, when considered in the broader context of socio-cognitive capacities, can help clarify when events occurred in the archaeological record. Extended development in humans allows both social skills and complex visuo-spatial/motor abilities to be acquired that are essential if a community is to survive and prosper, in that the practical expertise gained can be employed to sustain and create new essential technologies. Evidence as to when an extended childhood for achieving such skills first occurred would provide a marker as to when the MToMs initially became important and can also serve as a means for detecting signs of "MHB." In this regard, the teeth eruption of a 160-ka-old juvenile *Homo sapiens* suggests a developmental trajectory similar to that of contemporary adolescents (Smith et al. 2007). In contrast, evidence from *Homo erectus* and *Homo heidelbergensis* indicates a much shorter period of development (Coqueugniot et al. 2004; Rozzi et al. 2004). These findings also indicate that Neanderthals experienced a faster rate of childhood development than *Homo heidelbergensis*. This implies that, from the time of the last common ancestor of Neanderthals and anatomically modern humans (probably *Homo heidelbergensis*), a divergence occurred in developmental trajectories, with anatomically modern humans experiencing a longer juvenile period than Neanderthals, with all this implies for the ability to learn and fully exploit the potential inherent to the MToMs.

A recent morphometric study confirms this proposition where it was established that there is an earlier globularization phase in the brain of *Homo sapiens sapiens* neonates than is the case with Neanderthals that appears to be caused by an enlarged parietal area in humans (Gunz et al. 2012). Interestingly, in line with Bruner's finding that the parietal area seems to have expanded after the prefrontal cortex had reached its maximum in *Homo sapiens* 200 ka ago, the parietal area seems also to be one of the last areas to develop in children (Sowell et al. 2002). This scenario may be explained by the fact that Neanderthals seem to possess a reduced parietal area compared to anatomically modern humans (Bruner 2003, 2004, 2010; Bruner et al. 2003, 2010), which is precisely where the fronto-parietal mirror system interfaces with theory of mind i.e., the temporal parietal junction and intraparietal sulcus (Iriki 2006; Dubreuil 2010; Hodgson 2010). Perhaps, therefore, important changes occurred in the parietal area of anatomically modern humans that involved the integration of visuo-spatial/motor abilities with multi-modal capacities (Bruner 2010). This also implies that MHB may have depended on the enlargement and reorganization of the parietal area that led to the increased ability of *Homo sapiens sapiens* to engage in complex social interactions, thus allowing cultural innovations to accumulate when population rates rose to an optimum level.

As a result, anatomically modern humans were able to take greater advantage of the benefits deriving from social interaction than was the case for Neanderthals. In this sense, although the material culture of anatomically modern humans often seems to have been equivalent to Neanderthals (d'Errico 2003), when population levels rose in either species, it was *Homo sapiens sapiens* that benefited the most. This is reflected in the upper population limit at which anatomically modern humans were able to function as a coherent social unit of around 150 in number, which is thought to be larger than was the case for Neanderthals (Dunbar 2009; Gamble et al. 2011).

The enhanced social interactions from which *Homo sapien sapiens* were able to profit would have led to the ability to accumulate cultural information through the sharing of ideas that led to a re-calibration of evolutionary instantiated neural maps (brain areas specializing in particular kinds of information) that now became less constrained and more wide-ranging (Dehaene and Cohen 2007; Sperber and Hischfeld 2004; Donald 1998). The more free-ranging domains that arose out of greater cultural input allowed Upper Paleolithic groups to exploit communally derived information more effectively and, as a result, innovations accumulated. In this way, and given the raised population levels, MToMs provided the conditions that facilitated enhanced social transmission, from which the gains were able to be recycled to original neural macro-maps. This scenario demonstrates the complex ways in which neuro-cognition interacted with changing population rates, i.e., bottom-up from MToMs to externally derived socio-cultural components, and top-down from the socio-cultural to long-standing macro neural maps (see Figure 1) through a "parasitical" mechanism (Sperber 1996). Thus, according to Sperber (1996: 141) "cultural transmission causes, in the actual domain of any cognitive module, a proliferation of parasitic information that mimics the module's [evolutionary] proper domain." The output from such evolutionary instantiated domains can, however, give rise to a more reflective domain, referred to as a "meta-representational module" that arises from theory of mind. It is this meta-representational capacity that underlies human communication abilities. These insights provide further evidence that the neuro-cognition of *Homo sapiens sapiens*, more than in any other species, needs to be considered in tandem with enhanced socio-cultural criteria as part of a co-evolutionary framework (Richerson and Boyd 2005).

The above shows how it is necessary to take account of the flexible nature of human behavior in the context of the way neuro-cognitive systems dynamically interact with environmental and socio-cultural factors. In this regard, the systems that underpin mirror neurons and theory of mind appear to develop very early in childhood from about fourteen months onwards (Baron-Cohen 2007), which emphasizes the importance of pretend play and fictional enactment for the practicing of social skills by recourse to a meta-representational capacity (Leslie 1987). This corresponds with Donald's (1998) suggestion that the ability for fictional enactment occurred early, perhaps up to 500,000 years ago, and may have been intimately associated with mimesis and ritual. As Simon Baron-Cohen (2007) has argued, although the *content* of imagination may be determined more by culture than biology, the *capacity* to imagine owes more to biology than culture. It may have been that the capacity to imagine occurred very early, as Donald suggests, and derived from the need to engage in complex social interaction that led to the larger share of brain expansion and neural reorganization (Dunbar (2009). Such a raised level of social engagement may have also given rise to the need to try to imagine or guess the thoughts of others. Indeed, this is essential for normal communication to occur on a number of different levels, as is testified by the problems autistics have with social interaction due to deficits in theory of mind or mind reading (Baron-Cohen 2007).

The question arises: could these findings help to discern signs in the archaeological record of an imaginative faculty that was not tethered to the presiding moment or scaffolded by immediate environmental cues? Late Mode 2 Acheulian bifaces perhaps constituted the first tools that existed as such in the minds of the makers, in that the preceding Mode 1 Oldowan tools did not exist as a separate entity from the contexts in which they were employed. Mode 2 bifaces were carried from place to place by hominins, and as well as being reused they also served as a source of flakes. Thus, rather than being intimately associated with the context in which a procedure occurred, bifaces became permanent objects of hominin lifeways, even when not in use (Coolidge and Wynn 2009). The fact that Acheulian tools, from about 500,000 year onwards, seem to show more of a non-utilitarian concern for symmetry supports this contention, as the ability to imagine the form of an object from a number of different viewpoints using a mental template (allocentric perception) goes beyond the purely practical (Coolidge and Wynn 2009; Hodgson 2012)—which corresponds to the ability to imagine the viewpoints and perspectives of others; a propensity that probably led to a growing concern for shape for its own sake that was expressed in the more symmetrically shaped hand-axes. This raised concern for symmetry has been referred to as "the display hypothesis" by McNabb (2012) and seems to be related to a sensitivity to the attitudes of others in so far as the makers of the tools concerned seemed to have taken "pride" in the appearance of an object. It may therefore be the case that, with the coming of *Homo heidelbergensis,* the social imperative, which had led to brain expansion and reorganization, began to overflow into other spheres such as toolmaking. This meant that, because the human brain is essentially constructed out of the need to socialize in large groups, any activity that did not specifically involve social criteria nevertheless became socialized due to the fact that all areas of life had now become "infected" by such a proclivity. From this perspective, modern human cognition and its material embodiment seems to have been borne out of the social mind, of which working memory would have been one component.

A further problem with the enhanced working memory proposal is that it has led to a distorted notion of modern human behavior. As noted, MHB is extremely flexible in that it responds to ecological and population conditions according to situation that can give rise to very rudimentary Middle Paleolithic-like technologies or highly complex artifacts as a result of accumulated knowledge. This suggests that flexible human cognition rather than modern human cognition should be regarded as the main characteristic that defines human behavior. This also means that the idea of a fixed range of essential traits and material outcomes that might signify human behavior is inadmissible, not least because such behavior is liable to be expressed in various ways depending on context. The concept of MHB therefore needs to be either overturned or should be modified in a way that takes account of the flexibility that typifies the human condition. As human behavior is characterized by malleability, this goes some way to explain why the material record exhibits various degrees of complexity. The fact that the archaeological record appears to be less complex at earlier dates has not only been contradicted by finds such as Blombos but also the fact that seafaring occurred at an early date, which involves sophisticated planning and technological expertise (Bednarik 2003b).

There are also certain anomalies that are often ignored by those who favor a late cognitive event that underwrites purported MHB. The Berekhat Ram and Tan Tan figurines stand as obvious examples, not to mention the Schöningen spears (Thieme 1997). The spears are a particularly interesting example, as Coolidge and Wynn claim that all that was required to make such implements was a visuo-spatial procedural memory based upon manual dexterity acquired through actual engagement and involvement on a practical level. According to a number of authorities (Haidle 2010), however, the procurement and making of these ballistically refined objects entailed forward planning as well as a design sense. For example, the tips of the spears were deliberately fabricated from a particular part of the tree to promote function. There is also evidence that hafting probably took place at the same site, as grooved wooden tools were unearthed, making them the oldest composites on record at over 400,000 years old (Thieme 1997). Other commentators have also emphasized that evidence from the Middle Paleolithic indicates that enhancement to working memory had already evolved (Belfer-Cohen and Hovers 2010; Barham 2007, 2002). Perhaps Welshon (2010) is therefore correct in stating that enhanced working memory may have little to do with what separates Neanderthals and *Homo sapiens sapiens* cognitively. The veracity of this has recently been confirmed by the finding of Acheulian tools in Crete that are believed to date back from between 130,000 to 700,000 years ago. The only way the makers of these tools could have reached Crete is by sea, probably from Africa, which would have involved considerable seafaring and navigational expertise (Strasser et al. 2010). Similar evidence continues to come to light in other areas of activity, such as the Howiesons Poort bow and arrow technology and other associated implements that existed well before 60,000 years ago that attest to cognitive sophistication (Lombard and Parsons 2011; Lombard, in press; Lombard and Haidle, in press).

Lombard (Lombard and Parson 2011) puts forward the interesting idea that population rates, as they affect the rise and fall of technology throughout the Middle to Upper Paleolithic, can be compared to a rugged fitness landscape where the heights of various peaks represent a particular population density that is associated with various degrees of technical innovation. Thus, lower, more separated peaks represent dispersed populations with reduced densities that provide less opportunity for exchange of ideas, etc. In the case of more dense but isolated populations, when a peak is already beginning to be climbed by a population, it will be obliged to continue the same trajectory as there is little opportunity to change course or retrace steps (it is always more difficult to descend than ascend). Lombard regards this model as having greater explanatory and ecological validity than the ratchet effect but the two alternatives need not be mutually exclusive, as the latter can be seen as operating when a population is climbing a peak in that accumulation of innovations will occur along this trajectory depending on context. Interestingly, Lombard's model has been applied to understanding the way natural systems evolve in the Darwinian sense (Kauffman 1993; Dennett 1995). Specifically, various species survive or become extinct according to which trajectory is followed by a particular species, where once this has been adopted there is little opportunity for retraction as the physical systems will already have been formed in the light of the prevailing environment. Should the environment prove advantageous, the population of the species in question will be able to climb towards the targeted peak. It seems that the peak towards which humans strove was marked by advanced information processing abilities that allowed socio-cultural skills to be exploited according to context.

We can conclude from the above that the first glimmerings of a disposition that was not tied to the needs of the presiding environmental situation began at least 500,000 years ago with *Homo heidelbergensis* (Hodgson 2011). Moreover, this was a disposition that grew out of social needs where one was required to keep track of individuals in increasingly larger groups that called for greater brain resources in order to predict and deal with what others might be thinking. Working memory would have played a role in this process in the sense that it was but one node in a complex network of neural systems, including MToMs that allowed social competence to occur.

It is notable that the population densities of Europe during the Upper Paleolithic underwent a significant and sustained increase (Powell et al. 2009), thus providing an explanation for the accumulation of innovations that occurred at the time (and explains the appearance and endurance of representational art). Therefore, in order to fully understand how human behavior relates to the material record, the complete range of dynamically interacting factors needs to be considered. This will include the neural networks relating to social imperatives, memory, attention, cognitive control, emotion, that all interrelate with population levels and ecological factors in multifarious ways. The implication arising from this is that MHB derives from an interactive, flexible dynamic that depends on neuro-cognitive functions and population levels. As some modern human groups continue to rely on rudimentary technologies for survival, it seems it would be parsimonious to conclude that anatomically modern humans 180,000 to 200,000 BP already possessed a modern brain but required raised population levels for the inherent potential to be realized cumulatively in culture. A more effective strategy towards understanding human behavior in various contexts would, accordingly, be to define the level of competence for different population rates and the minimum level of expertise that would eventuate, given a lower rate and a more isolated situation. In this sense, the original Tasmanians may represent the minimum level of competence for the material expression of modern human flexibility. The definition as to what constitutes MHB based on trait lists thereby needs to be reassessed by taking account of the extensive flexibility of *Homo sapiens sapiens* in attaining different levels of cultural complexity. A more productive approach to this issue would be based on identifying the way in which the material expression of culture dynamically interacts with enduring cognitive abilities and population levels. In this sense, the archaeological record suggests MHB began to appear sporadically from around 500,000 BP onwards but only reached its full potential with the appearance of anatomically modern humans around 200,000 BP (Hovers and Belfer-Cohen 2007). In other words, there was no sudden break that heralded the appearance of modern human cognition, rather this was a product of a longstanding, gradual, evolutionary process. This analysis indicates that MHB from 200,000 BP onwards was not a fixed entity but varied in response to both population levels and isolation effects and how these interacted with multi-modal neuro-cognitive functions relating to socio-cultural abilities.

THE ROLE OF EMBODIED COGNITION

In this section, it will be shown how neuro-cognition and the population effects already alluded to can be assimilated with embodied or enactive cognitive accounts, which have increasingly been favored by archaeologists and anthropologists to explain material culture. Attention, however, will be drawn to the fact that embodied explanations need to be considered within a broader theoretical framework that includes disembodied cognition. In demonstrating this, it is hoped that a much better foundation can be formulated than is presently the case on which inferences about past human behavior can be made.

Due to the fact the MToMs is highly sensitive to population dynamics that affect rates of cultural transmission, it is essential that the implications of approaching the archaeological record from the perspective of embodiment is now carefully considered. Embodied, enactive, or grounded cognition have been proposed as a useful way of understanding the archaeological record that sees the extended mind as penetrating all aspects of material engagement (Malafouris 2010a, 2010b). This approach derives from embodied psychology that has come to the fore in archaeology over the recent past where many, if not all, aspects of thinking are deemed to be premised on the body situated in the world (Malafouris 2004; Renfrew and Malafouris 2008). Moreover, as the mirror system deals with the implicit understanding of actions that facilitates social abilities, it is thus held to be a classic example of embodied cognition (Malafouris 2010a). The concept of embodied cognition, however, requires a more nuanced reading not least in order to avoid the concept becoming redundant. Indeed, there is presently no common acceptance as to what exactly is meant be embodied cognition (Ziemke and Frank 2008; Goschler 2005). The following statement encapsulates the problem.

> It is of course possible to treat every kind of behavior as the interaction of a body in an environment. Thus, every experience we make could be called "embodied". But this would make the notion of the body trivial and we were better off with just calling it "experience" and nothing else. If one does not want the notion of embodiment to be a trivial one, which would lead to a non-falsifiable theory, "body" needs a narrower definition (Goschler 2005).

In order to address this problem, it is necessary to consider what neuroscience has to say about the brain. Although neuroscience has led to an improved understanding of brain function that has given rise to sub-disciplines such as neuroarchaeology, such insights need to be considered in terms of how the brain of humans has been recalibrated through socio-cultural feedback loops. Such recalibration has allowed the world to be interpreted and reinterpreted thanks to a cognitive capacity that can lead to the countermanding of certain long-standing embodied constraints (Dehaene and Cohen 2007). The interaction between embodied components and more abstract cognitive representations is, however, complex in that, depending on circumstances, embodied factors may preside whereas, in a different setting, more abstract cognitive domains may dominate. This reflects the difference between evolutionary defined functions and socio/cultural cognitive influences. It seems therefore inappropriate to regard human behavior and its effects as determined solely by embodiment, as some archaeologists and anthropologists have tended to (see, for example, Coward and Gamble 2008; Malafouris, 2010a), usually following Gallese (2005, 2007) and associates. Nor should behavior be regarded simply as dependent on higher-order disembodied cognition, as embodied and disembodied systems can function in parallel or separately depending on the prevailing situation (Mahon and Caramazza 2008; Meteyard 2010; Dove 2009). Having said this, it is probable that when population rates were low, embodied attributes exerted more of an influence compared to when population rates were high, when more abstract cognitive representations would have come to the fore thanks to increased social interaction. In addition, embodied attributes may be more relevant to earlier hominin evolution rather than when population rates had reached a critical size in modern humans, either before or during the Upper Paleolithic/Late Stone Age.

These insights are in line with a more restricted definition of embodiment (see, for example, Goldman and de Vignemont 2009; Vernon 2008; Mahon and Caramazza 2008; Adams and Aizawa 2010; Meteyard et al. 2010) than is employed by archaeologist and anthropologists. Thus, although embodiment may provide a novel way of understanding cognition and related material outcomes, representational approaches to cognition continue to be relevant, not least because the embodied thesis stems from J. J. Gibson's (1979) ideas regarding direct perception that continues to be of relatively minor importance within academic psychology (Wynn et al. 2009). What is meant by embodiment, nevertheless, seems to be close to what evolutionary psychologists refer to as enduring cognitive domains (Cosmides et al. 1992), which clearly continue to affect modern brains despite a highly technological society (Caramazza and Mahon 2003; Hodgson 2003).

In view of these observations, some researchers propose that representational and embodied approaches should be regarded as complementary rather than opposed (Mahon and Caramazza 2008; Meteyard 2010; Dove 2009). The fully embodied radicalism put forward by authorities, such as Lakoff and Nuñez (1999), has, therefore, been criticized as all cognition is regarded as embodied, including language and mathematics. Seen from a broader, more complementary perspective, embodied cognition can, however, be viewed as specifically linked to on-line bodily processes, i.e., somatosensory and visuo-spatial/motor abilities and basic interactions of the mirror system with social responses—an approach which has been referred to as "material embodiment" (Ziemke and Frank 2008). In contrast, the off-line conceptual/semantic aspects of higher thinking, visual memory, propositional reasoning, language, and where inferences regarding social information are made over time, seem to have more in common with disembodied cognition. Take, for example, the following statement:

> … cognition entails the manipulation of explicit representations of the state and behavior of the external world to facilitate appropriate, adaptive, anticipatory, and effective interaction, and the storage of the knowledge gained from this experience to reason even more effectively in the future. Reasoning itself is symbolic: a procedural process whereby explicit representations of an external world are manipulated to infer likely changes in the configuration of the world arising from causal actions (Vernon 2008).

In this sense, semantics would not be possible in the absence of the capacity for context-independent representations and symbolism in some form. Hence, a more interactive process, referred to as secondary/weak embodiment (Meteyard 2010), where elements of representation and embodiment exist alongside one another, seems to provide a more realistic way of understanding the dynamics of cognition.

The application of embodiment to all areas of cognition has also been criticized because it is unable to account for many abilities that are better accommodated by disembodied cognition (see Adams and Aizawa 2010; Chatterjee 2010; Mahon and Caramazza 2008; Zlatev 2008; Tversky and Hard 2009). For example, cognition that marks out humans may rely on recently evolved forward areas of the brain that operate as part of a multi-modal representation system for coordinating complex information (Barsalou 2008; Pessullo 2011)—what Halford et al. (2010) refer to as higher cognitive relational knowledge. It has also been established that social attribution recruits the medial prefrontal cortex and is involved in the meta-representation of complex social inferences (Van Overwalle 2009). So, although embodied processes may play an important role in cognition, "amodal" representations continue to be relevant by serving a unitary function (Barsalou 2008). In other words, and as Figure 1 illustrates, embodied attributes may operate at the lower to middle end of a hierarchy from which more abstract and flexible modes are constructed that may sometimes constrain thinking, but at other times abstract conceptual domains can lead to a release from such limitations (Goldman and de Vignemont 2009; Ikegami and Zlatev 2007). For example, the counter-intuitive principles of science, as exemplified by quantum mechanics, would not have been possible without disengagement from embodied constraints. Similarly, Deacon (1998) has argued that free-ranging symbolic expertise, although initially grounded on more constitutive elements (iconic to indexical), once constructed, allows originating modes to be transcended. The fact that information in the brain is bi-directionally also needs to be taken into account in that this involves feed-forward input from lower areas and feedback from higher levels with a significant degree of interaction taking place throughout the mid-levels (see Figure 1).

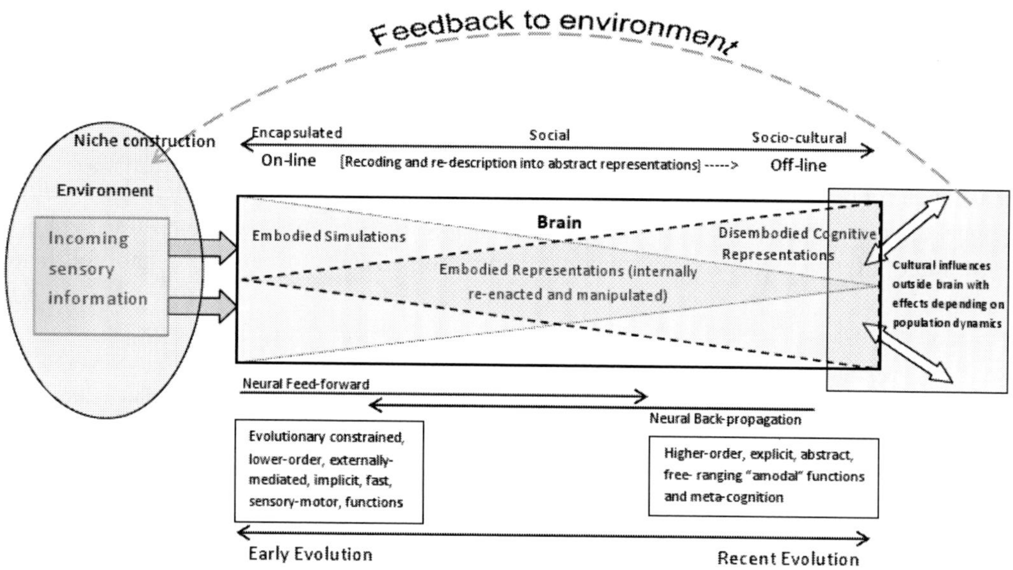

Figure 1. Three levels of organization indicating the interrelationship of embodied and disembodied cognition where the influence of the two factors grade into one another as indicated by the separate dashed triangles. The interaction of the two functions is highlighted by the shaded diamond-shaped area.

These observations suggest that higher order social functions should not always be regarded as embodied but also concern aspects of cognition that employ inferences (representations) regarding others. This corresponds to Dunbar's level 4–5 perspective taking, i.e., the ability to understand a series of embedded points of view, which underpins the ability of humans to engage in extended social groups involving complex interactions and abstract thinking on various levels of meta-cognition (Frith 2008). Interestingly, research by Dunbar (2010) has recently implicated the orbito-frontal prefrontal cortex in such inferences. This suggests that level 4–5 perspective taking, is mediated by sophisticated disembodied cognition that has been scaffolded by "lower" embodied processes (Goldman and de Vignemont 2009). Similarly, Dubreuil (2010) regards perspective taking as important for enhanced social abilities but sees this as associated more with neural restructuring rather than overall brain size (see also Hodgson 2010). In this sense, Dubreuil regards theory of mind as crucial to social abilities that appears to be related to a derived temporo-parietal junction, which is directly linked to the medial and orbito prefrontal cortex where sophisticated social abilities reside (Dunbar 2010; Iriki 2006). This is in line with Bruner's (2010) finding that the posterior parietal area and intraparietal sulcus have undergone enlargement in anatomical modern humans compared to Neanderthals.

The above suggests that disembodied cognition may have increasingly become important in determining the behavior of hominins, particularly from 200 ka onwards, especially when this interacted with cultural feedback as a function of raised population levels that led to niche construction (see Figure 1). In sum, what marked out *Homo sapiens sapiens* was the ability to benefit from the increased transmission of skills that came with rising population levels that seemed to have depended on an enhanced MToMs that led to more efficient ways of sharing and profiting from socially derived information. This, however, did not just derive from an embodied/extended mind as it engaged with the material world, but also the ability to exploit the benefits thereby through the flexibility of disembodied cognition that allowed highly efficient abstract thinking to occur, thus providing an economical way to deal with highly complex information. Although ideas may sometimes be expressed in embodied ways, as is reflected in material culture, the fact remains that disembodied representations (ideas) exist in an abstract form that may not always be realized materially. It is because such ideas can be exchanged intangibly that potential outcomes are able to be assessed without the need for material engagement. Although material culture may help to alter the way in which the world is regarded (Malafouris 2010b), it does not lead to a complete reshaping of all cognitive processes as certain long-standing cognitive domains continue to prevail even in modern humans (Dehaene and Cohen 2007), as evolutionary psychologists have repeatedly demonstrated (Barkow et al. 1992).

I wish to end this section by considering the relevance of phenomenology in relation to recent advances in neuroscience for understanding the past, as this concept has also had a marked influence on archaeological thinking over recent years. The penchant of archaeologists for phenomenology derives, in part, from a distaste of Descartes' mind-brain/body dichotomy that gave rise to the apparent reductive and positivist outlook of science. In addition, cognitive explanations as to how the brain relates to mind seemed to place great reliance on the scientific approach where mind/consciousness was seen as an illusion that could be explained by understanding how the brain functioned at various levels and which largely depended on preconscious/subconscious processes. As the "cognitive revolution" of the 1970s relied on understanding the brain by appealing either directly or indirectly to computer systems, this too came to be regarded as over reductionist—especially as J. J. Gibson's theory on direct perception seemed to be more in line with the phenomenology agenda that was concerned with the contents of immediate subjective experience rather than how it was arrived at (Merleau-Ponty 1961, 1964). However, due to the fact that most phenomenologists came from a philosophical tradition, much of their claims tended to be speculative and unverifiable. For example, there is no way an individual is able to enter the subjective experience of another to confirm what may have been sensed or perceived. The alternative means of investigation, despite the reductionist accusation, was through modern neuroscience where immediate sensory experience, which is referred to as qualia in psychology, has been shown to depend on fast-acting implicit neural processes. In fact, the direct sensory experience of J. J. Gibson (1979), although it might at first *appear not* to depend on much internal processing or representation, in reality, depends on evolutionary instantiated modes that determine what and how particular kinds of information deriving from the real world are processed. As a result, some Gibsonian supporters have come round to the view that a modicum of implicit processing is necessary for vision to proceed (Nakayama 2000). In this sense, the "automatic" evolutionary defined algorithms that the visual system employs to achieve visual discrimination can be interpreted as corresponding to Gibson's "formless invariants." Thanks to the fast-acting nature of these invariants, it might seem that perception is immediate but modern neuroscience has revealed that this occurs within a 150–200 mscs timeframe involving a complex hierarchy of stages. As a result, Gibson's theory can now be accommodated within the context of modern neuroscience. More specifically, although formless invariants were rather vaguely described by Gibson in terms of "resonance," they can now more readily be explained in terms of the weighting of neural networks. To quote Norman's (2002) account of Hatfield's (1988, 1990) interpretation of this:

> ... he [Hatfield] showed how a connectionist model can satisfy the claims of the constructivists that rule-like behavior underlies perception, but by being rule-instantiating without being rule-following the model can also satisfy the Gibsonian strictures against cognitive mediation. In other words, the connectionist network with its hidden units and the connection weights among them can respond (or resonate) as if it is making inferences without implementation of anything more than some changes in the weights in the model. These weight changes are the "representations" of the system. Hatfield suggested that representations of this sort are commensurate with Gibson's approach.

I would argue that the processes whereby neural networks become "weighted" are mediated mainly through phylogeny and are brought into play during ontogeny by way of maturation and interaction with the environment. There may be a degree of flexibility in this system but this does not imply an infinite adaptability rather than there are boundaries that, if crossed, would lead to a confused, unintelligible world. Weighted neuron assemblies thereby act together pre-consciously that gives rise to how the world is experienced phenomenologically. In order to have it both ways, as it were, archaeologists claim that the embodied approach to cognition complements phenomenology in that both deal with the immediate experience of the self as body situated in the world. As neuroscience has demonstrated that sensory experience at all levels can explain the immediate contents of consciousness, this provides a more robust way of understanding the underlying nature of human experience, and suggests the phenomenological approach may be based on a false premise.

Discussion

Altogether, the above deliberations highlight the need for archaeologists and anthropologist to take a more nuanced approach when appealing to neuroscience in order to understand human cognitive origins. By comprehending that human behavior is a flexible commodity that responds to environmental effects and socio-cultural factors in complex ways, one is thereby in a better position to make inferences about the archaeological record. It is clear that one of the main factors that seems to have been ignored until quite recently is the influence of population levels and densities on behavior that provides a more parsimonious way of disambiguating the archaeological record compared to approaches, such as enhanced working memory, that tend to rely on a single mechanism. The advantage of citing the importance of MToMs is to be found in the fact it seems to underpin the flexibility of human cognitive behavior through associative learning that is sensitive to population rates. Of course, working memory will play a role but only in so far as it is regarded as embedded in a multifarious, distributed system with some convergence points distributed throughout the brain. From this perspective, as well as taking account of what is happening in the brain, we also need to appreciate the significance of externally derived factors, not just in terms of population levels but also the way the artificially constructed niche created and inhabited by humans creates feedback to influence cognition in ways that directly impact on culture, as illustrated in Figure 1. Although a greater understanding of population dynamics and transmission effects may have led to important insights regarding variability in the archaeological record, a consideration of how neuro-cognition relates to such criteria can provide a more secure foundation on which inferences about past human behavior can be based.

A better understanding of the way in which cognitive functions relate to embodied processes and population trends can also help clarify underlying constraints and dynamics. Accordingly, although embodied concepts are often recruited by archaeologists and anthropologists for such purposes, this ignores the fact that there continues to be a great deal of dissent among psychologists and neuroscientists regarding the issue. A more balanced approach is therefore required that takes account of concepts such as disembodied cognition as this continues to be important to understanding human behavior. Although embodiment may have proved useful, only by considering its merits according to a wider framework will its applicability be fully realized. In the final analysis, MHB should not be regarded as fixed or restricted to a particular set of traits tied to the archaeological record; rather human behavior, because it responds in complex ways to population levels and the associated benefits to be gained from social interaction, needs to be reframed by taking into account the fact that MHB is determined by the fluctuating and complex nature of social relationships that may not always be either materially visible or embodied.

CONCLUSION

The primary objective of this chapter is to bring to the attention of readers the self-imposed limitations imposed by scholars interested in understanding the past. Such limitations have not only led to a distorted appraisal of human cognitive evolution but have also hampered a more exploratory and open assessment of the evidence. This has partly been a consequence of those concerned tending to remain within the parameters of a particular discipline, although this is now beginning to change with archaeologists and anthropologists now willing to take onboard the findings coming from neuroscience, neuropsychology, and the psychological sciences generally. The potential to be gained in greater interdisciplinary awareness for promoting a better understanding of the past cannot be over-emphasized but this has to be formulated in a way that takes into account the sub-disciplinary nuances that prevail in the various sciences concerned. Up to the present, interdisciplinary understanding has tended to cherry pick findings and theoretical insights when these often continue to be subject to controversy within a discipline. In the examples presented in this chapter, it is hoped that a better and more balanced analysis of the theoretical outlook from various fields will have helped provide a more fruitful way to interpret the past.

REFERENCES

Adams, F., and Aizawa, K. (2010). *The Bounds of Cognition.* Chichester, UK: Wiley-Blackwell.

Adolphs, R. (2009). The Social Brain: Neural Basis of Social Knowledge. *Annual Review of Psychology* 60, 693–716.

Allman, J. M. (1999). *Evolving brains.* New York: Scientific American Library.

Baddeley, A., and Hitch, G. J. (1974). Working memory. In G. A. Bower (Ed.), *Recent advances in learning and motivation* (pp. 47–90). New York: Academic Press.

Baddeley, A. (2007). *Working Memory, Thought, and Action.* Oxford: Oxford University Press.

Baddeley, A. (2012). Working memory: theories, models, and controversies. *Annual Review of Psychology* 63, 1–29.

Barham, L. S. (2002). Systematic pigment use in the Middle Pleistocene of south-central Africa. *Current Anthropology* 43,181–190.

Barham, L. S. (2007). Modern is as modern does? Technological trends and thresholds in the south-central African record. In P. Mellars, P., Boyle., O. Bar-Yosef and C. Stringer (Eds.), *Rethinking the human revolution* (pp. 165–176). Cambridge: McDonald Institute Monographs.

Barkow, J. H., Cosmides, L., and Tooby, J. (1992). *The adapted mind: evolutionary psychology and the generation of culture.* Oxford: Oxford University Press.

Baron-Cohen, S. (2007). The biology of the imagination. *Entelechy* 9. Available at: *http://www.entelechyjournal.com/simonbaroncohen.htm*

Barnard, P. J. (2010). From executive mechanisms underlying perception and action to the parallel processing of meaning. *Current Anthropology* 51(1), S39–54.

Barsalou, L. W. (2008). Grounded cognition. *Annual Review of Psychology* 59, 617–45.

Bednarik, R. G. (1994). A taphonomy of palaeoart. *Antiquity* 68, 68–74.

Bednarik, R. G. (1992). Palaeoart and archaeological myths. *Cambridge Archaeological Journal* 2(1), 27–43.

Bednarik, R. G. (2003a). The earliest evidence of palaeoart. *Rock Art Research* 20(2), 89–135.

Bednarik, R. G. (2003b). Seafaring in the Pleistocene. *Cambridge Archaeological Journal* 13, 41–66.

Belfer-Cohen, A. and Hovers, E. (2010). Modernity, enhanced working memory, and the Middle to Upper Paleolithic record in the Levant. *Current Anthropology* 51(1), S167–176.

Boyd, R., and Richerson, P. J. (1985). *Culture and the evolutionary process.* Chicago, IL: University of Chicago Press.

Boyd, R., and Richerson P. J. (2005). Culture, adaptation, and innateness. In P. Carruthers, S. Stich, and S. Laurence (Eds.), *The innate mind: culture and cognition* (pp. 22–38). Oxford: Oxford University Press.

Bruner, E. (2003). Fossil traces of the human thought: palaeoneurology and the evolution of the genus *Homo. Journal of Anthropological Science* 81, 29–56.

Bruner, E. (2004). Geometric morphometrics and paleoneurology: brain shape evolution in the genus *Homo. Journal of Human Evolution* 47, 279–303.

Bruner, E. (2010). Morphological differences in the parietal lobes within the human genus: a neurofunctional perspective. *Current Anthropology* 51, S77–S88.

Bruner, E., Manzi, G., and Arsuaga, J. L. (2003). Encephalization and allometric trajectories in the genus *Homo*: evidence from the Neandertal and modern lineages. *Proceedings of National Academy of Sciences USA 100* (6), 15335–15340.

Bruner, E., Martin-Loeches, M., and Colom, R. (2010). Human midsagittal brain shape variation: patterns, allometry and integration. *Journal of Anatomy* 216, 589–599.

Buckner, R. L., and Carroll, D. C. (2007). Self-projection and the brain. *Trends in Cognitive Sciences* 11(2), 49–57.

Buxbaum, L. J., Kyle, K. M., and Menon, R. (2005). On beyond mirror neurons: internal representations subserving imitation and recognition of skilled object-related actions in humans. *Cognitive Brain Research* 25, 226–239.

Caramazza, A., and Mahon, B. Z. (2003).The organization of conceptual knowledge: the evidence from category-specific semantic deficits. *Trends in Cognitive Sciences* 7(8), 354–361.

Catmur, C., Gillmeister, H., Bird, G., Liepelt, R., Brass, M., and Heyes, C.M. (2008). Through the looking glass: counter-mirror activation following incompatible sensorimotor learning. *European Journal of Neuroscience* 28: 1208–1215.

Catmur, C., Walsh, V., and Heyes, C. M. (2007). Sensorimotor learning configures the human mirror system. *Current Biology* 17, 1527–1531.

Catmur, C., Walsh, V., and Heyes, C. M. (2009). Associative sequence learning: the role of experience in the development of imitation and the mirror system. *Philosophical Transactions of the Royal Society B* 364, 2369–2380.

Chatterjee A. (2010). Disembodying cognition. *Language and Cognition* 2(1), 79–116.

Coolidge, F. L., and Wynn, T. (2009). *The rise of* Homo sapiens*: the evolution of modern thinking*. London: Wiley-Blackwell.

Coolidge, F. L., and Wynn, T. (2011). The implications of the working memory model for the evolution of modern cognition. *International Journal of Evolutionary Biology* 741357, 1–12. doi:10.4061/2011/741357.

Coqueugniot, H., Hublin, J.-J., Veillon, F., Houët, F., and Jacob, T. (2004). Early brain growth in *Homo erectus* and implications for cognitive ability. *Nature* 431, 299–302.

Constantinidis, C., and Procyk, E. (2004). The primate working memory networks. *Cognitive, Affective, and Behavioral Neuroscience* 4(4), 444–465.

Cosmides, L., Tooby, J., and Barkow, J. H. (1992). Introduction: evolutionary psychology and conceptual integration. In J. H. Barkow., L. Cosmides, and J. Tooby (Eds.), *The adapted mind: evolutionary psychology and the generation of culture* (pp. 3–15). Oxford: Oxford University Press.

Cowan, N. (1995). *Attention and memory: an integrated framework*. New York: Oxford University Press.

Cowan, N. (2005). *Working memory capacity*. New York: Psychology Press.
Cowan, N. (2000). The magical number 4 in short-term memory: a reconsideration of mental storage capacity. *Behavioral and Brain Sciences* 24, 87–185.
Coward, F., and Gamble, C. (2008). Big brains, small worlds: material culture and the evolution of the mind. *Philosophical Transactions of the Royal Society* B363, 1969–1979.
Deacon, T. (1998). *The symbolic species*. Harmondsworth: Penguin.
Dehaene, S., and Cohen, L. (2007). Cultural recycling of cortical maps. *Neuron* 56, 384–398.
Dennett, D. C. (1995). *Darwin's dangerous idea*. London: Penguin.
d'Errico, F. (2003). The invisible frontier. A multiple species model for the origin of behavioral modernity. *Evolutionary Anthropology* 12,188–202.
d'Errico, F., Zilhão, J., Baffier, D., Julien, M., and Pelegrin, J. (1998). Neanderthal acculturation in western Europe? A critical review of the evidence and its interpretation. *Current Anthropology* 39, S1–S44.
Diamond, J. (1978). The longest isolation, the simplest technology. *Nature* 273,185–186.
Donald, M. (1998). Hominid enculturation and cognitive evolution. In C. Renfrew and C. Scarre (Eds.), *Cognition and material culture: the archaeology of symbolic storage* (pp. 7–17). Cambridge: Cambridge University Press.
Dove, G. (2009). Beyond perceptual symbols: a call for representational pluralism. *Cognition* 110, 412–431.
Dubreuil, B. (2010). Paleolithic public goods games: why human culture and cooperation did not evolve in one step. *Biological Philosophy* 25, 53–73.
Dunbar, R. I. M. (2009). Mind the gap: or why humans aren't just great apes. *Proceedings of the British Academy* 154, 403–23.
Dunbar, R. I. M. (2010). Darwin and friends—Oxford abridged short talks (20th Oct). Available at: *http://www.youtube.com/watch?v=X5TkzhmVVVg*
Felleman, D. J., and Van Essen, D. C. (1991). Distributed hierarchical processing in the primate cerebral cortex. *Cerebral Cortex* 1, 1–47.
Ferrari, P. F., Rozzi, S., and Fogassi L. (2005). Mirror neurons responding to observation of actions made with tools in monkey ventral premotor cortex. *Journal of Cognitive Neuroscience* 17(2): 213–226.
Frith, C. D. (2008). Social cognition. *Philosophical Transactions of the Royal Society B* 363, 2033–2039.
Fuster, J. K. (2003). Thoughts from the long-term memory chair. *Behavioral and Brain Sciences* 26,734–35.
Fuster, J. K. (2006). Lecture 8 of 12 of IBM Research's Almaden Institute Conference on Cognitive Computing. Fuster's Powerpoint presentation is available at *http://www.almaden.ibm.com/institute/resources/2006/Almaden%20Institute%20Joaquin%20M.%20Fuster.ppt*.
Fuster, J. M. (2009). Cortex and memory: emergence of a new paradigm. *Journal of* Cognitive Neuroscience. 21(11), 2047–2072.
Gallese, V. (2005).Embodied simulation: from neurons to phenomenal experience. *Phenomenological Cognitive Science* 4, 23–48.
Gallese, V. (2007). Before and below 'theory of mind': embodied simulation and the neural correlates of social cognition. *Philosophical Transactions of the Royal Society* B362, 659–669.

Gamble, C., Gowlett, J., and Dunbar, R. (2011). The social brain and the shape of the Palaeolithic. *Cambridge Archaeological Journal*, 21(1), 115–135.

Gibson, J. J. (1979). *The ecological approach to visual perception*. Boston: Houghton Mifflin.

Goldman, A., and de Vignemont, F. (2009). Is social cognition embodied? *Trends in Cognitive Sciences* 13(4), 154–159.

Goschler J. (2005). Embodiment and body metaphors. *Metaphorik* 9, 33–52. Available at: *http://www.metaphorik.de/09/*

Grèzes, J., Costes, N., and Decety, J. (1998). Top down effect of the strategy on the perception of human biological motion: a PET investigation. *Cognitive Neuropsychology* 15, 553–582.

Grove, M., and Coward F. (2008). From individual neurons to social brains. *Cambridge Archaeolical Journal. 18*(3), 387–400.

Gunz, P., Neubauer, S., Golovanova, L, Doronichev, V., Maureille, B., and Hublin, J. J. (2012). A uniquely modern human pattern of endocranial development. Insights from a new cranial reconstruction of the Neandertal newborn from Mezmaiskaya. *Journal of Human Evolution* 62(2), 300–313.

Haidle, M. N. (2010). Working-memory capacity and the evolution of modern cognitive potential: implications from animal and early human tool use. *Current Anthropology* 51(1): S149–166 .

Halford, G. S., Wilson, W. H., and Phillips, S. (2010). Relational knowledge: the foundation of higher cognition. *Trends in Cognitive Sciences* 14(11), 497–505.

Hatfield, G. (1988). Representation and content in some (actual) theories of perception. *Studies in History and Philosophy of Science* 19, 175–214.

Hatfield, G. (1990). Gibsonian representations and connectionist symbol processing: prospects for unification. *Psychological Research* 52(2–3), 243–52.

Henrich, J. (2004). Demography and cultural evolution: how adaptive cultural processes can produce maladaptive losses—the Tasmanian case. *American Antiquity* 69,197–214.

Henrich, J. (2006). Understanding cultural evolutionary models: a reply to Read's critique. *Amercian Antiquity* 71, 771–782.

Henshilwood, C. S., d'Errico, F., Yates, R., Jacobs, Z., Tribolo, C., Duller, G. A. T., Mercier, N., et al. (2002). Emergence of modern human behavior: Middle Stone Age engravings from South Africa. *Science* 295(5558), 1278–1280.

Henshilwood, C.S., d'Errico, F., and Watts, I. (2009). Engraved ochres from the Middle Stone Age levels at Blombos Cave, South Africa. *Journal of Human Evolution* 57(1), 27–47.

Heyes, C. (2003). Four routes of cognitive evolution. *Psychological Review* 110(4), 713–727.

Heyes, C. (2010). Where do mirror neurons come from? *Neuroscience and Biobehavioral Reviews* 3, 575–583.

Hill, K., Barton, M., and Hurtado, A. M. (2009). The emergence of human uniqueness: characters underlying behavioral modernity. *Evolutionary Anthropology* 18:187–200.

Hodgson, D. (2003). The biological foundations of Upper Palaeolithic art: stimulus, percept and representational imperatives. *Rock Art Research* 20(1), 3–22.

Hodgson, D. (2010). Determining the behavioral profile of early modern humans: assimilating population dynamics and cognitive abilities. *Before Farming 2*(1). Available at: *http://www.waspjournals.com/journals/beforefarming/about/index.php*

Hodgson, D. (2011). The first appearance of symmetry in the human lineage: where perception meets art. *Symmetry* 3(1), 37–53. Available at: *http://www.mdpi.com/2073-8994/3/1/37/*

Hodgson, D. (2012). Hominin tool production, neural integration and the social brain. *Human Origins* 1, 41–64.

Hodgson, D., and Helvenston, P. (2006). Hunting disguises, ritual and animals in Palaeolithic art: a response to critics. *Rock Art Research* 23(1), 26–40.

Holloway, R. L. (1966). Cranial capacity, neural reorganization, and hominid evolution: a search for more suitable parameters. *American Anthropologist* 68, 103–120.

Hovers, E., and Belfer-Cohen, A. (2007). "Now you see it, now you don't"—modern human behavior in the Middle Palaeolithic. In E. Hovers and S. Kuhn (Eds.), *Transitions before the transition—evolution and stability in the Middle Palaeolithic and Middle Stone Age* (pp. 295–304). New York: Springer.

Ikegami, T., and Zlatev, J. (2007). From pre-representational cognition to language. In T. Ziemke., J. Zlatev, and R. Frank (Eds.), *Cognitive linguistics research: body, language, and mind. Volume: Embodiment* (pp. 197–239). Berlin: Mouton de Gruyter.

Iriki, A. (2006). The neural origins and implications of imitation, mirror neurons and tool use. *Current Opinion in* Neurobiology16, 660–667.

Jerison, H. J. (1973). *Evolution of the brain and intelligence.* New York and London: Academic Press.

Jones, R. (1977). The Tasmanian paradox. In R. V. S. Wright (Ed.), *Stone tools as cultural markers: change, evolution and complexity* (pp. 189–204). Canberra: Australian Institute of Aboriginal Studies.

Jones, R. (1995). Tasmanian archaeology: establishing the sequences. *Annual Review of Anthropology* 24, 423–246.

Jonides, J., Lewis, R. L., Nee, D. E., Lustig, C. A., Berman, M. G., and Moore, K. S. (2008). The mind and brain of short-term memory. *Annual Review of Psychology* 59,193–224.

Kauffman, S. (1993). *The origins of order.* New York: Oxford University Press.

Keysers, C., and Gazzola, V. (2011). Social neuroscience: mirror neurons recorded in humans. *Current Biology 20*(8), 353–354.

Kline, M. A., and Boyd, R. (2010). Population size predicts technological complexity in Oceania. *Proceedings of the Royal Society, London* B277 (1693), 2559–2564.

Lakoff , G., and Nuñez, R. (1999). *Where mathematics comes from.* New York: Basic Books.

Lombard, M. (in press). Thinking through the Middle Stone Age of sub-Saharan Africa. *Quaternary International.* Available at: *http://dx.doi.org/10.1016/j.quaint.2012.02.033*

Lombard, M., and Haidle, M. N. (in press). Thinking a bow-and-arrow set: cognitive implications of Middle Stone Age bow and stone-tipped arrow technology. *Cambridge Archaeological Journal.*

Lombard, M., and Parsons, I. (2011). What happened to the human mind after the Howiesons Poort? *Antiquity* 85, 1433–1443.

Leslie, M. (1987). Pretense and representation: the origins of "theory of mind." *Psychological Review* 94, 412–426.

Mahon, B. Z., and Caramazza, A. (2008). A critical look at the embodied cognition hypothesis and a new proposal for grounding conceptual content. *Journal of Physiology – Paris,* 102, 59–70.

Malafouris, L. (2004). The cognitive basis of material engagement: where brain, body and culture conflate. In E. DeMarrais, C. Gosden, and C. Renfrew (Eds.), *Rethinking materiality: the engagement of mind with the material world* (pp. 53–62). Cambridge: The McDonald Institute for Archaeological Research.

Malafouris, L. (2010a). Metaplasticity and the human becoming: principles of neuroarchaeology. *Journal of Anthropological Science* 88, 49–72.

Malafouris, L. (2010b). The brain–artefact interface (BAI): a challenge for archaeology and cultural neuroscience. *Social Cognitive and Affective Neuroscience* 5(2–3), 264–273.

McBrearty, S. (2007). Down with the revolution. In P. Mellars, K. Boyle, O. Bar-Yosef, and C. Stringer (Eds.), *Rethinking the human revolution* (pp. 133–151). Cambridge: McDonald Institute Monographs.

McBrearty, S., and Brooks A. S. (2000). The revolution that wasn't: a new interpretation of the origin of modern human behavior. *Journal of Human Evolution* 39,453–563.

McDougall, I., Brown, F. H., and Fleagle, J. G. (2005). Stratigraphic placement and age of modern humans from Kibish, Ethiopia. *Nature* 433, 733–736.

McNabb, J. (2012). The importance of conveying visual information in Acheulean society: the background to the visual display hypothesis. *Human Origins* 1, 1–23.

Merleau-Ponty, M. (1961). *L'Œil et l'esprit.* Paris: Gallimard.

Merleau-Ponty, M. (1964). Eye and mind. In J. M. Edie (Ed.), *The primacy of perception* (pp. 159–190). Evanston: Northwestern University Press.

Meteyard, L., Rodriguez, C. S., Bahrami, B., and Vigliocco, G. (2010). Coming of age: a review of embodiment and the neuroscience of semantics, *Cortex* 1–17. Available at: *doi:10.1016/j.cortex.2010.11.002*

Mithen, S. (1996). *The prehistory of the mind: the cognitive origins of art, religion and science.* London: Thames and Hudson.

Nakayama, K. (2000). James J. Gibson—an appreciation. In M. S. Gazzaniga (Ed.), *Cognitive neuroscience* (pp. 140–152). Malden, Mass.: Blackwell.

Nairne, J. S. (2002). Remembering over the short-term: the case against the standard model. *Annual Review of Psychology* 53, 53–81.

Norman, J. (2002). Two visual systems and two theories of perception: an attempt to reconcile the constructivist and ecological approaches. *Behavioral and Brain Sciences* 25,73–144.

Pardoe, C. (1991). Isolation and evolution in Tasmania. *Current Anthropology,* 32(1), 1–21.

Pessulo, G. (2001). Grounding procedural and declarative knowledge in sensorimotor anticipation. *Mind and Language* 26(1), 78–114.

Petraglia, M., Clarkson, C., Boivina, N., Haslama, M., Korisettard, R., Chaubeye, G., Ditchfielda, P., Fullerg, D., James, H., Jonesi, S., Kivisildh, T., Koshyd, J., Lahr, M. M., Metspalu, M., Roberts, R., and Arnoldj, L. (2009). Population increase and environmental deterioration correspond with microlithic innovations in South Asia ca. 35,000 years ago. *PNAS* 106(30), 12261–12266.

Postle, B. R. (2006). Working memory as an emergent property of the mind and brain. *Neuroscience.* 139, 23–38.

Powell, A., Shennan, S., and Thomas, M. G. (2009). Late Pleistocene demography and the appearance of modern human behavior. *Science* 324,1298–1301.

Powell, A., Shennan, S. J., and Thomas, M. G. (2010). Demography and variation in the accumulation of culturally inherited skills. In M. J. O'Brian and S. J. Shennan (Eds.),

Innovation in cultural systems: contributions from evolutionary anthropology (pp. 137–160). Cambridge, MA: MIT Press.
Ranganath, C., and Blumenfeld, R. S. (2005). Doubts about double dissociations between short- and long-term memory. *Trends in Cognitive Sciences* 9(8), 374–380.
Renfrew, C. and Malafouris, L. (2008). Steps to a "neuroarchaeology" of mind. *Cambridge Archaeological Journal* 18(3), 381–385.
Richerson P. J., and Boyd, R. (2005). *Not by genes alone: how culture transformed human evolution.* Chicago: University of Chicago Press.
Rizzolatti, G., Fogassi, L., and Gallese, V. (2001). Neurophysiological mechanisms underlying the understanding and imitation of action. *Nature Reviews Neuroscience 2*, 661–670.
Rozzi, F. V. R., and de Castro, J. M. B. (2004). Surprisingly rapid growth in Neanderthals. *Nature 428*, 936–939.
Shea, J. J. (2011). *Homo sapiens* is as *Homo sapiens* was: behavioral variability versus "behavioral modernity" in Paleolithic archaeology. *Current Anthropology* 52(1), 1–35.
Shennan, S. (2001). Demography and cultural innovation: a model and its implications for the emergence of modern human culture. *Cambridge Archaeological Journal* 11, 5–16.
Shennan, S. J., and Steele, J. (1999). Cultural learning in hominids: a behavioral ecological approach. In H. Box and K. Gibson (Eds.), *Mammalian social learning: comparative and ecological perspectives* (pp. 367–388). Cambridge: Cambridge University Press.
Smith, T. M., Tafforeau, P., Reid, D. J., Gru, R., Eggins, S., Boutakiout, M., and Hublin, J. J. (2007). Earliest evidence of modern human life history in north African early *Homo sapiens*. *Proceedings of the National Academy of Science USA* 104(15): 6128–6133.
Sowell, E. R.,Trauner, D. A., Gamst, A., and Jernigan, T. L. (2002). Development of cortical and subcortical brain structures in childhood and adolescence: a structural MRI study. *Developmental Medicine and Child Neurology* 44, 4–16.
Sperber, D. (1996). *Explaining culture.* Oxford: Blackwell.
Sperber, D., and Hirschfeld, L.A. (2004). The cognitive foundations of cultural stability and diversity. *Trends in Cognitive Sciences* 8, 40–46.
Stout, D. (2002a).Thinking and doing in cognitive archaeology: Giving skill its due. Commentary on "Wynn: archaeology and cognitive evolution." *Behavioral Brain Sciences* 25, 421–422.
Stout, D. (2002b). Skill and cognition in stone tool production: an ethnographic case study from Irian Jaya. *Current Anthropology* 45(3), 693–722.
Strasser, T., Panagopoulou, E., Runnels, C., Murray, P., Thompson, N., Karkanes, P., McCoy, F., and Wegmann, K. (2010). Stone Age seafaring in the Mediterranean: evidence for Lower Palaeolithic and Mesolithic inhabitation of Crete from the Plakias region. *Hesperia* 79(2), 145–190.
Straus L. G. (2009). Has the notion of "transitions" in Paleolithic prehistory outlived its usefulness? The European record in wider context. In M. Camps and P. Chauhan (Eds.), *Sourcebook of Paleolithic transitions* (pp. 3–18). New York: Springer.
Teufel, C., Fletcher, P. C., and Davis, G. (2010). Seeing other minds: attributed mental states influence perception. *Trends in Cognitive Sciences* 14, 376–382.
Thieme, H. (1997). Lower Palaeolithic hunting spears from Germany. *Nature* 385, 807–810.
Tomasello, M. (1999). *The cultural origins of human cognition.* Cambridge, MA: Harvard University Press.

Turk, M., and Dimkaroski, L. (2011). Neandertalska piščal iz Divjih bab I: stara in nova spoznanja [Neanderthal flute from Divje babe I: old and new findings]. In B. Toškan (Ed.), *Drobci ledenodobnega okolja. Zbornik ob življenjskem jubileju Ivana Turka [Fragments of Ice Age environments. Proceedings in Honour of Ivan Turk's Jubilee]* (pp. 251–265). Ljubljana: Založba ZRC, ZRC SAZU. *http://www.cpa.si/tidldibab.pdf*

Tversky, B., and Hard, B. M. (2009). Embodied and disembodied cognition: spatial perspective-taking. *Cognition* 110, 124–129.

Van Overwalle, F. (2009). Social cognition and the brain: a meta-analysis. *Human Brain Mapping* 30, 829–858.

Vernon, D. (2008). Cognitive vision: the case for embodied perception. *Image Vision Computing* 26, 127–140.

Weber, G. (2009). The Andamanese. In *Lonely islands*. Available at: *http://www.andaman.org/BOOK/text-group-BodyChapters.htm*

Welshon, R. (2010). Working memory, neuroanatomy, and archaeology. *Current Anthropology* 51(10), S191–199.

Wynn, T., and Coolidge, F. L. (2010). How Levallios reduction is similar to, and not similar to, playing chess. In A. Nowell and I. Davidson (Eds.), *Stone tools and the evolution of human cognition* (pp. 83–103). Boulder: University Press of Colorado.

Wynn, T., Coolidge, F. L., and Bright, M. (2009). Hohlenstein-Stadel and the evolution of human conceptual thought. *Cambridge Archaeological Journal* 19(1), 73–83.

Zlatev, J. (2008). Embodiment, language, and mimesis. In T. Ziemke, J. Zlatev, and R. Frank (Eds.), *Cognitive linguistics research: body, language, and mind, Volume 1: Embodiment* (pp. 297–337). Berlin: Mouton de Gruyter.

Ziemke, T., and Frank, R. M. (2008). Introduction: the body eclectic. In T. Ziemke, J. Zlatev, and R. Frank (Eds.) *Cognitive linguistics research: body, language, and mind, Volume 1: Embodiment* (pp. 1–16). Berlin: Mouton de Gruyter.

In: The Psychology of Human Behavior
Editor: Robert G. Bednarik
ISBN: 978-1-62257-901-3

Chapter 5

Rock Art and Human Behavior

Ben Watson*
Melbourne, Australia

Abstract

Human ethology, or the study of the biological bases of human behavior, has important implications for understanding various aspects of pre-historic rock art. This chapter reviews current literature on the relationship between rock art and human ethology. The isolation and depiction of characteristic features of natural sign stimuli as non-figurative motifs and patterns, and the significance of figurative depictions as sign stimuli capable of triggering typical behavioral and emotional responses are considered. The importance of innate neurophysiological mechanisms that underlie perceptual biases is highlighted, and it is suggested that these biases have influenced the nature of rock art around the world.

The rock art of pre-historic hunter-gatherer societies is a phenomenon capable of informing our understanding of human psychology and behavior in new ways. Paleoart in fact provides the primary source of empirical data available to study human cognition and behavior in the deep past. Conversely, the study of the psychology of human behavior reveals a great deal about art-like phenomena. Human behavior may be studied in the same way as other animal behaviors by considering underlying principles. Human ethology, or the biological bases of human behavior, is based largely in evolutionary theory and concerned in part with certain ubiquitous psychological and behavioral patterns or tendencies that are relatively stable in the human species (Eibl-Eibesfeldt 1989). Of particular interest in the present context are those behavioral patterns or tendencies that relate to visual stimuli. For example, eyes and faces elicit smiles in infants because they attract attention (Robson 1967), and experiments have demonstrated that the consistent, predictable reaction of smiling extends to schematic face-like configurations (e.g., Kagan et al. 1966). Other studies have demonstrated that certain visual configurations relating to predatory animals, such as snake-

*email: watson.benjamin@hotmail.com

like curves, the stalking pose of predatory cats and eye-spot patterns, can evoke universally appropriate behavioral responses such as fear or excitement (Coss 1965). The use of such visual configurations in art can evoke similar responses, and indeed, visual arts throughout time and space exploit imagery types that were of vital interest and great biological importance to Pleistocene hominins (Dissanayake 1998: 490). It appears that this is the case for rock art, displaying many characteristic features that may be understood in this light.

This chapter aims to outline some of the potential implications for the application of the study of human behavior to rock art studies. Specifically, it considers the significance of typical behavioral responses to biologically relevant visual stimuli, and presents the argument that evolved perceptual sensitivities to specific visual forms and patterns have been exploited by humans in the past, influencing the nature of the imagery they created. Two main types of rock art imagery are discussed as examples: abstract-geometric motifs and patterns; and zoomorphs, including the representation of animals and animal-like imagery. The rock art in question is attributed to past societies where ethnographic access to meaning is absent. This chapter is therefore not concerned with how markings were originally interpreted by their authors or what they were intended to mean, which is exceptionally difficult to determine (Bednarik 2003; Watson 2010a). However, the importance of higher cognitive factors and culturally-laden interpretations is by no means denied, and must be seen as complementary to the approach taken here. The interpretation of rock art has drawn extensively on ethnographic analogy in recent years (e.g., Watson 2007), and may provide useful data against which ethological hypotheses could be tested, although this is beyond the scope of this chapter. Although the exact cultural uses and attribution of symbolic meaning(s) to pre-historic rock art by its makers or others during pre-history may no longer be understood, the underlying neurobiological and behavioral frameworks are able to reveal important information concerning its production.

ABSTRACT-GEOMETRIC IMAGERY

The basic units of behavior derived from phylogenetic adaptations are fixed action patterns (FAPs), or stereotyped behavioral responses in animals that are activated by triggering stimuli known as “sign stimuli” or “releasers” via neuro-sensory mechanisms in the central nervous system (Eibl-Eibesfeldt 1975, 1989; Hinde 1982). These neuro-sensory mechanisms are known as innate releasing mechanisms (IRMs), and remain latent until activated by exposure to sign stimuli. Sign stimuli may trigger a reflexive response or IRM that is characteristic of a species. IRMs are thus perceptual mechanisms that function to recognize and identify a stimulus without prior experience (Curio 1993). Since the inception of ethological theory, advances in neuroscience have allowed for the mapping of IRMs in controlled experiments in support of the theory originally proposed by ethologists: that such basic units of behavior are the basis of complex behaviors such as predator avoidance.

Animals may exhibit stereotypical behavioral response patterns to certain stimuli, but these patterns are also flexible; responses may not be as “fixed” as the term “fixed action pattern” implies, but may be subtly influenced by experience and environment (Aiken 1998: 52). In humans, instinctual behavior may be particularly influenced by cognitive intervention. Hodgson (2003) has recently considered the manifestation of rock art in terms of FAPs and sign stimuli, and notes that this flexibility, mediated by the higher brain (i.e., the cerebral cortex, responsible for the most complex cognitive capacities such as thought) is an adaptive specialization that serves to increase perceptual capabilities. Although this makes the innate determinants difficult to assess, particularly because no humans are without experience, they are strongly suggested by cultural invariability, and this is reflected in parallels observable in the typical characteristics of rock art imagery throughout time and space (Watson 2009). Like other animals, humans are found to respond in predictable ways to biologically relevant visual stimuli, and this helps in understanding the determinants that shape the nature of rock art imagery around the world.

The properties of visual stimuli that are most interesting and tend to be used most often in graphics are those that "resonate" with certain properties of the human visual system. These are forms that either isolate or exaggerate a specific process of the visual system by hyper-stimulating neurons selectively responsive to their attributes. Hodgson's (2006b) "neurovisual resonance" theory for early mark making proposes that repetitive patterns and lines are capable of hyper-stimulating certain areas of the visual brain leading to an "undifferentiated sense of arousal" because these areas of the brain have evolved to selectively respond to such forms due to their importance for object discrimination in the visual world (Hodgson 2006b: 56). This provides an important basis for understanding the selection of such forms for depiction by rock artists. Simple geometric motifs may be more likely to appear in graphics through intuition by corresponding with patterns that excite "visual form neurons" more intensely than natural stimuli for which the neurons originally developed. The theory also provides an explanation for aesthetic preference, whereby preferences are influenced by the amount of neural activity generated by the stimuli presented, i.e., the greater the neural activity generated, the greater the preference for the stimuli.

These notions may be further understood in terms of the IRMs that are activated by sign stimuli. Artificial releasers, or graphic configurations representing key visual features of objects, may isolate and/or exaggerate the most salient characteristics of natural releasers, evoking a neurological response more effectively. From an ethological standpoint, a fundamental source for the aesthetic experience afforded by certain configurations of line can thus be understood as integral to universal reflexive responses to biologically significant stimuli (Dissanayake 1988: 150).

The perceptual ability to detect characteristic features of potentially dangerous visual stimuli would have been imperative to the survival of early humans. In addition to flora and minerals, regular patterns of elements such as spots, stripes, and other configurations of lines form the structural basis of signal properties in animals. Examples include a leopard's spots or a tiger's stripes. Despite their role in camouflage, these patterns are thus "well-readable" as crucial visual cues for survival (Sütterlin 2003: 141). The importance of the ability to detect static images by early humans over thousands of years appears to have resulted in the development of neural specialization for the extraction of visual information relevant to those patterns commonly exhibited on potentially dangerous animals. For example, Tanaka et al. (1991) discovered the existence of cells specialized for the processing of dot-patterns in the macaque inferotemporal cortex, for which humans are likely to have analogous neural structures. These cells are found to respond most strongly in response to the viewing of spot patterns similar to those occurring in the natural environment (Kruizinga and Petkov 2000). One reason for this evolved sensitivity may have been the importance for primates to avoid predators such as leopards by rapidly identifying them (Coss 2003: 111; Coss and

Coss and Ramakrishnan 2000). Experiments with the visual pattern preferences of infants have in fact shown an inherent interest in leopard spots and python scales, supporting the notion of inherent factors at play. Coss (2003: 112) randomly presented infants with plastic jars containing paper that was patterned with either plaid fabric print, leopard rosettes, rock-python patches and scales, or was plain yellowish-orange in color. It was found that the jars with python and leopard patterns were initially poked and prodded (actions interpreted as investigative) prior to handling them with significantly higher frequencies than the plain and plaid jars (Coss 2003: 113). Further empirical studies on recognition and response to graphic configurations relating to predators may provide more statistically significant results. However, as visual cues of possible danger, it is apparent that such features of animals are immediately compelling to the visual brain (Aiken 1998; Coss 2003; Üher 1991). The common use of spotted, crosshatch, and other patterns in rock art and other paleoarts may therefore be explained in terms of their related perceptual salience and human attraction toward them.

Reptiles commonly feature distinctive tessellated scales, including crosshatch or grid-like patterns, the repetitive properties of which act as reliable visual cues for potential danger, even if partially obscured in the animal's habitat. This is possible due to the human ability to preattentively detect the segregation of patterned regularity in cluttered scenes. An innate recognition system attuned to these cues appears to have evolved in humans throughout the long history of coexistence with reptiles (Coss 2003: 105). The vital ability to detect the visual properties of reptilian scales in peripheral vision to ensure avoidance is demonstrated in neuroimaging studies showing that checkerboard and diamond-shape patterns evoke greater neural responses than others when viewed outside direct visual gaze (Kastner et al. 2000; Okusa et al. 2000).

It is also possible that a perceptual bias toward zigzag lines has been exploited by paleoartists in their selection for use in graphics. Zigzag lines occur as markings on early portable art-like objects such as the c. 75,000-year-old engraved ochre piece from Blombos Cave, South Africa (d'Errico et al. 2001; Henshilwood et al. 2002), the middle Paleolithic bone fragment from Bacho Kiro, Bulgaria (Marshack 1976), and many Upper Paleolithic portable art objects, as well as commonly in rock art throughout the world (e.g., Dowson and Holliday 1989; Lewis-Williams and Dowson 1988, 1989; Marshack 1977). Like other simple geometric designs they occur both in isolation and in association with complex figurative depictions.

In addition to vertical and horizontal orientation detectors, there are many cells in the human visual cortex that respond selectively to diagonal lines. However, in contrast to vertical and horizontal lines, oblique lines are handled by a more complex level of visual processing in the extrastriate regions of the brain where lines of various orientations are equally represented—a feature of perception thought to have been exploited by 20th century abstract artists such as van Doesberg (Hodgson 2005). The generation of zigzag lines as fortification illusions (visual effects commonly experienced in migraines and occipital-lobe epilepsy) and similar forms of subjective mental imagery has been suggested as a possible source of imagery for some bodies of rock art (e.g., Dowson and Holliday 1989). However, the real importance of subjective visual phenomena of this type is that they demonstrate the physiological structuring of the visual apparatus giving rise to abstract-geometric patterns, which may have evolved partly in response to certain significant stimuli in the environment. Apart from suggesting a preoccupation with the depiction of angle (and relating to orientation-selective cells discussed), "sharp" and "piercing" forms may appear in rock art and other artistic traditions as the result of the exploitation of the evolved perceptual sensitivity to these forms (Bar and Neta 2006; Coss 2003: 92; Üher 1991).

Üher (1991, 1994) argues that the use of the zigzag motif in the art of many cultures is a replacement of depiction of the bite threat (the showing of canines in anger), and that this may result in the same response as the realistic stimulus. In humans, the "startle" involving the baring of teeth is most likely a by-product of hominid evolutionary history when canines played a more active role in threat displays. Exposure of canines is seen in many primates other than humans as a defense mechanism. Interestingly, it has been noted that such graphic imagery is used commonly in apotropaic (warding-off) symbolism (Sütterlin 1989; Üher 1991, 1994). Canines have much the same visual properties as tusks, horns, antlers, claws and other sharp, pointed forms that are common to mammals. Crocodylidae, Alligatoridae and Gavialidae also exhibit zigzag patterns of teeth, and osteoderms on their dorsal scales (Coss 1965, 2003: 105). The visual properties of such parts of animals are innately recognized as dangerous and evoke emotional arousal in humans, including fearsome reactions and aversive behavior (Coss 1965). Üher (1991, 1994) also reports the results of an experiment in which zigzags and wavy lines were presented to a large number of people of varying ages and gender and requested descriptions and ratings of emotional qualities of the motifs using a set of 24 antagonistic or affiliative adjectives. Zigzag motifs were found to be more significantly associated with antagonistic characteristics (e.g., "aggressive" or "harsh"), whereas wavy lines were more significantly associated with affiliative ones. This might explain a preference for zigzags over other motifs, and perhaps indicate the representation of events of tension, particularly in antagonistic contexts (Üher 1994). A bias is reflected not only in the semantic categorization of a visual object, but also in relation to low-level perceptual properties. Bar and Neta (2006) similarly compared subjective preferences for pictures of objects with sharp-angled and curved contours, and found a negative bias toward those with sharp-angled features. Coss (1965, 1968: 277) also measured pupillary dilation as an indicator of emotional state within the hypothalamus in response to the presentation of slides with various pointed and rounded shapes, and found that the viewing of zigzag patterns resulted in a significantly greater pupillary dilation than patterns with rounded contours. Coss (2003: 92–93) further devised a survey to record the responses to silhouettes of pointed and rounded contours, and found that pointed shapes were rated as more aesthetically beautiful than a rounded counterpart.

The results of these studies suggest that pointed shapes and patterns are perceptually and emotionally significant, elevate physiological arousal and are physically and aesthetically attractive in addition to signaling caution. The use of sharp or piercing forms such as zigzags in pre-historic rock art and other artistic traditions, may therefore be understood as influenced by evolved perceptual biases, attracting attention and increasing sympathetic nervous system arousal, and enhancing the aesthetic appreciation of culturally meaningful objects or markings (Coss 2003: 115).

ZOOMORPHOUS IMAGERY

In addition to the isolation and depiction of characteristic features of natural releasers as non-figurative motifs and patterns, the significance of figurative depictions as sign stimuli capable of triggering IRMs and typical behavioral and emotional responses is also important to consider. The rapid, accurate and reliable detection and recognition of important visual information, such as potential food sources, dangerous animals, or conspecifics, and the making of appropriate responses to such stimuli, is crucial for the survival of a species. Accordingly, humans are biologically predisposed or "prepared" to respond to animals and their perceptual characteristics in appropriate ways (Gray 1971; Öhman and Mineka 2001; Seligman 1971). These responses involve the rapid activation of specialized neural circuitry in order to evaluate them preattentively or with minimal thought (Guthrie 1993; Öhman et al. 1975; Yen and Finkel 2002).

Living animals clearly differ from non-living inanimate objects in various ways, and separate regions of the brain are accordingly predisposed for the perception, recognition and identification of living (animate) and non-living (inanimate) things. Clinical observations of neurological patients and neuroimaging studies suggest that animate and inanimate conceptual categories represent domain-specific knowledge systems based in distinct neural networks (e.g., Caramazza and Mahon 2003; Chao et al. 2002; Farah et al. 1991; Laiacona and Capitani 2001; Martin 2007). For example, subjects with damage to the left temporal lobe and left inferotemporal cortex have been reported to have a selective deficit restricted to the category of animate objects (involving visual and functional/associative knowledge of animals) (Caramazza and Shelton 1998; Damasio et al. 1996). This suggests that a neural network is specifically dedicated to processing conceptual knowledge about living things. Positron emission tomography (PET) scans have also shown that the naming of animals and the recognition of visual stimuli representing animals strongly activates parts of the temporal cortex, including the inferior and medial temporo-occipital areas, bilaterally (Caramazza and Mahon 2003; Damasio et al. 1996; Humphreys and Forde 2001; Martin et al. 1996; Perani et al. 1995; Tranel et al. 1997). This finding accords with evidence for category-specific deficits for living things in patients with posterior occipitotemporal damage (Forde et al. 1997; Humphreys et al. 1997; Riddoch et al. 1999), and the strong activation of the occipital lobes in the naming of animals (Caramazza and Shelton 1998). Studies have also shown that the lateral fusiform gyri and superior temporal sulcus respond differentially to the presentation of pictures of animals (Caramazza and Mahon 2003; Chao et al. 1999a, 1999b; Martin and Chao 2001; Price et al. 2003). Further, single cell recordings taken from medial temporal regions of the brain have demonstrated the existence of neurons in the entorhinal cortex that respond selectively to pictures of different animals (Kreiman et al. 2000). Distinct neural systems common to all humans thus respond explicitly to this specific category of visual stimuli.

The existence of multiple neural networks dedicated to animate objects may reflect the particularly complex visual processing required for the perception of animals (Gibson 1979). It may, however, also reflect the interpretation of data derived from existing neuroscientific investigations, or the need for further studies (see Moore and Price 1999). Nonetheless, specific structures of the brain are clearly specialized for the visual processing of living and non-living things, as well as the classification of animal types according to their perceptual attributes (see also Hodgson 2003a; Hodgson and Helvenston 2007). Neuropsychological evidence further suggests that the neural substrates representing knowledge concerned with living and non-living things are innate and fixed at birth (Farah and Rabinowitz 2003). An innate and unlearned ability to differentiate between animate and inanimate is further supported by the demonstrated predisposition for infants to distinguish between different categories of objects (e.g., Gelman 1990; Poulin-Dobois et al. 1996; Quinn and Eimas 1996; Quinn et al. 1993). Certain predispositions, including the ability to detect and predict animals and their behavior, as well as a strong motivation to learn about animals, are also observed in young children.

Despite the existence of category-specific perceptual mechanisms for biological forms such as fauna, Bradshaw (2003: 9) argues that the difference between classes of objects is not particularly significant, and that perceptual categorization is more general and not restricted to particular types of objects. This point highlights the notion that there must be additional reasons apart from a perceptual predisposition for the selection of faunal themes for depiction by rock artists. Of course, there may be any number of reasons for the depiction of animals, many of which may stem from the great importance of fauna in the lives of hunter-gatherers in the past. In response to this criticism, Hodgson (2003b: 16) has made the important point that because they are typically structured by curved lines and thus have more similar features than artificial objects, the perceptual disambiguation of animals can take longer than artificial objects.

Greater neural resources appear to be required for the perceptual processing of animals, reflecting their importance in the lives of early humans during the Pleistocene. The basic level of organization in neural systems undoubtedly reflects an evolutionary adaptation providing for the rapid and accurate recognition of animals. This can be understood both from an ontogenetic and phylogenetic perspective (Hodgson 2003c). Chimpanzees, for example, have similar innate capacities for the categorization of animal types, as well as animals and non-animals, and it is very likely that early hominins were also capable of this type of neural processing (Hodgson and Helvenston 2007). The neural structures around which perceptual, conceptual and linguistic knowledge are organized are very likely a result of evolutionary adaptations for recognizing animals, plants, and artifacts (Caramazza and Shelton 1998).

Of course, learning and exposure to specific animals in different environments undoubtedly play important roles. Learning from experience is essential to survival, and human neural networks may adapt to the perception of certain dangerous animals that co-inhabit a particular environment. This ensures that they may be successfully avoided, but also strengthens preferences for giving them visual attention. This in turn may strengthen preferences for their depiction in rock art (Onians 2007). Because hunter-gatherers are specialists in the recognition of animals in their environment and require only minimal visual cues for the identification of certain species, the categorization of fauna may be neurologically differentiated at a relatively early stage of visual processing. This is supported by electrophysiological studies monitoring the brain activity of people with expert knowledge of birds and dogs while they categorize pictures of commonly known species (Tanaka and Curran 2001). Different parts of the visual system may therefore adapt to respond selectively to certain visual information (and the structural properties of a particular object class), including ecologically important stimuli. For hunter-gatherers, including those in the past, this includes the expert recognition of many animals in the environment in which they lived. This "perceptual tuning" demonstrates the importance of learning and the modification of neural activity associated with object perception in response to experience and environmental concerns (Tanaka and Curran 2001).

Learning, however, essentially involves an enrichment of core psychological principles and corresponding neural architecture, as well as the "perceptual entrenchment" or "imprinting" of visual stimuli (Carey and Spelke 1994). Learning helps to refine categories, whereas the tendency to categorize appears to be innate. From an ethological perspective, the capacity for the recognition of significant visual stimuli may be enhanced by this neural imprinting as a result of individual experience, memory, and cultural appropriation. Importantly, in addition to genetic predispositions and susceptibilities, this imprinting appears to be largely stable in humans, resulting in cross-cultural constants. The capacity to manipulate responses to visual stimuli by conscious reflection is also a characteristic that differentiates humans from other animals. Furthermore, because animals became a visual cue intrinsic to human perception, throughout human evolution concomitant neural substrates of the perceptual/recognition system are likely to have become increasingly inbuilt, meaning that the need for learning was significantly reduced and significant environmental stimuli could be responded to appropriately with minimal experience (Hodgson 2003a).

Animals are also given priority for attentional selection by the brain. New et al. (2007) demonstrated experimentally that participants were substantially faster and more accurate at detecting changes in animals relative to motor vehicles, even though the participants had learned during the course of their lives to monitor the trajectories of motor vehicles for sudden changes in order to avoid collision. Similarly, a survey of American school children has shown that wild animals are feared most in contrast to things they have been taught to be careful of, such as cars and germs (Maurer 1965). This provides additional support for the existence of innate, preconscious neural mechanisms for the detection of animals. It further shows that animals as a category of information in the visual environment were also time-sensitive in relation to the survival and reproduction of hominins during the Pleistocene. In other words, the rapid identification of animals and what they signify (predatory danger, food, etc.) would have been imperative to adaptive problems at this time (New et al. 2007). With a basis in evolved prioritization, it appears that animals recruit more attention than other categories of objects.

It appears that certain enduring cues became more deeply ingrained throughout hominin evolution as opposed to simply reflecting the experience of individuals during their lifetimes. The capacity to perceive and identify animal forms during the Pleistocene ultimately resulted from the evolutionary refinement of the visual faculty and its structural configuration in response to the human interrelationship with animals. Innate neural structures may thus act as a constraint on learning potential, resulting in a predisposition to learn some things (in areas of evolutionary significance for the species) rather than others (Hinde and Stevenson-Hinde 1973; Laughlin and d'Aquili 1974: 107–113; Seligman and Hager 1972).

Approached from a perceptual-neurophysiological perspective, rock art may be understood as reflecting processes of human categorization, and confirms neuroscientific evidence for conceptual organization in the brain (Hodgson 2008: 345). The approach is important in terms of the depiction of animals generally, but also the ways in which animals are classified. For example, humans classify animals based on their size and ferocity (Atran 1998), which may partly explain the general lack of small animals such as rodents in rock art despite their importance in the diet of the artists. In addition to the experience of fauna in everyday life of hunter-gatherers in the past, the pre-existence of innate neural structures concerned with animals helps to explain their prevalence in rock art as determining factors in their perception, recognition, identification, and recall, as well as the greater likelihood of meaningful associations and concepts being attributed to them.

There are several other factors relating to behavioral response mechanisms that should be considered, particularly those relating to the emotional brain. Located in the anteroinferomedial part of the temporal lobes, the amygdala, in connection with the visual and limbic systems, is central to the detection and evaluation of potential dangers (Adolphs and Tranel 1999; Amaral 2003). It is also central to reflexive and emotional responses to important visual stimuli such as animals (LeDoux 1994, 1998). It receives sensory input before an object has been consciously identified, explaining startle responses to ambiguous visual stimuli and significant visual cues such as potentially dangerous or threatening animals. Visual stimuli such as these are preferentially processed by the brain by way of the amygdala, allowing for appropriate behavioral responses to be made (Phelps and LeDoux 2005). Dedicated neural structures that are preferentially activated and centered on the amygdala include the limbic, paralimbic, and autonomic nervous systems, as well as subcortical, thalamic-amygdaloid connections (Öhman and Soares 1993; Pissiota 2003). In addition, an innate and preattentive mechanism in the midbrain, including sensorimotor-orienting systems involved in the shifting of gaze and attention, is involved in rapid reactions to potentially dangerous stimuli (Carrive 1993; Hodgson 2003: 6–7; Öhman 1986). When triggered, these systems give rise to fear, anxiety, and a heightened state of awareness and preparedness involving freezing and crouching, and fight-or-flight responses. Many physiological changes rapidly take place in the face of danger, some of which, such as increases in heart rate, pupillary dilation, adrenaline secretion, and electrical resistance of the skin, are measureable biochemical reactions that have been recorded in humans responding to the presentation of certain visual stimuli (e.g., Coss 1965; May 1977; Schroeder and Rich 1976).

Another aspect of threat response is the perception of an object as a single unit, i.e., the extraction of a particular feature of the visual world when focus on it is required (Ramachandran and Hirstein 1999: 24–25). The visual system allows for an attentional bias and special focus on a potentially dangerous animal, allowing immediate action to be taken (Hodgson 2006a: 33; Öhman and Soares 1998). This has important implications for the depiction of animals in hunter-gatherer rock art. As Hodgson and Helvenston (2006: 8) explain, the state of heightened awareness experienced in the face of a threat

> -enables [one] to focus on the object of concern with greater acumen, almost to the exclusion of neighbouring stimuli (some researchers also claim that the object under scrutiny appears to move as if in slow motion). The increased arousal also facilitates the memory storage of numerous details about the event and the slow motion effect would solidify the memory of the animal's specific behaviour and form, enhancing the ability to reproduce it in visual representations.

The physiological response mechanisms outlined are common to all humans and are largely beyond cognitive control. The emotional responses that are governed by inherent human biology are also unaffected by cultural differences. Because visual and limbic system structures are closely connected through neural networks, it is likely that in mediating aesthetic experience, the emotional brain influences the production of graphic art

(Baumgartner 1988: 178). Of course, emotional responses will only result on the presentation of appropriate visual stimuli, such as those graphic configurations characteristic of predators or potentially dangerous animals (Coss 1965; Mundkur 1983: 211–212). The human sensitivity to these visual forms undoubtedly contributes to their selection for depiction. As opposed to the attribution of top-down cognitive associations, these bottom-up, elementary responses to animal or animal-like imageries are independent in origin and are largely the result of innate, genetically determined neurophysiological mechanisms. They thus have the potential to give rise to a prevalence of zoomorphous imagery in art cross-culturally.

Snakes are a particularly good example of the type of animal eliciting strong physiological, behavioral, and cognitive responses in humans. Snakes and snake-like motifs and themes are also recurrent features of hunter-gatherer rock art throughout the world. They appear throughout southern Africa (e.g., Vinnicombe 1976: 229–237) and the Americas (e.g., Benton 1984; Ewing 1989; Smith 1986), and are characteristic of Australian rock art, including those associated with the Rainbow Serpent mythology from c. 10,000 years ago (Flood 1997; Radcliffe-Brown 1926; Taçon et al. 1996; Taylor 1990). Snakes powerfully excite human emotion and the physiological response to fear, including strong sympathetic nervous system arousal (Mundkur 1978, 1983). It has recently been suggested that the human visual system actually developed during evolutionary adaptation as a means for better detecting venomous and dangerous snakes that posed a threat to primates (Isbell 2006). Experiments with nonhuman primates, including chimpanzees, gorillas, and vervet monkeys, suggest that fear of snakes is not socially acquired, although group psychology and social communication is thought to play some role in avoidance behavior (Mineka 1987; Seyfarth et al. 1980). Mineka and Cook (1989) found experimentally that fearful responses to evolutionarily relevant stimuli including snakes were vicariously acquired in rhesus monkeys by observing the behavior of other monkeys of their species. In humans, social communication and learning are also very important, but innate perceptual sensitivities and evolutional predispositions underlying fearful behavioral responses remain fundamental factors. Experiments have demonstrated that humans and other primates react in much the same way to snakes even if they have never had previous contact or experience with them (e.g., Morris and Morris 1965; Sackett 1966). Studies on phobic responses in humans and other animals have further demonstrated that similar neural mechanisms are responsible for the comparable responses to potential predatory threats (LeDoux 1994).

Curiosity toward dangerous carnivores serves as a form of attraction, and enables humans and other animals to learn about danger and behave in appropriate ways. The fascination with dangerous animals is reflected in material culture with probable survival value (Kruuk 2002: 179). For example, the choice of particular animal types for depiction may involve the cultural reinforcement of an avoidance message through art to further enhance chances of survival within a population (Wilson 1998). In a social context, the depiction of fauna allows knowledge and recognition skills to increase, including the discrimination between threatening and useful animals (Hodgson 2000; Hodgson and Helvenston 2006: 33). For example, in western Arnhem Land, northern Australia, many of the animal species depicted in rock art include preferred food sources (e.g., Chaloupka 1993; Flood 1997: 289; Taylor 1989). The depiction of food sources may also explain the prevalence of particular animals in different regions of the world and the values invested in them (Anati 1994: 134–138). Indeed, the iconic representation of prey or predators may be necessary for both survival and well-being (Conkey 1982: 120).

In addition to snakes, large cats and predatory birds also elicit automatic responses in primates as a result of evolutionary adaptation to environmental pressures (Bednarik 1990/91: 71–72; Öhman 1986: 128–129). For example, African vervet monkeys signal the presence of a leopard, snake, or eagle with automatic warning vocalizations (Seyfarth et al. 1980; Struhsaker 1967). This primate/predator relationship is in fact found globally with few exceptions (Jones 2000). The appearance of snake, predatory bird and feline forms in rock art may be explained partly because of their visual salience and entrenchment in the visual system as a result of the evolutionary history of the species (Hodgson 2003: 8). Significantly, these are some of the most frequently depicted subjects in some rock art concentrations such as the petroglyphs at Toro Muerto, Peru (Bednarik 1990/91: 72; Linares Málaga 2004).

Examples of carnivore depictions in the parietal art of Upper Paleolithic Europe include the cave lion (*Panthera [Leo] spelaea*), e.g., at Les Trois Frères, France; and cave bear (*Ursus spelaeus*), e.g., at Les Combarelles, France (Ucko and Rosenfeld 1967). Felines also feature at La Colombiere, Labouiche, and La Marche, France, in addition to the 73 depictions of lions in Chauvet Cave (Clottes 2003; Packer and Clottes 2000). Some of these felines are depicted in crouching/stalking postures (Fig. 1). Significantly, these postures are thought to be the most conspicuous characteristic of felines in terms of evoking innate nervous system reactions (Coss 1965: 23–24).

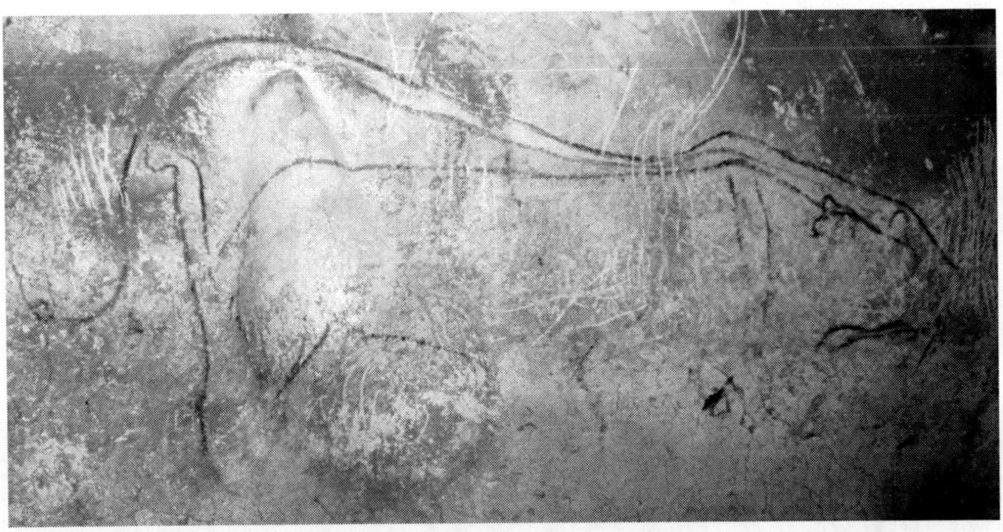

Figure 1. Lions depicted in stalking posture, Chauvet Cave, France (photograph by Jean Clottes).

Clottes (1998) has also noted that depictions of fauna during the Aurignacian period in Europe commonly include threatening species such as rhinoceroses, lions, mammoths, and bears that constitute 61 per cent of identifiable animals in Chauvet Cave. However, this bias is no longer apparent in later Upper Paleolithic cultures in the region, although they are very occasionally represented until the end of the Magdalenian (e.g., at La Vache). This suggests that cultural factors may have played a greater role in influencing the choice of animals for depiction. Although this may be the case in some contexts, predatory animals are depicted in most major rock art corpora throughout the world. For example, paintings of felines (lions and leopards), some with extended claws, also occur in 14 per cent of recorded shelters in the Drakensberg area of South Africa (Vinnicombe 1976: 215). These are often depicted as if in pursuit of hunters (Fig. 2). Although they are not represented as often as other animals, their appearance is consistent and repeated throughout the area. Although depictions of carnivores and other typically dangerous animals may be comparatively rare in contrast to herbivores in some regions and time periods, it should also be kept in mind that *potentially* dangerous animals (e.g., bison and horses in Upper Paleolithic Europe) feature prominently, and can be understood in the same light. Large mammals may be very dangerous when wounded, and also appear in poses traditionally interpreted as aggressive, such as the "charging" bulls of Lascaux (Fig. 3) and Pech-Merle (e.g., Graziosi 1960: 163).

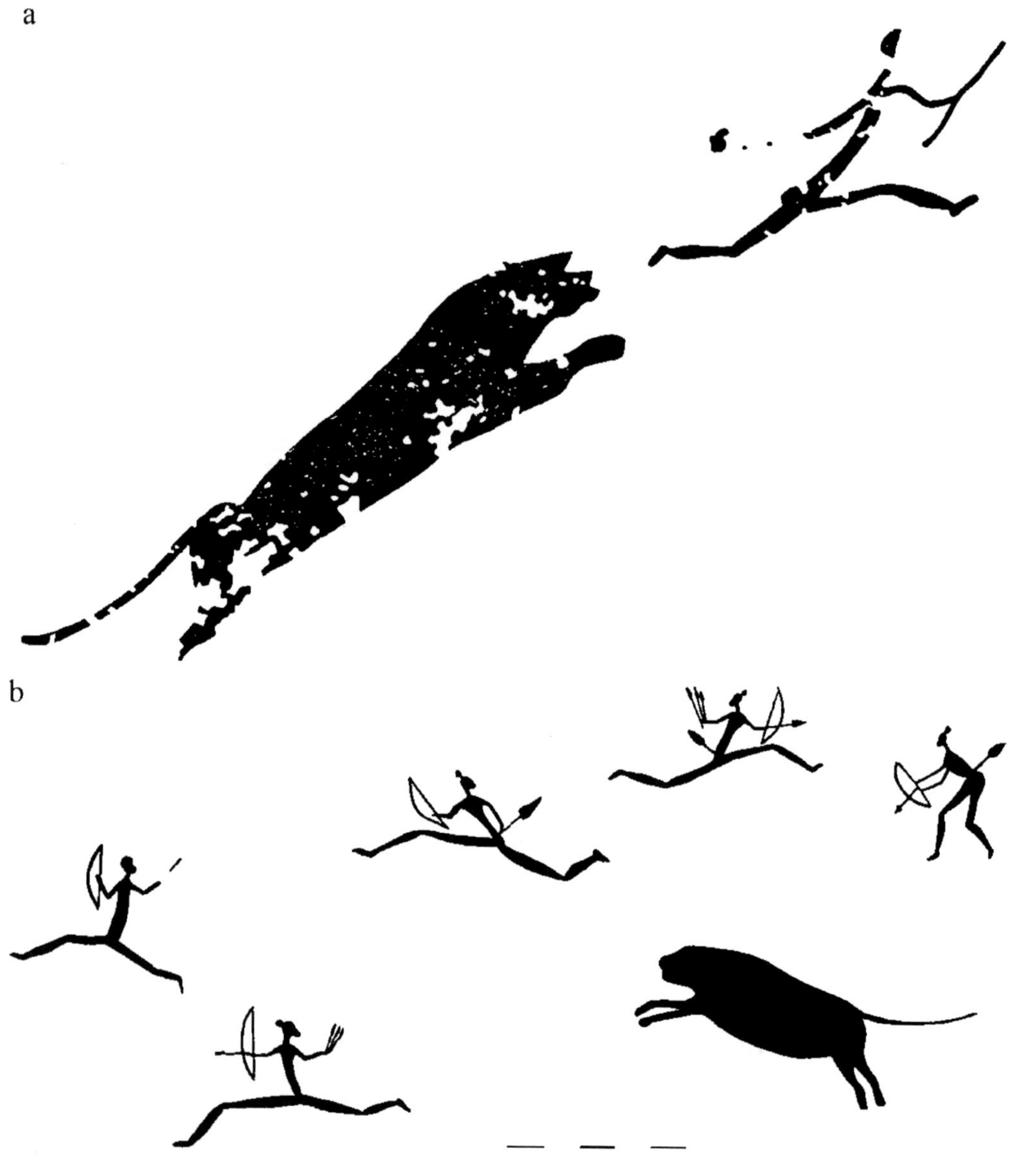

Figure 2. Depictions of felines in pursuit of humans. Drakensberg, South Africa. (a) after Pager 1972: 184; (b) after Vinnicombe 1976: 214.

Figure 3. Painting in Lascaux Cave, France, suggesting a bull savaging a man.

A similar case is found in the portable art of Upper Paleolithic Europe, including the many instances of carnivores such as bears and felines. For example, the portable engraving from Pechialet, France, appears to depict a bear on its hind legs threatening two humans (Bahn and Vertut 1988: 129). Paleolithic statuettes from southwest Germany also include predatory animals such as lions and bears represented in aggressive postures (Dowson and Porr 2001). Half of the 77 terracotta figurines of Dolni Věstonice and Pavlov, Czech Republic, are of carnivores such as bears, lions, wolves, and foxes (Bahn and Vertut 1988: 129). It is also clear that the canines and other teeth of carnivores were valued by people during the Paleolithic (and more recently), as indicated by their use in personal adornment (e.g., Bednarik 2001; Leavesley 2007). The size of canines is also often exaggerated when they are included in depictions of carnivores (Bahn and Vertut 1988: 130).

Of course, snakes and snake-like forms appear in higher frequencies at some sites and in some regions than in others. Because statistical studies (e.g., Leaky 1983; Leroi-Gourhan 1965; Vinnicombe 1976) reveal that a majority of rock art in some regions consists of less aggressive or non-dangerous animals such as the horse, bison or eland, the arguments presented certainly do not provide an all-encompassing theory. A lack of dangerous animals in some bodies of rock art may reflect their absence or rarity in a particular environment or time period, although the shared neurobiology of those producing the images and the behavioral response of producing the images themselves clearly reflects comparable responses to similar environmental circumstances (Onians 2000). It should also be stressed that the frequency with which certain animal types are depicted is not necessarily indicative of the significance they were attributed by any one artist or society, nor can it be said to have meaning without direct ethnographic insight. Mundkur (1983: 59) makes this observation for rock art in southern Africa:

> Antelope of all kinds are the most frequently depicted of the Drakensberg regional art forms and constitute 77 percent of the total. The eland alone constitutes 35 percent, is the principal focus of interest because of its important religious and mythic roles, and is often drawn painstakingly. The much more easily depicted serpent constitutes a mere 1 percent, but this numerical deficiency is fortuitous, for the animal's actual importance is as great as the eland's.

This is supported by the fact that both eland and snakes are strongly linked through mythology and beliefs of the San who created the art, including strong associations with rain and rain-making, as well as having close conceptual links through depiction (e.g., Bahn 2010: 51; Dowson 1998: 75, 80). For example, mythological deities such as Cagn of the Bushmen of southern Africa are believed to shape-shift, taking the form of any number of animals, including both eland and snakes (Lewis-Williams 2000: 143; Moore et al. 2004: 113). Snakes are similarly rare in the Paleolithic art of Europe, but this does not necessarily suggest that the more frequently depicted bison or horses were any more significant (Mundkur 1983: 205).

There are undoubtedly numerous motivations for the depiction of certain animal types, including the predominance of non-threatening species such as the eland in southern Africa (see e.g., Hodgson and Helvenston 2006). Animals were significant to hunter-gatherer peoples in the past for several reasons, such as the use of their various parts for utilitarian purposes. Cultural factors determined any number of symbolic meanings and interpretations given to them. The emphasis of non-threatening animals in rock art in some cases was very likely prompted by their social and ontological significance, and association with beliefs and attitudes, with some animals having more prominent roles in myth, ritual, and symbolism (e.g., James 1990; Lewis-Williams and Dowson 1989; Vinnicombe 1976).

The associated meaning(s) and significance(s) given to zoomorphous imagery of any type are also contingent upon cultural context. Differences in the symbolism attributed to snakes, for example, may have quite opposite meanings depending on their cultural context (Willis 1990). Dangerous or aggressive animals have taken significant roles in mythology, ritual, and symbolism throughout time. In Native California, animal symbolism closely related to shamanistic rituals, beliefs and practices often includes particularly dangerous or aggressive species such as the grizzly bear (*Ursus arctos*) and rattlesnake (*Scrotalus spp.*) (Whitley 1994, 2001). Inciting a powerful physiological and emotional response, these animals and their depictions are attributed great cultural significances in many cultures, taking on the form of gods, spirits, and other powerful supernatural entities. Ethnographic data thus demonstrates the special socio-cultural significance given to predatory and dangerous animals, and by analogy, suggests possible reasons for their frequent depiction in rock art in contexts where direct ethnographic insight is absent.

Cultural experience may result in the importance of such animals in cultural imagery, mediated by the higher brain (Hinde 1998), although their choice for depiction and use in cultural symbolism is likely to have an ultimate basis in perceptual salience and innate physiological and emotional responses (Hodgson 2003: 14–15; Mundkur 1983). In light of the above discussion, the choice of particular animals for symbolic roles may be understood as influenced by their visual salience, mediated by shared human perceptual-neurophysiological structuring and associated behavioral responses. The existence of specialized neural structures that respond strongly to certain types of animals can help to explain a bias toward their choice for depiction, and strongly suggest reasons for their appearance in rock art.

Depiction and Emphasis of Animal Parts

In addition to the depiction of complete animal figures, the emphasis and exaggeration of certain parts of animals such as horns is quite common in rock art throughout the world. Parts of animals are also thought to appear as isolated and repeated motifs. Existing interpretations have centered on the notion that animal depictions with oversized horns relate to phosphenes—autogenous, nonfigurative subjective images generated by structures within the human visual system. For example, the oversized horns of quadruped depictions (thought to represent mountain sheep) in North America have been associated with nested curves and meandering lines experienced as subjective visual imagery in altered states of consciousness (e.g., Faulstich 2000; Lewis-Williams and Dowson 1988). This interpretation has also been given to the apparent isolation and repetition of mountain sheep horns (Whitley 1994, 2000). Repeated engravings and paintings of comparable motifs have recently been discovered in Chauvet Cave, France (Azéma and Clottes 2008). These most likely depict isolated mammoth tusks, suggested by the association of one such motif with a mammoth depiction.

Rather than the depiction of subjective visual imagery, the horns and tusks are more likely to be repeated and exaggerated due to factors on which the salience of parts of an object depend, including the size of a part relative to the whole object depicted, the degree to which it protrudes, and the strength of its boundaries (Hoffman and Singh 1997). Relatedly, the "peak shift effect," or neurologically inherent propensity to exaggerate, offers a more convincing explanation. As Ramachandran and Hirstein (1999: 18) explain, the peak shift effect is observed in the animal kingdom as a form of discrimination learning:

> If a rat is taught to discriminate a square from a rectangle (of say, 3:2 aspect ratio) and rewarded for the rectangle, it will soon learn to respond more frequently to the rectangle. Paradoxically, however, the rat's response to a rectangle that is even longer and skinnier (say, of aspect ratio 4:1) is even greater than it was to the original prototype on which it was trained.

A similar phenomenon is observed in seagull chicks:

> a seagull chick will beg for food by pecking at its mother's beak. Remarkably, it will peck just as vigorously at a disembodied beak with no mother attached or even a brown stick with a red dot at the end (the gull's beak has a vivid red spot near the tip). The stick with the red dot is an example of a 'releasing stimulus' or 'trigger feature' since, as far as the chick's visual system is concerned this stimulus is as good as the entire mother bird. What is even more remarkable, though, was Tinbergen's discovery (Tinbergen 1954) that a very long, thin brown stick, with *three* red stripes at the end is even more effective in eliciting pecks than the original beak, even though it looks nothing like a beak to a human observer (Ramachandran and Hirstein 1999: 18).

The experimental studies undertaken by Tinbergen and others have thus demonstrated the possibility of isolating and exaggerating sign stimuli to produce "supernormal stimuli" that elicit supernormal responses. As in other animals, natural behavioral responses in humans may be increased by the exaggeration of certain characteristics of visual stimuli. The relevance of these findings in art has been discussed by several authors (e.g., Bedaux 1996; Gombrich 1977, 1978; Hodgson 2003; Sütterlin 2003), and there are many examples of the phenomenon throughout all periods. For example, the mechanisms can operate by the isolation and exaggeration of the eyes represented schematically as large concentric circles, which activate strong aesthetic (i.e., neurophysiological) responses. These motifs may be considered the equivalent of the red stripes to the herring gull chicks. The depiction of eyes in this way is characteristic of rock art traditions in several parts of the world, such as the petroglyphs of the Northwest Coast, North America, and the "archaic faces" of the Australian arid zone (Watson 2011).

Exaggerations and distortions also stimulate the brain's aesthetic response to the human body, which may explain the typically unnaturalistic representation of the human form in rock art (Watson 2012). This is evidenced particularly in the creation of grossly exaggerated features of the human form in many regions of the world (Ucko and Rosenfeld 1972: 170). The effect is also achieved by the depiction of the human body in motion, where overly "dynamic" postures strongly suggestive of vigorous movement are commonly used (Watson 2010b). Further examples may include the depiction of human form in contorted postures and those that emphasize or accentuate salient curves of the body, such as the low-relief sculptures of reclining women at La Magdelaine (Guthrie 2005: 331; Ucko and Rosenfeld 1967: 210–211).

Artists may be similarly biased in their exaggeration of certain features of animals in their depiction. These do not appear to be random distortions but structurally and instinctually governed alterations. The exaggerations and distortions stimulate the brain's "aesthetic" response to features of animals, creating supernormal stimuli. It is a natural behavioral tendency to depict subjects in these ways because the brain is "hard-wired" to give more attention to these features due to their perceptual salience.

In addition to functioning as a possible communicative device, the exaggeration of salient features of animals in rock art may serve as supernormal stimuli, acting primarily on the instinctive responses to dangerous attributes of certain animal types, such as reptiles and large quadrupeds (Kruuk 2002: 178). The neurophysiological response may be a generalized one that is adapted to the visual characteristics of particular species. The response afforded (i.e., the intensity of the reaction) may be greater or lesser depending on the size of the animal and its attributes. A less dramatic response may be afforded by smaller animals with smaller dangerous features (Kruuk 2002: 178–179), which might help to explain why depictions of smaller animals are not always as prevalent as larger ones in rock art, as is the case for the Paleolithic cave art of southwestern Europe.

As noted, the fragmentary depiction and exaggeration of salient parts of animals such as canines, tusks, horns and claws of animals can be explained in these terms. (These need not have been intended by rock artists to represent parts of animals, although their form may still elicit an emotional response and may have been chosen for depiction either consciously or unconsciously.) This interpretation can further extend to other instances of exaggerated animal appendages, including occasional examples from Upper Paleolithic sites in Europe such as the antlers of red deer at Lascaux, France, the horns of bison at several sites (see

Guthrie 2005: 107), and those of rhinoceroses in Chauvet Cave, France (Fig. 4). Although the depiction of rhinoceroses with large horns may suggest the animals depicted are old males, the horn is clearly emphasized by repetition in at least one instance (Fig. 4b). Great attention was also given to the horns of rhinoceroses in rock engravings of southern Africa, where extensions and additions to them have been made over time (Dowson 1992: 81–87) (Fig. 5). The types of features of animals that are most often exaggerated or depicted in isolation, such as the horns of rhinoceroses or antlers of deer, correspond with aspects that are most salient and facilitate recognition.

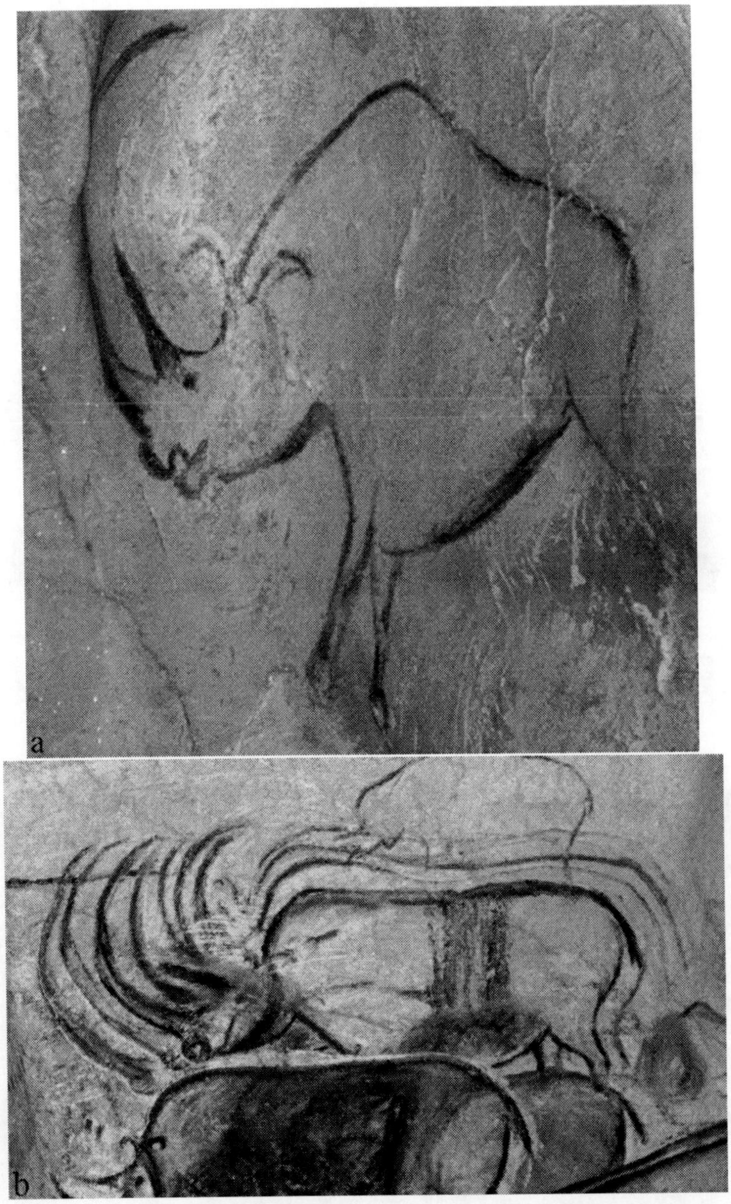

Figure 4. Rhinoceroses depicted with exaggerated horns, Chauvet Cave, France (photographs by Jean Clottes).

An additional factor that should be taken into account is the process of translation of the perception of an object into its depiction. In this process the artist may exaggerate features of an animal in order to communicate its image effectively (particularly in canonical outline drawings that contain more salient information about an object), or make ordinary features appear special (Johnson 1993). Of course, the interpretations given do not deny the symbolic importance exaggerated horns or other appendages may have had for the societies that created the images. Exaggeration of horns may stress their importance in myth, magic, ritual, or shamanistic practices and beliefs (Le Quellec 2004: 162–163; Ouzman 1995). But the reason they are chosen for these roles, either consciously or unconsciously, is very likely a result of their perceptual potency and the inherent human behavioral responses they afford as a result of evolved, underlying neurophysiology.

Figure 5. Rhinoceroses depicted with exaggerated horns in southern Africa. (a) Bristown District; (b) Klerksdorp District (after Dowson 1992: 86, 87).

Conclusion

Rock art reveals fundamental psychological and behavioral characteristics of human beings around the world over vast periods of time. However, there remains much to learn about the nature of pre-historic artistic phenomena, and the study of the neurobiological bases of human behavior has major implications for understanding their fundamental characteristics. The study of human ethology helps in understanding how the nature of hunter-gatherer rock art may be influenced by perceptual sensitivities to specific visual forms and patterns resulting from environmental pressures during evolutionary adaptation. A preference for certain abstract-geometric graphics reflects perceptually significant aspects of the natural world, including forms of biological importance or sign stimuli that elicit innate neurophysiological responses. A perceptual bias for certain forms is evident, and the production of these forms in graphics exploits the allocation of perceptual resources toward them. Innate connections with appropriate emotional responses and instinctual behavioral reactions such as avoidance are also likely to have influenced the representation of certain animal types, and affected cultural choices and the importance given to certain forms of imagery. The innate perceptual sensitivity to animal forms is also able to explain the exaggeration and emphasis of particular features of animals; the neural substrates underlying typical human behavioral responses to animals and their parts provide a particularly important basis for their representation. Importantly, these interpretations are applicable without denying the socially determined attitudes toward rock art motifs and the diverse symbolic associations they were undoubtedly given in the past, and are complementary to approaches that take these factors into consideration more closely.

Acknowledgments

Jean Clottes is thanked for kindly providing photographs from Chauvet Cave and permission to reproduce them, and for comments that helped to improve this chapter.

References

Adolphs, R. and Tranel, D. (1999). Preferences for visual stimuli following amygdala damage. *Journal of Cognitive Neuroscience* 11(6), 610–616.

Aiken, N. E. (1998). *The biological origins of art.* Westport: Praeger.

Amaral, D. G. (2003). The amygdala, social behavior, and danger detection. *Annals of the New York Academy of Science* 1000, 337–347.

Anati, E. (1994). Archetypes, constants, and universal paradigms in prehistoric art. *Semiotica* 100(2–4), 125–140.

Atran, S. (1998). Folk biology and the anthropology of science: Cognitive universals and cultural particulars. *Behavioral and Brain Sciences* 21(4), 547–609.

Azéma, M., and Clottes, J. (2008). Chauvet-type signs. *International Newsletter on Rock Art* 50, 2–7.

Bahn, P. G. (2010). *Prehistoric rock art: Polemics and progress*. Cambridge: Cambridge University Press.

Bahn, P. G., and Vertut, J. (1988). *Images of the Ice Age*. Leicester: Windward.

Bar, M., and Neta, M. (2006). Humans prefer curved visual objects. *Psychological Science* 17(8), 645–648.

Baumgartner, G. (1988). Physiological constraints on the visual aesthetic response. In I. Rentschler, B. Herzberger and D. Epstein (Eds.), *Beauty and the brain: Biological aspects of aesthetics* (pp. 165–180). Basel: Birkhäuser.

Bedaux, J. P. (1996). From normal to supranormal: Observations on realism and idealism from a biological perspective. In R. Woodfield (Ed.), *Gombrich on art and psychology* (pp. 171–195). Manchester: Manchester University Press.

Bednarik, R. G. (1990/91). Epistemology in palaeoart studies. *Origini* 15, 57–78.

Bednarik, R. G. (2001). Beads and pendants of the Pleistocene. *Anthropos* 96, 545–55.

Bednarik, R. G. (2003). Creating futile iconographic meanings: *http://mc2.vicnet.net.au/home/interpret/web/icono.html*. Retrieved 2012-3-17.

Benton, J. (1984). Seeing snakes. *Rock Art Papers (San Diego Museum Papers)* 18(2), 107–112.

Bradshaw, J. L. (2003). The roots of art and the European Upper Palaeolithic. *Rock Art Research* 20(1), 9–10.

Caramazza, A., and Mahon, B. Z. (2003). The organization of conceptual knowledge: The evidence from category-specific semantic deficits. *Trends in Cognitive Sciences* 7(8), 345–361.

Caramazza, A., and Shelton, J. R. (1998). Domain-specific knowledge systems in the brain: The animate-inanimate distinction. *Journal of Cognitive Neuroscience* 10, 1–34.

Carey, S., and Spelke, E. (1994). Domain-specific knowledge and conceptual change. In L. A. Hirschfeld and S. A. Gelman (Eds.), *Mapping the mind: Domain specificity in cognition and culture* (pp. 169–200). Cambridge, Cambridge University Press.

Carrive, P. (1993). The periaqueductal gray and defensive behavior: Functional representation and neuronal organization. *Behavioral Brain Research* 58, 27–47.

Chaloupka, G. (1993). *Journey in time: The world's longest continuing art tradition – the 50,000-year story of the Australian Aboriginal rock art of Arnhem Land.* Sydney: Reed.

Chao, L. L., Haxby, J. V., and Martin, A. (1999a). Attribute-based neural substrates in posterior temporal cortex for perceiving and knowing about objects. *Nature Neuroscience* 2, 913–919.

Chao, L. L., Martin, A., and Haxby, J. V. (1999b). Are face-responsive regions selective only for faces? *Neuroreport* 10, 2945–2950.

Chao, L. L., Weisberg, J., and Martin, A. (2002). Experience-dependent modulation of category-related cortical activity. *Cerebral Cortex* 12(5), 545–551.

Chauvet, J. -M., Deschamps, E. B., and Hillaire, C. (1996). *Dawn of art: The Chauvet Cave: The oldest known paintings in the world*. London: H.N. Abrams.

Clottes, J. (1998). The 'Three C's': Fresh avenues towards European Palaeolithic art. In C. Chippindale, and P. S. C. Taçon (Eds.), *The archaeology of rock art* (pp. 112–129). Cambridge: Cambridge University Press.

Clottes, J. (2003). *Chauvet Cave: The art of earliest times*. Trans. by P.G. Bahn. Salt Lake City, UT: University of Utah Press.

Conkey, M. W. (1982). Boundedness in art and society. In I. Hodder (Ed.), *Symbolic and structural archaeology* (pp. 115–128). Cambridge: Cambridge University Press.

Coss, R. G. (1965). *Mood provoking visual stimuli: Their origins and applications*. Los Angeles, CA: University of California Press.

Coss, R. G. (1968). The ethological command in art. *Leonardo* 1, 273–287.

Coss, R. G. (2003). The role of evolved perceptual biases in art and design. In E. Voland and K. Grammer (Eds.), *Evolutionary aesthetics* (pp. 69–130). Berlin: Springer.

Coss, R. G., and Ramakrishnan, U. (2000). Perceptual aspects of leopard spot recognition with wild bonnet macaques (*Macaca radiata*). *Behaviour* 137, 315–335.

Curio, E. (1993). Proximate and developmental aspects of antipredator behavior. *Advances in the Study of Behavior* 22, 135–238.

d'Errico, F., Henshilwood, C., and Nilssen, P. (2001). An engraved bone fragment from c. 70,000-year-old Middle Stone Age levels at Blombos Cave, South Africa: Implications for the origin of symbolism and language. *Antiquity* 75, 309–318.

Damasio, H. G., Grabowski, T. J., Tranei, D., Hichwa, R. D., and Damasio, A. R. (1996). A neural basis for lexical retrieval. *Nature* 380, 499–505.

Dissanayake, E. (1988). *What is art for?* Seattle, WA: University of Washington Press.

Dissanayake, E. (1998). Komar and Melamid discover Pleistocene taste. *Philosophy and Literature* 22(2), 486–496.

Dowson, T. A. (1992). *The rock engravings of southern Africa*. Johannesburg: Witwatersrand University Press.

Dowson, T. A. (1998). Rain in Bushmen belief, politics and history: The rock-art of rain-making in the south-eastern mountains, southern Africa. In P. S. C. Taçon and C. Chippindale (Eds.), *The archaeology of rock art* (pp. 73–89). Cambridge: Cambridge University Press.

Dowson, T. A., and Holliday, A. L. (1989). Zigzags and eland: An interpretation of an idiosyncratic combination. *South African Archaeological Bulletin* 44, 46–48.

Dowson, T. A., and Porr, M. (2001). Special objects – special creatures: Shamanistic imagery and the Aurignacian art of southwest Germany. In N. Price (Ed.), *The archaeology of shamanism* (pp. 165–177). London: Routledge.

Eibl-Eibesfeldt, I. (1975). *Ethology: The biology of behavior*. New York, NY: Holt, Rinehart and Winston.

Eibl-Eibesfeldt, I. (1988). The biological foundations of aesthetics. In I. Rentschler, B. Herzberger and D. Epstein (Eds.), *Beauty and the brain: Biological aspects of aesthetics* (pp. 29–68). Basel: Birkhäuser.

Eibl-Eibesfeldt, I. (1989). *Human ethology*. New York, NY: Aldine de Gruyter.

Ewing, E. (1989). Serpiente: New discoveries. *Rock Art Papers (San Diego Museum Papers)* 24(6), 48–58.

Farah, M. J., McMullen, P. A., and Meyer, M. (1991). Can recognition of living things be selectively impaired? *Neuropsychologia* 9, 189–193.

Farah, M. J., and Rabinowitz, C. (2003). Genetic and environmental influences on the organisation of semantic memory in the brain: Is 'living things' an innate category? *Cognitive Neuropsychology* 20(3), 401–408.

Faulstich, P. (2000). An inquiry into the nature of sacred places: The petroglyph sites of the Pipkin Lava Flow, San Bernardino County, California. *Rock Art Papers (San Diego Museum Papers)* 39(15), 43–53.

Flood, J. (1997). *Rock art of the Dreamtime: Images of ancient Australia*. Sydney: Angus and Robertson.

Forde, E. M. E., Francis, D., Riddoch, M. J., Rumiati, R., and Humphreys, G. W. (1997). On the links between visual knowledge and naming: A single case study of a patient with a category-specific impairment for living things. *Cognitive Neuropsychology* 14(3), 403–458.

Gelman, R. (1990). First principles organize attention to and learning about relevant data: Number and the animate-inanimate distinction as examples. *Cognitive Science* 14, 79–106.

Gibson, J. J. (1979). *The ecological approach to visual perception*. Boston, Houghton Mifflin.

Gombrich, E. H. (1977). *Art and illusion: A study in the psychology of pictorial representation*. London: Phaidon.

Gombrich, E. H. (1978). *Meditations on a hobby horse, and other essays on the theory of art*. London: Phaidon.

Gray, J. A. (1971). *The psychology of fear and stress*. London: Weidenfeld and Nicholson.

Graziosi, P. (1960). *Palaeolithic art*. London: Faber.

Guthrie, R. D. (2005). *The nature of Palaeolithic art*. Chicago, IL: University of Chicago Press.

Guthrie, S. (1993). *Faces in the clouds: A new theory of religion*. New York, NY: Oxford University Press.

Henshilwood, C. S., d'Errico, F., Yates, R., Jacobs, Z., Tribolo, C., Duller, G. A. T., Mercier, N., Sealy, J. C., Valladas, H., Watts I., and Wintle, A. G. (2002). Emergence of modern human behavior: Middle Stone Age engravings from South Africa. *Science* 295, 1278–1280.

Hinde, R. A. (1982). *Ethology*. London: Fontana.

Hinde, R. A. (1998). Humans and human habitats: Reciprocal influences. In B. Cartledge (Ed.), *Mind, brain, and the environment: The Linacre Lectures* 1995–6. Oxford: Oxford University Press.

Hinde, R. A., and Stevenson-Hinde, J. (Eds.) (1973). *Constraints on learning: Limitations and predispositions*. London,: Academic Press.

Hodgson, D. (2000). Art, perception and information processing: An evolutionary perspective. *Rock Art Research* 17(1), 3–34.

Hodgson, D. (2003a). The biological foundations of Upper Palaeolithic art: Stimulus, percept and representational imperatives. *Rock Art Research* 20(1), 3–22.

Hodgson, D. (2003b). Perception, recognition, evolution and palaeoart: Interactive hierarchies and reciprocal correspondences. *Rock Art Research* 20(1), 14–18.

Hodgson, D. (2003c). Seeing the 'unseen': Fragmented cues and the implicit in Palaeolithic art. *Cambridge Archaeological Journal* 13(1), 97–106.

Hodgson, D. (2005). Graphic primitives and the embedded figure in 20th-century art: Insights from neuroscience, ethology and perception. *Leonardo* 38(1), 55–58.

Hodgson, D. (2006a). Altered states of consciousness and palaeoart: An alternative neurovisual explanation. *Cambridge Archaeological Journal* 16(1), 27–37.

Hodgson, D. (2006b). Understanding the origins of palaeoart: The neurovisual resonance theory and brain functioning. *PaleoAnthropology* 2006: 54–67.

Hodgson, D. (2008). Visual dynamics of Upper Palaeolithic cave art. *Cambridge Archaeological Journal* 18(3), 341–353.

Hodgson, D., and Helvenston, P. A. (2006). The emergence of the representation of animals in palaeoart: Insights from evolution and the cognitive, limbic and visual systems of the human brain. *Rock Art Research* 23(1), 3–40.

Hodgson, D., and Helvenston, P. A. (2007). *The neuropsychological basis of rock art: Hyperimagery and its significance for understanding the archaeological record.* Paper presented at the Archaeological Invisibility and Forgotten Knowledge: Ethnoarchaeology, Hunter-Gatherers, Ephemeral Cultural Aspects WAC Inter-Congress, 5–8 September 2007, Institute of Archaeology, University of Lódz, Lódz, Poland.

Hoffman, D. D., and Singh, M. (1997). Salience of visual parts. *Cognition* 63, 29–78.

Humphreys, G. W., Riddoch, M. J., and Price, C. (1997). Top-down processes in object identification: Evidence from experimental psychology, neuropsychology and functional anatomy. *Proceedings of the Royal Society of London. Series B, Biological Sciences* 352, 1275–1282.

Humphreys, G. W., and Forde, E. M. E. (2001). Hierarchies, similarity, and interactivity in object recognition: 'Category-specific' neuropsychological deficits. *Behavioral and Brain Sciences* 24, 453–509.

Isbell, L. A. (2006). Snakes as agents of evolutionary change in primate brains. *Journal of Human Evolution* 51, 1–35.

James, W. (1990). Antelope as self-image among the Uduk. In R. G. Willis (Ed.), *Signifying animals: Human meaning in the natural world* (pp. 196–203). London: Unwin Hyman.

Johnson, M. (1993). A cognitive model for the perception and translation of a three-dimensional object/array onto a two-dimensional surface. *Visual Arts Research* 19, 85–99.

Jones, D. E. (2000). *An instinct for dragons*. London,: Routledge.

Kagan, J., Henker, B. A., Hen-Tov, A., and Levine, J. (1966). Infants' differential reactions to familiar and distorted faces. *Child Development* 37(3), 519–532.

Kastner, S., De Weerd, P., and Ungerlieder, L. G. (2000). Texture segregation in the human visual cortex: A functional MRI study. *Journal of Neurophysiology* 83, 2453–2457.

Kreiman, G., Koch, C., and Fried, I. (2000). Category-specific visual responses of single neurons in the human medial temporal lobe. *Nature Neuroscience* 3(9): 946–953.

Kruizinga, P., and Petkov, N. (2000). Computational model of dot-pattern selective cells. *Biological Cybernetics* 83, 313–325.

Kruuk, H. (2002). *Hunter and hunted.* Cambridge: Cambridge University Press.

Laiacona, M., and Capitani, E. (2001). A case of prevailing deficit of nonliving categories as a case of prevailing sparing of living categories? *Cognitive Neuropsychology* 18(1), 39–70.

Laughlin, C. D., and d'Aquili, E. G. (1974). *Biogenetic structuralism.* New York,: Columbia University Press.

Le Quellec, J. -L. (2004). *Rock art in Africa: Mythology and legend.* Trans. by P. G. Bahn. Paris: Flammarion Press.

Leaky, M. G. (1983). *Africa's vanishing art: The rock paintings of Tanzania.* New York, NY: Doubleday.

Leavesley, M. G. (2007). A shark-tooth ornament from Pleistocene Sahul. *Antiquity* 81(312), 308–316.

LeDoux, J. E. (1994). Emotion, memory and the brain. *Scientific American* 270, 32–39.
LeDoux, J. E. (1998). *The emotional brain*. London: Weidenfeld and Nicolson.
Leroi-Gourhan, A. (1965). *Treasures of prehistoric art*. New York, NY: Harry Abrams.
Lewis-Williams, J. D. (2000). Stories that float from afar: Ancestral folklore of the San of southern Africa. Cape Town: New Africa Books.
Lewis-Williams, J. D., and Dowson, T. A. (1988). The signs of all times: Entoptic phenomena in Upper Palaeolithic art. *Current Anthropology* 29(2), 201–245.
Lewis-Williams, J. D., and Dowson, T. A. (1989). *Images of power: Understanding Bushman rock art*. Johannesburg: Southern Book Publishers.
Linares Málaga, E. (2004). *Arte rupestre en arequipa y se sur del Perú*. San Agustín: UNSA, Universidad Nacional de San Agustín.
Marshack, A. (1976). Implications of the Paleolithic symbolic evidence for the origin of language. *American Scientist* 64, 136–145.
Marshack, A. (1977). The meander as a system: The analysis and recognition of iconographic units in Upper Palaeolithic compositions. In P. J. Ucko (Ed.), *Form in Indigenous art: Schematisation in the art of Aboriginal Australia and prehistoric Europe* (pp. 286–317). Canberra: Australian Institute of Aboriginal Studies.
Martin, A. (2007). The representation of object concepts in the brain. *Annual Review of Psychology* 58, 25–45.
Martin, A., and Chao, L. L. (2001). Semantic memory and the brain: Structure and process. *Current Opinion in Neurobiology* 11, 194–201.
Martin, A., Wiggs, C. L., Ungerleider, L. G., and Haxby, J. V. (1996). Neural correlates of category-specific knowledge. *Nature* 379, 649–652.
Maurer, A. (1965). What children fear. *Journal of Genetic Psychology* 106, 265–277.
May, J. R. (1977). A psychophysiological study of self and externally regulated phobic thoughts. *Behavior Therapy* 8, 849–861.
Mineka, S. (1987). A primate model of phobic fears. In H. Eyesenck and I. Martin (Eds.), *Theoretical foundations of behavior therapy* (pp. 81–111). New York-, NY: Plenum.
Mineka, S. and Cook, M. (1989). Observational conditioning of fear to fear-relevant versus fear-irrelevant stimuli in Rhesus monkeys. *Journal of Abnormal Psychology* 98(4), 448–459.
Moore, E., Lewis-Williams, J. D., and Pearce, D. G. (2004). San spirituality: Roots, expression, and social consequences. Rowman: Altamira.
Moore, C. J., and Price, C. J. (1999). A functional neuroimaging study of the variables that generate category-specific object processing differences. *Brain* 122(5), 943–962.
Morris, R., and Morris, D. (1965). *Men and snakes*. London: Hutchinson.
Mundkur, B. (1978). The roots of ophidian symbolism. *Ethos* 6(3), 125–158.
Mundkur, B. (1983). *The cult of the serpent*. Albany, NY: State University of New York Press.
Mundkur, B. (1988). Human animality, the mental imagery of fear and religiosity. In T. Ingold (Ed.), *What is an animal?* (pp. 141–184). London: Unwin Hyman.
New, J., Cosmides, L., and Tooby, J. (2007). Category-specific attention for animals reflects ancestral priorities, not expertise. *Proceedings of the National Academy of Sciences of the United States of America* 104(42), 16598–16603.
Öhman, A. (1986). Face the beast and fear the face: Animal and social fears as prototypes for evolutionary analyses of emotion. *Psychophysiology* 23(2), 123–145.

Öhman, A., Erikkson, A., and Olofsson, C. (1975). One-trial learning and superior resistance to extinction of autonomic responses conditioned to potentially phobic stimuli. *Journal of Comparative and Physiological Psychology* 88, 619–627.

Öhman, A., and Mineka, S. (2001). Fears, phobias, and preparedness: Towards an evolved module of fear and fear learning. *Psychological Review* 108, 483–522.

Öhman, A., and Soares, J. J. F. (1993). On the automatic nature of phobic fear: Conditioned electrodermal responses to masked fear-relevant stimuli. *Journal of Abnormal Psychology* 102(1), 121–132.

Öhman, A., and Soares, J. J. F. (1998). Emotional conditioning to masked stimuli: Expectancies for aversive outcomes following nonrecognized fear-relevant stimuli. *Journal of Experimental Psychology: General* 127(1), 69–82.

Okusa, T., Kakigi, R., and Osaka, N. (2000). Cortical activity related to cue-invariant shape perception in humans. *Neuroscience* 98, 615–624.

Onians, J. (2000). The biological and geographical bases of cultural borders: The case of the earliest European prehistoric art. In S. Muthesius and K. Murazka-Muthesius (Eds.), *Borders in art: Revisiting kunstgeographie* (pp. 27–33). Warsaw: Warsaw Institute of Art.

Onians, J. (2007). Neuroarchaeology and the origins of representation in the Grotte de Chauvet. In C. Renfrew and I. Morley (Eds.), *Image and imagination: A global prehistory of figurative representation* (pp. 307–320). Cambridge,: McDonald Institute for Archaeological Research.

Ouzman, S. (1995). Spiritual and political uses of a rock engraving site and its imagery by San and Tswana Speakers. *South African Archaeological Bulletin* 50(161), 55–67.

Packer, C., and Clottes, J. (2000). When lions ruled France. *Natural History* 11, 52–57.

Pager, H. (1972). *Ndedema: A documentation of the paintings at the Ndedema Gorge*. Portland: International Scholarly Book Services.

Perani, D., Cappa, S. F., Bettinardi, V., Bressi, S., Gorno-Tempini, M., Matarrese, M., and Fazio, F. (1995). Different neural systems for the recognition of animals and man-made tools. *Neuroreport* 6, 1637–1641.

Phelps, E. A., and LeDoux, J. E. (2005). Contributions of the amygdala to emotion processing: From animal models to human behavior. *Neuron* 48, 175–187.

Pissiota, A. (2003). *Fear, startle, and fear-potentiated startle: Probing emotion in the human brain*. Uppsala: Acta Universitatis Upsaliensis.

Poulin-Dobois, D., Lepage, A., and Ferland, D. (1996). Infants' concept of animacy. *Cognitive Development* 11, 19–36.

Price, C. J., Noppeney, U., and Phillips, J. (2003). How is the fusiform gyrus related to category-specificity? *Cognitive Neuropsychology* 20, 3–6.

Quinn, P. C., and Eimas, P. D. (1996). Perceptual cues that permit categorical differentiation of animal species by infants. *Journal of Experimental Child Psychology* 63, 189–211.

Quinn, P. C., Eimas, P. D., and Rosenkrantz, P. D. (1993). Evidence for representations of perceptually similar natural categories by 3-month-old and 4-month-old infants. *Perception* 22, 463–475.

Radcliffe-Brown, A. R. (1926). The Rainbow-Serpent myth of Australia. *The Journal of the Royal Anthropological Institute of Great Britain and Ireland* 56, 19–25.

Ramachandran, V. S., and Hirstein, W. (1999). The science of art: A neurological theory of aesthetic experience. *Journal of Consciousness Studies* 6(6/7), 15–51.

Robson, K. S. (1967). The role of eye-to-eye contact in maternal-infant attachment. *Journal of Child Psychology and Psychiatry* 8, 13–25.

Riddoch, M. J., Humphreys, G. W., Gannon, T., Blott, W., and Jones, V. (1999). Memories are made of this: The effects of time on stored visual knowledge in a case of visual agnosia. *Brain* 122, 537–559.

Sackett, G. P. (1966). Monkeys reared in isolation with pictures as visual input: Evidence for an innate releasing mechanism. *Science* 154, 1468–1473.

Schroeder, H. E., and Rich, A. R. (1976). The process of fear reduction through systematic desensitization. *Journal of Consulting and Clinical Psychology* 44, 191–199.

Seligman, M. E. P. (1971). Phobias and preparedness. *Behavior Therapy* 2, 307–320.

Seligman, M. E. P., and Hager, J. L. (Eds.) (1972). *Biological boundaries of learning*. New York,: Appleton-Century-Crofts.

Seyfarth, R. M., Cheney, D. L., and Marler, P. (1980). Monkey responses to three different alarm calls: Evidence of predator classification and semantic communication. *Science* 210, 801–803.

Smith, R. (1986). Serpent Cave. *Rock Art Papers (San Diego Museum Papers)* 20(3), 27–50.

Struhsaker, T. T. (1967). Auditory communication among vervet monkeys (*Cercopithecus aethiops*). In S. A. Alman (Ed.), *Social communication among primates* (pp. 281–324). Chicago, IL: University of Chicago Press.

Sütterlin, C. (1989). Universals in apotropaic symbolism: A behavioral and comparative approach to some medieval sculptures. *Leonardo* 22(1), 65–74.

Sütterlin, C. (2003). From sign to schema to iconic representation: Evolutionary aesthetics of pictorial art. In E. Voland and K. Grammer (Eds.), *Evolutionary aesthetics* (pp. 131–170). Berlin: Springer.

Taçon, P. S. C., Wilson, M., and Chippindale, C. (1996). Birth of the Rainbow Serpent in Arnhem Land rock art and oral history. *Archaeology in Oceania* 31(3), 103–124.

Tanaka, J. W., and Curran, T. (2001). A neural basis for expert object recognition. *Psychological Science* 12(1), 43–47.

Tanaka, K., Saito, H. -A., Fukada, Y., and Moriya, M. (1991). Coding visual images of objects in the inferotemporal cortex of the macaque monkey. *Journal of Neurophysiology* 66, 170–189.

Taylor, L. (1989). Seeing the 'inside': Kunwinjku paintings and the symbol of the divided body. In H. Morphy (Ed.), *Animals into art* (pp. 18–389). London: Unwin Hyman.

Taylor, L. (1990). The Rainbow Serpent as visual metaphor in western Arnhem Land. *Oceania* 60(4), 329–344.

Tinbergen, N. (1954). *Curious naturalists*. New York, NY: Basic Books.

Tranel, D., Damasio, H., and Damasio, A. (1997). A neural basis for the retrieval of conceptual knowledge. *Neuropsychologia* 35(10), 1319–1327.

Ucko, P.J., and Rosenfeld, A. (1967). *Palaeolithic cave art*. London: Weidenfeld and Nicholson.

Ucko, P. J., and Rosenfeld, A. (1972). Anthropomorphic representations in Palaeolithic art. In M. B. Almagro and M. A. Garcia Guinea (Eds.), *Santander Symposium, Symposium Internacional de Arte Rupestre 1970* (pp. 149–211). Santander: Patronato de las cuevas prehistoricas de Santander and Direccion General de Bellas Artes.

Ühër, J. (1991). On zigzag designs: Three levels of meaning. *Current Anthropology* 32, 437–439.

Üher, J. (1994). Zigzag rock art: An ethological perspective. In T. A. Dowson and J. D. Lewis-Williams (Eds.), *Contested images: Diversity in southern African rock art research* (pp. 293–313). Johannesburg: Witwatersrand University Press.

Vinnicombe, P. (1976). *People of the eland.* Pietermarizburg: Natal University Press.

Watson, B. (2007). Dreaming phenomena and palaeoart. *Before Farming* 2007(4), 81–94.

Watson, B. (2009). *Universal visions: Neuroscience and recurrent characteristics of world palaeoart.* Unpublished Ph.D. dissertation. Centre for Classics and Archaeology, University of Melbourne.

Watson, B. (2010a). Psychoanalysis and prehistoric art. *Journal of Iberian Archaeology* 13, 35–49.

Watson, B. (2010b). The neuropsychology of animism and implied motion in rock art. *Rock Art Research* 17(1), 79–80.

Watson, B. (2011). The eyes have it: Human perception and anthropomorphic faces in world rock art. *Antiquity* 85(327), 87–98.

Watson, B. (2012). The body and the brain: Neuroscience and the representation of anthropomorphs in palaeoart. *Rock Art Research* 29(1), 3–18.

Whitley, D. S. (1994). Shamanism, natural modeling and the rock art of far western North America. In S. Turpin (Ed.), *Shamanism and rock art in North America* (pp. 1–43). San Antonio, TX: Special Publication 1, Rock Art Foundation, Inc.

Whitley, D. S. (2000). *The art of the shaman: Rock art of California.* Salt Lake City, UT: University of Utah Press.

Whitley, D. S. (2001). Science and the sacred: Interpretive theory in U.S. rock art research. In K. Helskog (Ed.), *Theoretical perspectives in rock art research* (pp. 124–152). Oslo: The Institute for Comparative Research in Human Culture.

Willis, R. G. (Ed.) (1990). *Signifying animals.* London,: Unwin Hyman.

Wilson, E. O. (1998). *Consilience: The unity of knowledge.* New York, NY: Alfred A. Knopf.

Yen, S. -C., and Finkel, L. H. (2002). Salience. In V. S. Ramachandran (Ed.), *Encyclopedia of the human brain* (pp. 237–250). San Diego, CA: Academic Press.

In: The Psychology of Human Behavior
Editor: Robert G. Bednarik
ISBN: 978-1-62257-901-3

Chapter 6

COPING WITH THE ADVERSITY OF CHRONIC DISORDER: THE DEVELOPMENT OF RESILIENCE

Ashley Craig**, *Elaine Blumgart and Yvonne Tran
Rehabilitation Studies Unit, Sydney Medical School,
The University of Sydney, Ryde, NSW Australia

ABSTRACT

Chronic diseases and disorders include a diverse range of conditions that often impose a considerable burden on mental health and quality of life. Stuttering (or stammering) is a chronic communication disorder with suspected neural causes. It involves involuntary disruption to the fluency of speech beginning in childhood and for many it persists into adulthood. Recent research suggests that chronic stuttering can impose a significant burden with subsequent adverse conditions, such as avoidant behavior and social disengagement. This chapter will explore the behavioral and mental impact of stuttering and will discuss recent research the authors have conducted on the development of resilience in the face of adversity associated with this chronic disorder. The chapter will also explore resilience factors such as helpful social support and self-efficacy that will protect people from the adversity of a chronic condition like stuttering. The importance of these factors is discussed in the light of coping with and adjusting to the potential negative impacts of stuttering on the behavior and mental health of people who stutter.

INTRODUCTION: RESILIENCE AND COPING WITH ADVERSITY

Chronic disorder is often associated with negative adverse outcomes such as psychopathology and lowered quality of life (Bonanno and Mancini 2008; Chodosh et al. 2005; Craig 2012; Monroe and Reid 2009; Rutter 1985). Substantial individual differences exist in the way people cope with and adjust to adversity. Some cope and adjust adaptively

* Rehabilitation Studies Unit, Sydney Medical School, The University of Sydney, PO Box 6, Ryde, NSW Australia, 1680, a.craig@sydney.edu.au

(e.g., they seek out helpful support), while others cope badly (e.g., abuse alcohol to forget unpleasantness), often becoming depressed and highly anxious (Monroe and Reid 2009). As an example, depression is believed to be a prevalent response to a severe adverse event such as traumatic spinal cord injury (Craig et al. 2009). Surprisingly, almost 60 out of every 100 adults living with a chronic spinal cord injury (SCI) and its permanent impairment do not develop major depressive disorders or any anxiety disorder within 12 months of their injury (Craig et al. 2009). In fact, many will go on to thrive, adjusting positively to the demands of their injury and impairment (Craig et al. 2009). These people are demonstrating resilience, which is a dynamic process involving adjusting and coping in an adaptive manner when confronted with significant and challenging life events (Coifman and Bonanno 2010; Craig 2012; Garmezy and Masten 1991; Luthar, Cicchetti and Becker 2000). It stands to reason also, that resilient behavior will be related to maintaining an acceptable quality of life (QOL) while grappling with the stresses and strains of daily living (Taylor et al. 2010).

Risk and Protective Factors

Resilience-based research commonly adopts a risk and protective factor model (Craig 2012). This model involves examining risks of a poor outcome such as employed in a risk deficit model. However, this model also asserts the importance of examining factors that are related to beneficial outcomes, that is, resilient behavior. Factors that enhance resilient behavior are labeled protective factors. Protective factors, by definition, reduce the negative impact of risk factors or act as buffers in opposition to distress that follows adversity (Cummins 2010). For instance, multiple sclerosis (MS) imposes significant hardship and carries many risks of negative (that is, non-resilient) outcomes (Chwastiak and Ehde 2007). However, if a person with MS has managed their disease in the past, believes they can manage their disease in the future and also has someone close who will support and care for them, then these protective factors will begin to outweigh risk factors, assisting the person to cope and adjust to their MS. Protective factors "restrain", "buffer", and "reduce" the negative impact of adversity (Chwastiak and Ehde 2007). The strength of a protective factor will, of course, depend on the level of risk exposure (Fergus and Zimmerman 2005). That is, if a chronic disorder is very severe, then it will require additional or strong protective factors to help a person cope and adjust.

The use of a risk and protective factor model has provided substantial benefits for the study of chronic disorders. For instance, researchers began the search for factors that contributed to people surviving severe adversity (perhaps against all odds) instead of merely focusing on risks. They invested time into determining those factors that may defend a person against distress and hardship (Coifman and Bonanno 2010; King et al. 1999; Rutter 1985). As an example, Coifman and Bonanno (2010) recently explored factors that protected people from becoming depressed when they experienced bereavement. They found that during the time of bereavement, the ability to distract by employing positive emotions when dealing with events unrelated to the loss actually enhanced their resilience. Further, King et al. (1999) studied protective factors in combat veterans with a diagnosed post-traumatic stress disorder (PTSD). Typical risks included elevated distress and a pre-war history of trauma. However, they also found that factors like helpful social support and a resilient personality (e.g., hardiness) protected a person from developing PTSD. Southwick, Vythilingam and Charney (2005) concluded that factors that protect against depression include optimism, regular exercise, social support, positive role models, and positive coping styles. Risk factors for depression include severity of the disorder, lack of social support, poor financial capacity, poor health status, low quality of life and a sense of helplessness (Craig 2012; Rutter 1985; Southwick et al. 2005). Taylor et al. (2010) studied protective factors in people with epilepsy, a chronic disorder involving potential significant social embarrassment and social impairment. Protective factors included fewer adverse treatment effects and a sense of self-mastery. Finally, Anzarut, Chen, Shankowsky, and Tredget (2005) found that adults with severe burns on more than 50% of their total body surface area were protected by helpful social support.

CHALLENGES ASSOCIATED WITH CHRONIC STUTTERING

Effective verbal communication is vital for social interaction and integration (Kagan et al. 2008). It therefore follows that sustaining a chronic communication disorder could constitute a serious barrier to successful social interaction. Stuttering is a Communication Disorder in which a person has involuntary disruptions to the fluency of their speech (American Psychiatric Association *2000*). Stuttering begins early, usually by two to three years of age, and except for rare cases of traumatic brain injury that causes disruption to speech fluency, stuttering is believed to be related to a genetic-based speech processing capacity deficit (Bloodstein and Bernstein-Ratner 2008). For about 1% of those who stutter as a child, stuttering becomes chronic and continues to develop into adulthood (Bloodstein and Bernstein-Ratner 2008; Craig et al. 2002).

Adverse reactions to stuttering are known to begin early. For instance, negative peer reactions to stuttering have been found in young children, and children and adolescents who stutter experience significantly elevated rates of bullying (Blood et al. 2010; Langevin et al. 2009). Children who stutter have been shown to develop abnormally elevated communication fears by mid to late adolescence (De Nil and Brutten 1991). Recent work by Eggers, De Nil, and Van den Bergh (2010) showed that children who stutter (mean age 5 years) were at risk of developing higher levels of anger and frustration. Research by Mulcahy, Hennessey, Beilby, and Byrnes (2008) with adolescents who stutter showed that stuttering imposed significant psychosocial conflict regardless of its severity.

ADVERSITY ASSOCIATED WITH STUTTERING IN ADULTS

By late adolescence and into adulthood, people who stutter have been found to have significant risks of elevated trait and social anxiety (Craig et al. 2003; Craig and Tran 2006; Ezrati-Vinacour and Levin 2004; Iverach et al. 2009a; Mulcahy et al. 2008). Chronic stuttering can impose significant adversity, with a consequent risk of emotional and social distress (Blumgart et al. 2010a; Eggers et al. 2010; Iverach et al. 2009a; Iverach et al. 2009b; Mulcahy et al. 2008). For example, Tran, Blumgart, and Craig (2011) studied negative affect in 200 adults with chronic stuttering using the Revised Symptom Checklist-90 (SCL-90-R;

Derogatis 1994). Compared to a non-stuttering control group (n=200) with a similar age and sex ratio, the stuttering sample had significantly elevated levels of distress across a broad range of psychopathology constructs such as interpersonal sensitivity, anxious mood, phobic anxiety, somatization, obsessive compulsiveness tendencies, depressive mood, hostility, psychoticism tendencies and paranoid ideation. Figure 1 demonstrates the extent of distress across these constructs in the stuttering sample. Based on these findings, Tran et al. (2011) concluded that stuttering does impose a severe challenge to a person's capacity to cope and adjust, and thus be resilient. Tran et al. (2011) argued that it comes as no surprise that an involuntary chronic disorder like stuttering has a negative personal and social impact. They emphasized, however, that the broad-ranging distress shown in Figure 1 is more likely due to adverse reactions to their chronic disorder, rather than some psychopathological mechanism unrelated to the Communication Disorder. Reactions to stuttering such as anticipating difficulties when talking to others in social contexts, extreme embarrassment and frustration, loneliness and shyness and difficulties feeling close to others, are clearly prevalent in adults who stutter.

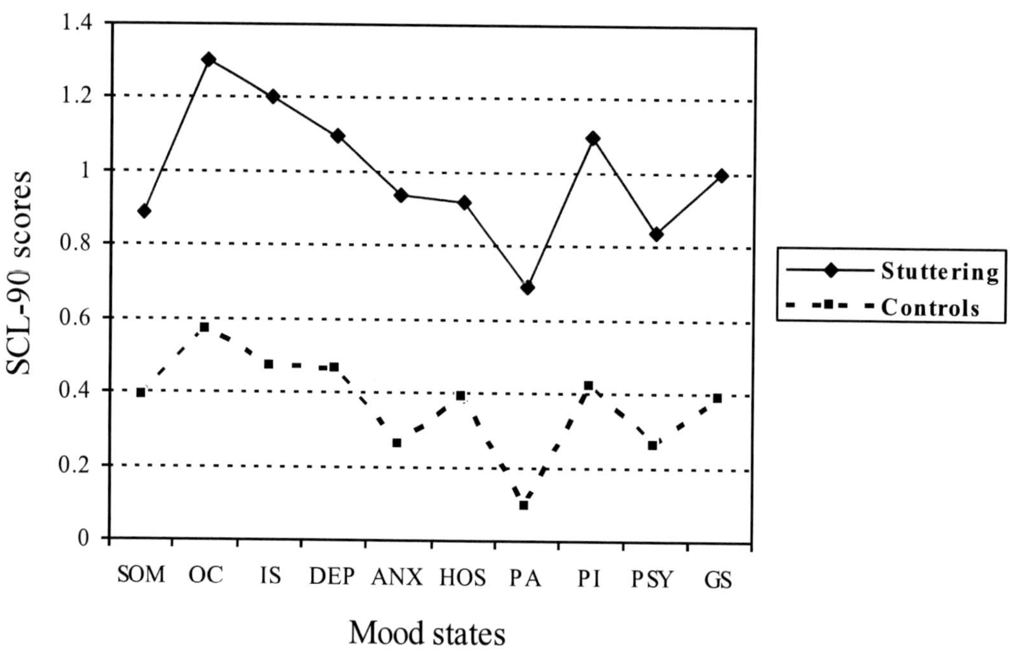

Figure 1. Shows the extent of distress across multiple constructs for 200 adult persons who stutter compared to 200 non-stuttering adult controls. All constructs were significantly elevated ($p < .05$) in the stuttering sample—close to levels seen in psychiatric outpatient samples (Derogatis 1994). Note: SOM=somatization; OC=obsessive compulsive tendency; IS=interpersonal sensitivity; DEP=depressive mood; ANX=anxiety; HOS=hostility; PA=phobic anxiety; PI=paranoid ideation; PSY=psychoticism tendencies; GS=global severity.

Evidence also suggests that QOL is significantly reduced in domains such as vitality, emotional, social, and mental health functioning (Craig et al. 2009). Craig et al. (2009) measured QOL with The Medical Outcomes Study Short Form-36 (SF-36; Ware and Gandek 1998). Figure 2 shows the extent of reduced QOL in adults who stutter. Note that the reduced QOL did not occur in QOL domains such as physical function or role, pain, or general health, but was significantly reduced in vitality, social and emotional function, and mental health domains. This data makes it clear that stuttering negatively impacts social and psychological aspects of QOL. Craig et al. (2009) argued that the extent of the impact of stuttering on QOL becomes evident when compared to the impact of other chronic disorders such as tetraplegia or traumatic head injury (Middleton et al. 2007). The reduced QOL found in the above four domains in the people who stutter was similar to the reduced QOL in these same domains in people with tetraplegia and traumatic brain injury (Middleton et al. 2007). It is sobering news that stuttering, a Communication Disorder, can negatively impact QOL similar to life threatening chronic diseases.

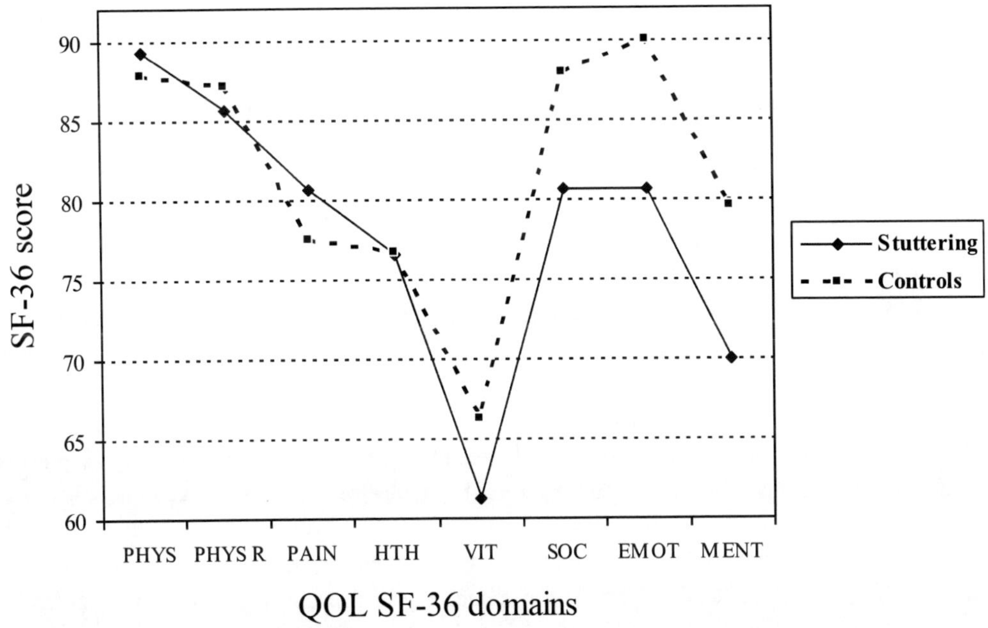

Figure 2. Shows the extent of reduced QOL across multiple QOL domains for 200 adult persons who stutter compared to 200 non-stuttering adult controls. High scores suggest better QOL. Note that PHYS=physical function; PHYS R=physical role; PAIN=pain; HTH=general health; VIT=vitality; SOC=social function; EMOT=emotional function; MENT=mental health. Vitality, social and emotional function and mental health were significantly reduced ($p < .05$) in the stuttering sample, close to levels seen in severe chronic disorder such as neuro-trauma (Craig et al. 2009).

Of further concern was the finding that adults who stutter have elevated risks of social phobia (SP; Blumgart et al. 2010a; Schneier et al. 1997; Stein et al. 1996). SP involves extreme and intense anticipatory anxiety in response to perceived embarrassment in social contexts where a person believes they will be or are being scrutinized by others (American Psychiatric Association 2000). Stein et al. (1996) found a SP spot prevalence of 44% in a small group of adults who stutter. Blumgart et al. (2010a) investigated prevalence rates of SP in a large sample of adults who stutter, with comparisons made to a non-stuttering sample of adults. They found a reliable SP prevalence estimate of 40% compared to a prevalence of 4% in the non-stuttering control group. Blumgart et al. (2010a) also identified the prevalence of SP participants meeting DSM criteria for Generalized SP, a recognized more severe form of

SP (American Psychiatric Association 2000). They found a rate of 85% of the SP stuttering sample met DSM criteria for Generalized SP, while 15% met DSM criteria for Specific SP. In comparison, 50% of the non-stuttering SP controls met DSM criteria for Generalized SP. They concluded that the majority of adults who stutter with SP have a Generalized SP diagnosis. The adults who stutter feared entering a broad range of specific social contexts, including eating in public (odds ratio of 6.8, meaning they had 6.8 times greater risk of fearing eating in public), asking questions in a group (odds ratio of 9.1), attending a social gathering or party (odds ratio of 9.8), and attending a work related meeting (odds ratio of 4.3). Clearly, stuttering can negatively influence social interaction. Stuttering has also been found to impose a significant financial cost burden related to paying for treatment or buying treatment related items (Blumgart et al. 2010b).

Resilience Research in Adult Stuttering

The above risk-based research demonstrates the adversity associated with chronic stuttering. Unfortunately, there has been scarce research that has adopted a risk and protective factor model; that is, a model delineating specific factors that are related to coping and adjusting over time. Such a model outlines and describes those factors that protect people from negative outcomes associated with living with a chronic fluency disorder. In reality, this lack of research has created a deficit in our knowledge about resilience processes in adults who stutter. One exception involved grounded theory research conducted by Plexico, Manning, and Levit (2009a; 2009b). For instance, they reported that protective mechanisms used by people who stutter consisted of strategies such as action oriented coping responses. They reported also that the use of these strategies would enhance positive outcomes (i.e., resilience). Clearly, we believe that considerable benefits would result from identifying factors that may protect adults who stutter from experiencing severe distress in their lives related to their chronic disorder. The present chapter will present and summarize controlled research (Craig et al. 2011) that was designed to determine those protective factors that may operate in adults who stutter which will enhance the resilience process when dealing with the challenges of a chronic fluency disorder.

Methodology

Participants

The detailed methodology has been presented elsewhere (Craig et al. 2011). In summary, the study involved the same participants reported in Craig et al. (2009) and in Tran et al. (2011). The participants comprised 200 adults who stuttered and 200 non-stuttering controls. However, no further detail about the control sample will be presented in this chapter. Table 1 presents demographic information for the participants. Most of the 200 stuttering participants had received treatment for stuttering in their lifetime (n=187; 94%). For the few that had never sought treatment for stuttering, reasons included treatment not available, believing they were not severe enough, and lack of faith in treatment.

Table 1. Demographics (age and age diagnosed with stuttering), severity of stuttering (assessed by percent syllables stuttered or %SS and syllables per minute or SPM), and cumulative health risks assessed by the Lifestyle Appraisal Questionnaire (LAQ1) for the stuttering group. Higher LAQ1 scores mean increased health risks. Risks increase when LAQ1 scores rise above 20.

	Age (yrs) mean (SD)	Age Diag mean (SD)	%SS mean (SD)	SPM (mean SD)	LAQI mean (SD)
Males (n=151)	46.7 (16)	5.8 (2.6)	3.6 (2.7)	178 (15)	15.1 (6)
Females (n=49)	42.5 (16)	5.5 (3.2)	3.9 (3.2)	178 (23)	14.2 (7)
Total (N=200)	45.7 (16)	5.7 (2.8)	3.7 (2.8)	178 (17)	14.9 (6)

The ratio of male to female (M: F) participants entered into the study was based on epidemiological data from research conducted in New South Wales (NSW), Australia (Craig et al. 2002). The Craig et al. (2002) findings suggest that a NSW adult male to female ratio lay within the range of 2:1 to 4:1. Participants were recruited proportionally to NSW adult age distribution population statistics in 2006 (www.abs.gov.au). Eligibility criteria for the participants consisted of: (a) lack of history of a physical or neurological disorder or condition that was independent of stuttering and which could dominate the impact of stuttering, for instance, a diagnosed neurodegenerative disorder such as Parkinson's disease or a traumatic neurological injury, (b) aged between 18 years and 85 years at the time of interview, and (c) able to speak English. Research ethics approval was received from a university institutional human research ethics committee and written consent was obtained before participation in the study.

Definition and Assessment of Stuttering

Stuttering was defined as a disorder in the rhythm of speech, in which the individual knows what he or she wishes to say, but at the same time is unable to say it because of an involuntary, repetitive prolongation or cessation of sound (Andrews et al. 1983). Stuttering included repetition of syllables, part-or-whole words or phrases; avoidance of words; substitutions, prolongations of speech or blocking of sounds (Craig et al. 1996a). Three-minute samples of conversational speech were taken for all participants and from this, severity of stuttering (e.g., percent syllables stuttered or %SS) was calculated. In order to confirm the reliability of the speech measures, an experienced clinician randomly reassessed 10% of the speech samples. Inter-rater reliability was established for %SS: mean %SS for rater 1 = 3.37 (SD = 3.4); mean %SS for rater 2 = 3.66 (SD = 3.5); df=38, t= 0.25, p=ns; Pearson correlation coefficient r=0.99, p< .01.

Design and Procedure

A population group cohort design was used to ensure participants were recruited according to the proportion of the age distribution for the community in which the study was conducted, with samples stratified for age and sex as explained above. All 200 participants attended a 2–3 hour interview conducted in a relaxed environment in which an interviewer assessed severity of stuttering. Participants also completed a regimen of standardized psychological questionnaires.

Demographic Measures

Age, sex, level of education, age at which stuttering was diagnosed; country of birth (Australia or overseas), and employment status were assessed. All participants were also asked to provide an estimate (within $10,000) of their annual income over the past five years. The educational breakdown of the group was as follows: 20% completed secondary school or less, 25% completed technical or trade education, and 55% completed tertiary studies. At the time of the interview, 62% of participants were working full-time, 11% were employed part-time, about 4% were students, 10% were self-employed, about 10% had retired, and three participants were unemployed. About one third (33.5%) of the 200 earned less than $50,000 per annum, 35% earned between $50,000 and $99,999, while just under one-third (31.5%) earned over $100,000 per annum.

In summary, the participants were well educated with a similar health risk profile to the Australian adult community. Males and females were similar in terms of health. The great majority of the sample was employed at the time of the study. At least 50% of the stuttering sample earned equal to or above the median full time Australian wage of around $56,000 in 2010 (Australian Bureau of Statistics 2010).

Psychological Measures

All participants completed a suite of measures. For the purposes of this paper, only the following will be presented:

(i) *Symptom Checklist* – Revised (SCL-90-R, Derogatis 1994). The SCL-90-R is a widely used 90-item self-report measure of psychopathology, assessing symptoms for nine psychopathology domains as well as a measure of global severity of psychopathology called the Global Severity Index (GSI). Items are scored using a 5-point Likert scale. The reliability of the SCL-R-90 has been well established (Kennedy et al. 2001), with an acceptable internal consistency demonstrated by coefficient alpha scores ranging between .79 and .90, and excellent test-retest reliabilities for the nine symptom dimensions ranging between .68 and .90 (Derogatis 1994). Construct and convergent-discriminate validity has been demonstrated (Derogatis 1994), and it has been shown to be a valid screen for detecting psychopathology (Schmitz et al. 1999). The SCL-R-90 symptom domains include: somatization (distress, pain and discomfort arising from perceptions of bodily dysfunction); obsessive-compulsiveness (thoughts, impulses and behavior experienced as irrepressible and uncontrollable); interpersonal sensitivity (feelings of inadequacy and inferiority); depressive mood (presence of dysphoric mood); anxiety (feelings of nervousness and tension); hostility (feelings of resentment; aggression and irritability; phobic anxiety (persistent fear response to a specific person or place); paranoid ideation (suspiciousness, delusiveness and perceived loss of autonomy); and psychoticism (from mild interpersonal alienation to severe psychoses). Factor analytic studies of the SCL-90-R have demonstrated that the SCL-90-R GSI provides a general global measure of psychopathology or negative affectivity (Vassend and Skrondal 1999; Watson et al. 1988).

While psychometric measures of resilience exist (e.g., the Connor-Davidson Resilience Scale; Connor and Davidson 2003), we employed the participant's level of global psychopathology as an indication of resilience. It was assumed that high GSI scores indicate poor resilience and that a low or normal GSI score indicates healthy resilience. This assumption has been supported by recent research by Sexton, Byrd, and von Kluge (2010) who studied resilience in women suffering infertility. They found that high levels of subjective distress (as measured by the SCL-R-90 GSI score) of the infertile women was strongly related to lower levels of resilience. Bonanno and Mancini (2008) have also supported the use of subjective distress levels or psychopathology symptoms as an indicator of resilience.

(ii) The *Lifestyle Appraisal Questionnaire* (LAQ) is a standardized self-report measure of health risk (Craig et al. 1996b). Items are scored using a Likert scale. The LAQ consists of two parts. The LAQ1 assesses multiple sources of health risks such as body mass index, diet, alcohol and nicotine intake, blood pressure level, drug intake, and so on. A higher score indicates elevated health risks, while a score of less than 20 indicates normal levels of health risks (Craig et al. 1996). The LAQ2 measures a person's sense of mastery (self-efficacy) over their ability to influence their life challenges and stress. High scores indicate low self-efficacy. The LAQ 1 and 2 have been shown to have acceptable test-retest reliability and an acceptable internal reliability confirmed by a Cronbach coefficient alpha of 0.5 and 0.89 for LAQ1 and LAQ2 respectively (Craig et al. 1996). The LAQ has also been shown to have acceptable construct validity and low social desirability (Craig et al. 1996).

(iii) *Quality of life* (QOL) was measured using The Medical Outcomes Study Short Form-36 (SF-36; Ware and Gandek 1998; Ware et al. 1993). The SF-36 measures eight QOL dimensions including: (a) physical functioning, indicating the extent to which a person's health limits their day to day physical activities; (b) role limitations at work or in the home due to physical health problems, (c) pain, indicating the extent to which pain interferes with daily activities; (d) health status and perception of health; (e) vitality, a measure of a person's energy levels or conversely, fatigue; (f) social functioning, indicating the extent to which health limits social activities; (g) role limitations due to emotional problems, indicating the extent to which a person's emotional problems impact on daily and work activities; and (h) mental health, indicating the amount of time a person experiences feelings of nervousness, depression, happiness and so on. The SF-36 is scored so that a high score indicates a better QOL. The SF-36 questionnaire was scored by summing up and transforming raw data for each of the eight domains, as per the formula in the SF-36 manual (Ware et al. 1993). It has been shown to have acceptable reliability and validity with a variety of populations in Australia and normative Australian data are available (Australian Bureau of Statistics 1997; McCallum 1995; Sanson-Fisher and Perkins 1998). Validity and reliability of this instrument have been well established (Sanson-Fisher and Perkins 1998; Ware et al. 1993). For example, it has been shown to have acceptable internal reliability shown by Chronbach's alpha score of around 0.85; acceptable test-retest reliabilities after two weeks, and excellent construct validity demonstrated by its ability to distinguish between groups with expected health differences (Brazier et al. 1992).

(iv) The *Significant Others Scale* (SOS). The SOS scale (Power et al. 1988) assesses actual and ideal levels of perceived social support. The SOS assesses the emotional, social, protective and practical support of up to seven people, who the respondent believes are close to them. Responses are rated on a Likert scale of 1 to 7, with high scores indicating high levels of actual or ideal social support. Only actual social support scores for Person 1 were reported in this paper, as all participants provided scores for Person 1. The reliability and validity of this subtest has been established (Power et al. 1988).

Analysis

In order to examine factors that operate to protect people from the adversity of chronic disorder, the 200 stutter participants were divided into two groups based on their GSI score (Derogatis 1994). Derogatis (1994) reported non-patient norms for the SCL-90-R GSI to be .3 (*SD*= .3). Therefore, stutter participants were considered to be resilient if their GSI score was equal to or fell below .6, that is, within or below one standard deviation of the mean. Participants were considered to be non-resilient if their scores fell above .6 on the GSI measure, that is, they scored more than one standard deviation above the mean. Eight factors believed to be protective based on prior research were investigated (Bloodstein and Bernstein Ratner 2008; Rutter 1985), included stuttering frequency (ie. severity), health risks, self-efficacy, physical role limitations, vitality, social function, perceived social support, and annual income. Overall differences between the two sub-groups were first tested by a MANOVA and then, if the MANOVA was significant, ANOVA tests were used to determine where differences existed between the two sub-groups. The SF-36 domains of general health, pain and physical function were not examined because health risk status (LAQ1) was already assessed. The SF-36 domains of emotional and mental health functioning were not examined, as they are similar constructs to the SCL-90-R GSI measure. Eta-squared (η^2) values are provided as estimates of the size of the difference between the two samples. An η^2 of around .03 is considered small, .13 is considered a medium difference and over .2 is considered a large and substantial difference (Cohen 1988). Last, a standard multiple regression analysis was used to determine if any factors uniquely contributed to psychopathology (and thus to resilience) in the 200 participants.

Table 2. Data for the resilient and non-resilient stutter sub-groups, include stuttering frequency or %SS (higher scores indicate greater severity), health risks (LAQ1: higher scores indicate higher levels of risk), self-efficacy (LAQ2: higher scores indicate poor self-efficacy), social support (SOS: lower scores indicate poorer social support) and global psychopathology score (GSI: higher scores indicate more severe psychopathology).

	Age (yrs) Mean (*SD*)	Age (yrs) diagnosed Mean (*SD*)	%SS Mean (*SD*)	LAQ I Mean (*SD*)	LAQ II Mean (*SD*)	SOS Mean (*SD*)	GSI Mean (*SD*)
Resilient (n=76)	47.8 (16)	5.6 (2.6)	3.5 (2.6)	13.4 (6)	16.8 (9)	25.0 (4.3)	.23 (.18)
Non resilient (n=124)	44.3 (16)	5.8 (2.8)	3.8 (2.9)	15.8 (7)	25.1 (14)	22.6 (5.2)	1.47 (.58)

FINDINGS OF THE STUDY

Detailed results for this study can be found in Craig et al. (2011). Table 2 shows data for the resilient and non-resilient sub-groups. The global psychopathology score (mean SCL-90-R GSI score) for the resilient group was .23 (*SD*= .18, n=76), and the mean SCL-90-R GSI score for the non-resilient group was 1.47 (*SD*= .58, n=124). In comparison, a mean score of .3 (*SD*= .3) has been found for a non-clinical group, while a mean GSI score for a psychiatric outpatient group was found to be 1.3 (*SD*= .7) (Derogatis 1994). Factors such as sex, age, age diagnosed with stuttering, stuttering severity, education, birthplace, and employment were not significantly associated with the global measure of psychopathology (GSI measure) in either group using a Pearson correlation analysis, with probability set at .01 to control for Type 1 errors.

Table 3. Factors found to protect adults who stutter from the adversity of stuttering. Significance of difference is marked.

Factors	Resilient sub-group (n=76) SCL-90-R GSI score ≤ .6				Non-resilient sub-group (n=124) SCL-90-R GSI score >.6			
	Mean	SD	SE	±95% CI	Mean	SD	SE	±95% CI
%SS	3.5	2.6	.30	2.9-4.2	3.8	2.9	.26	3.2-4.3
LAQ1	13.4	5.5	.63	12.1-14.7	15.8	6.9	.62	14.6-17.1 *
LAQ2	16.8	9.1	1.04	14.7-18.8	25.1	14.3	1.29	22.5-27.6 **
Phys R	92.8	21.1	2.42	87.9- 97.6	81.4	32.0	2.87	75.8-87.1 **
Soc fn	90.9	13.6	1.56	87.8-94.1	74.5	25.3	2.27	69.9-78.9 **
Vitality	65.5	16.4	1.88	61.7-69.2	58.6	18.6	1.67	55.3-61.9 **
SOS	25.0	4.3	.49	24.0-26.0	22.6	5.2	.47	21.6-23.5 **
Ann inc	81,973	36,597	4142	73,721-90,225	76,693	36,112	3286	70,188-83,199

Note. *p<.05 **p<.01

%SS=stuttering severity; LAQ1=health risks; LAQ2=self-efficacy; Phys R=SF-36 physical role domain; Soc fn=SF-36 social functioning domain; Vitality=SF-36 vitality domain; SOS=social support measure; Ann inc=annual income in $Australian

Differences between the Resilient and Non-Resilient Sub-Groups

A number of factors were found to distinguish between the resilient and non-resilient sub-groups. MANOVA results indicated significant overall differences between the two groups: Wilks Lambda = .83, $F(8,191) = 4.97, p< .001$. ANOVA tests were then performed to determine where the difference occurred. Table 3 shows data for eight possible protective factors (stuttering frequency or %SS, health risks or LAQ1, self-efficacy or LAQ2, SF-36 physical role limitations, SF-36 vitality, SF-36 social function, perceived social support or SOS, and annual income in Australian currency) for both the resilient and non-resilient sub-groups. The resilient group was shown to be significantly different from the non-resilient group in the following factors: lower health risk status $F(1,198) = 6.5, p < .05; \eta^2=.03$, power = 72%; higher self-efficacy: $F(1,198) = 20.2, p < .01; \eta^2=.09$, power = 99%; higher perceived social support: $F(1,198) = 11.2, p < .01; \eta^2=.05$, power = 91%; fewer physical limitations due to physical health $F(1,198) = 7.5, p < .01; \eta^2=.04$, power = 77%; superior social functioning:

$F(1,198) = 27.3, p < .01; \eta^2=.12$, power = 99%, and superior levels of vitality: $F(1,198) = 7.0, p < .01; \eta^2=.03$, power = 75%. Frequency of stuttering (%SS): $F(1,198) = 2.2$, p=ns, and annual income $F(1,198) = 1.4$, p = ns, were not found to be significantly different between the two sub-groups. There were no significant age or sex interaction effects.

Contributors to Resilience

Using the psychopathology score (the SCL-90-R GSI) as the indicator of resilience (the dependent variable), a standard multiple regression (MR) analysis was performed on the sample of 200 participants to determine factors that may significantly contribute to resilience. Table 4 shows details for the MR analysis, as well as the individual contribution to global psychopathology severity (the square of the semi partial correlation statistic or Spc^2) for each of the eight potential resilience factors. Altogether, the eight factors explained 34% of the variance in the global psychopathology severity index: $R= .58, R^2= .34, F(8,191) = 12.1, p< .001$. Of the eight, three significant contributors were found. These included self-efficacy ($p< .001$, contributing 10.5%), social support ($p< .01$, contributing 2.0%), and social functioning ($p< .05$, contributing 2.3%). High self-efficacy (i.e., low LAQ2 scores) contributed to low global psychopathology, that is, to superior resilience. Superior perceived social support (SOS) contributed to reduced global psychopathology, that is, to superior resilience. Superior social functioning contributed to low global psychopathology, that is, to superior resilience. The remaining five factors did not contribute significantly with individual contributions of less than 1%, though vitality came close (p= .09) explaining almost 1% of the variance in psychopathology. There was also a trend for annual income to contribute to resilience, with higher salaries related to lower psychopathology scores (i.e., higher resilience).

Table 4. Factors found to contribute significantly to the resilience process, isolated by standard multiple regression analysis results. The dependent variable was global psychopathology (SCL-90-R global severity index) with eight continuous independent variables.

$R= .58, R^2= .34, F(8,191)=12.1, p<.001$

Factor	*ß*	*Std Error of ß*	*B*	*Std Error of B*	*t*	*p level*	*Spc^2*
%SS	.024	.060	.006	.016	.39	0.69	.05%
Self -efficacy	.423	.078	.023	.004	5.45	0.00	10.5%
Health risks	-.004	.065	-.001	.007	-.064	0.95	.01%
Social supp	-.149	.062	-.022	.001	-2.38	0.02	2.0%
Physical role	-.027	.066	-.001	.002	-.42	0.67	.06%
Social Funct	-.198	.077	-.006	.002	-2.57	0.02	2.3%
Vitality	-.126	.075	-.005	.003	1.67	0.09	.96%
Annual inc	-.066	.062	-.000	.000	-1.07	0.13	.40%

Note. The semi-partial correlation variance (Spc2) indicates the amount of variance that each factor individually contributes, to the dependent variable, in this case, to the level of psychopathology

CONCLUSIONS: WHAT DISTINGUISHES THOSE WHO ARE RESILIENT?

A number of factors were isolated that were related to lowered risk of psychopathology (thus to resilience) when coping with a chronic disorder like stuttering. Table 5 shows the factors believed to enhance resilience. The resilient group had superior levels of protective factors shown in Table 5. Minor protective factors in the Resilient Group included lower levels of health risks, fewer physical role limitations, higher vitality (or lower levels of fatigue), a higher income and lower severity of the chronic disorder. Major protective factors included a greater sense of perceived self-mastery (or self-efficacy) over stress in their lives, greater access to helpful social support, and superior social functioning (meaning fewer limitations in their ability to mix socially). Factors like self-efficacy are not just consequences of experiencing adversity, but have been shown to act in a protective manner (Kendler et al. 2005; Maciejewski et al. 2000; Rutter 1985). Also, independent researchers have concluded that many of the protective factors listed in Table 5 have been found in people experiencing severe trauma and distress, as well as in people with chronic disorder such as epilepsy and burns (Anzarut et al. 2005; Bonanno and Mancini 2008; Rutter 1985; Southwick et al. 2005; Taylor et al. 2010). Importantly, the eight factors shown in Table 5 accounted for over one-third of the psychopathology variance (R^2=34%). However, this also means that other factors contribute to resilience given that around two-thirds of the resilience variance is unaccounted for, and therefore further research will be required to isolate what these factors are.

Table 5. Known resilience factors in people with a chronic Communication Disorder.

Protective factors	Nature of the contribution
Minor protective factors	
Severity of the disorder	Lower severity: increased resilience
Annual income	Higher income: increased resilience
Vitality	Higher vitality (or low fatigue): increased resilience
General health.	Better health: increased resilience
Physical role	Greater physical function: increased resilience
Major protective factors	
Self-efficacy	High self-efficacy: increased resilience
Helpful social support	Greater social support: increased resilience
Social integration	Greater social activity: increased resilience

Self-efficacy is an important resilience factor crucial for adaptive coping and adjustment. It has been found to be an important mediating factor in the resilience process, determining the severity of psychopathology (Maciejewski et al. 2000). It has also been shown to enhance a person's management of stressful life experiences such as chronic pain (Arnstein et al. 1999) and in lessening the risk of depressive mood following traumatic SCI (Craig et al. 2009). Maciejewski et al. (2000) showed that a higher level of self-efficacy resulted in fewer depressive mood symptoms, concluding that maintaining a healthy self-efficacy, that is, a strong sense of control over one's life and environment, serves to protect a person from psychopathology, perhaps by ameliorating the negative effect of stressful life events experienced (Maciejewski et al. 2000). Internal attitudes such as an active sense of self-control have been shown to act as a buffer against distress, and to be an important factor in maintaining quality of life and happiness (Cummins 2010). The findings of the current study presented in this chapter support the notion that resilience is much more likely to occur if a person believes they can manage their life and any challenging life events they experience daily.

Social support is also a crucial resilience factor and was found to be protective in this study. Participants in the resilient group believed they had superior levels of actual social support compared to the non-resilient group. Supportive social networks have been found to act as a protective buffer against distress and psychopathology (Kendler et al. 2005; Kessler et al. 1985). Social support is believed to be beneficial because it enhances a person's sense of belonging. For example, when a person has a social contact that provides quality emotional support, they perceive they have access to help in difficult times, and this no doubt boosts their confidence, mood, and ultimately their resilience capacity (Kessler et al. 1985). Rutter (1985) argued that social support would only buffer against adversity when the quality of the support is helpful, and of course, if the person makes use of the support. Bloom (1990) suggested that social networks provide access to information and enhance motivation to engage in adaptive behavior. She also suggested social networks will benefit a person indirectly, for instance, by encouraging adherence to goals of treatment, and by assisting in the maintenance of health-promoting behaviors such as exercise and a regular and balanced diet. Social support may also enhance resilience by small acts of support such as driving someone to a medical appointment, or by providing fluency support to a friend who stutters.

High levels of social functioning and activity were also found to act in a protective manner. Social functioning has been found to be protective in people with chronic disorder (de Leon et al. 2003; Southwick et al. 2005; Rutter 1985), while the reverse is possible, that is, people can begin to avoid and reduce their social functioning when faced with adversity (Cardozo et al. 2004; Middleton et al. 2007). Research by de Leon et al. (2003) found those who were more socially active reported lower levels of disability, independent of age, gender, and physical activity. Clearly, a very desirable goal for people with chronic disorder is to become more socially active. This finding has important implications for people who stutter, especially when many are at risk of developing social anxiety (Blumgart et al. 2010a). Evidence-based strategies will be needed to help them overcome barriers and fears of social interaction (Menzies et al 2008).

These findings raise possibilities for improving treatment for people who stutter. Given a large percentage of older adolescents and adults who stutter have high risks of developing social phobia as well as elevated negative mood states, the findings presented in this chapter suggest that stuttering treatment would benefit from the addition of components such as:

i. Psycho-education about protective factors such as self-efficacy, helpful social support, and social activity and engagement.
ii. Self-control strategies known to enhance self-efficacy (Andrews and Craig 1988).
iii. Anti-anxiety treatments to enhance control over communication fears of social anxiety (Menzies et al. 2008).
iv. Socially-based strategies like social skills and assertion training, problem solving and conflict resolution techniques, all of which should enhance motivation to mix socially.

These components should be applied to varied social contexts including speaking in front of others in public contexts, interacting in informal gatherings, speaking at meetings, and interacting at family gatherings. Treatment should also encourage the involvement of people who stutter in helpful social networks such as self-help groups (Ramig 1993; Yaruss et al. 2002).

In conclusion, this chapter has presented firm results on factors that optimize resilience behavior in people with a chronic disorder. It will be beneficial for future research to concentrate on revealing other factors that may also contribute to the resilience process. It is highly recommended that a risk and protective factor model be employed to accomplish this. Not only has such a model the potential to uncover factors that may be potential risks, but it also has the capacity to identify factors that can defend against the adverse impact of chronic stuttering.

REFERENCES

American Psychiatric Association *(2000). Diagnostic and statistical manual of mental disorders, fourth edition* (*DSM-IV-TR*). Washington, DC: Author.

Andrews, G., and Craig, A. (1988). Prediction of outcome after treatment for stuttering. *British Journal of Psychiatry* 153, 236–240.

Andrews, G., Craig, A.R., Feyer, A. M., Hoddinott, S., Howie, P., and Neilson, M. (1983). Stuttering: A review of research findings and theories circa 1982. *Journal of Speech and Hearing Disorders* 48, 226–246.

Anzarut, A., Chen, M., Shankowsky, H., and Tredget, E. (2005). Quality-of-life and outcome predictors following massive burn injury. *Plastic and Reconstructive Surgery* 116, 791–797.

Arnstein, P., Caudill, M., Mandle, C. L., Norris, A., and Beasley, R., (1999). Self-efficacy as a mediator of the relationship between pain intensity, disability and depression in chronic pain patients. *Pain* 80, 483–491.

Australian Bureau of Statistics (1997). *National Health Survey: SF-36 population norms*, Australia. Canberra: Author.

Australian Bureau of Statistics (2010). 1350.0. Australia's economic indicators. *http://www.abs.gov.au*

Blood, G. W., Boyle, M. P., Blood, I. M., and Nalesnik, G. R. (2010). Bullying in children who stutter: speech-language pathologists' perceptions and intervention strategies. *Journal of Fluency Disorders* 35, 92–109.

Bloodstein, O., and Bernstein-Ratner, N. (2008). *A handbook of stuttering* (6th Ed.). New York: Thomson Delmar Learning.

Bloom, J. R. (1990). The relationship of social support and health. *Social Sciences Medicine* 30, 635–637.

Blumgart, E., Tran, Y., and Craig, A. (2010a). Social anxiety disorder in adults who stutter. *Depression and Anxiety* 27, 687–692.

Blumgart, E., Tran, Y., and Craig, A. (2010b). An investigation into the personal financial costs associated with stuttering. *Journal of Fluency Disorders* 35, 203–215.

Bonanno, G. A., and Mancini, A. D. (2008). The human capacity to thrive in the face of potential trauma. *Pediatrics* 121, 369–375.

Brazier, J. E., Harper, R., Jones, N. M. B., O'Cathain, A., Thomas, K. J., Usherwood, T., et al., (1992). Validating the SF-36 health survey questionnaire: new outcome measure for primary care. *British Medical Journal* 305, 160–164.

Cardozo, B. L., Bilukha, O. O., Crawford, C. A. G, Shaikh, I., Wolfe, M. I., Gerber, M. et. al., (2004). Mental health, social functioning, and disability in postwar Afghanistan. *JAMA* 292, 575–584.

Chodosh. J., Morton, S. C., Mojica, W., Maglione, M., Suttorp, M. J., Hilton, L., et al., (2005). Meta-analysis: Chronic disease self-management programs for older adults. *Annals of Internal Medicine* 143, 427–438.

Chwastiak, L. A., and Ehde, D. M. (2007). Psychiatric issues in multiple sclerosis. *Psychiatric Clinics of North America* 30, 803–817.

Cohen, J. (1988). *Statistical power analysis for the behavioral Sciences*. New Jersey: LEA.

Coifman, K. G., and Bonanno, G. A. (2010). When distress does not become depression: emotion context sensitivity and adjustment to bereavement. *Journal of Abnormal Psychology* 119, 479–490.

Connor, K. M., and Davidson, J. R. T. (2003). Development of a new resilience scale: the Connor-Davidson Resilience Scale (CD-RISC). *Depression and Anxiety* 18, 76–82.

Craig, A. (2012). Resilience in people with physical disabilities (Chapter 26). In P. Kennedy (Ed.). *The Oxford handbook of rehabilitation psychology*. Oxford: Oxford University Press.

Craig, A., Blumgart, E., and Tran, Y. (2009). The impact of stuttering on the quality of life in adult people who stutter. *Journal of Fluency Disorders* 34, 61–71.

Craig, A., Blumgart, E., and Tran. Y. (2011). Resilience and stuttering: factors that protect people from the adversity of chronic stuttering. *Journal of Speech, Language, and Hearing Research* 54, 1485–1496.

Craig, A., Hancock, K., Chang, E., McCready, C., Shepley, A., McCaul, A., et al., (1996a). A controlled clinical trial for stuttering in persons aged 9 to 14 years. *Journal of Speech and Hearing Research* 39, 808–826.

Craig, A., Hancock, K., and Craig, M. (1996b). The lifestyle appraisal questionnaire: a comprehensive assessment of health and stress. *Psychology and Health* 11, 331–343.

Craig, A., Hancock, K., Tran, Y., Craig, M., Peters, K. (2002). Epidemiology of stuttering in the community across the entire lifespan. *Journal of Speech, Language and Hearing Research* 45, 1097–1105.

Craig, A., Hancock, K., Tran, Y., Craig, M., Peters, K. (2003). Anxiety levels in people who stutter: a randomized population study. *Journal of Speech, Language and Hearing Research* 46, 1197–1206.

Craig, A., and Tran, Y. (2006). Chronic and social anxiety in people who stutter. *Advances in Psychiatric Treatment* 12, 63–68.

Craig, A., Tran, Y., and Middleton, J. (2009). Psychological morbidity and spinal cord injury: a systematic review. *Spinal Cord* 47, 108–114.

Cummins, R. A. (2010). Fluency disorders and life quality: subjective wellbeing vs. health related quality of life. *Journal of Fluency Disorders* 35, 161–172.

de Leon, C. F. M., Glass, T. A., and Berkman, L. F. (2003). Social engagement and disability in a community population of older adults. The New Haven EPESE. *American Journal of Epidemiology* 157, 633–642.

DeNil, L. C., and Brutten, G. J. (1991). Speech-associated attitudes of stuttering and nonstuttering children. *Journal of Speech Hearing Research* 34, 60–65.

Derogatis, L. R. (1994). SCL-90-R. Symptom checklist-90-R. *Administration, scoring and procedures manual-3rd Edition*. Minneapolis: National Computer Systems, Inc.

Eggers, K., De Nil, L. F., and Van den Bergh, B. R. H. (2010). Temperament dimensions in stuttering and typically developing children. *Journal of Fluency Disorders* 35, 355–372.

Ezrati-Vinacour, R., and Levin, I. (2004). The relationship between anxiety and stuttering: a multidimensional approach. *Journal of Fluency Disorders* 29, 135–148.

Fergus, S., and Zimmerman, M. A. (2005). Adolescent resilience: a framework for understanding healthy development in the face of risk. *Annual Reviews of Public Health* 26, 399–419.

Garmezy, N., and Masten, A. S. (1991). The protective role of competence indicators in children at risk. In E. M. Cummings, A. L. Greene, and K. H. Karraker (Eds.). *Life-span developmental psychology: perspectives on stress and coping* (pp. 151–174). Hillsdale, NJ: Lawrence Erlbaum Publishers.

Iverach, L., Jones, M., O'Brian, S., Block, S., Lincoln, M., Harrison, E., et al., (2009a). The relationship between mental health disorders and treatment outcomes among adults who stutter. *Journal of Fluency Disorders* 34, 29–43.

Iverach, L., Jones, M., O'Brian, S., Block, S., Lincoln, M., Harrison, E., et al., (2009b). Screening for personality disorders among adults seeking speech treatment for stuttering. *Journal of Fluency Disorders* 34, 173–186.

Kagan, A., Simmons-Mackie, N., Rowland, A., Huijbregts, M., Shumway, E., McEwen, S., et al., (2008). Counting what counts: a framework for capturing real-life outcomes of aphasia intervention. *Aphasiology* 22, 258–280.

Kendler, K. S., Myers, J., and Prescott, C. A. (2005). Sex differences in the relationship between social support and risk for major depression: a longitudinal study of opposite-sex twin pairs. *American Journal of Psychiatry* 162, 250–256.

Kennedy, B. L., Morris, R. L., Pedley, L. L., and Schwab, J. J. (2001). The ability of the Symptom Checklist SCL-90 to differentiate various anxiety and depressive disorders. *Psychiatric Quarterly* 72, 277–288.

Kessler, R. C., Price, R. H., and Wortman, C. B. (1985). Social factors in psychopathology: stress, social support and coping processes. *Annual Reviews Psychology* 36, 531–572.

King, D. W., King, L. A., Foy, D. W., Keane, T. M., and Fairbank, J. A. (1999). Posttraumatic stress disorder in a national sample of female and male Vietnam veterans: risk factors, war-zone stressors, and resilience–recovery variables. *Journal of Abnormal Psychology* 108, 164–170.

Langevin, M., Packman, A., and Onslow, M. (2009). Peer responses to stuttering in the preschool setting. *American Journal of Speech-Language Pathology* 18, 264-276.

Luthar, S. S., Cicchetti, D., and Becker, B. (2000). The construct of resilience: the construct of resilience: a critical evaluation and guidelines for future work. *Child Development* 71, 543–562.

Maciejewski, P. K., Prigerson, H. G., and Mazure, C. M. (2000). Self-efficacy as a mediator between stressful life events and depressive symptoms. *British Journal of Psychiatry* 174, 373–378.

McCallum, J. (1995). The SF-36 in an Australian sample: validating a new, generic health status measure. *Australian Journal of Public Health* 19, 160–166.

Menzies, R.G., O'Brien, S., Onslow, M., Packman, A., St Clare, T., and Block, S. (2008). An experimental clinical trial of a cognitive-behavior therapy package for chronic stuttering. *Journal of Speech, Language, Hearing Research* 51, 1451–1464.

Middleton, J., Tran, Y., and Craig, A. (2007). Relationship between quality of life and self-efficacy in persons with spinal cord injuries. *Archives Physical Medicine and Rehabilitation* 88, 1643–1648.

Monroe, S. M., and Reid, M. W. (2009). Life stress and major depression. *Current Directions in Psychological Science* 18, 68–72.

Mulcahy, K., Hennessey, N., Beilby, J., and Byrnes, M. (2008). Social anxiety and the severity and typography of stuttering in adolescents. *Journal of Fluency Disorders* 33, 306–319.

Plexico, L. W., Manning, W. H., and Levit, H. (2009a). Coping responses by adults who stutter: Part I. Protecting the self and others. *Journal of Fluency Disorders* 34, 87–107.

Plexico, L. W., Manning, W. H., and Levit, H. (2009b). Coping responses by adults who stutter: Part II. Approaching the problem and achieving agency. *Journal of Fluency Disorders* 34, 108–126.

Power, M. J., Champion, L. A., and Aris, S. J. (1988). The development of a measure of social support: the Significant Others (SOS) Scale. *British Journal of Clinical Psychology* 27, 349–358.

Ramig, P. R. (1993). The impact of self-help groups on persons who stutter: a call for research. *Journal of Fluency Disorders* 18, 351–361.

Rutter, M. (1985). Resilience in the face of adversity. Protective factors and resistance to psychiatric disorder. *British Journal of Psychiatry* 147, 598–611.

Sanson-Fisher, R. W., and Perkins, J. J. (1998). Adaptation and validation of the SF-36 Health Survey for use in Australia. *Journal of Clinical Epidemiology* 51, 961–967.

Schmitz, N., Kruse, J., Heckrath, C., Alberti, L., and Tress, W. (1999). Diagnosing mental disorders in primary care: the General Health Questionnaire (GHQ) and the Symptom Check List (SCL-90-R) as screening instruments. *Social Psychiatry and Psychiatric Epidemiology* 34, 360–366.

Schneier, F. R., Wexler, K. B. and Liebowitz, M. R. (1997) Social phobia and stuttering. *American Journal of Psychiatry* 154, 131.

Sexton, M. B., Byrd, M. R., and von Kluge, S. (2010). Measuring resilience in women experiencing infertility using the CD-RISC: Examining infertility-related stress, general distress, and coping styles. *Journal of Psychiatric Research* 44, 236–241.

Southwick, S. M., Vythilingam, M., and Charney, D. S. (2005). The psychobiology of depression and resilience to stress: implications for prevention and treatment. *Annual Reviews Clinical Psychology* 1, 255–291.

Stein, M. B., Baird, A., and Walker, J. R. (1996). Social phobia in adults with stuttering. *American Journal of Psychiatry* 153, 278–280.

Taylor, J., Jacoby, A., Baker, G. A., Marson, A. G., Ring, A., and Whitehead, M. (2010). Factors predictive of resilience and vulnerability in new-onset epilepsy. *Epilepsia*, DOI: 10.1111/j.1528-1167.2010.02775.x

Tran, Y., Blumgart, E., and Craig, A. (2011). Subjective distress associated with chronic stuttering. *Journal of Fluency Disorders* 36, 17–26.

Vassend, O., and Skrondal, A. (1999). The problem of structural indeterminacy in multidimensional symptom report instruments. The case of SCL-90-R. *Behaviour Research and Therapy* 37, 685–701.

Ware, J. E. Jr., and Gandek, B. (1998). Overview of the SF-36 Health Survey and the International Quality of Life Assessment (IQOLA) *Project. Journal of Clinical Epidemiology* 51, 903–912.

Ware, J. E., Snow, K. K., Kosinski, M., and Gandek, B. (1993). SF-36 *Health Survey: Manual and interpretation guide.* Boston: The Health Institute, New England Medical Centre.

Watson, D., Clark, L. A., and Carey, G. (1988). Positive and negative affectivity and their relation to anxiety and depressive disorders. Journal of Abnormal Psychology 97, 346–353.

Yaruss, J. S., Quesal, R. W., and Murphy, B. (2002). National Stuttering Association members' opinions about stuttering treatment. Journal of Fluency Disorders 27, 227–242.

INDEX

A

B

C

D

E

F

G

H

I

J

K

L

N

O

P

Q

R

S

T

X

Y

Z